PRESENTED TO

_____

ON

_____

BY

_____

# Pursuit of His Presence

DAILY DEVOTIONS TO STRENGTHEN YOUR WALK WITH GOD

# Pursuit of His Presence

## Daily Devotions to Strengthen Your Walk With God

*Kenneth and Gloria Copeland*

**Harrison House**
Tulsa, Oklahoma

*Pursuit of His Presence*
*Daily Devotions to Strengthen Your Walk With God*
ISBN 1-57794-137-3
Copyright © 1998 by Kenneth and Gloria Copeland
Kenneth Copeland Ministries
Fort Worth, Texas  76192-0001

Published by Harrison House, Inc.
P.O. Box 35035
Tulsa, Oklahoma  74153

# Preface

*But we all, with open face beholding as in a glass
the glory of the Lord, are changed into the same image
from glory to glory, even as by the Spirit of the Lord.*

2 Corinthians 3:18

God is doing mighty works in believers everywhere. He is changing His people because they are giving Him entrance into their lives. He is changing us from Glory to Glory into His image.

As we spend time hearing the Word of God preached, as we read and meditate on the Word, as we spend time in prayer, as we listen to the Holy Spirit and follow His instructions, we are changed.

In His presence, we overcome, we break through, we experience the victory, we develop our faith, we experience signs and wonders, we grow to a higher level spiritually, we walk in the supernatural in every area of our lives.

For more than 30 years Gloria and I have been on our journey...and daily we are still being transformed into His image. It's an ongoing process that lasts our entire lifetime. While we have changed, the process that changes us never has...spending time in His Word, putting it first place and obeying it.

*Pursuit of His Presence* is a devotional designed to help you spend time in God's Word every day and make it first place. It's designed to daily lead you down the right road on your personal journey of faith.

Each devotion is designed to take you to a higher level, to teach you, to challenge you, to encourage you. Take each day's devotion as food. Feed your spirit man. Meditate on the key Scripture verse. Study the daily Bible reading. The Word will change you...from day to day, from week to week, from month to month...from glory to glory, as you actively continue in *Pursuit of His Presence*.

*Kenneth and Gloria Copeland*

## How to Use Your New Devotional

As you read each day's devotion, receive it as food nourishing your spirit man. Meditate on the day's **KEY SCRIPTURE VERSE,** located at the top of each devotion, and receive revelation knowledge from the Holy Spirit.

Each day, **SPEAK THE WORD** by reading the daily confession aloud. Allow God's power to be activated in your life through the Spoken Word.

At the end of each devotion, you will find **FOR FURTHER STUDY,** which is designed to help you go deeper into God's Word concerning that day's devotion topic. Read it and allow God's Word to speak to you personally.

Reading through the Bible in a year is a marvelous way to see the reality of the Scriptures unfold before you. The **DAILY SCRIPTURE READING** is an excellent plan to read a portion of the Bible every day, enabling you to have read the entire Bible in a year's time.

If you have a specific need at times and want to build up your faith in that area of your life, turn to the **TOPICAL INDEX** in the back of the devotional. Here you will find all of the devotions listed by practical topics. It's an excellent, quick, helpful tool to find the answers you need right away.

Enjoy your new *Pursuit of His Presence* devotional. Use it to its fullest and receive all that God has for you!

> ❧
>
> "For God so loved the world, that he gave his only begotten Son, that whosoever believeth in him should not perish, but have everlasting life."
> JOHN 3:16

# God Loves YOU!

Something's missing. You feel it. You know it. You trust God's power. You know His promises. But inside you're wavering. How can you be sure He'll come through for you?

To answer that question, you need more than a knowledge of God's power and promises. You need a personal relationship with Him. You need a personal revelation of His love.

*"For God so loved...that he gave..."* (John 3:16). And He gave and He gave.

Everlasting, unconditional, never-failing love. God's love. Our natural minds cannot grasp it. Yet Paul prayed in his letter to the Ephesians that we might *"know the love of Christ, which passeth knowledge, that ye might be filled with all the fulness of God"* (Ephesians 3:19). How is that possible? How can we comprehend the incomprehensible?

We can't! At least not with simple human understanding. To know something as vast as the love of God requires a revelation from the Holy Spirit.

Revelation is comprehension imparted into our spirits from the Holy Spirit and transmitted into our minds. It doesn't pass from the head to the heart. It must come from the heart to the head.

The story of Abram is a perfect example. When God first began to make promises to Abram, he didn't understand God's love. Until God approached him, Abram had worshiped the moon—and the moon had certainly never seemed interested in doing anything for him. Then Abram encountered *El Shaddai*, the greatest being he had ever known, and the first thing *El Shaddai* wanted to do was give to him!

God wants to give to you. It is His desire that every person know His vast love for them. If you've never known God's unconditional love, start the new year off right—ask Him for a personal revelation. If you've never asked Jesus to be the Lord of your life, ask Him into your heart. You can pray like this:

*"O God in heaven, I come before You and ask for Your forgiveness for my sins. Jesus, I ask You to come into my life and save me. I make You Lord of my life. I give myself to You. I receive You into my life. I am a believer. Thank You, Lord."*

Now, walk by faith into His arms of love. Receive the revelation of His unconditional love for you. God really does love *you.*

## Speak the Word

*God loves me so much that He gave His only Son for me. I believe in Jesus, therefore, I will not perish. I have everlasting life.*
*John 3:16*

FOR FURTHER STUDY:

1 John 4:8-19

❧

DAILY SCRIPTURE READING:

Genesis 1-3;
Matthew 1-2

*Gloria*

# Jesus Is Inside YOU!

I believe you are about to receive a revelation from God that will turn you inside out and upside down. It's a mystery hidden in God from the beginning of time. It's *"Christ—the Anointed One and His Anointing—in you, the hope of glory."*

Before you shrug that off as something you already know and understand, I want to ask you a question: Do you really—really realize—that Jesus Christ, the Anointed One Himself, lives in YOU? Do you realize that at this very moment *you* are His Body on the earth?

You and I are not just Jesus' representatives. We're His literal, physical Body on this earth! If the people of today's world are going to see Him, they'll have to see Him through your body. They'll have to see Him through my body.

It's a staggering thing to think about—so staggering it would be unbelievable if it weren't in the Bible. But 1 Corinthians 12:27 says it so plainly, even a child can understand it: *"Now ye are the body of Christ."*

When you or I lay hands on someone, Jesus is in us to bring that healing to pass. When we open our mouth to utter words, He's in there to give us utterance in the Holy Ghost. The Word says, *"He that is joined unto the Lord is one spirit"* with Him (1 Corinthians 6:17).

Think about that! You are one spirit with Jesus and Jesus has never changed. He hasn't lost any of His power. And He is in you, able to do the very same things He did when He walked the earth Himself 2,000 years ago!

Why then aren't we doing those things? Why isn't His power being revealed in our lives?

Because we're not expecting it to be! We're not exercising our faith and believing Jesus Christ is to be revealed in us.

That shouldn't surprise you. After all, nothing in God's kingdom just drops on you automatically. To receive healing, you have to believe for it. Not even the new birth was dropped on you. You had to receive it by faith.

FOR FURTHER
STUDY:

Mark 16:15-20;
Romans 12:4-5;
1 John 4:4

DAILY SCRIPTURE
READING:

Genesis 4-5;
Matthew 3

Everything we get from God takes faith. So, for the Lord Jesus Christ to be revealed in you, you're going to have to believe He's in there and begin expecting Him to manifest His presence through you.

So start doing it. Get the revelation on the inside of you...Christ in YOU, the hope of Glory!

## Speak the Word

*Christ, the Anointed One and His Anointing, is in me.*
*He is my hope and expectation of Glory.*
*Colossians 1:27*

> "Be not conformed to this world: but be ye transformed by the renewing of your mind, that ye may prove what is that good, and acceptable, and perfect, will of God."
> ROMANS 12:2

# Take a Crash Course— And Then Expect More

If you're just getting started in the things of God, you may be wondering exactly how you "jump into faith." It's simple. Romans 10:17 says faith comes by hearing and hearing by the Word of God.

When Ken and I first learned about the life of faith, we were so hungry for it that we took a crash course in the Word of God. Day and night, we listened to tapes of the preached Word.

In fact, for the biggest part of that first year, we hardly did anything but read and study and listen to the Word of God. We were so tired of being failures that we weren't interested in anything else. Ken was traveling at the time and I was staying home with the children. But I was having revival all by myself!

I was in my own little world of God's Word and faith. I spent all my extra time in the Word and listening to tapes. One day I was hanging clothes on the line to dry, thinking about what I'd been learning, when the telephone rang. I ran inside to answer it but I was so caught up in my excitement about the Word, that instead of saying "Hello," I accidentally said, "Hallelujah!" My well was overflowing.

You may think that's extreme—but I recommend being extreme. I recommend you so saturate yourself with the Word of God that there's not room in your thinking for unbelief, doubt and fear. Saturate your heart until the Word naturally begins to flow out of your mouth. Let it completely take over and renew your mind.

Then, when Satan lies to you and tells you that God is not listening to your prayers, that you won't receive your healing or get that new job, don't listen to him. Instead, begin to tell him about God's mercy. Tell him, "The Lord is good to all. He's full of compassion. His tender mercy is over all His works—and that includes me! I'm one of God's favorites!"

If you've been afraid to come to God with your needs...afraid to expect His blessings to come your way, start meditating on His mercy today. Spend some time thinking about the ocean of goodness He's longing to pour into your life. Then open the door of faith and let it in!

Take a crash course in His Word and let the blessings flow until you've reached the limit of your expectations. Then expect more. Experience the good life God has prepared for you!

## *Speak the Word*

*I am not conformed to this world. I am transformed as I renew my mind to God's Word. I experience the good and acceptable and perfect will of God.*
*Romans 12:2*

FOR FURTHER STUDY:

Psalm 1

DAILY SCRIPTURE READING:

Genesis 6-7;
Matthew 4

*Kenneth*

# Protect the Anointing

If you're in Christ, there's an anointing for everything you're called to do, no matter how small or great the task. Notice in this verse Paul didn't say, "through Christ who strengtheneth me"?

He said, *"which strengtheneth me."*

He was talking about the anointing! The anointing will empower you to prosper spirit, soul, body and in every aspect of your life.

I can prove that to you from the Bible. Do you remember the account recorded in Luke 5 about the palsied man who went down through the roof into Jesus' meeting to be healed? When Jesus told him, *"Man, thy sins are forgiven thee"* (verse 20), the scribes and Pharisees took offense at that and said, *"Who can forgive sins, but God alone?"*

Then Jesus answered them by saying, *"That ye may know that the Son of man hath power upon earth to forgive sins, (he said unto the sick of the palsy,) I say unto thee, Arise, and take up thy couch, and go into thine house"* (verse 24).

Why did healing the man prove Jesus had power to forgive sins? Because it was the same anointing that accomplished them both!

You see, there is not *an* anointing. There is only *the* Anointing of the Anointed One, and it is present within you to empower you to do whatever God has called you to do.

Once you understand that, it will shed an entirely new light on the instructions God has given us about how we're to conduct ourselves.

In Ephesians 4, for example, Paul says, *"Walk worthy of the vocation wherewith ye are called.... Endeavoring to keep the unity of the Spirit.... Sin not.... Let no corrupt communication proceed out of your mouth....grieve not the holy Spirit of God.... Be ye kind one to another, tenderhearted, forgiving one another, even as God for Christ's sake hath forgiven you"* (verses 1, 3, 26, 29-30, 32).

Why is it so important that we follow these instructions? It is for *Christ's* sake. It's for the sake of the anointing! The reason God forgave you is so He could put His burden-removing, yoke-destroying power in you and on you!

> "I can do all things through Christ [the Anointed One and His Anointing] which strengtheneth me."
> PHILIPPIANS 4:13

Our calling is to keep ourselves in a place where we can be anointed with the Holy Ghost and power, so we can go everywhere healing all who are oppressed of the devil. When you realize that, you'll stop a lot of that junk you've been doing. You'll protect that anointing. You'll say, "Oh, wait a minute. I don't want to do that. It will quench the anointing, and the anointing is in me, my hope of experiencing God's Glory. It's the anointing that keeps me healed and prosperous and free of the devil's yoke. I don't want to say or do anything to block that anointing!"

FOR FURTHER STUDY:

Ephesians 4:26-32

DAILY SCRIPTURE READING:

Genesis 8-9;
Matthew 5

## *Speak the Word*

*I can do all things through the Anointed One and
His Anointing which strengthens me!*
*Philippians 4:13*

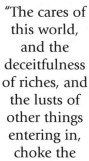

> "The cares of this world, and the deceitfulness of riches, and the lusts of other things entering in, choke the word, and it becometh unfruitful."
>
> MARK 4:19

# Kick the Habit

Most people these days don't think much about worry. They're so accustomed to it. To them it's *normal.* Some people are proud that they worry. They seem to think that to love their family is to worry about them.

But Jesus considered it deadly! He listed it as one of the few things that can kill off your harvest—even after the Word has taken root in your life.

No doubt the coming year will fly by as quickly as the past year, but, praise God, you can make it more glorious and more victorious than any year in your life. How? By making one decision, right now, before the year gets underway. You can decide that this is the year you'll quit worrying!

"Quit worrying?" you ask. "Gloria, you might as well tell me to quit breathing! I've worried all my life. And this year I have more reason to worry than ever!"

On the contrary. The more problems you're facing, the more reason you have not to worry! You see, the Word of God can overcome any problem in your life. If you'll plant it in the good soil of your heart, and let it grow unhindered, it will eventually grow up and produce a harvest greater than any problem.

Notice I said it must grow unhindered. The greatest tool of the devil to hinder the Word from working in your life is described in Mark 4:19. The "cares of this world" in that verse mean one word: *worry.*

"OK, Gloria, I'm ready to quit worrying. This is the year for me!"

If you're ready to make that decision, great! But let me warn you up front—worry is a habit. If you're going to rid yourself of it, you'll have to be diligent. I know that from experience. I come from a long line of worriers. I'll never forget the verse that helped me kick the habit: *"Roll your works upon the Lord—commit and trust them wholly to Him; [He will cause your thoughts to become agreeable to His will, and] so shall your plans be established and succeed"* (Proverbs 16:3, AMP).

When I read that verse, I decided to believe it. Once I did, I began to quit worrying like an alcoholic quits drinking—one moment at a time. I'd have a worried thought and I'd roll it over on the Lord. About 60 seconds later, I'd have another worried thought so I'd roll that one over on the Lord too.

I did that over and over every few minutes. But as I continued to resist worried thoughts and to feed on God's Word, those thoughts began to be further apart. I hardly ever have a worried thought anymore!

So kick the habit! Apply Proverbs 16:3 every time worry knocks at your door. Pretty soon, it'll be normal for you *not* to worry! You'll be free!

FOR FURTHER STUDY:

Psalm 55:22;

1 Peter 5:7

DAILY SCRIPTURE READING:

Isaiah 32-33;

Psalm 43

## *Speak the Word*

*I do not allow the worries of this world or the deceitfulness of riches or the lusts of other things to enter into my heart and choke the Word. I am determined to bear much fruit.*

*Mark 4:19*

*Kenneth*

# Get Out From Under the Barrel!

JANUARY 6

"All these blessings shall come on thee, and overtake thee, if thou shalt hearken unto the voice of the Lord thy God."
DEUTERONOMY 28:2

These days, when I say the Word of God can heal your body, pay off your debts and bring you victory in every area of your life, not everyone believes me. Most wouldn't admit it outright, but it's true nonetheless.

They don't intentionally doubt the Word, of course. They're just so overwhelmed by the problems in their own lives, they're not sure anything (natural or supernatural) can help.

When they see Gloria and me so blessed and prosperous, they think, *Sure it's easy for you to live by faith. You have a great life. But what can God do with a life as messed up as mine?*

If you struggle with that question, let me tell you, God can do for you exceedingly, abundantly above all that you can ask or think. After 30 years of ministry, I can say that, not only because it's the Word of God, but also because it's a living reality for me.

You see, I wasn't always blessed. When I first learned about faith, I was a failure going somewhere to happen. I wasn't just scraping the bottom of the barrel, I was underneath with the barrel on top of me! Then one day I was reading Deuteronomy 28, and I saw all the blessings God's people are supposed to have in their lives.

To be quite honest, I got mad. *Where are all these blessings that are supposed to belong to me?* I thought. As far as I could see, I didn't have even one of them. Yet Deuteronomy clearly said I was to have them.

I didn't have any land. I didn't have any storehouse. In fact, I'd heard that God wouldn't bless you with a storehouse at all because He didn't want you to have anything.

But verses 11-12 of Chapter 28 said God would make me plenteous in all kinds of ways and that I would lend to nations and not borrow!

I don't mind telling you, that looked good to me. All I'd ever known how to do was borrow, and I had even depended on borrowed money all my adult life. (Gloria always says I must have borrowed on my tricycle!)

FOR FURTHER STUDY:

Haggai 2:7-9

DAILY SCRIPTURE READING:

Genesis 12-13;
Matthew 7

Religion may try and rob you of these blessings. Your friends and family may try and talk you out of them...but you turn your eyes and ears to the Word. Get out from under that barrel and dare to believe God for your needs, your finances, your healing. Receive Deuteronomy 28 as God's will for your life. And watch God do exceedingly, abundantly above all that you can ask or think!

## *Speak the Word*

*I hearken unto the Word of the Lord my God.*
*All the blessings of the Word come on me and overtake me!*
*Deuteronomy 28:2*

❧

"All things are
possible to
him that
believeth."
MARK 9:23

# The Root of Hopelessness

Have you ever felt hopeless...ready to give up? Maybe you've already given up...felt that there were no answers and that you were simply trapped right where you sit. Well, according to the Word of God, you don't have to stay there.

According to the Word, hopelessness isn't caused by lack of money. It isn't caused by lack of education. It isn't caused by negative circumstances. Hopelessness comes from being without God in the world. It comes from being a stranger to His covenant (Ephesians 2:12).

Anybody anywhere can have hope if they know Jesus and the covenant promises of God. Your background, race or financial status doesn't matter. You can live in the worst slum in the world and still have hope in God because He isn't limited by man's resources. He isn't limited by man's prejudices. God is an equal opportunity employer!

Some people have said to me, "You ought not preach that prosperity message in poverty-stricken areas. You'll get those people's hopes up, and they don't have the same opportunity to prosper that you do."

Yes they do!

I've seen God prosper people in places where there was absolutely nothing. No food. No jobs. No welfare program. Nothing! There is one country in Africa where the government wanted a tribe to die out, so they just stopped the flow of food and began to starve them to death. But that plan failed because some Holy Ghost-filled, African Christians refused to give up hope. They knew their covenant, so they prayed "Give us this day our daily bread." Do you know what happened? The people were fed and the government went under!

The Apostle Paul said in Philippians 1:20, *"According to my earnest expectation and my hope, that in nothing I shall be ashamed...."* If you'll look up the two Greek words translated "earnest expectation and hope," you'll find that both mean the same thing. So hope is earnest expectation.

"But how can you so intensely expect to prosper when the unemployment rate is up and the economy is down?" you ask.

Because what I'm earnestly expecting isn't dependent on the world's economy. It's based on what God has promised in His covenant. Because He said it, I earnestly expect it! I have a covenant with Almighty God and I can be filled with hope. If you need hope today, ask God into your heart. If you are already a believer, take authority over the devil and cast hopelessness away from you. Stand on God's Word, His personal promises to you, and let hope rise up within you. With God all things are possible to him that believes!

## Speak the Word

*I am a believer. All things are possible to me!*
*Mark 9:23*

FOR FURTHER
STUDY:

Ephesians 2:11-18

❧

DAILY SCRIPTURE
READING:

Genesis 14-15;
Matthew 8

*Gloria*

# Tap Into the Mind of the Spirit

Most believers don't realize it, but praying in the spirit, or praying in other tongues, is a spiritual exercise that strengthens your inner man. Just like barbells build up your arms, praying in tongues will build up your spirit. If you'll do it faithfully, it will help to keep that flesh body of yours in line.

"Well, Gloria," you may ask, "why can't I just do that praying in my native language?"

Because the Bible says your "weakness" gets in the way. Many times your natural mind doesn't have the first idea how to say a prayer that will strengthen you against temptations or bring the answer you need.

Your mind is not informed like your spirit is. Your spirit is in contact with God. That's why, as Romans 8:26-27 says, the Holy Spirit comes to our aid because we do not know how to pray as we ought.

Praying in tongues enables you to pray the perfect will of God for your life. It allows you to step out of the realm of the flesh and into the realm of the spirit so that no matter how weak or ignorant you may be in the natural, you can pray exactly what you need.

Praying in tongues is the tool God has given us to tap into the mind of the Spirit. When we pray in tongues, we activate our spirit to understand as the Holy Spirit enlightens us.

But be warned, it won't work for you unless you put it to work. The Holy Spirit is a gentleman. He's not going to come storming in and make you pray in the spirit. He's going to wait for you to put your will in gear.

So yield to the Holy Spirit today. Begin to pray in tongues every day and build yourself up. Tap into the mind of the Spirit. You'll be blessed to have the strength, ability and answers you need for every situation!

## Speak the Word

*The Holy Spirit comes to my aid and bears me up in my weakness when I do not know how to pray as I ought. He intercedes on my behalf according to the will of God.*
Romans 8:26-27, AMP

FOR FURTHER
STUDY:

1 Corinthians
14:1-4

DAILY SCRIPTURE
READING:

Genesis 16-18;
Matthew 9-10

"The (Holy) Spirit comes to our aid and bears us up in our weakness; for we do not know what prayer to offer nor how to offer it worthily as we ought, but the Spirit Himself goes to meet our supplication and pleads in our behalf with unspeakable yearnings and groanings too deep for utterance. And He Who searches the hearts of men knows what is in the mind of the (Holy) Spirit...because the Spirit intercedes and pleads [before God] in behalf of the saints according to and in harmony with God's will."
ROMANS
8:26-27, AMP

> "For the Son of God, Jesus Christ...was not yea and nay, but in him was yea. For all the promises of God in him are yea, and in him Amen...."
> 2 CORINTHIANS 1:19-20

# Be Answer-Minded

"Oh, God, I feel so sick. My head hurts. My skin hurts. My stomach hurts. I need You to heal me!"

Have you ever prayed like that? If so, don't ever again!

One of the operating principles of faith is to go to God on the basis of His provision—not on the basis of your need.

I learned this years ago in the area of healing. I don't ever go to God and tell Him how sick I am, and then ask for healing.

Isaiah 53:5 assures me that Jesus already provided for my healing on the cross. So when my body is experiencing symptoms of illness, I pray by saying:

"I am thanking You, Lord, for providing healing for me. By faith I receive that provision now, in Jesus' Name. I set myself in agreement with Your Word which says, *By His stripes I was healed*" (see 1 Peter 2:24).

Remember this: If you continue to rehearse your need, you will be so need-minded that it will stunt your faith, and you won't be able to receive God's supply. But if you continue to rehearse God's promise, you'll become so answer-minded that it will be the most natural thing in the world to simply reach out by faith and receive His provision.

## *Speak the Word*

*All God's promises to me are yes and Amen.*
*2 Corinthians 1:20*

FOR FURTHER STUDY:

Luke 13:11-17

DAILY SCRIPTURE READING:

Genesis 19-20;
Matthew 11

# Read the Will and Receive Your Inheritance

Have you ever been invited to an attorney's office for the reading of a will? I haven't. Where I come from, there was never enough money left for the relatives to fight over when somebody died.

But, glory to God, that's not the case anymore. I became an heir to a fortune more than 30 years ago in Little Rock, Arkansas, when I gave my life to Jesus. At that moment I was born again into the richest family ever known. I was born into the royal family that owns and operates the universe. I received an inheritance so vast, it will take me all of eternity to fully comprehend it.

Some people get excited about tracing their natural family history. They like to know if they have great people in their family tree because it makes them feel they've come from good stock.

You and I ought to be that way about our heritage as believers. Our ancestors are the greatest men and women who ever walked the face of the earth. We can trace our lineage back to Abraham, Isaac, Jacob, Joseph, King David...all the way to Jesus. Think about that! Those are our forefathers.

"Now, wait a minute," you may say. "Those are Jewish men. They lived in the land of Canaan and Israel. You're an American from Arkansas! You're not part of that family."

> "That the blessing of Abraham might come on the Gentiles through Jesus Christ; that we might receive the promise of the Spirit through faith.... And if ye be Christ's, then are ye Abraham's seed, and heirs according to the promise."
> GALATIANS 3:14, 29

No, not physically. But spiritually, according to the Bible, yes, I am. And if you've made Jesus Christ the Lord of your life, you are too. Galatians 3 says so.

As a Christian, you are the seed of Abraham! That means everything God promised him belongs to you. It has been passed down to you through Jesus.

Abraham's blessing is your inheritance! It has been willed to you by the Word of God. And while you need to read the will—the Word—to find out what is rightfully yours, you can only receive it by faith. Faith gives us access to the favor and grace of God...and it gives God access to our lives. It opens the door to our inheritance.

FOR FURTHER
STUDY:

Hebrews 6:13-30

DAILY SCRIPTURE
READING:

Genesis 21-22;
Matthew 12

So start reading the Word with a new perspective—not like a book of stories, but as the record of your forefathers. Read it and believe it like you would a will that detailed your inheritance. Enjoy the riches that are yours by virtue of the new birth. Discover for yourself that you truly are an heir to the limitless resources of the family of God!

## *Speak the Word*

*The blessing of Abraham comes on me through Jesus Christ. I receive the promise of the Spirit through faith. I am an heir to the promise!*
*Galatians 3:14, 29*

> "As we have therefore opportunity, let us do good unto all men, especially unto them who are of the household of faith."
>
> GALATIANS 6:10

# The Household of Faith

According to Galatians 6:10, if you are born again, you are a member of the household of faith.

"But, Brother Copeland, I just don't think I have any faith."

You have to! You couldn't possibly be of the household of faith unless you had faith! And you can't be born again and not have faith. Settle it right now in your mind and your heart that God has given you His faith. He hasn't shortchanged you. He has put in you enough faith to blast through every mountain that gets in your way.

He expects you to use it, and He will develop it to the point where it can keep your body healed and your family prosperous and blessed. He expects you to use it to get your kinfolk saved and obtain every other promise given you in the Word of God.

If you haven't had much success in those areas, it isn't because you don't have enough faith. It's because what you have has never developed. You've been lying around on your sofa, eating spiritual junk food and watching videos all day. So when the devil kicked your door in and announced he was taking over your household by bringing sickness and calamity to it, you didn't have enough strength to stop him.

But don't let that discourage you. Come over to God's gym with the rest of us and start working out. Start studying your Bible, listening to tapes, fellowshiping with the Lord and exercising your faith until you're a spiritual Schwarzenegger.

Then, the next time the devil comes bursting through your door, you can stand up, flex those faith muscles and say, "Stop, thief! You're not taking over this household. It belongs to me and don't you touch one thing in it. I'll cut you up one side and down the other with the Word of God. Now, get out and don't let me see your ugly face on this block again!"

Now that's what I call acting like who you are...a member of the household of faith!

## *Speak the Word*

*My Heavenly Father provides me with the measure of faith and I am determined to build my faith by meditating on His Word.*
*Romans 12:3*

FOR FURTHER STUDY:

Ephesians 2:4-10

DAILY SCRIPTURE READING:

Genesis 23-24;
Matthew 13

# Don't Just Open the Door— Take It Off the Hinges

"We have access by faith into this grace wherein we stand...."
ROMANS 5:2

When people came to Jesus and asked, *"What shall we do, that we might work the works of God? Jesus answered and said unto them, This is the work of God, that ye believe on him whom he hath sent"* (John 6:28-29). All through the Old Testament, every mighty exploit that was done, every time the mercy of God flooded into a situation, every time a miracle was performed, somebody had to have faith. Somebody had to believe God enough to act on His Word and open the door.

That's what happened to me the day I was born again. I read that scripture in Matthew 6:26 that God cares for the birds of the air, and faith came into my heart. I didn't know anything about the new birth, yet when I spoke that faith out, I opened the door just a crack and God's mercy flooded my heart and changed it forever.

The same thing is true today. However wide you open that door of faith is how much of God's mercy and goodness will flow into your life. He'll fill up every inch you'll give Him.

I'm telling you, He's ready. He is eagerly yearning to bless you. He is hovering over you in mercy. He has an ocean full of salvation benefits and He's longing to pour them out on you.

When I say *salvation*, I'm not just talking about a ticket to heaven. Salvation denotes deliverance. From what? Oppression, poverty, sickness, danger, fear—anything from which you need to be delivered!

Salvation also means "soundness, protection, liberty, health and restoration." Glory to God!

Psalm 68:19 says God daily loads us with benefits of salvation. When you wake up in the morning, you ought to start the day thanking God for the salvation that's going to happen to you today. You ought to start by opening the door of faith. And don't just open it a crack—take it off the hinges!

Say, "Lord, here I am. Pour it on me!"

That's what Ken and I did. We didn't just ease into this. Once we heard it, we jumped into it with both feet. And we've never stopped!

FOR FURTHER STUDY:

Psalm 103:1-12

~∽~

DAILY SCRIPTURE READING:

Genesis 25-26; Matthew 14

## *Speak the Word*

*I have access by faith into the grace of God.*
*Romans 5:2*

> "Why are ye so
> fearful? how is
> it that ye have
> no faith?"
> MARK 4:40

# You Can't Blame It on Luck!

*"It doesn't matter how hard I try, everything I do turns out wrong!"*

Have you ever felt that way? I certainly have. There was a time in my life when everything I put my hand to fell apart. Back then, I chalked it up to "bad luck."

But I was wrong. I found out in the 25 years since then, that there's no such thing as luck—good or bad. In fact, I don't even use that word anymore.

It's not luck that determines how things turn out in our lives—it's choices. When we make good ones, things go well for us. When we make bad ones, things go wrong.

Now some would dispute me on that, but no matter how "right" you think you are at any given time, a decision that brings trouble is a poor decision.

*"Oh, but Brother Copeland, there's no way in the world I could have known in advance what would happen in that situation!"*

No, there may not have been any way in this natural world you could have made a better choice. But, if you're a born-again believer, you aren't restricted to making choices according to this natural world. You have another, far more powerful option.

Consider the disciples and Jesus in the boat during the storm in Mark 4:36-41. There were the disciples facing this fierce storm. No doubt they were doing everything they knew to do in the natural to stay afloat. They were bailing; they were paddling.

But they didn't say a word to Jesus, even though He was right there in the boat with them! They didn't call on His power until the boat was full of water and they were about to sink. Why? They'd made a wrong choice. They had chosen to look to natural solutions instead of supernatural ones. Faith never even entered their minds until they were about to drown!

If they'd thought supernaturally, any one of them could have drawn by faith on the Anointing and the words of Jesus and stopped that storm. But they made the wrong choice.

Many well-meaning believers are making that same mistake today. They have Jesus right there in the boat with them, but they're depending on natural resources to get them through. They're making wrong choices, and are chalking it up to bad luck. If you're living like that, stop. Get in the Word. Start living according to the supernatural. Then, when the storms of life come, you'll know what to do. Instead of just grabbing a bucket and starting to bail, faith will rise up within you and you'll say, "Look here, Storm. Peace, be still." It will work for you just like it would have worked for the disciples. After all, you have Jesus in your boat!

## *Speak the Word*

*I have faith in God. I will not fear.*
*Mark 4:40*

FOR FURTHER
STUDY:

Mark 4:36-41

DAILY SCRIPTURE
READING:

Genesis 27-28;
Matthew 15

# Go the Other Way

"Repent: for
the kingdom
of heaven is at
hand."
MATTHEW 4:17

When Jesus came preaching the good news of the gospel, He said to the people, *"Repent: for the kingdom of heaven is at hand."*

What did Jesus mean by this?

Change your mind and come My way. Turn around and go a different direction. Come into the kingdom of heaven. He was offering life to the people of His day, but for them to receive it, they had to repent—or change their will. They had to choose God's way of doing and being right.

That's what repentance is. It's not just being sorry for something you've done, or sorrowful over a situation. It's changing your mind. It's changing your will. It's changing your direction. It's choosing God and His way. It is a return to obedience.

When we sin and miss the mark, to make things right, we have to repent. Jesus then forgives us of our sins and we are cleansed by His blood (1 John 1:7). He is our advocate with our Heavenly Father.

Romans 2:4 says the goodness of God leads men to repentance. If you've never been born again, repent and ask Jesus to be your Savior. Make Jesus the Lord of your life right now and begin to move in God's direction.

If you are a believer, repentance includes choosing to obey God. It is turning back to God's ways when you realize you've sinned and missed the mark. As a Spirit-filled Christian, you know deep down inside what God wants you to do. Now, you may not want to do it, but that knowing is on the inside of you.

When you repent, you not only ask for forgiveness, but you put away from yourself that which displeases God. It includes submitting to doing something God has asked you to do. It's turning from the direction you've been going, and turning to the direction God's told you to go.

I don't care what you've done...or what you may do in the future...whether you are a believer or not, if you repent, God will forgive you and receive you cleansed and made new by the blood of Jesus. You can live a life of obedience to Him.

Don't condemn yourself, or live a life full of guilt. Repent! That's all you have to do. Just ask God for forgiveness, and change. Go the other way. Go toward God in that area of your life.

FOR FURTHER
STUDY:

Luke 15

DAILY SCRIPTURE
READING:

Genesis 10-11;
Matthew 6

## *Speak the Word*

*I repent and turn away from sin for the kingdom of heaven is at hand.*
*Matthew 4:17*

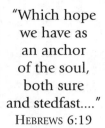

> "Which hope
> we have as
> an anchor
> of the soul,
> both sure
> and stedfast...."
> HEBREWS 6:19

# You Have Hope!

You may be in the deepest hole of your life. But if the Word says you have hope, then, glory to God, you have hope!

You may think your circumstances are tearing you apart, but I have news for you. Your circumstances are not the problem! All circumstances, I don't care what they are, must bow their knee and submit to the Name of Jesus and the Word of God when faith, hope and love are brought to bear on them.

When circumstances are very bad, get your Bible and some teaching tapes and go off by yourself until you stop negative thoughts from bombarding your mind. Gloria and I have done that many, many times. Years ago, we did that where our children are concerned. It was obvious from the circumstances that the devil was after them and the pressure was getting worse and worse.

Finally, we decided to deal with the situation head on. We spent time piled up in the middle of the bed with our Bibles and our notebooks, looking up every scripture we could find about children. We wrote them all down, prayed over them and made an irrevocable declaration.

We said, *"On the basis of the promises of God and by the blood of Jesus, our children are not going to hell. The Word of God says our children are taught of the Lord and great is their peace, and that settles it forever."*

Then, no matter what happened, we stood our ground in the Name of Jesus. To keep from wavering, we had to cast down imaginations and every high thing that exalted itself against the Word God had given us about our children. We had to bring *all* our thoughts into captivity and into obedience to that Word. *All* our thoughts!

*"Well, I try to do that, but sometimes I just can't help what I think."*

You most certainly can. God's Word says you can (Philippians 4:8). God's Word tells you to choose what you think, and cast down what you shouldn't think. When you do that, hope will have a place to work. In fact, if you'll guard your mind, there will come a moment when hope suddenly rises up. Add to that, faith and the love of God, and complete the transaction in the realm of the spirit. Suddenly, that hole you are in won't be deep at all. You can walk right out.

When that happens, you'll suddenly know that what you're hoping for is yours. It's yours and all the demons of hell can't keep you from receiving it. You'll find yourself saying, "It's done! It's mine, glory to God!"

## *Speak the Word*

*Hope is the anchor of my soul. Hope keeps me sure and steadfast.*
*Hebrews 6:19*

FOR FURTHER
STUDY:

Psalm 71

DAILY SCRIPTURE
READING:

Genesis 31-33;
Matthew 17-18

*Gloria*

# Fear the Lord

> "O fear the Lord, ye his saints: for there is no want to them that fear him."
> PSALM 34:9

What does it mean to fear the Lord? It means to give Him total respect, to honor Him, to let Him be God in your life. If you fear the Lord, whatever He says, you'll do. When you find something in His Word, you implement it immediately. You're quick to make changes.

God says people who live that way have no want. *No want!* That's a vast statement. But read the Bible and you can see that it's true. God has always taken total care of His people. When Israel followed Him, there was no lack in the whole nation. They had everything they needed. They were strong. They were prosperous. No enemy could stand before them. There was no sickness or disease among them.

God doesn't have any problem backing up His Word. The only problem He's had since the Garden of Eden has been finding people who would do what He says and allow Him to be God in their lives.

Listen to me closely. God knows exactly how to get you out of trouble. He hasn't forgotten how to part the Red Sea. He never changes. When He finds somebody who is loyal to Him, He's loyal to them.

Second Chronicles 16:9 says, *"For the eyes of the Lord run to and fro throughout the whole earth, to show himself strong in the behalf of them whose heart is perfect toward him."* That word *perfect* doesn't mean one who doesn't make mistakes. It means "one who is loyal."

God isn't just *willing* to deliver you from trouble, He *wants* to deliver you. He is constantly searching for opportunities to show Himself strong on your behalf! But He won't force it on you. You'll have to fear Him, give Him total respect and honor Him. If you want to walk in the delivering power of God, you will have to want it enough to let God be God every day of your life.

## Speak the Word

*I reverently fear the Lord. I respect and honor Him therefore I do not lack!*
*Psalm 34:9*

FOR FURTHER STUDY:

Proverbs 2:1-6

DAILY SCRIPTURE READING:

Genesis 34-35;
Matthew 19

*Kenneth*

# Grace Will Shake Your Life

"By the grace of God I am what I am: and his grace which was bestowed upon me was not in vain; but I laboured more abundantly than they all: yet not I, but the grace of God which was with me."

1 CORINTHIANS 15:10

Brother Paul wasn't just using a figure of speech in this verse. He was referring to a very real power that was operating in his life. That power can be called *favor*. Could you possibly believe that you're God's favorite? Well, you are!

Even though we committed great sin against Him, He didn't turn away from us. He just kept coming. He just kept reaching for us. God is determined He is not going to lose us.

He is so willing to get involved with you, that He swore an oath in the blood of His own Son that He would personally carry out *through you* everything that is required *of you,* if you'll allow Him to be your Lord and take over your affairs. Glory to God, that's grace!

I know I'm just scratching the surface here, but if you'll get your Bible and begin to study it, you'll get a revelation of it—a revelation that will come into your spirit, becoming very real to you and making you very bold. The longer you meditate on it, the bolder you will get.

I've had people accuse me of being on an ego trip because I talk confidently about what God will do for me. But that's not my ego talking, it's my faith talking! I'm not bragging on me, I'm bragging on God.

When you get a revelation of grace, you'll have that same kind of boldness. You'll just reach out and take the promises of God by faith because you'll know they're yours. Romans 4:16 says, *"Therefore it is of faith, that it might be by grace; to the end the promise might be sure to all the seed."* Who's the seed? Galatians 3:29 says, *"If ye be Christ's, then are ye Abraham's seed, and heirs according to the promise."*

You are just as much an heir to the promises of God as Jesus is!

How can that be? By grace—that's how!!

You want to see great power? You want to see the miracles of God happening around you? You want to see the gospel flooding the streets? Then, reach out for a revelation of grace...it will shake your life!

## *Speak the Word*

*God has bestowed His grace upon me. By His grace, I am what I am.*
*1 Corinthians 15:10*

FOR FURTHER STUDY:

Ephesians 2:8-10

DAILY SCRIPTURE READING:

Genesis 36-37; Matthew 20

*Gloria*

# Take Authority

God has given you authority over the things in your life just like He gave Adam authority in the Garden of Eden. You have authority over your family and your household. But if you don't exercise your authority, the devil will come in and take over your garden just like he took over Adam's garden.

When Ken and I were first born again, we didn't understand that. We just kept bumping around in the same old ruts we'd been in before we were saved. We stayed just as broke and as sick as everybody else in the world.

Oh, we knew God worked miracles. Ken saw them firsthand when he was working as a co-pilot, flying Oral Roberts to his healing meetings. When they would arrive at the meeting, it was Ken's job to get the people in the invalid tent ready before Brother Roberts came in to minister to them.

The invalid tent was the place where the people went who were too sick to go into the regular meeting. Most of them were on stretchers or in the last stages of some terminal illness.

Yet, as Brother Roberts laid his hands on those people, Ken saw amazing miracles. One woman spit the cancer up, right in the middle of the floor. A girl, who came in strapped to a board because she was totally paralyzed, jumped straight up when Brother Roberts touched her, and began to run around the tent totally healed.

Ken saw those miracles with his own eyes. But do you know what? They didn't do anything for our family. It was when we heard that Jesus had already borne our sicknesses and carried our diseases that our personal lives changed.

It was when we saw in the Word of God that we had authority over sickness and began to say so, that we began to get free. When we realized that we weren't the sick trying to get healed, and the devil was trying to steal our health, we began to take dominion and say, "Devil, get out of here!" And he would flee and take his sickness with him.

Of course, it's a thrill to see God work miracles. But you can't live day in, day out on miracles. What will change your life is taking hold of the authority that belongs to you in the Word of God and releasing that authority from your mouth. If you'll do that, you can keep the devil under your feet where he belongs.

> "All authority in heaven and on earth has been given to me. Therefore [you] go...."
> MATTHEW 28:18-19, NIV

FOR FURTHER STUDY:

Genesis 2:15-17, 3:1-6

DAILY SCRIPTURE READING:

Genesis 38-39; Matthew 21

## *Speak the Word*

*All authority in heaven and on earth has been given to me by Jesus Christ.*
*Matthew 28:18*

> "And when ye
> stand praying,
> forgive, if ye
> have ought
> against any."
> MARK 11:25

# "I love you, Brother."

"Brother Copeland, some time ago I was deeply hurt by another Christian. I've tried to forgive, yet every time I see that person, I still feel angry and resentful. Will I ever be able to truly forgive?"

I've been asked that question many times. And the answer is, "Yes, you can, and you must!"

Unforgiveness is downright dangerous. It will make your spirit feeble and your prayers ineffective. It will pull the plug on your faith so completely that you won't have enough power to move the molehills in your life—much less the mountains.

In Mark 11, Jesus didn't say, "When you stand praying, *try* to forgive" or "When ye stand praying, *forgive if you can.*" He simply said, *"Forgive."* Period.

Jesus made forgiveness a command. It would be unjust for Him to command us to do something we couldn't do. So you can be sure it's within your power to obey His command and forgive—no matter how badly you've been wronged.

Most people don't realize it, but unforgiveness is actually a form of fear. Quite often we don't forgive because we're afraid of getting hurt again. We're afraid we're never going to recover from the damage that person has done to our lives.

If you want to freely forgive, get rid of those fears. Cleanse yourself from them by the *"washing of water by the word"* (Ephesians 5:26). Fill your mind and heart with promises of God that apply to your situation.

If you'll do that, I can assure you from my own experience, your feelings will change. It may not happen overnight...but it will happen. One of these days, almost without thinking, you'll throw your arms around that person, give him a big hug and say, "I love you, Brother." What's more, you'll mean it from the bottom of your heart.

## *Speak the Word*

*I forgive those whom I have anything against*
*so that my prayers are not hindered.*

*Mark 11:25*

FOR FURTHER
STUDY:

Luke 6:27-36,
17:3-4

DAILY SCRIPTURE
READING:

Genesis 40-41;
Matthew 22

# Put Your Foot on Healing Ground

If you need healing in your body today, you need to possess it like the children of Israel possessed the Promised Land. Joshua and the people of Israel had to put their foot on what belonged to them, if they were going to enjoy the blessing of God. The same thing is true today with healing and every other blessing.

> "Every place that the sole of your foot shall tread upon, that have I given unto you...."
> JOSHUA 1:3

If you are a believer, healing already belongs to you. Isaiah 53 clearly says Jesus has borne our griefs, sickness, weakness and pain, and carried our sorrows, and that by His stripes we are healed and made whole.

As far as God is concerned, healing is yours. Jesus has already paid the price for it. But for you to receive it, you have to put your foot on it. You have to go in and possess the land!

That's not always easy. It wasn't necessarily easy for Joshua either. To do it, God told him he would have to be *"strong and very courageous"* (Joshua 1:7). The people of Israel had to arm themselves and go up before their enemy. They had to put their foot on that land.

In the same way, taking the land of healing requires spiritual strength and courage. Why? Because the manifestation of healing doesn't always come instantly. We want it instantly—and many times it comes that fast—but other times it takes longer.

When you think about it, that's not so unusual. After all, in most cases, sickness and disease do their destructive work gradually. They don't just appear one moment—and kill you the next. They take effect over time. So it's not surprising that healing often displaces their effects gradually as well.

If you need healing today, you need to put your foot on the healing land. You need to step out on the Word, take it and say, "Healing is mine. The devil is not going to steal it from me. No one is going to talk me out if it. It belongs to me. Today, this day, I receive my healing!"

Once you've said that, don't ever say anything contrary to it. Don't be moved by time or by symptoms or by anything else. Just stay with it. Continue to take God's medicine—the Word—every day and you will continually improve.

When the devil comes back next week and tells you you're not going to get your healing, laugh at him and say, "Too late! I've already gotten it. I received my healing last week. I put my foot on healing ground and it's mine."

Just refuse to give up, keep on taking the land and your healing will come to pass.

FOR FURTHER STUDY:

Isaiah 53:1-5

DAILY SCRIPTURE READING:

Genesis 42-43;
Matthew 23

## *Speak the Word*

*God has given me every place that my feet tread upon. Therefore, I have dominion over sin, sickness and poverty.*

*Joshua 1:3*

*Kenneth*

# The Good News of the Anointing

> "The Spirit of the Lord is upon me, because he hath anointed me to preach the gospel to the poor; he hath sent me to heal the brokenhearted, to preach deliverance to the captives, and recovering of sight to the blind, to set at liberty them that are bruised, To preach the acceptable year of the Lord."
>
> LUKE 4:18-19

The message Jesus preached was this: *"The Spirit of the Lord is upon me, because he hath anointed me...."* That may not mean a great deal to you right now, but if you'll keep reading for a few minutes, that one verse will make you shout for joy!

The word *anoint* actually means "to pour on, smear all over or rub into." So Jesus was telling the people in Nazareth that day, "God is poured on, smeared all over and rubbed into Me." He was telling them from the book of Isaiah that He had come with the yoke-destroying, burden-removing power of Almighty God all over Him.

He didn't just make that statement either. He began to preach a sermon saying: "Hey, I have good news for you! Poverty is a yoke and I'm anointed to destroy it! Brokenheartedness is a yoke and I'm here to destroy it! Being captive to sin, sickness, demons and fear is a yoke, and I'm here with the yoke-destroying power and presence of God. I'm here to get the burden off your back! I'm here to set you free!"

That's the gospel Jesus preached. It is the good news of the anointing!

And it's available to you today. Whatever Satan is throwing your way, you don't have to put up with one more second of it. If you'll draw on that anointing power within, if you're born again, you can be free. That anointing is available to deliver you from every stronghold of the devil. It can tell you things you never knew before. It can destroy the bondages you've fought for years. It can obliterate and utterly destroy as to powder every burden of condemnation, guilt, fear, lack, poverty, abuse, addiction, torment, hatred and anger, just to name a few.

I mean, whatever it is you've wanted to be free of, the Anointing of Jesus is what will do it. And, if you've made Jesus the Lord of your life, it's right there on the inside of you. Receive it. Receive the good news of the anointing!

## *Speak the Word*

*The Spirit of the Lord is upon me. He has anointed me with the same anointing that Jesus has. The anointing in me removes every burden and destroys every yoke in my life.*
*Luke 4:18; Isaiah 10:27*

FOR FURTHER STUDY:

Luke 4:14-19

DAILY SCRIPTURE READING:

Genesis 44-45; Matthew 24

*Gloria*

# From a Seed to a Force

Many times, people think, *I just wish I had faith like Ken and Gloria. Then I wouldn't be in this mess.*

Well, you do have faith like Ken and me. You just have to develop it. Everyone who's been born again has been given a measure of faith...the same measure. But not everyone spends the time necessary to develop it from a seed to a powerful force.

> "God hath dealt to every man the measure of faith."
> ROMANS 12:3

Faith comes in response to the promise of God. On the other hand, whatever God promises you in His Word, you can count on because He is *"alert and active, watching over [His] word to perform it"* (Jeremiah 1:12, AMP).

So, if you want to learn to use your faith, start finding out what God has already said. Open your Bible and discover what already belongs to you according to His Word.

Then take that Word and keep it in front of your eyes. Keep it in your ears and in your mouth. Proverbs 4:20-22 puts it this way: *"My son, attend to my words; incline thine ear unto my sayings. Let them not depart from thine eyes; keep them in the midst of thine heart. For they are life unto those that find them, and health to all their flesh."*

The word *attend* in that passage means "to pay close attention to something." The nurse who is attending to a sick patient watches diligently over that patient. Faith comes when you give that same kind of diligence to the Word.

It comes when you do what God told Joshua to do, when you let the Word of God *"not depart out of your mouth, but...meditate on it day and night, that you may observe and do according to all that is written in it; for then you shall make your way prosperous, and then you shall deal wisely and have good success"* (Joshua 1:8, AMP).

So do what it takes to develop your faith from a seed to a force. Then, when you get in a fix and need help, you can use your faith. You can speak the Word of God, and watch your faith go to work.

Or, better yet, learn to use your faith ahead of time and all the time, and you can avoid most of those "fixes." When you learn to live in the blessing continually, fewer miracles are needed!

FOR FURTHER STUDY:

2 Timothy 1:1-5

DAILY SCRIPTURE READING:

Genesis 46-48; Matthew 25-26

## Speak the Word

*God has dealt to me the measure of faith. I have the God kind of faith.*

*Romans 12:3*

*Kenneth*

"Ask of the Lord rain in the time of the latter or spring rain. It is the Lord Who makes lightnings, which usher in the rain and give men showers of it, to every one grass in the field."
ZECHARIAH 10:1, AMP

# Look Out for the Rain

Some years ago, the Lord showed me a vision of the Glory that was destined to be released on the earth before Jesus' return. It was vast and very heavy, and it was being held back by what looked to me like a thin, elastic sheet of some kind.

As I looked at it, I was reminded of a balloon filled with water, so filled that the pressure of the water makes it stretch thin and appear to be ready to burst.

That's what the coming Glory looked like to me. It was hanging over the earth and had a big swag in it. When I saw it, I asked the Lord what it was.

*That membrane is filled with My Glory, He said. In it are more signs and wonders, an outpouring of the Holy Spirit, the gifts of the Spirit, and more souls to be won than the human race has ever seen. All that will have to happen is for that membrane to get one little hole in it, and it won't be able to hold back the Glory anymore. So continue to pray. Keep poking at that spiritual membrane with prayer and with faith until it breaks and spills the Glory all over the earth.*

During those years following, the "pray-ers" of Kenneth Copeland Ministries have prayed about that Glory. Many others have too.

Then a couple of years ago something happened. That "balloon" burst in the spirit. Since that occurred, there have been spiritual breakthroughs on every hand. People who had preached on the streets for years suddenly saw more people saved than they'd ever seen in all their lives. Sinners whose hearts had been hardened toward God began to turn to Him in staggering numbers.

There was a surge in the response to our prison ministry...we went from 3600 letters received in 1994 to well over 100,000 in 1995.

In light of the vision God gave me, I believe only one thing can account for such a supernatural increase. The membrane that held back the Glory had burst! A powerful change has taken place in the realm of the spirit. The storm of God's Glory has been released in the earth. The earth is now filling up with that Glory.

We're still only in the beginning stages of it. It's only going to increase more and more in these days before His return. Pray about it. Ask God for the Glory to be manifested in your life...then look out for the rain.

## *Speak the Word*

*I expect the Glory of God to be poured out on my life like the rain.*

*Zechariah 10:1*

FOR FURTHER STUDY:

Deuteronomy 11:13-15

❧

DAILY SCRIPTURE READING:

Genesis 49-50; Matthew 27

*Gloria*

# Funny, Funky and Far-Out

Natural man cannot understand Christians. Unbelievers say we are funny, funky, far-out, messed up, have-no-fun kind of people, who have nothing to do.

But natural man does not and has never experienced what the Bible calls *peace*. The Bible word for *peace* means everything that makes for man's highest good. Natural man has never experienced that.

People in the world don't understand what we do in honor to God, that we do the things we do because we love God, and because God says it is right. They don't understand the reward of the kind of life we live—a life whose reward is well-being, good health, having your children serve God, having things work right in your life. The people of the world around you don't feel like they have anything in common with you. They just don't understand you.

They think, *When you could commit adultery, why do you remain faithful to your husband or wife? When you go on business trips with others who are in the world and are committing adultery, why don't you do it? Why don't you want to have any "fun"?* They don't understand that adultery brings death. From Proverbs we know that adultery and death are tied together. They think adultery brings excitement through lust. But you know better.

First Corinthians 15:33 tells you that keeping the companionship of evil will wrongly influence you. When you are born again, you shouldn't want to hang out in the same places you once did. You're now learning and taking on a new life.

Later on, as you grow stronger, you might walk back through the middle of that life and there'll be no temptation. But you have to walk very carefully until you learn how to walk completely free of your old lifestyles. Many times you have to break off old associations. You have to listen to God regarding where you're to go and to fellowship. You can love your old friends and people in the world, but you can't fellowship with them the same way you once did.

Fellowship is where you are relaxed. It's where you don't need your guard up. You feel at home. Fellowship now where you're comfortable and being built up in the Word of Truth.

> "Do not be so deceived and misled! Evil companionships, (communion, associations) corrupt and deprave good manners and morals and character."
> 1 CORINTHIANS 15:33, AMP

You know the way to peace. You know the right way to live. You know in your heart where you should fellowship, and the places you need to avoid. Follow your heart. Follow the Holy Spirit on the inside of you. It doesn't matter that no one around you understands. It's OK to be called funny, funky, far-out and messed up—especially when you're full of God's peace.

FOR FURTHER STUDY:

2 Corinthians 6:14-18

DAILY SCRIPTURE READING:

Exodus 1-2; Matthew 28

## Speak the Word

*I refuse to be deceived or misled by having evil associations or companions. I choose to fellowship with those who believe in the Lord Jesus Christ.*

*1 Corinthians 15:33, AMP*

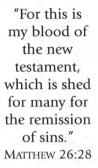

*Kenneth*

> "For this is my blood of the new testament, which is shed for many for the remission of sins."
> MATTHEW 26:28

# He Destroyed the Note

For every believer, Jesus' death and resurrection provided complete freedom from the curse of sin and death. But until we learn what that means and how to apply it, we don't know how to lay hold of all that is ours.

To walk in complete freedom from sin, guilt, condemnation and defeat is like an unattainable dream to some people. They have no idea of the freedom and joy that is already theirs—if they only knew how to tap into it.

When Jesus died, His shed blood ratified the covenant you and I have with God. His blood was the ultimate and final sacrifice for our sins. You don't have to "do" things to make up for your sins. You don't have to punish yourself, or offer up a sacrifice like they did in the Old Testament.

In the Old Testament, the Hebrew sacrifices of the blood of animals was atonement. It covered for sin, it did not destroy it. *Atonement* means "to cover over or cover up." Animal blood only temporarily hid sin away for one year.

Under the New Covenant, the blood of Jesus did not just cover our sin, it remitted or did away with it. In the Greek language in the New Testament, the word is never atonement, it's God reconciling by totally wiping out. The Greek word for *atonement* doesn't occur in the New Testament when referring to the sacrifice of Jesus.

To use the word *atonement* in referring to the blood of Jesus is totally inaccurate. In ignorance we've used it. People in religious circles have talked about the great atonement. I did for years until I learned the truth.

It was an atonement in the basic understanding of it, but not in the real description of it. The blood of Jesus did far more than just cover up sin.

Colossians 2:14 explains *remittance:* It rendered invisible the ink of the note that was written against us in sin. The *King James Version* says, it "blotted it out." Atonement would have stamped "paid in full" on the note. Atonement would have covered the note. But remittance wiped out the ink of the note. Remittance means there's no evidence now that there ever was a note. The note is not only paid, it doesn't exist anymore. The blood of Jesus destroyed it.

Are you getting this? It means when you confess your sins and they are put under the blood of Jesus, and you mention it to God the next day, He doesn't know what you are talking about. It's been destroyed! It's no longer in existence. You are worrying and fretting over something that doesn't exist. You are living under condemnation of something that isn't there. You're letting something hold you back that isn't real. You've been redeemed! You've been set free!

FOR FURTHER STUDY:

Colossians 1:9-23;
1 Peter 1:18-25

DAILY SCRIPTURE READING:

Exodus 3-4;
Mark 1

## *Speak the Word*

*Jesus shed His blood for the remission of my sins and now they no longer exist!*

*Matthew 26:28*

*Gloria*

# Fulfill Your Destiny

A sense of urgency has been implanted in the Body of Christ, in our spirits, by the Spirit of God, because the end of this age is very near. Time is running out, and God is fulfilling His plan in us. He is preparing for Himself a glorious Church without spot or wrinkle. He is raising up a people who will walk in the things He has prepared for them.

God is bringing forth a multitude of believers who will fulfill the divine destiny prepared for them since the beginning of time. That destiny is defined clearly in Romans 8:29. Our destiny as believers is to grow up in Jesus. It's to be fully conformed to His image, which was placed within us the moment we were born again.

It's a staggering thought that you and I could ever truly be transformed into that divine image. It seems almost impossible that we could be like Jesus. But God says we can be. In fact, the Bible says He has equipped us with everything necessary so that we might continue growing and developing and being conformed into His image (Romans 8:29).

Not only is God able to do that, but it is His will for us. It is His end-time plan. But whether or not that divine will comes to pass in our own individual lives is up to us. If we want to *be a part* of God's plan, we must *do our part* of God's plan. Our part is simply this: *to walk pleasing before Him—to think His thoughts, to speak His Words. In other words, to walk in His ways.*

When we do that, we will fulfill His will, and then He can manifest Himself in our lives just as He manifested Himself in Jesus' life.

If we truly want to fulfill our divine destiny and enjoy the fullness of the power of God in our lives, we must make a decision and a determination to start living every moment of every day to please our Father. We must walk out the prayer the Apostle Paul prayed for the Colossians: *"That ye might be filled with the knowledge of his [God's] will in all wisdom and spiritual understanding; That ye might walk worthy of the Lord unto all pleasing, being fruitful in every good work, and increasing in the knowledge of God; Strengthened with all might, according to his glorious power..."* (Colossians 1:9-11).

> "For those whom He [God] foreknew—of whom He was aware and loved beforehand—He also destined from the beginning (foreordaining them) to be molded into the image of His Son [and share inwardly His likeness], that He might become the first-born among many brethren."
>
> ROMANS 8:29, AMP

Make your decision today...and fulfill your divine destiny!

## Speak the Word

*I am filled with the knowledge of God's will in all wisdom and spiritual understanding.*

Colossians 1:9, AMP

FOR FURTHER STUDY:

Daniel 1:8-17

DAILY SCRIPTURE READING:

Exodus 5-6;
Mark 2

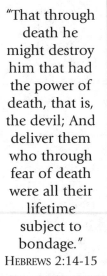

Kenneth

# The Lord Is on Your Side

> "That through death he might destroy him that had the power of death, that is, the devil; And deliver them who through fear of death were all their lifetime subject to bondage."
> HEBREWS 2:14-15

If you were the navigator of a ship, you'd be at a great disadvantage if you didn't know south existed, wouldn't you? If the only direction you were aware of was north, you'd get off track very easily.

That sounds silly but the truth is, many Christians are trying to do that very thing in the realm of the spirit. They are trying to navigate by faith without taking into consideration the reciprocal force that can, and will, take them in the opposite direction if they do not guard against it.

What is this reciprocal force I'm talking about? It's the force of fear.

"Oh, I don't feel like I'm afraid of anything," you may say.

That doesn't really matter because fear is not a feeling. It is not an emotion. It is a spiritual force. And although it can and does affect your emotions, it can be in operation even when you don't feel it.

Just as *"faith is the substance of things hoped for"* (Hebrews 11:1), fear is the substance of things not desired. Faith reaches into the unseen realm of the spirit and manifests the promises of God. Fear reaches into the unseen realm and manifests the threats of the devil. Faith is the power God uses to create. Fear is the power the devil uses to destroy.

Hebrews 2:14-15 says Jesus became flesh and blood to destroy the power of death and deliver those who were in bondage to it. It is the fear of death that keeps us in bondage.

You must understand, however, that fear of death does not necessarily mean you're afraid to leave your body to go to heaven, as believers do when they die physically. The fear of death referred to in Hebrews has a much broader meaning than that. It includes the fear of sickness, lack, failure and everything else that is included under the Master Law of Sin and Death.

If you grew up in a poor family, for example, you might spend your lifetime in bondage to the fear of poverty. You might even try to apply the principles of God—giving and confessing and doing all the things that bring prosperity—but if you retain the underlying fear of being poor, it won't matter how much wealth you accumulate, the devil will rob you every time you turn around. You have to repent and get free!

As Ephesians 6:12 says, we wrestle not against flesh and blood, but against principalities, powers, rulers of the darkness of this world. What do those rulers use to rule? Fear! Fear is their source of power. So, if we'll take authority over it and break its power, then poverty, sickness and failure that fear was designed to bring will never have the opportunity to manifest itself in our lives! You can take authority over fear. You can be free from its grip. You can live in freedom. Simply go before God and repent and use your God-given authority over that fear. Then stand in faith in your freedom. Confess the truth. In Psalm 118:6 David said, *"The Lord is on my side; I will not fear."*

## Speak the Word

*Jesus came and destroyed the power of death and the works of the devil in my life. He has delivered me from the bondage of fear.*
*Hebrews 2:14-15*

FOR FURTHER STUDY:

Psalm 118:1-6

DAILY SCRIPTURE READING:

Exodus 7-8;
Mark 3

*Gloria*

# Race for the Final Frontier

Today the Church is standing at the edge of a great frontier. I believe it is the final frontier that stands between us and the fullness of God's Glory. On the other side lie the greatest manifestations of God's power this earth has ever seen. What is the last great, spiritual frontier?

Holiness.

That's right. Holiness is the final frontier. And we will cross it before Jesus comes to catch us away. I know we will because the Bible says that He is coming for a glorious Church without spot or wrinkle (Ephesians 5:27). In other words, He is coming for a Church that is holy.

Some people get more excited about being the glorious Church than they do about being the holy Church. They have the idea that the Glory of God is exciting, while holiness is boring. But that's not true! Glory and holiness are both wonderful things—and you can't have the fullness of one without the other.

The reason is simple. Holiness is what allows the Glory of God to be manifested. So the more we walk in holiness, the more God will be able to pour forth His Glory through us! *Holiness* is a formidable word to many. But it simply means "separation to God for His use."

Knowing that should make us hungry for holiness. It should make us more eager than ever to separate ourselves from the things of the world unto the things of the Spirit. It should give us an intense desire to obey Romans 12:1-2.

So commit yourself to being holy. Present yourself to God as a living sacrifice. Move on into the spiritual realm—race for the final frontier.

## Speak the Word

*I present my body to God as a living sacrifice.*
*I will live a holy life, acceptable unto Him,*
*which is my reasonable service.*
*Romans 12:1*

> "I beseech you therefore, brethren, by the mercies of God, that ye present your bodies a living sacrifice, holy, acceptable unto God, which is your reasonable service. And be not conformed to this world: but be ye transformed by the renewing of your mind, that ye may prove what is that good, and acceptable, and perfect, will of God."
> ROMANS 12:1-2

FOR FURTHER STUDY:

Ephesians 5:23-33

DAILY SCRIPTURE READING:

Exodus 9-10;
Mark 4

> "Thou art the Christ [the Anointed One, the One with the burden-removing, yoke-destroying power], the Son of the living God."
> MATTHEW 16:16

# Translate and Meditate

When the Bible was translated into English, the translators failed to translate the Greek word *Christ*. Through this error, the devil has been able to steal a major revelation from the Church.

The word *Christ* is a Greek translation of the Hebrew word *Messiah*. Translated into English it means "anointed" or "the Anointed One."

If you want to see just how much this translation has cost us, read through the New Testament and find every time the word Christ is mentioned. (It will take awhile because it's in there 341 times!) In each instance translate Christ into *the Anointed One and His Anointing*. Then meditate on the new meaning it gives each scripture.

Take, for example, Colossians 1:27, *"Christ in you, the hope of glory."* Translate and meditate. *"The Anointed One and His Anointing in you, the hope of glory."* Hallelujah, it's the anointing in us—the same yoke-destroying power that's on Jesus—that gives us the earnest, intensive expectation of experiencing the Glory of God in our lives!

Therefore, when the New Testament refers to the gospel of Christ, it's talking about the gospel of the anointing, the good news of the sin-annihilating, sickness-crushing, poverty-pulverizing, bondage-breaking, yoke-destroying power of God. Jesus brought that anointing into our midst. That's the reason it's called *the gospel of Jesus Christ!*

Can you see how this can transform our thinking? Can you see what revelation has been kept from the Church? Get your Bible out. Go through the New Testament. Just mark it every time you see Christ. Translate and meditate. Christ, the Anointed One and His Anointing. You'll never be able to just read over Christ again. You will understand the revelation of that anointing in you, on you and poured all over you, if you'll translate and meditate!

## Speak the Word

*Jesus is the Christ—the Anointed One—the Son of the living God. He removes every burden and destroys every yoke of the devil.*

*Matthew 16:16; Isaiah 10:27*

FOR FURTHER STUDY:

Matthew 16:13-25

DAILY SCRIPTURE READING:

Exodus 11-13;
Mark 5-6

*Gloria*

# No Voice Mail in the Throne Room

Have you ever called out to God and received an answer like this?... "Hello, this is God. I'm away from the throne right now. But if you'll leave a number and a brief message at the sound of the beep, I will return your call."

Of course not! God is on call 24 hours a day, every day. He is always ready to listen and respond to you. You never get voice mail when you call God. Never! Even at 3 o'clock in the morning, He is right there, ready to visit with you.

In fact, He sent His Spirit to live in you so He could communicate with you every moment of the day.

If you haven't already done so, it's time you woke up to that fact and started taking advantage of it! Set aside special time to pray and commune with God every day.

I'll never forget when I first began to do that without fail. It was after I had heard a prophecy given by a man of God. At that time John was just a teenager, and I was concerned about him. He wasn't a bad boy, but he was doing things I knew he shouldn't do.

A word from the Lord said that if we'd spend just an hour or two in fellowship with Him each day, all would be well.

You know, just an hour or two a day is not very much to invest in order to have everything in your life be well. And I can vouch for the fact that it really works because today, all is well in our lives. All of our children, including John, are dedicated to the Lord and serving Him with us in ministry.

So make a quality decision to spend time with God every day. I guarantee, when you call out to Him, you won't get voice mail!

## Speak the Word

*I am constant in prayer.*

*Romans 12:12,* AMP

FOR FURTHER
STUDY:

John 16:5-16

DAILY SCRIPTURE
READING:
Exodus 14-15;
Mark 7

# Power Containers

"Death and
life are in the
power of the
tongue: and
they that love
it shall eat the
fruit thereof."
PROVERBS 18:21

The power of God's Word has a profound effect on our lives. But most believers don't really understand the degree to which this is true. Most believers only know that words convey information. But they are far more powerful than that. They actually serve as containers for spiritual power. According to Proverbs 18:21, they have the ability to carry faith or fear, blessing or cursing, life or death.

People sometimes speak idle or empty words, but God never does. Every word He has ever spoken has been filled with faith, power and life. In fact, God's Word actually contains within it the power to bring itself to pass. For example in Isaiah 55:11, He says, *"My word...shall not return unto me void, but it shall accomplish that which I please, and it shall prosper in the thing whereto I sent it."*

Every word God has ever spoken is backed by His faith and is as full of power today as it was the moment He said it. So when you believe that Word, and your faith comes together with His faith, the power of that Word is released, the Holy Spirit goes into action, and the Word explodes into this natural realm and becomes a reality in your life!

That's what happened when you were born again. You heard or read God's Word *"That if thou shalt confess with thy mouth the Lord Jesus, and shalt believe in thine heart that God hath raised him from the dead, thou shalt be saved"* (Romans 10:9). You believed that word, spoke it in faith and the power of the Holy Spirit was released, transforming your dead, fallen spirit into a reborn spirit, re-created in the image of Jesus Himself.

My, what a miracle! You were snatched from the dominion of darkness, and there was nothing the devil could do to stop it. The Words of God did the same thing for you that they did for Jesus when He was in the pit of hell. They demolished the devil's power over you and raised you up together with the Lord Jesus to sit together in heavenly places with Him!

Now think about this a minute. If His Word can save you...it can accomplish everything else you need...healing, finances, spiritual growth, a new job, a new home, a new car, restored relationships, a better marriage...whatever it is that you need TODAY...you can speak words of life and blessing and truth in faith, and as spiritual containers, they will begin to effect a change in the spiritual realm...which will eventually manifest in the natural realm.

In other words, you have the power to effect change in your life, by SPEAKING, because your words are containers of power. So get started. Speak God's Word. Speak words of life and power and faith. Things will never be the same!

## *Speak the Word*

*Death and life are in the power of my tongue.*
*I determine to speak only words of life.*

Proverbs 18:21

FOR FURTHER
STUDY:

James 3:1-6

DAILY SCRIPTURE
READING:

Exodus 16-17;
Mark 8

*Kenneth*

# Get In On the Power!

FEBRUARY 1

"But ye shall receive power, after that the Holy Ghost is come upon you."
ACTS 1:8

If you've been seeking the Baptism in the Holy Spirit and seem to have hit a brick wall, then hang on. Help is on the way! The promise of receiving the Holy Spirit with the evidence of speaking in tongues is for the entire Body of Christ—it's for you!

God wants you to have it. He knows how the Holy Spirit will empower your spiritual walk, how He will help you get the answers you need for day-to-day living. The enemy will rob you of this gift. Well-meaning saints will try to force it on you or tell you all kinds of "tactics" and "exercises" to get it. But your Heavenly Father just wants to give it to you. He wants to pour out His Spirit on you. He wants to flood your life with His life and power.

After you make Jesus the Lord of your life, it is the will of God that you experience the fullness of the Holy Spirit. Ephesians 5:18 says, *"Be not drunk with wine, wherein is excess; but be filled with the Spirit."* It is the Holy Spirit's ministry not only to impart the nature of God to the spirit of man at salvation, but also to come and live in the new creature. His job is to reveal exact knowledge of God from the heart of the Father. A believer cannot understand, by his own spirit alone, the profound wisdom of God. This is why Jesus said in John 14:26 that the Father would send us the Comforter to teach us "all things."

When you receive the Holy Spirit, you receive the ability of God. The word *power* in Acts 1:8 is translated *dunamis,* which means "ability" and "might." It is through the energizing force of the Holy Spirit living in us that we are transformed into effective witnesses.

If you haven't yet received the Baptism in the Holy Spirit, pray the following and release your faith. God is faithful! Just ask in faith.

*"My Heavenly Father, I am a believer. I am Your child and You are my Father. Jesus is my Lord. I believe with all my heart that Your Word is true. Your Word says that if I ask, I will receive the Holy Spirit. So in the Name of Jesus Christ my Lord, I ask You to fill me to overflowing with Your precious Holy Spirit. Because of Your Word, I believe that I now receive the Holy Spirit and I thank You for Him. I believe that the Holy Spirit is within me and by faith I accept Him. Holy Spirit, rise up within me as I praise my God. I fully expect to speak with other tongues as You give me utterance. Amen."*

Now begin to praise God. Worship Him and let the Spirit rise up within you as you speak in other tongues. Just receive and get in on the power!

FOR FURTHER STUDY:

Acts 2:1-13

≈

DAILY SCRIPTURE READING:

Exodus 18-19; Mark 9

## Speak the Word

*I have the Holy Ghost in me. Therefore, I have power!*
*Acts 1:8*

> "So, since Christ suffered in the flesh [for us, for you], arm yourselves with the same thought and purpose [patiently to suffer rather than fail to please God]. For whoever has suffered in the flesh...has stopped pleasing himself and the world, and pleases God."
> 1 PETER 4:1, AMP

# Live to Please Him

God was able to say of Jesus, *"Thou art my beloved Son, in whom I am well pleased"* (Mark 1:11). In the same way, there is no reason why we as believers can't please God as much as Jesus did. We have a reborn spirit made in His image. We've been given His righteousness. We've been filled with the same Holy Spirit. We have all the capacity that Jesus had in the earth to be just like Him and to do the works that He did because He lives in us (Colossians 1:27).

He was dedicated. He was totally sold out to God. He was without sin. The Bible tells us that many times He ministered all day and then prayed all night, yet He had a flesh-and-blood body just like you. He enjoyed a good night's sleep just as much as you do. So there was an element of crucifying the flesh involved in giving up that sleep and doing what pleased God. He said no to His flesh, and yes to His Father.

*"Well, Gloria, I know Jesus did that, but God doesn't expect that kind of self-sacrifice from us."*

Yes, He does. First Peter 4:1 says so. You see, it's time for the Church to stop living like Gentiles (those in the world without God and without hope)! It's time for the Church to live like God says, regardless of what the world around us is doing. Just because the morals of the world slip doesn't mean the morals of the Church should slip.

It doesn't matter how dark this world gets, we are to be the light of this world. We need to fight against compromise by arming ourselves with the commitment to suffer in the flesh rather than fail to please God in any area of our lives. Suffering in the flesh is making your flesh do something it doesn't want to do. It's dedicating yourself to do what's pleasing to God even when it causes your flesh discomfort. When you are ready to do that, you'll go beyond just "not sinning" and into a life that is pleasing to God. You'll be ready to lay down those things that you enjoy, things that aren't necessarily bad in themselves, but are hindering your walk with God.

If you want to walk in the best God has for you, those are the kinds of sacrifices you must make. You have to step into that higher life by faith. You have to lay down your life because the Word says to do it. Then, and only then, will you discover the wonders that are waiting on the other side of your obedience.

I know this can sound harsh...but I know you want to go on with God. I know you want to hunger and thirst after righteousness...so make some adjustments in your life. When you do, you'll live to please Him!

## *Speak the Word*

*I suffer in the flesh rather than fail to please God.*
1 Peter 4:1, AMP

FOR FURTHER STUDY:

1 Peter 4:1-7

DAILY SCRIPTURE READING:

Exodus 20-21;
Mark 10

*Kenneth*

# Let Not Your Heart Be Troubled

FEBRUARY 3

❧

"Let not your heart be troubled."
JOHN 14:1

People everywhere—many believers included—are running around wringing their hands, worrying about what to do. But there's really no need for it. After all, Jesus has already told us what to do. He said, *"Let not your heart be troubled."*

*"Yes, but Brother Copeland, He said that thousands of years ago. They didn't have the kind of trouble back then that we're facing today."*

Friend, when Jesus said those words to His disciples, they were about to face more trouble than most of us can even imagine. Jesus was about to be crucified before their eyes. Peter was about to deny Him. Who can even imagine how distressing those days must have been?

Yet Jesus said to them, *"Let not your heart be troubled."*

But, praise God, He didn't stop there. He went on to teach us the key to having an untroubled heart even in the most troubling times.

He goes on to say...*abide.* "Abide in Me, and I in you. As the branch cannot bear fruit of itself, unless it *abides* in the vine, neither can you, unless you *abide* in Me. I am the vine, you are the branches.... If you *abide* in Me, and My words *abide* in you, you will ask what you will, and it shall be done for you. By this My Father is glorified, that you bear much fruit..." (read John 15:4-10).

When you *abide* in Jesus, He's not just your Sunday God. He's not just the One you think about when you get in trouble. No, when you *abide* in Him, He's your Monday Lord. He's your Tuesday Lord. He's your Wednesday, Thursday, Friday and Saturday Lord. He's your daytime Lord and nighttime Lord. He's Lord of your life 24 hours a day, seven days a week. He's involved with you every moment.

When you rest in the Word all day long like that, then the Word begins to *abide* in you, and it will constantly teach you the ways and wisdom of God. It will keep your heart from being troubled.

## *Speak the Word*

*I do not let my heart be troubled because I trust and abide in Jesus.*

John 14:1

FOR FURTHER
STUDY:

Proverbs 8:10-17

❧

DAILY SCRIPTURE
READING:

Exodus 22-23;
Mark 11

> "Many are the afflictions of the righteous: but the Lord delivereth him out of them all."
> PSALM 34:19

# Set Your Angels Free!

I don't think it's any exaggeration to say that every one of us, or someone we know, is facing some kind of problem today—some kind of trouble we can't escape without the help of God. For one person, that trouble may be a disease that medical science can't cure. For another, it may be financial problems or a family crisis.

But no matter what kind of wall the devil has backed you up against, you can count on one thing: God has promised to deliver you. That's right. The Word says the afflictions of the righteous are many, but the Lord delivers him out of them all. How I love the word ALL in the Bible!

Psalm 91:9-11 AMP says, *"Because you have made the Lord your refuge, and the Most High your dwelling place, There shall no evil befall you, nor any plague or calamity come near your tent. For He will give His angels [especial] charge over you, to accompany and defend and preserve you in all your ways [of obedience and service]."*

God gives His angels charge over you. He charges them to protect you...to keep you...to minister to you.

"To me?" Yes, to you! Does that surprise you? It shouldn't. As Hebrews 1:14 (AMP) says, *"Are not the angels all (servants) ministering spirits, sent out in the service [of God for the assistance] of those who are to inherit salvation?"*

If you are an heir of salvation, angels are sent out in service to you. And their ministry can literally be a lifesaver. (Read about Shadrach, Meshach and Abednego in Daniel 3.) I've noticed something about people whose angels supernaturally delivered them. They were faithful people.

If you need deliverance today, be faithful. You can do this with the words you speak. When you speak words of defeat instead of victory, the angels assigned to you are bound by your words of unbelief. They have been charged to hearken to God's Word—words of faith (Psalm 103:20).

If you haven't been getting the action you need in your finances, your health or any other area, look to your words. There's no shortage of angel power, although you may be experiencing a shortage of Word power on your part.

Solve that shortage by putting God's promises of deliverance in your heart and in your mouth. Continually give the angels the Word they need to protect you. When you're tempted to discuss how bad your situation is...stop. Remember your great salvation. Remember the angels. Remember what God's Word says about your situation. Open your mouth and set your angels free to minister to you!

## *Speak the Word*

*The Lord delivers me out of all my afflictions.*
*Psalm 34:19*

FOR FURTHER STUDY:

Daniel 3

DAILY SCRIPTURE READING:

Exodus 24-25;
Mark 12

*Kenneth*

# Put Your Power Tools to Work

> "If two of you agree on earth about anything that they may ask, it shall be done for them by My Father who is in heaven."
> MATTHEW 18:19, NAS

The prayer of agreement is one of the most powerful tools God has given us as believers. It is the prayer that Jesus Himself guaranteed would bring results every time. It's especially powerful in marriages. When a husband and wife come into agreement about something, it is so powerful!

But sometimes couples don't seem to be getting results. Maybe you and your spouse have prayed the prayer of agreement, perhaps over your finances or your children, and nothing appears to be happening. I have found, when that occurs, that the problem usually lies in one of four areas.

1) *Run a harmony check.* The word *agreement* in Matthew 18:19 can also be translated "to harmonize or make a symphony." When the members of a symphony are tuning their instruments, the sound isn't much to hear. But when they all begin to harmonize, the sound they make is tremendously powerful. The same is true in prayer. Believers agreeing together in the Holy Spirit are a powerful, unstoppable force. That's why Satan fights Christian families. That's why he doesn't want men and women unified in marriage. He wants us fussing and fighting all the time because he knows it will hinder our prayers (1 Peter 3:7).

2) *Establish your heart on God's Word.* The prayer of agreement should be based on the Word. Find scriptures that cover your request. That word from God is the faith foundation of your prayer. Now you are agreeing on something God has already said.

3) *Fix your mind on the Word.* Soak your mind in it. Keep it before your eyes. When the devil tells you something contrary to the Word, speak. Bring every thought captive (2 Corinthians 10:5). Think on what the Bible says (Philippians 4:8).

4) *Act as if it's done.* This is where many people miss it. You have to act on your faith. Don't leave your prayer closet and start wringing your hands and speaking fear and unbelief. Speak the desired end result. Speak what you just agreed on. Refuse to act like that issue is a problem anymore. When someone asks you about it, say: "Glory to God, that issue is handled. My wife/husband and I have agreed in prayer. God is honoring our agreement. And as far as we're concerned, that problem is behind us."

The prayer of agreement is a powerful tool. So don't despair if you're not seeing results. Go through this list and check your heart. Then, put your power tools to work!

FOR FURTHER STUDY:

Matthew 18:18-20

DAILY SCRIPTURE READING:

Exodus 26-28;
Mark 13-14

## Speak the Word

*When I agree with another in prayer about anything that we ask, it shall be done for us by our Father in heaven.*
*Matthew 18:19, NAS*

# Loose Me and Let Me Go!

> "And when he thus had spoken, he cried with a loud voice, Lazarus, come forth. And he that was dead came forth, bound hand and foot with graveclothes: and his face was bound about with a napkin. Jesus said unto them, Loose him, and let him go."
>
> JOHN 11:43-44

Do you remember the account in John 11 of Jesus' raising Lazarus from the dead? If you'll go back and read it, you'll see that when Jesus stood before the tomb, He called out, *"Lazarus, come forth!"* Sure enough, Lazarus came forth. But the Bible says he was still bound up. The grave clothes were wrapped around him. So Jesus said, *"Loose him, and let him go!"*

That's a good illustration of our situation. When we were born again, our spirit man came forth. We were born of God. But the self-centered habits we had acquired while living under the Law of Sin and Death were still in place. They still had us bound.

Well, Jesus wants the same thing for us that He wanted for Lazarus. He not only wants us alive, He wants us free! He wants us walking in love because that's the only way the new life He's put within us can get out!

When we walk in love, we step out of the natural realm into the supernatural. Nothing can hold us back anymore. But the grave clothes, those deadly habits of unforgiveness, impatience, irritation and selfishness, have to go.

Do you want to be free from the habits of hostility that have you bound? Then say the same thing Jesus is saying. Get into agreement with Him and say to each one of those deadly habits, *"Loose me and let me go! I will go on with God. I refuse to be held down. I will walk in love. I put hate and unforgiveness and selfishness behind me. I will go forward in the power and the Glory of God. SO LOOSE ME AND LET ME GO!"*

It doesn't take weeks or months to switch over from natural to supernatural living. For a born-again follower of Jesus, all it takes is a decision to yield to the force of love. After all, God has already placed it within you. But love won't do any good if you keep it locked inside.

"Put on the new man created after God," the Bible says (Ephesians 4:24). Don't leave him trapped inside. Bring him to the outside. Dare to release what God has put within you. Strip off those graveclothes and live the life He has called you to live.

Dare to step into the supernatural. Dare to give yourself over to love.

## *Speak the Word*

*Deadly habits of unforgiveness, impatience, irritation
and selfishness, loose me and let me go.
I choose to walk free by the power of God's Word.
John 11:43-44; Romans 8:2-6*

FOR FURTHER STUDY:

Galatians 5:13-15

DAILY SCRIPTURE READING:

Exodus 29-30;
Mark 15

*Kenneth*
# Settle it at the Table

Faith has never changed. God has never changed. The only ones who need to do some changing are you and I. We need to make some adjustments.

First, we need to get off our religion and get on the Word of God. We need to find out what God has provided and walk in it in an indelible manner.

We need to learn to take advantage of what Hebrews 6:18 calls the two immutable things in which it was impossible for God to lie—God's sworn oath in the blood and the body of Jesus. We need to start thinking in terms of God's blood oath that can't be broken. That's what the New Testament is.

That's what you're dealing with when you take Communion. Bread and wine—body and blood. It's the securing of the covenant.

When you want something settled once and for all, go to God about it. Come to Him with all your homework done and go over His Word with Him. Rehearse before Him His promises about that situation, then seal it with Communion. That will finalize it in your mind.

> "That by two immutable things, in which it was impossible for God to lie, we might have a strong consolation, who have fled for refuge to lay hold upon the hope set before us."
> HEBREWS 6:18

I can tell you from experience, it is a powerful thing. Gloria and I have done it many times over some very serious issues. It sealed our faith so completely that at the moment of Communion, those things ceased to be issues for us in our own minds. They were settled in the blood of Jesus.

If you're facing something today that, in the natural, looks overwhelming, go to the table. Whether it's cancer, a serious financial need or direction you're needing, settle it in the blood of Jesus. Settle it at the Communion table.

## *Speak the Word*

*As I receive Communion, I put myself in remembrance of what Jesus did for me through His death on the cross. Because of Jesus I am redeemed from the curse of the law.*
*1 Corinthians 11:25-26; Galatians 3:13*

FOR FURTHER
STUDY:

Matthew 26:26-29

DAILY SCRIPTURE
READING:

Exodus 31-32;
Mark 16

> "But if ye have bitter envying and strife in your hearts, glory not, and lie not against the truth. This wisdom descendeth not from above, but is earthly, sensual, devilish. For where envying and strife is, there is confusion and every evil work."
>
> JAMES 3:14-16

# An Open Door to the Devil

The most hazardous weapon the devil uses against us is a foremost enemy of love. The weapon: *strife*.

*Strife* means "vigorous or bitter conflict, discord and antagonism; to quarrel, struggle or clash; competition; rivalry." Strife is of the devil. It is an open door to the devil. It licenses him to bring confusion and evil into your life. That's why he's always pushing for us to argue with one another and get offended or critical of one another. It gives him access to us!

You see, when you were born again, the Bible says you were delivered out of the control and the dominion of darkness and into the kingdom of God's Son (Colossians 1:13). At that time, the devil lost his right of lordship over you and you received salvation.

Salvation doesn't just include the new birth, it includes all the blessings of God. Peace, healing, well-being, finances and provision for every area of your life belong to you the moment you become a child of God.

But Satan doesn't want you to enjoy those blessings. He doesn't want you to be healed, happy and prosperous, because if you are, other people will notice and want the same quality of life you have. They'll give their hearts to God because of the goodness of God they see in your life.

In order to stop that from happening, the devil tries to steal those blessings from you. But since he has no authority over you anymore, to successfully do that, he has to trick you into opening the door of your life to him. So what does he do? He tries to get you into strife. He brings you an opportunity to have a conflict with someone because he knows that the moment you step into strife, he can begin to gain the mastery over you.

I remember when Ken and I first received that revelation years ago. We realized that if we wanted to walk in the full blessing of God, we would have to stay out of strife. We wouldn't be able to argue with people. We wouldn't be able to fight back when people criticized us or wronged us. We'd have to respond in love.

So we made up our minds to put strife out of our family. We kept it out of our ministry. When we did mess up and exchange harsh words, we determined we had to be quick to repent or the devil would have a foothold in our lives.

You do the same thing. Don't open the door to the devil in your life. Shut it! Put strife out of your life. Put it out of your family. Put it out of your church. When you do, you'll enjoy the blessings of God like never before!

## *Speak the Word*

*I refuse to allow envy and strife into my heart.*
*I refuse to give the devil a license to bring confusion and*
*every evil work into my life.*
*James 3:16*

FOR FURTHER
STUDY:

Romans 13:11-14

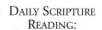

DAILY SCRIPTURE
READING:

Exodus 33-34;
Luke 1

*Kenneth*

# Choose Your Profession

Your confession is what you say all the time. That's why you'll see the word for confession translated in the New and Old Testaments as both *confession* and *profession*.

A professional is a person who devotes himself to a particular occupation. A professional athlete, for example, is not a person who participates in a sport every now and then. He or she is a person who plays that sport full time.

Our profession of faith, the profession of our mouths and our actions, is the way we act and talk continually—not just when we stop for a few glorious moments and speak to the mountain, but all the time.

Jesus said, *"Whosoever shall say unto this mountain...and shall not doubt in his heart, but shall believe that those things which he saith shall come to pass..."* (Mark 11:23). Notice He said "those things," not just "that one thing."

Everything you do and say all day long ought to be an answer to the mountain. What do you do all the time when no one is watching? What do you say when you first get up in the morning? How do you talk about that mountain when there's nobody around to hear you? That's your profession.

If your profession isn't one of faith, then go to the Word, find God's promise that applies to your situation, and meditate on it until it becomes God speaking to you. Then the hope of God will rise up on the inside of you. You'll hook your faith to the living Word of God and you'll start acting and speaking in strength and power.

Let me tell you, when you speak the Word of God with real faith, mountains move, fig trees die and the devil runs for cover. Why? Because Jesus is the High Priest over your profession. He is anointed and appointed by Almighty God to bring it to pass. He is ready, willing and able to move on your profession of faith-filled words and actions. So give Him some! Talk to your problems in faith. Speak the desired end result and nothing more. Then continually offer thanksgiving and praise to the Lord for the answer:

> "Seeing then that we have a great high priest, that is passed into the heavens, Jesus the Son of God, let us hold fast our profession."
> HEBREWS 4:14

*"Lord Jesus, You're the High Priest of my confession. You're the Administrator over the words I've spoken to this situation. I want You to know I appreciate it. I thank You for being my Lord. I'm standing on the living Word of God and I refuse to change my stand. I know the Word of God will never change. God will never change. The blood of Jesus will never change. The Name of Jesus will never change. So that means the devil and this situation will have to change. Lord God, I thank You for it. From here on, I consider this problem solved! Amen."*

FOR FURTHER STUDY:

Matthew 17:14-20

DAILY SCRIPTURE READING:

Exodus 35-36; Luke 2

## *Speak the Word*

*Jesus is the High Priest of my profession; therefore, I hold fast to it.*
*Hebrews 4:14*

> "But the fruit of the Spirit is love, joy, peace, longsuffering, gentleness, goodness, faith, Meekness, temperance: against such there is no law."
> GALATIANS 5:22-23

# Flow in the Fruit

Wouldn't it be wonderful if the power of God were flowing through you all the time? Wouldn't it be marvelous if you could walk in His supernatural might every day of your life?

There's no question about it. That would be a glorious way to live. But most Christians don't believe it's possible. That's because they think God's supernatural power comes only through the gifts of the Spirit, and the Bible says those gifts are given only as God wills.

While it's true that we can't operate in the gifts of the Spirit—such as words of wisdom and knowledge, gifts of healing and miracles—24 hours a day, God has given us a well of supernatural power that is continually bubbling up within us. He has made resident within our born-again spirit mighty forces that can enable us to overcome anything the devil might throw our way any moment of the day or night.

Galatians 5:22-23 calls these unbeatable forces the fruit of the spirit. They include love, joy, peace, long-suffering (or patience), gentleness, goodness, faith, meekness and temperance (or self-control).

Contrary to popular belief, the fruit of the spirit aren't just nice qualities we should adopt so we'll be pleasant company—although people who have those fruit are delightfully pleasant! The fruit of the spirit actually release the supernatural power of God in our lives.

Love, for example, is God's power to overcome every obstacle, for as 1 Corinthians 13:8 (NIV) says: *"Love never fails."* Joy fortifies you with supernatural power when you start to weaken, for Nehemiah 8:10 says, *"The joy of the Lord is your strength."* Peace undergirds you and helps you make supernaturally correct decisions, for Colossians 3:15 (AMP) says, *"Let the peace...from the Christ rule (act as umpire continually) in your hearts—deciding and settling with finality all questions that arise in your minds...."*

And on down the list I could go.

The fruit of the spirit are God's provision for the strength of your character to be developed, so you can be overcoming in all circumstances. Study them. Learn to yield to them. Watch those life forces come out of you and put you over as you grow. When you do, you'll flow in the fruit...the fruit of the spirit!

## Speak the Word

*I flow in the fruit of the spirit. I allow love, joy, peace, longsuffering, gentleness, goodness, faith, meekness and temperance to grow and develop in my life.*
Galatians 5:22-23

FOR FURTHER STUDY:

2 Peter 1:5-11

DAILY SCRIPTURE READING:

Exodus 37-38;
Luke 3

*Kenneth*

# Dare to Be Courageous!

"My brethren,
be strong in
the Lord, and
in the power
of his might."
EPHESIANS 6:10

In the face of impossible challenges, God gives us the same instruction He gave to Joshua and Solomon. "Be strong and very courageous."

He does not say, "You pray and I'll make you strong."

He says, "You be strong—not in your own power, but in My might."

Clearly, being courageous is our responsibility, and it's not a take-it-or-leave-it proposition. It's a command.

The word translated *courage* in the Hebrew means "to be sharp, alert or clearheaded." It also means "to be strong or confirmed." When I looked up the word *confirmed* in the dictionary, I found it means, "to be strengthened, established and made more firm."

The word *virtue* in 2 Peter 1:5 carries this same idea. There, the Apostle Peter tells us, *"Giving all diligence, add to your faith virtue."* In other words, "Add to your faith courageous, moral energy."

There's a conspicuous lack of courageous, moral energy among many believers today. Great numbers of Christians know the Word says that by the stripes of Jesus we were healed (1 Peter 2:24). They believe it. They have been taught that if they'll fill their hearts and mouths with that Word—and stick with it long enough—healing will be certain to manifest in their bodies.

Why then don't more people take hold of that Word and stay with it until they're healed? No courage. No moral energy.

You see the same problem in the area of finances. Christians everywhere want to be debt free. They know the truth. So they confess, "I'm the head and not the tail. I lend to many, but I don't borrow! God meets all my needs...." and so on.

But when it comes time to buy a car, a house or build a church, they wilt. "Oh my, that's a lot of money. There's no way in the world I'll ever be able to believe God for that much money."

What makes people back off their faith like that? A lack of courage. A lack of moral energy.

You may be facing some serious circumstances today. It may be your health, your family, your finances. Whatever it is, being courageous to believe the Word of God can put you over. But, you have to choose to stand up to the fear, to stand up to that doubt. Boldly declare, "Fear, you have no place in me. I'll not serve you. I dare to believe the Word of God! I dare to stand on it and not back off! I dare to be courageous!"

FOR FURTHER STUDY:

Psalm 31

DAILY SCRIPTURE READING:

Exodus 39-40; Luke 4

## *Speak the Word*

*I am strong in the Lord and in the power of His might.*
*Ephesians 6:10*

> "A new commandment I give unto you, That ye love one another; as I have loved you, that ye also love one another."
>
> JOHN 13:34

# Love Is Not an Option

Have you ever wondered why Jesus commanded us to live by love? It's because He desires for us to succeed and be blessed—spirit, soul and body. And He knows love is the primary key to that success.

If we actually understood the blessing that walking in love brings, we wouldn't be so willing to abandon it when we encounter pressure or aggravation. If we knew, for example, that becoming fretful or resentful was going to cost us a great, supernatural revelation, we might be more apt to set those unloving attitudes aside.

"What does love have to do with spiritual revelation?" you ask.

Plenty! Read Colossians 2:2 and you can see for yourself how closely they are tied together. But the benefits of love don't stop with wisdom and revelation. They also include divine power. Jesus said in John 14:21 that He will manifest Himself to the person who walks in love.

I think this verse in John is very interesting, especially in light of how eager we are to have Jesus manifest Himself among us in power. We long for Him to reveal Himself by signs and wonders and miracles. And, surely, as the time of His Second Coming draws closer, those signs and wonders must come in greater manifestation.

But do you know where they will manifest in greatest power? Among the people who are living and walking in love. That's what happened in the book of Acts. God poured out His Spirit in mighty power at Pentecost with tongues of fire and the sound of a mighty, rushing wind, not upon people who were squabbling and arguing with one another, but among people who *"continued with one accord"* (Acts 1:14).

He shook the building and filled every believer with the Holy Ghost and boldness—not when the Church was fussing and working up denominational splits, but when they were *"of one heart and of one soul"* (Acts 4:32).

Need power in your life today? Need harmony in your family, in your marriage and among your children? Then walk in love. Walk in love at all costs...walk in love and decide that for your life, love is a command, not an option.

## *Speak the Word*

*I am obedient to the commandment of Jesus.*
*I love others as He has loved me.*
*John 13:34*

FOR FURTHER STUDY:

1 Corinthians 13:1-3

DAILY SCRIPTURE READING:

Leviticus 1-3;
Luke 5-6

*Kenneth*

# You Are Loved!

What I'm about to share with you, more than any single revelation, has changed my life. It has changed the way I read the New Testament. It has settled every question I have ever had—or could have—about prosperity, healing and every other blessing of God.

The revelation I'm referring to is as big as eternity, yet it can be summed up in one small, Hebrew word—*hesed*. That word may mean nothing to you right now, but once you gain insight into it, your spirit will take off like a bird out of a cage.

> "O give thanks unto the Lord; for he is good: for his mercy *[hesed]* endureth for ever."
>
> PSALM 136:1

What truth could be that powerful? Read it for yourself: *"For I desired mercy, and not sacrifice; and the knowledge of God more than burnt offerings. But they like men have transgressed the covenant"* (Hosea 6:6-7).

The word *mercy* in that verse is actually the Hebrew word *hesed* (spelled *chesed*, pronounced kheh'-sed). It is translated in the Old Testament as "mercy, kindness, tender mercies, lovingkindness and fidelity." Its counterpart in the Greek language is *agape*. Although *agape* was in the Greek language in Jesus' day, until He used it, most people didn't know what it meant. It was not heard on the streets.

To be quite honest, people still don't know what it means. You talk to most of them about unconditional love or real mercy, and they just bat their eyes at you like a frog in a hailstorm. Yet, without that understanding, we can't even begin to grasp the nature of our relationship with God.

If you doubt it, take some time and read all of Psalm 136. *Hesed* is mentioned in all of the 26 verses. Obviously the psalmist was driving home a point. He was telling us that the compelling force behind all of God's actions was *hesed*. More than just a quality He possesses, *hesed* is God's very nature. The New Testament puts it this way: "God is *agape*" (1 John 4:16).

In the natural realm, *hesed* can be compared to that tender yet fiercely protective love a mother has when she holds her baby in her arms and her heart goes out to it. It's the love that causes her to say, "I'll nurse you, little one. I'll care for you. I'll teach you all that I know. I'll see to it that no one harms you."

That is a picture of *hesed*. It's a picture of God Almighty saying to you, "I'll never leave you nor forsake you."

**FOR FURTHER STUDY:**

Psalm 136

**DAILY SCRIPTURE READING:**

Leviticus 4-5; Luke 7

No matter how you feel today, you are loved. Your feelings may tell you otherwise, but your Heavenly Father has loved you with His *hesed* from the beginning of your life. He loves you unconditionally, just the way you are, every day of your life. He never changes...He never leaves nor forsakes you. Receive His embrace today. Receive His love.

## Speak the Word

*I give thanks to the Lord for He is good. His love and mercy endure forever.*

*Psalm 136:1*

> "Love never
> fails."
> 1 CORINTHIANS
> 13:8, NKJV

# The Greatest Quest

What is the number one goal in your life? What are the things you're aiming to accomplish, the dreams you want to achieve?

If you're a businessperson, you may be pursuing the goal of building a business so successful, you can pour millions of dollars into the work of God. If you're called to the ministry, you may be dreaming of preaching the gospel around the world.

Yet, as wonderful as those goals might be, there is something even more important you can accomplish. It is something that you as a believer should *"eagerly pursue and seek to acquire."* It should be *"your aim, your great quest"* (1 Corinthians 14:1, AMP).

What is this great quest? The goal of having your life ordered by and overflowing with the love of God.

You see, human love is so changeable, it can turn to hate overnight. It is so undefined that it can behave with tender affection one moment and then with jealous rage the next, and be called "love" all the while.

But the love of God, which is the kind of love you and I are called to live, is altogether different. It is not changeable. It does not act one way today and another way tomorrow. It does not vary according to our circumstances or emotions. On the contrary, its characteristics are distinct and consistent.

First Corinthians 13:4-8 tells us precisely what its characteristics are. This passage of Scripture sets a very high standard for love—so high that you might be tempted to think it's beyond your reach. But it's not. In fact, if you're a believer, that God kind of love is a natural part of your supernatural disposition. It's in your heart now. You may not be yielding to it, but it's there. When you were born again, God put Himself and His own nature of love inside you. Romans 5:5 says He poured out His love in your heart through the Holy Spirit.

Without the constant influence of the Spirit of God and the Word of God, you will have a natural pull toward selfishness. We all have a natural mind that has been trained to believe things like, "You have to look out for yourself...and stick up for your own rights." On top of that, the devil continually works full time to draw us out of love, because he knows if he succeeds, he can pull the plug on our faith and steal the answers to our prayers. In short, he can make a "place" for himself.

The bottom line: Love is the foundation for the Christian life. When you walk in love, you put yourself in a position where God Himself can protect you. When you quit seeking your own, He seeks your own for you. And He is a great One to have on your side, because when He is for you, no one can stand against you (Romans 8:31-34). Love is our one and only commandment. Love is the key to God's wisdom, power and protection. No wonder the Word says, *"Make it your aim, your great quest."*

## *Speak the Word*

*I eagerly pursue and seek to acquire love.*
*I make it my aim and my great quest in life.*
*1 Corinthians 14:1, AMP*

FOR FURTHER
STUDY:

1 Corinthians
13:4-8

DAILY SCRIPTURE
READING:

Leviticus 6-7;
Luke 8

*Gloria*

# Make the Switch

If you've been born again, you can walk in love and be so loving to people all the time! Even those people who really get to you. You have the power to do that! Did you know that?

"Oh, no, Gloria. Not me. I could never switch from being selfish to walking in the love of God. I've tried it...I just don't know how to break this habit!"

I'm happy to tell you, the key to developing your love life is wonderfully simple. You do it by maintaining contact with God. You do it by fellowshiping with Him in the Word and in prayer—by staying in union and communion with Him and letting His life flow through you.

As Christian writer Donald Gee says, "Fruit is the result of life. Loss of communion is the explanation of most of our failure in spiritual fruit-bearing, and no amount of Christian work, or even exercise of spiritual gifts, can ever be a substitute for walking with God. It is encouraging to remember that sustained [continual] communion with Christ in our daily walk produces the fruit of the spirit unconsciously" (Donald Gee, *The Fruit of the Spirit* [Springfield: Gospel Publishing House, 1928], p. 60, used by permission of the publisher).

Jesus Himself taught us that principle of communion. He said, *"Just as no branch can bear fruit of itself without abiding in (vitally united to) the vine, neither can you bear fruit unless you abide in Me. I am the Vine, you are the branches. Whoever lives in Me and I in him bears much (abundant) fruit. However, apart from Me—cut off from vital union with Me—you can do nothing"* (John 15:4-5, AMP).

Actually, when we maintain living contact with God, we enter a glorious cycle that continually lifts us higher. The more we fellowship with God, the more we are changed by His presence and empowered to walk in love. And the more we walk in love, the more intimate our fellowship with Him becomes.

Are you longing for greater measures of God's power in your life? Are you yearning for greater manifestations of His victorious presence? Then eagerly pursue and seek to walk in love. Determine above all else to live in union with Jesus and be ruled by His love. Then, you CAN make the switch!

> "God is love, and he who dwells and continues in love dwells and continues in God, and God dwells and continues in him. In this [union and communion with Him] love is brought to completion and attains perfection with us...because as He is, so are we in this world."
> 1 JOHN 4:16-17, AMP

## Speak the Word

*God is love. As I dwell and continue in God, He dwells and continues in me; and love is brought to completion and attains perfection in me.*
*1 John 4:16-17, AMP*

FOR FURTHER STUDY:

John 15:9-11

DAILY SCRIPTURE READING:

Leviticus 8-9; Luke 9

*Gloria*

# It's Not What You Know

Notice Jesus didn't say we should believe we've received what we ask for when we see it. He said to believe you receive *when you pray*.

Now, if you follow His instructions, how do you think you're going to act? Are you going to walk around all depressed and joyless? Are you going to stand around wringing your hands worrying?

No! You're going to rejoice and praise God for the answer to your prayer. You're going to act like you've already received it.

Right here is where many people miss it. They know God's Word works, but they fail to act on it.

You may have been studying the Word for 20 years. You may know how to live by faith better than anyone around. But remember, it's not what you know that will bring you through in victory—it's what you do.

You can walk in faith consistently through 10 trials that come your way and experience great success. Yet on the 11th one, if you neglect to act on the Word, you'll fail. Although the string of victories in your past is a wonderful thing, it's what you do today that will get you through today's test or trial.

So set your heart and mind on doing what the Word says...in every situation. Believe you receive when you pray...and enjoy the victory!

## *Speak the Word*

*What things soever I desire, when I pray,*
*I believe that I receive, and I shall have them!*
*Mark 11:24*

FOR FURTHER STUDY:

1 John 3:19-22

DAILY SCRIPTURE READING:

Leviticus 10-11;
Luke 10

*Gloria*

# By the Grace of God

It doesn't matter what kind of trouble you may find yourself in from time to time, God's grace is always strong enough to get you out! All you have to do is tap into it...by faith.

If you want to enjoy God's grace—His unconditional favor—then start releasing your faith. Get into God's Word. Put that Word into your heart and speak it out of your mouth. Begin to believe it and act on it.

If you'll do that, you won't have to be defeated in any area of your life. Because there is no situation, no circumstance, no disaster—nothing Satan has ever done or can do—that is stronger than the grace of God.

> "For thou, Lord, wilt bless the righteous; with favour wilt thou compass him as with a shield."
>
> PSALM 5:12

The Apostle Paul proved that. He faced more trouble than most of us could ever imagine. He gives a list of the things that happened to him in 2 Corinthians 11:23-29—beatings, stonings, jail, shipwrecks.

Paul said those things came to him because a demonic messenger had been sent to stop him. This evil spirit came to stop him from preaching the gospel. Paul called the messenger *"a thorn in the flesh"* (2 Corinthians 12:7).

That demon worked hard to shut Paul's mouth and throw him off course, but nothing worked. Why? Grace. God's favor.

Remember that when circumstances come against you. When the devil is trying to mess up your life and it looks like there's absolutely no way out of the problem, don't despair. God's power excels in those situations. His favor is always enough to bring you out on top.

Don't ever be intimidated by the devil. The Bible says he is limited to the things of this natural world. But grace is without limit. It releases heaven's supernatural power on your behalf.

Speak to what you are facing today. Say: *"I'm a born-again child of Almighty God. His supernatural favor surrounds me like a shield this very moment. It is more than enough to deliver me out of this trouble. My faith is in God's Word and I'm coming out of this triumphantly by the grace of God!"*

## Speak the Word

*The Lord blesses me for I am righteous.*
*He surrounds me with favor as with a shield.*
*Psalm 5:12*

FOR FURTHER
STUDY:

Acts 7:8-10

DAILY SCRIPTURE
READING:

Leviticus 12-13;
Luke 11

> "And he arose, and rebuked the wind, and said unto the sea, Peace, be still. And the wind ceased, and there was a great calm."
>
> MARK 4:39

# Speak the End Result

I've preached for years that believers are to speak directly to the situations that they want to change in their lives. And some people have asked me a very good question. They've asked, "Well, what do you say?"

The answer is simple. You speak the desired end result. Nothing more. *"Peace, be still."* That's all Jesus had to say to end a violent storm. *"No man eat fruit of thee hereafter for ever."* That's all He said to eliminate the fig tree (Mark 11:13-14, 20-21).

We need to imitate His example and quit talking so much. If that had been us talking to the fig tree, we wouldn't have just said, "No man eat fruit of thee...." We'd have said, "Fig tree, in the Name of Jesus, I curse you. I send you to hell in the Name of Jesus. Fig tree, you die. I'm telling you, devil, come out of that fig tree...." And on and on we'd go.

Jesus didn't say we are heard because of much talk. We are heard because of faith in the Name of Jesus.

There's no telling what we would have said to that fig tree before we got through.

But not Jesus. He just spoke the end result and never looked back.

What enabled Him to operate with such simple certainty? He was confident in the authority His words carried. He knew without question that the power of Almighty God backed Him and caused His every word to come to pass.

When you operate in faith, you can be just as confident. God is backing your faith just as surely as He backed Jesus' faith. So speak to your situation with authority. Speak confidently. And speak the end result.

## Speak the Word

*As I speak in faith, I do not doubt in my heart. I believe those things*
*which I say shall come to pass. I have what I say.*
*Mark 11:23*

FOR FURTHER STUDY:

Mark 11:13-14, 20-21

DAILY SCRIPTURE READING:

Leviticus 14-15; Luke 12

# More Than a Goose Bump

The signs of the times are all around us. It's time for the outpouring of the Glory of God. Both in the natural and in the spirit realm, you can sense the pulse beat of it growing more and more rapid.

Things are happening. Prophecies are being fulfilled. We are seeing events the prophets of old only longed to see. We need to get our spiritual antennae up. We need to wake up and *expect* the Glory of God!

When I say expect the Glory of God, most Christians will nod their heads and say, "Yes, amen, Brother Copeland." But they won't have any idea what I'm talking about.

> "Glory and honour are in his [God's] presence; strength and gladness are in his place."
> 1 CHRONICLES 16:27

To them, God's Glory is just a vague, religious term. Or some kind of spiritual thrill that leaves them with goose bumps every now and then.

Listen, the Glory of God isn't a goose bump. It's much more vast and powerful than that. And before we can truly begin to expect it, we must know what it is.

First Chronicles says glory and honor are in God's presence. However, the word *glory* in the English language is really kind of pitiful. It can mean splendor, but also it can refer to boasting and pride. Those things have nothing to do with the Glory of God.

The Hebrew words translated *glory* mean "desire, adornment, honor, beauty, majesty, cleanliness, purity, preciousness, rarity, weight and heaviness." So when you say God is glorious, you're really saying that God is a heavyweight—heavy with everything good. He is heavy in prosperity. Heavy in healing. Heavy in deliverance. Heavy in salvation. Hallelujah! If you need to be saved from anything, God is heavy enough to do it!

What we're talking about here is living in the heavy weight of God's goodness, desire, adornment, honor, beauty, majesty, cleanliness, purity, preciousness and rarity. When you walk in Glory, you literally walk in God Himself!

Of course, that power is going to break through to the natural realm more and more, and you're going to see physical manifestations of God's presence. Just keep standing in grace by faith expecting the Glory of God. Who knows, you may even get some goose bumps.

FOR FURTHER STUDY:

Matthew 17:1-8

DAILY SCRIPTURE READING:

Leviticus 16-18; Luke 13-14

## *Speak the Word*

*In the presence of God there are glory and honor and strength and gladness.*
*1 Chronicles 16:27*

> "Blessed shalt thou be when thou comest in, and blessed shalt thou be when thou goest out."
>
> DEUTERONOMY 28:6

# Building God's Dreams

People always talk about building their "dream home." But did you know that you can begin to build dreams out of God's Word? A good foundation for them is Deuteronomy 28. I can tell you from experience, it is good dream-building material.

God intended for man to be a dreamer. He built into us the capacity to do it. But He didn't intend for us to be limited by natural thoughts and circumstances. He meant for us to dream beyond them.

That's what Abraham did. He locked into God's dream—and it was bigger than anything he could have thought on his own.

It will be that way for you too. God's dream for you is bigger than your dream for yourself. It is exceedingly, abundantly beyond all you can ask or think! (See Ephesians 3:20.)

Once you get that dream inside you, things will begin to change. No, all your problems won't disappear overnight any more than mine did. But you'll respond to them differently.

When they rise up in front of you and threaten to defeat you, God's dream will stir in your heart.

You'll start saying, "Wait just a minute. I'm the head, not the tail. I'm blessed, not cursed. I don't have to tolerate this situation. I happen to be a child of the King Himself. He sets my table in the presence of my enemies. No weapon formed against me can prosper!" (See Deuteronomy 28:13; Psalm 23:5 and Isaiah 54:17.)

Building your dream home is great! But building God's dreams inside of you, and then seeing those dreams come to pass is GLORIOUS!

## *Speak the Word*

*I am blessed when I come in and blessed when I go out.*
*Deuteronomy 28:6*

FOR FURTHER STUDY:

Psalm 23

DAILY SCRIPTURE READING:

Leviticus 19-20; Luke 15

*Gloria*

# Live Like a King

In Deuteronomy 28, God told the Israelites if they would hearken diligently to His voice and do what He said, He would set them high above all nations. He told them to be diligent about His Word. That's because the curse, also listed in Deuteronomy 28, is out there working 24 hours a day. The devil is diligent in his destructive work, so they had to be diligent about the things of God.

If they obeyed God, He promised to bless them—not just a little here and there, but in every area of their natural lives. He said they'd be blessed in the city and in the field. Their children would be blessed. Their crops and livestock would be blessed. Their baskets and storehouses would be blessed. He said they'd be blessed when they came in and when they went out. Their enemies would flee before them in all directions. Their finances and everything they put their hand to would be blessed.

God didn't leave anything out of that blessing! In spite of Satan's authority over the world at that time, God made a way through His Word for His people to have the most wonderful life that anyone could imagine—the life of a king! He desired for His people to be so blessed that the whole world would know, just by looking at them, they belonged to God.

Think about that. When God's people are blessed, He receives the respect He deserves from the rest of the world. Even the ungodly are forced to say, "Hey, those people serve a living, powerful God. They might start out at the bottom of the barrel, but their God always makes them rise to the top!"

> "For if, because of one man's trespass... death reigned through that one, much more surely will those who receive [God's] overflowing grace...and the free gift of righteousness... reign as kings in life through the One, Jesus Christ, the Messiah, the Anointed One."
> ROMANS 5:17, AMP

Romans 5:17 clearly says He wants us to live and reign like kings. And now, because of the covenant of the blood of Jesus and the power of the indwelling of the Holy Spirit, we can do it—not just physically, but spiritually too. He has done everything He can to get us to raise our expectations higher. He wants us to know that He is willing and able to do for us *"superabundantly, far over and above all that we [dare] ask or think—infinitely beyond our highest prayers, desires, thoughts, hopes or dreams"* (Ephesians 3:20, AMP).

FOR FURTHER STUDY:

Psalm 67

DAILY SCRIPTURE READING:

Leviticus 21-22; Luke 16

He wants us to believe His Word and act on it. He wants us to walk upright before Him. He wants us to fully take advantage of His covenant of blessing that we astonish the world. He wants us to be so assured of His blessings that we will stop being concerned about ourselves and start being a blessing to all the families of the earth. He wants us to live like kings!

## Speak the Word

*I have received God's overflowing grace and the free gift of righteousness. Therefore, I reign in life as a king through Jesus Christ.*
*Romans 5:17, AMP*

> "Be sober,
> be vigilant;
> because your
> adversary the
> devil, as a
> roaring lion,
> walketh about,
> seeking whom
> he may devour:
> Whom resist
> stedfast in the
> faith, knowing
> that the same
> afflictions are
> accomplished
> in your
> brethren
> that are in
> the world."
> 1 PETER 5:8-9

# Talk...Talk...Talk

Satan is like a salesman. He makes you a presentation and tries to sell you a bill of goods. He tells you God doesn't really love you. He tells you the Word won't work this time. He tells you that you don't have the strength to go on. He'll even try to sell you on the idea that it would be easier for you just to curl up and die than to see this trial through in faith.

All he does is talk...talk...talk! And lie...lie...lie, and we don't have to listen.

Now that talk can get very annoying, but remember, that's all he can do! He doesn't have any real power or authority over you.

According to 1 Peter, he walks around as a roaring lion, *"seeking whom he may devour."* It doesn't say he is a lion. He just acts like one. Therefore, he can't devour you, unless you let him.

First Peter 5:9 says we are to resist the devil steadfastly! That means you have to use patience to resist him. He is, after all, a persistent fellow. He may pester you a thousand times a day, but if you'll resist him every time, he will flee from you every time (James 4:7).

He and all the low-level demons he sends to aggravate you have already *"come to nought"* (1 Corinthians 2:6). Jesus has stripped them of all their power and authority and left them with nothing (see Colossians 2:15).

So the next time Satan starts his sales pitch, *talk back.*

"I am a new creature in Christ Jesus. I am born of God. I am filled with the Holy Spirit Who proceeds from the Father. I am endowed with the Name of Jesus, which is *'far above all principality, and power, and might, and dominion, and every name that is named, not only in this world, but also in that which is to come!'"* (Ephesians 1:21). "Greater is He that is in me, than he that is in the world" (1 John 4:4). "Leave my presence in Jesus' Name!" (James 4:7).

If you're short of time, just say, "Get out of here, devil, in the Name of Jesus." He has to bow his knee at the Name of Jesus uttered in faith!

## *Speak the Word*

*I resist the devil steadfastly. He will not devour me, because greater is He that is in me than he that is in the world!*
*1 Peter 5:8-9; 1 John 4:4*

FOR FURTHER
STUDY:

Psalm 112

DAILY SCRIPTURE
READING:

Leviticus 23-24;
Luke 17

*Kenneth*

# Free of Condemnation

There's one serious mistake we often make that trips us up and keeps us from winning our victory...it's letting the devil put us under condemnation.

The condemnation of the carnal mind will weaken the spirit man. Yet we use condemnation on ourselves and each other all the time.

That's what happened to me. I fought cigarettes with everything I had. I threw away more than I smoked. I knew I ought not be smoking those things, but after I got saved, I went from 1½ packs a day to three packs a day.

Some people would say that was proof I wasn't saved, but they'd be wrong. I was born again. I knew it!

Two and a half months later, I received the Baptism in the Holy Ghost and spoke with other tongues. Still, I was fighting those cigarettes with both hands and feet. Why? My spirit was trying to get me to believe God and quit, but my body was fighting to keep doing what it had been trained to do.

Every time I lit a cigarette, it would tear me up inside. Yet I was walking in all the light I had.

I finally went to a meeting in Houston and heard godly men preach under the Anointing of God that Jesus was coming back. You know, the Word says when a man puts his hope in the return of Jesus, it will purify him, and that's what it did for me. I walked away from that meeting without any desire for tobacco. Years have come and gone since then and I haven't had any desire for it at all.

If you're struggling with something, you need to develop your own spirit and become skillful in the Word of righteousness regarding condemnation.

Learn to confess, "There is no condemnation to those who are in Christ Jesus—and that's me. Therefore, there is no condemnation to me, praise God. I'm walking after the dictates of my spirit, not after the dictates of my flesh."

Before long, you'll be free of that thing...and free of condemnation.

> "There is therefore now no condemnation to them which are in Christ Jesus, who walk not after the flesh, but after the Spirit."
> ROMANS 8:1

## Speak the Word

*I am in Christ Jesus. I do not walk after the flesh, but after the Spirit. Therefore, I am free of condemnation.*

Romans 8:1

FOR FURTHER STUDY:

Hebrews 10:1-17

DAILY SCRIPTURE READING:

Leviticus 25-26; Luke 18

*Gloria*

"My son,
attend to my
words; incline
thine ear unto
my sayings.
Let them [the
Words of God]
not depart
from thine
eyes; keep
them in the
midst of thine
heart.... Keep
thy heart with
all diligence;
for out of it
are the issues
of life."
PROVERBS
4:20-21, 23

# Trust the Great Physician

There is a medicine so powerful it can cure every sickness and disease known to man. It has no dangerous side effects. It is safe even in massive doses. And when taken daily according to directions, it can prevent illness altogether and keep you in vibrant health.

Does that sound too good to be true? It's not. I can testify to you by the Word of God and by my own experience that such a supernatural medicine exists. Even more importantly, it is available to you every moment of every day.

You don't have to call your doctor to get it. You don't even have to drive to the pharmacy. All you have to do is reach for your Bible, open it to Proverbs 4:20-24 and follow the instructions there.

As simple as they might sound, those five verses contain the supernatural prescription to divine health. It's a powerful prescription that will work for anyone who will put it to work.

If you have received healing by the laying on of hands, following this prescription will help you maintain that healing.

If you have believed for healing, but are experiencing lingering symptoms, it will help you stand strong until you are completely symptom free.

And if you are healthy now, it will help you stay that way—not just for a day or a week, but for the rest of your life!

These five verses teach you to keep your attention trained on the Word of God—not on lingering symptoms. Be like Abraham who *"considered not his own body"* (Romans 4:19). Instead of focusing on your circumstances, focus on what God has said to you. Develop an inner image of yourself with your healing fully manifested.

See yourself well.

See yourself whole.

See yourself healed in every way.

Since what you keep before your eyes and in your ears determines what you will believe in your heart and what you will act on, make the Word your number one priority. Keep taking God's medicine as directed and trust the Great Physician to do His wonderful healing work in you!

## *Speak the Word*

*I attend to God's Word, and incline my ear to His sayings. I will not let
His Word depart from my eyes. I will keep it in the midst of my heart.
I keep my heart with all diligence for out of it are the issues of life.*
*Proverbs 4:20-21, 23*

FOR FURTHER
STUDY:

Deuteronomy
7:8-15

DAILY SCRIPTURE
READING:

Leviticus 27;
Numbers 1;
Luke 19

*Kenneth*

# The Anointed House

Did you know that you could live in a household and not partake of everything given to you? Sure you could. But who would want to do such a thing?

Well, being a part of the household of the anointing is no different. You can live in it, if you're born again, and never draw on the benefits of it. Or, you can tap into it!

And the way you do that is the same way you do everything else. By faith!

"Well, I just don't have much faith."

Yes, you do. If you've made Jesus the Lord of your life, you have great faith. To consider just how great it is, read Hebrews 11. That's where all the Old Testament heroes of faith are listed. Usually when we read about those people, we want to be like them, but Hebrews 11:40 says God has *"provided some better thing for us!"*

That means you have more faith than the Old Covenant patriarchs. Think about that. You have more faith inside you than what split the Red Sea! God gave it to you when you were born again. First John 5 says, *"Whosoever believeth that Jesus is the Christ [Anointed One] is born of God.... For whatsoever is born of God overcometh the world: and this is the victory that overcometh the world, even our faith"* (verses 1, 4).

You're born of God. You have His spiritual genes and they include world-overcoming faith! What's more, according to Hebrews 3:1-6, you have the anointing to use that faith. You and I are the house of the Anointed. We are the anointed house!

> "But Christ [the Anointed One and His Anointing]... was faithful over His [own Father's] house as a Son [and Master of it]. And it is we who are [now members of] this house, if we hold fast and firm to the end our joyful and exultant confidence and sense of triumph in our hope [in Christ]."
> HEBREWS 3:6, AMP

## Speak the Word

*I believe that Jesus is the Christ—the Anointed One.*
*I am born of God and I overcome the world.*
*1 John 5:1,4*

FOR FURTHER STUDY:

Hebrews 11

DAILY SCRIPTURE READING:

Numbers 2-3; Luke 20

> "As the One Who called you is holy, you yourselves also be holy in all your conduct and manner of living."
> 1 PETER 1:15, AMP

# Be Holy!

Let me ask you a question. Do you want to see Jesus when He comes to catch His Church away? Do you want to see and move in manifestations of His power and Glory in the days that lead up to His coming? Then you must live a holy life.

That's just the truth and we all need to know it. As wonderful and vast as this great move of God is going to be, the fact is, not everyone will be a part of it. Only those who have sanctified themselves unto God will be used of Him in the days ahead. Only those who are obedient to Him will be able to stand in the midst of this great work.

In other words, if you and I want in on this great move of God, we must follow after holiness.

What exactly does the word *holiness* mean? It simply means "separation to God" or "conduct befitting those so separated." To *separate* means "to set apart, to disunite, to divide, to sever, to disconnect, to part company, to go in a different direction, to cease to be associated, to become distinct, or disengage as cream separates from milk and rises to the top."

If we want to be holy, we must be disconnected from the world and its ways—and connected to God and His ways.

"But we're just human beings. Is it really possible for us to be holy?"

Yes, it is, because we've been born again. When that happened, we were separated to God on the *inside.* Now God expects us to walk out that separation so it can be seen on the *outside.* Holiness isn't a strange thing that just a few people achieve. Holiness is the way everyone in the Body of Christ ought to be walking.

We ought not look like the world and talk and act like the world. We ought to look and talk and act like God! We've been commanded: *Be holy! In all your conduct and manner of living.* So set your course. Set your mind and your spirit. You can do it. Live from the inside out. Walk holy before the Lord.

## *Speak the Word*

*God is holy. Therefore I am also holy in all my conduct and manner of living.*
*1 Peter 1:15, AMP*

FOR FURTHER STUDY:

2 Timothy 2:19-21;
Hebrews 12:14

DAILY SCRIPTURE READING:

Numbers 4-6;
Luke 21-22

*Kenneth*

# Sitting on the Edge of His Seat

FEBRUARY 27

All my adult life Mama used to say, "Kenneth, Jesus is coming this year."

I would say, "Is that right, Mama?"

"Yes," she'd say, "He's coming this year. And you had better get yourself straightened out!"

Even though Jesus didn't come when Mama said, she was right—JESUS IS COMING! I don't know if it's this year. I don't know if it's next year. I don't know if it's next week. But I *do* know He's coming and it's a whole lot sooner than most people really think.

Just take a good look around you. It doesn't matter where on this planet you live—there is more Glory, more outpouring, more preaching, more Word, more believers, and even more hell on this earth than there has ever been before. It's nothing like mankind has ever seen.

You and I are now living and operating in a whole new time frame. When we made Jesus the Lord of our lives, we moved over into His time schedule and He came into ours. But what I really want you to grasp is that Jesus' time frame and the world's time frame do not function the same. Oh, we're in the same space as the rest of the world, but we're not functioning on the same schedule.

From the very beginning, God has given us the time frame in which He will work with mankind. It is a seven-day time frame—and a day is as a thousand years. For example, we see in Genesis that God created the earth in six days, and rested on the seventh. Then He gave mankind a 6,000-year lease on the earth. Jesus was born 4,000 years into that time frame—or on the fourth day. For all practical purposes, 2,000 years have come and gone since Jesus' birth and ministry—which is 6,000 years since Adam was created.

Where does that put us on our spiritual clock? We have entered that little sliver of time between Adam's lease on earth—and Satan's dominion in this earth as a consequence of Adam's Fall—and the period of time we read about in Acts 2:19-20. You and I are being squeezed between 6,000 years of time behind us and another 1,000 years ahead of us. The 1,000 years facing us is the millennial reign of Jesus of Nazareth, which is the first time in human existence since the Fall of Adam that humanity will be totally and completely out of contact with Satan.

I'm telling you, Jesus is coming! He's about to arise from His heavenly throne and return to earth. He may not have stood up yet, but I guarantee you He is out on the edge of His seat!

> "And I will shew wonders in heaven above, and signs in the earth beneath; blood, and fire, and vapour of smoke: The sun shall be turned into darkness, and the moon into blood, before that great and notable day of the Lord come."
> ACTS 2:19-20

FOR FURTHER STUDY:

1 Thessalonians 4:13-5:11

DAILY SCRIPTURE READING:

Numbers 7:1-48; Luke 23

## Speak the Word

*The day of the Lord is coming soon.*
*He will show wonders in heaven above, and signs in the earth beneath.*
*I prepare myself for that great and notable day.*
*Acts 2:19-20*

> "For we are members of his body, of his flesh, and of his bones."
> EPHESIANS 5:30

# The Greater One Lives in You!

Today, if the world is going to see Jesus, they'll have to see Him through us. We're His physical Body! If His Body doesn't preach the gospel, the gospel doesn't get preached. If His Body does not lay hands on the sick, then His ministry to them is cut short.

That thought surprises some people. They think Jesus changed somehow after He was resurrected and went to heaven. They think He stopped being interested in ministering personally to people like He did on the shores of Galilee. But Jesus didn't change. He is the same yesterday, and today and forever (Hebrews 13:8). He still wants to preach the Word of God to people. He still wants to cast out demons and heal the sick. And He still has the power to do all those things—and even greater things (John 14:12)!

How does He get them done? Through you and me.

Point your finger at yourself right now and say out loud, "I am the Body of the Anointed One. He is living right now in me!"

When that truth becomes a reality to you, impossible tasks won't overwhelm you anymore. You won't faint or give up, because you'll know that God is in you, and He has the power to get the job done. When He calls you to preach and you can't talk very well, you'll just say, "Well, that's all right. The Anointed One is in me and He'll give me utterance." When someone who's sick comes to you for prayer, you won't want to bolt and run. You'll be eager to lay hands on that person because you'll know the Healer lives in you, and when you lay hands on someone, He's there to bring that healing to pass!

The Greater One lives in you! Now, believe it! Live like it!

## *Speak the Word*

*Greater is He Who lives in me than he that is in the world.*
*1 John 4:4*

FOR FURTHER STUDY:

1 John 4:1-6

DAILY SCRIPTURE READING:

Numbers 7:49-78; Luke 24

*Kenneth*

# You Are His Disciple

> "The Father hath not left me alone; for I do always those things that please him."
> JOHN 8:29

Jesus lived by faith. Did you know that? Some people don't seem to realize that. They think that because He was the Son of God, He just floated through life with some mystical, supernatural power we could never have.

But Jesus Himself said that the Father hadn't left Him alone...and that He always did those things that please His Father.

Jesus walked by faith—and He got that faith the same way we get it. *"Faith cometh by hearing, and hearing by the word of God"* (Romans 10:17).

How do you think His mother knew to tell the leaders of the wedding feast at Cana to do whatever He told them? (See John 2:1-11.) How did she know He could solve the problem of lack?

The Bible tells us He had never done a miracle at that time—a miracle of suspension of the normal course of nature. Yet He had always lived by faith. He was living by faith when He was just a young fellow of 12 years old saying, "I have to be about My Father's business."

Year by year, He kept growing in faith, just as He grew physically. He wasn't born a faith giant. He had to develop, just as we do. He said, *"As my Father hath taught me, I speak these things"* (John 8:28).

Jesus had to be taught. How was He taught? By the Holy Spirit through the written Word!

Luke 4:16 says that when Jesus came to Nazareth, *"as his custom was, he went into the synagogue on the sabbath day, and stood up for to read."*

Jesus was a Bible reader! That was His custom. He studied. He meditated. He continued in the Word of God. He preached the Word of God. He knew the truth and the truth made Him free!

Now more than ever before, it is vital that you and I follow in His footsteps. We simply cannot afford to cast aside our Bibles and go skipping off after signs and wonders.

No! Our Father needs us to grow up in Him. He needs those who will dare to stand on the Word and develop their faith so that, instead of seeking miracles at the hands of others, they will *become* the hands that deliver those miracles. That, my friend, is the greatest thrill of all. And that is the day we're living in.

Get in the Word today. Meditate in it. Then go out and live by faith. Jesus did...and you are His disciple.

## Speak the Word

*Without faith it is impossible to please God. Therefore,*
*I am determined to live by faith so that I will always please Him.*
*Hebrews 11:6*

FOR FURTHER
STUDY:

John 2:1-11

> "For he that speaketh in an unknown tongue speaketh not unto men, but unto God: for no man understandeth him; howbeit in the spirit he speaketh mysteries."
> 1 CORINTHIANS 14:2

# Unlock the Mysteries

What are mysteries? Mysteries are things we don't know. Sometimes we don't know what the perfect will of God is for our lives. We don't know exactly what steps to take and what moves to make each day to fulfill the plan God has laid out for our lives. And nobody in the world can tell us!

As 1 Corinthians 2:9-10 says, *"Eye hath not seen, nor ear heard, neither have entered into the heart of man, the things which God hath prepared for them that love him. But God hath revealed them unto us by his Spirit!"*

When you pray in the spirit—in other tongues—you'll get answers. The answers to your circumstances will begin to come up inside you. You'll get a word. A sentence. You'll begin to receive understanding on things you've never understood before. That's what you need, revelation from God!

God has things that are so far better than what we've seen that we can't even figure them out. But if we'll pray in the spirit, we'll get beyond our natural knowledge and receive supernatural understanding. Spend time praying in the spirit every day. Tap into the mind of God. Receive wisdom from heaven. And unlock the mysteries of God's plan for your life!

## *Speak the Word*

*When I speak in an unknown tongue, I do not speak unto men, but unto God.*
*In the spirit I speak mysteries and receive understanding.*
*1 Corinthians 14:2*

FOR FURTHER STUDY:

Jude 1:17-21

DAILY SCRIPTURE READING:

Numbers 7:79-89, 8; John 1

*Kenneth*

# Separate Unto Him

The fast God is talking about here has very little to do with simply going without food. This fast is a lifestyle. It is a commitment that says, "I'm breaking the hold of wickedness on my life. I will not partake of the things of the world that have kept me bound. I'll turn off the television, and I'll turn on teaching tapes instead. I'll put down the newspaper and pick up my Bible. Instead of sitting down at the table, I'll get down on my knees and pray until the sin is burned out of me and I'm 100 percent committed to Jesus. Then, once I'm free, I will give myself in intercession for others so they can get free too!"

Do you know what that kind of fast will do for you? It will heal you. It will cause the light of God to shine from your life. It will cause the Glory of God to be your total covering! In the words of Isaiah, it will cause you to *"be like a watered garden, and like a spring of water, whose waters fail not"* (Isaiah 58:11).

If you want to see an example of the kind of Glory that accompanies this kind of life, all you have to do is look at Jesus. He went out, led by the Spirit, into the wilderness for 40 days. While He was out there, He fasted, prayed and interceded just as Isaiah described.

> "Is not this the fast that I have chosen? to loose the bands of wickedness, to undo the heavy burdens, and to let the oppressed go free, and that ye break every yoke?"
> ISAIAH 58:6

We know He did because Isaiah 59 tells us that when God could find no one to intercede in that way, He sent "His arm." In other words, He sent Jesus.

When Jesus left that place of fasting, His ministry exploded into power. What did that power look like? From the earthly perspective, it looked like people being healed of sickness and disease. It looked like the dead being raised. It looked like people's needs being met in supernatural ways.

But in the world of the spirit, it looked like a dam had broken and a flood of spiritual power had been released.

Right now, God is calling His Church to the same place of fasting that He called Jesus. He's calling us to a fast of separation to Him that will give us such a hunger to know Him and walk in His Spirit, that we'll not be satisfied until we're raptured.

Don't wait another moment. Answer that call right now. Get down on your knees and say, "Lord, I'll do anything You want me to do. I'll be everything You've made me to be. No matter what it takes, I want the rivers of Your Spirit to flow through me."

In the ears of heaven, such prayer sounds like a symphony of triumph. In the ears of hell, it sounds like the rushing mighty waters—a thunderous announcement that, despite the best efforts of the devil, the dam has broken and the flood is on the way.

FOR FURTHER
STUDY:

Matthew 4:1-11

DAILY SCRIPTURE
READING:

Numbers 9-10;
John 2

## *Speak the Word*

*I live a separated life unto God and I am like a watered garden,
and a spring of water, whose waters fail not.
Isaiah 58:11*

> "If a man abide not in me, he is cast forth as a branch, and is withered."
> JOHN 15:6

# Overflow With His Fruit

Jesus said if we want to bear fruit we must abide in Him. The word *abide* has a sense of permanency about it. It doesn't mean to come in and go out. It refers to the place where you remain and dwell continually.

Contrary to what many people seem to think, you cannot live from Sunday to Sunday without spiritual food. You can't fellowship with the Lord once a week at church, ignore Him the rest of the time, and still have the new man on the inside be the dominant part of you. John 15:6 makes that clear.

The moment a branch is broken off from the vine, it begins to die. It doesn't matter how close they are to one another. You can lay that branch beside the vine, but if the union has been broken, there will be no life flow. There will be no sap (no life) flowing from the vine into the branch.

The same is true for us. When we get too busy to spend time with God in prayer and in His Word, when we get preoccupied with natural, earthly things and disconnect from communion with Him, we immediately begin to wither.

The word *wither* means "to shrivel, to lose or cause to lose energy, force or freshness." That's a vivid picture of what happens to us when we aren't living in vital contact with the Lord. We still belong to Him. We still have His life within us, but His energy is not flowing through us so we can't produce anything.

We lose our capacity for spiritual action. We may know what to do, but we find ourselves lacking the power to do it. We haven't the strength to bear fruit!

On the other hand, when you do abide in the Vine, you are certain to bear fruit. In fact, it is inevitable! The power of the Holy Spirit flowing through you will just naturally bring forth that which God has placed within you. And you will begin to act like the loving, joyful, peaceful, patient, gentle, good, faithful, meek and self-controlled person you really are! You will overflow with His fruit!

## *Speak the Word*

*I abide and dwell in Jesus so that I bear abundant fruit.*
*John 15:5, AMP*

FOR FURTHER STUDY:

John 15:1-8

DAILY SCRIPTURE READING:

Numbers 11-12;
John 3

*Kenneth*
# Now, *That's* Good News!

Ever since the Fall of Man, the devil has been using people as pack mules. He has clamped his yoke around their necks and burdened them down with sin, sickness, failure, poverty and every other damnable thing hell could devise.

Everyone has felt the terrible weight of that yoke. We've all experienced the pain and frustration that comes from struggling free of one burden, just to have the devil yank us around and pile on even more.

For thousands of years, that yoke of bondage was the inescapable tragedy of man's existence. To natural eyes it looked as though there would never be a way out. But by the Spirit of God the prophet Isaiah looked forward to a time and saw that a redeemer was coming. One Who would finally free us from the oppression of the devil.

To fully appreciate just how good that news is, you must realize that Isaiah doesn't say the yoke will be broken because of the anointing. Many people read the verse that way, but that's not what it says. It says the yoke will be *destroyed*.

> "And it shall come to pass in that day, that his burden shall be taken away from off thy shoulder, and his yoke from off thy neck, and the yoke shall be destroyed because of the anointing."
> ISAIAH 10:27

When you look it up in the Hebrew, you'll find the word translated *destroyed* means "absolutely useless." It's possible that a broken yoke could be repaired and put back. But Isaiah said this anointing would annihilate the devil's yoke so completely, there would no longer be any evidence that it was ever on your neck!

That means every time you allow the Anointing of God to destroy a yoke in your life, whether it's in the realm of your health, your finances, your relationships or your past, it is literally, utterly destroyed and cannot be repaired to be used again. The devil can't pick it up and hold you in bondage with it again. Whom the Son sets free, is free indeed!

Now, that's good news!

## Speak the Word

*Jesus, the Anointed One and His Anointing, has removed every burden and destroyed every yoke in my life.*
*Isaiah 10:27*

FOR FURTHER STUDY:

Isaiah 61:1-3

DAILY SCRIPTURE READING:

Numbers 13-14; John 4

> "Fear not, Abram: I am thy shield, and thy exceeding great reward."
> GENESIS 15:1

# Put Your Name in the Promise

God promised Abraham many things. Genesis 12 records God's first promise to him: *"I will make of thee a great nation...I will bless thee, and make thy name great; and thou shalt be a blessing..."* (verse 2).

To fully grasp what God was saying here, you must realize that when He blesses someone, He is not just telling them to have a good day. He is conferring upon them the power to increase and prosper in every area of life. According to W. E. Vine and *Webster's Dictionary,* the true definition of *bless* is "to cause to prosper, to make happy, to bestow favor upon, to consecrate to holy purposes, to make successful, to make prosperous in temporal concerns pertaining to life, to guard and preserve." It was actually the blessing of God that made Abraham rich! It caused him to prosper wherever he went.

But this wasn't the only benefit God's blessing brought Abraham. It also made him an overcomer. Abraham could conquer any enemy that came against him or his family.

Genesis 14 tells of the time when Lot and his family were taken captive by wicked kings who made war on Sodom and Gomorrah. Abraham and his servants single-handedly whipped four kings and their armies, then recovered everything and everyone they had taken captive!

What gave Abraham the boldness to go after those kings? He knew he had a covenant with God. He knew God had promised to be an enemy to his enemies, and he dared to act on that promise. Abraham understood that God was God! Abraham took God at His Word when God told him not to fear in Genesis 15:1.

We need to do the same thing. We need to take that promise and put our name on it. After all, it's ours! We're the seed of Abraham. We're heirs of the promise.

Years ago, when Ken and I first started to walk with the Lord, we were facing debts and problems that seemed overwhelming. So I took that promise from God to Abraham and put my name in it. I read it like this: *Fear not, Gloria. I am your shield, your abundant compensation, and your reward shall be exceedingly great!*

I determined that since I was an heir of Abraham, those words were just as true for me as they were for him. And sure enough, they have been. In the years since, God has protected me and rewarded me beyond anything I could ask or think. He has been faithful to me as He was to Abraham! And He will be to you too!

God keeps His promises. Whatever you need today, His Word has a promise to cover your need. Find it and put your name in it. Confess it by faith...and receive your inheritance as a seed of Abraham.

## *Speak the Word*

*I do not fear for God is my shield and my exceeding great reward!*
*Genesis 15:1*

FOR FURTHER STUDY:

Genesis 14:12-15:1

DAILY SCRIPTURE READING:

Numbers 15-17; John 5-6

*Kenneth*

# Generation Faith Is Here

The devil has done everything he could in this generation to steal our children, but, thank God, his day with our children is over. We have a generation of young people growing that is really something. They are taking their stand and moving out in the Spirit. They are bringing countless multitudes into the kingdom of God.

Gloria and I were at a meeting at Brother Jerry Savelle's ministry once, when God poured out His Spirit on the children. They were lying on the floor praising God, interceding in the spirit for one another, laying hands on and praying for the adults...it was one of the most powerful things we've ever witnessed. These children were 8 to 13 years old.

One young man came up to me at the close and asked if he could lay hands on me. I said, "Sure, I wish you would." When he touched me, the power of God shot through me from head to foot. I'm telling you it was glorious!

"Brother Copeland, I surely do wish my children would move more in the things of God."

Well, don't wait until you see the Spirit of God moving on them to begin confessing Isaiah 54:13 over them. Start saying that about them now! "All my children are taught of the Lord and great is the peace of God on them." The peace of God is the Anointing of God.

Begin to treat them like they are God's anointed NOW! Don't wait until you see evidence of it. It makes no difference whether they are 3 or 43, release your faith! Treat them as if they were already walking in that anointing. I'm telling you, Generation Faith is here! And your child can be part of it, starting today.

## Speak the Word

*All my children are taught of the Lord and great is their peace.*
*Isaiah 54:13*

FOR FURTHER STUDY:

Psalm 128

DAILY SCRIPTURE READING:

Numbers 18-19;
John 7

# Turn the World Right Side Up

> "He that believeth on me, the works that I do shall he do also; and greater works than these shall he do; because I go unto my Father."
>
> JOHN 14:12

If you want to receive the gifts of the Spirit, it won't happen until you start ministering. As much as you might want to, you can't wait around until you receive the gift of healing and then go lay hands on the sick.

The power manifests as you give out. Once you step out to do the works of Jesus, the Spirit of God will back you up with His power.

When it comes down to it, power is what people of the world are looking for today. They have problems with no answers. They're sick. They're hooked on alcohol and drugs. Their relationships are tearing them apart. The devil has turned their lives so upside down, they don't know where to go or what to do to get things fixed.

People like that don't care very much about what you believe. They don't care if you talk in tongues and dance in the aisles or sit up straight and sing out of a hymnal. But if you have the power to get their bodies healed and their lives straightened out, they'll come wherever you are. Not only that, they'll listen to what you say.

That's the kind of credibility God wants to establish. He wants the Church in our day to have the same reputation Jesus had when He was on the earth. He wants people to say about us what they said about those first-generation disciples, "If you go where they are, you can get healed."

Now that's exciting. In fact, you haven't had any excitement until you've started doing the works of Jesus. It's fun to be spiritually on fire, going all-out for God. When you live like that, you never know what's going to happen. You don't know where you'll wind up or who you'll be ministering to or what amazing things the Spirit of God will be doing next.

But you will know this: You're doing what God sent you to do. You're destroying the works of the devil. And in Jesus' Name, you're turning this old upside-down world right side up again!

## *Speak the Word*

*I do the works of Jesus because I believe on Him.*
*John 14:12*

FOR FURTHER STUDY:

Luke 10:17-20

DAILY SCRIPTURE READING:

Numbers 20-21; John 8

*Kenneth*

# Break the Fear Threshold

> "He hath said, I will never leave thee, nor forsake thee. So that we may boldly say, The Lord is my helper, and I will not fear what man shall do unto me."
>
> HEBREWS 13:5-6

Without courage, you'll never be able to stand on the Word of God for anything. You won't be able to receive what God has promised you, because fear will come and steal the faith right out of your heart.

You see, your point of fear is your point of failure. Wherever fear begins, faith ends. It takes courage to break that fear threshold, to push it back further and further until "I will not fear" is a reality in your life.

I can't count how many times I have had to break through that threshold. One of the most memorable was the time God instructed us to put our broadcast on television. I really struggled with it when God first put it on my heart. I wanted it, but I knew how expensive it was, and I couldn't even figure out where to start—much less how.

So Gloria and I began to meditate on what God said about it. We prayed over it. We talked about it in faith. We meditated on God's Word and on His ability instead of our inability.

This went on for a long time. Then one morning, as we were driving back to Texas from Arkansas, we stopped for breakfast. When we stepped out of the car, I didn't have any more insight into how we could be on television than I had the month or the year before.

But in an instant, as we ate our breakfast and discussed the television ministry, the faith I needed dropped into my heart. I looked at Gloria and realized by the look on her face that the same thing had happened to her.

"Gloria," I said, "tomorrow is Monday. Let's go home and make arrangements to put our broadcast on television."

Suddenly, it looked easy. We didn't have the money, but we had the faith, and if you have the faith, the money will come. We didn't call the bank. The bank would have laughed at us. But God wasn't laughing.

Now, someone might say, "Boy, it must take a lot of courage to go on television when you don't have the money in the bank to pay all the expenses."

Yes, it does. But that courage came as I meditated on the Word of God. As I meditated on the Word, my capacity for faith grew bigger, until one day I thought, *There's not any reason not to do this! I can do all things through the Anointed One and His Anointing that strengthens me!* I broke through that threshold of fear. I broke through to faith. It takes courage to do that... courage that comes from meditating on the Word of God.

FOR FURTHER STUDY:

Psalm 27

DAILY SCRIPTURE READING:

Numbers 22-23; John 9

## *Speak the Word*

*The Lord is my helper, and I do not fear what man shall do to me.*
*The Lord never leaves me, nor forsakes me.*
*Hebrews 13:5-6*

# It's Who You Really Are!

When I realized what these verses were saying, I determined to have these powerful forces called the "fruit of the spirit" flowing in my life because I don't want to fall. I don't want to stumble and miss my destiny. I want to run my God-appointed course and finish it in victory!

"I do too, Gloria," you may say. "But I have a problem. I'm just not a very patient person. My personality is harsh—not gentle. And I have a major lack of self-discipline. In other words, these fruit of the spirit just don't come naturally to me."

Yes, they do.

If you're born again, the fruit of the spirit are a part of your new nature. They're your natural "supernatural" disposition!

When you made Jesus the Lord of your life, you became *"a new creature"* (2 Corinthians 5:17). Your spirit was reborn in the image of your Heavenly Father. You were made a partaker of His divine nature (2 Peter 1:4).

• God is loving by nature. First John 4:8 says, *"God is love."* • God is joyful by nature. Psalm 16:11 says, *"In thy presence is fulness of joy."* • God is good by nature. Exodus 34:6 says the Lord is *"abundant in goodness."* • God is peaceful by nature. Philippians 4:9 says He is *"the God of peace."* • God is patient by nature. Numbers 14:18 says, *"The Lord is longsuffering [patient], and of great mercy."* • God is gentle by nature. David said to Him in Psalm 18:35, *"Thy gentleness hath made me great."* • God is faithful by nature. Psalm 119:90 says, *"Thy faithfulness is unto all generations."* • God is meek by nature. Jesus—Who is exactly like the Father—said, *"I am meek"* (Matthew 11:29).

We know God is temperate by nature because if He were not, none of us would be here.

The reason I went through the entire list of the fruit is because I wanted to impress firmly on your mind that they are all attributes of God. And since you've been born again in His image, they are also your attributes! Because God is love, you are love. Because God is patient, you are patient. Because all the fruit of the spirit are His nature, they are yours too! It's your nature. It's who you really are!

## *Speak the Word*

*I am not barren or unfruitful in the knowledge of the Lord for I give diligence to let the fruit of the spirit abound in my life.*
*2 Peter 1:5-8*

FOR FURTHER STUDY:

Psalm 101

DAILY SCRIPTURE READING:

Numbers 24-25;
John 10

*Kenneth*

# God Honors the Blood

Born-again people make mistakes. I mean, we sometimes flat-out miss God. That doesn't mean we're looking for a way to sin and get away with it. No, we're looking for a way to get sin out of our lives and grow in the righteousness of God.

That's why it is so vitally important to realize the Bible is not a religious book. It is the copy of a covenant between you and God, and it's sworn in blood.

Both the Old Covenant and the New were ratified in blood. Both of them are blood-sworn oaths to certain people. But there is a big difference between them.

The Old Covenant, first recorded in Genesis, was between Abraham and God, and sworn in the blood of animals. God told Abraham to kill specific animals and lay them out a certain way. It was God walking in the blood and passing between those animals that convinced Abraham that God was serious about fulfilling what He had promised to Abraham and his seed.

Later, under Old Testament Law, a priesthood and ministry was set in motion in order to continue to sacrifice animals. Galatians 3 says it was done because of man's transgression—he kept breaking the covenant.

> "How much more shall the blood of Christ, who through the eternal Spirit offered himself without spot to God, purge your conscience from dead works to serve the living God?"
>
> HEBREWS 9:14

In relation to that covenant, Jesus came and established the New Covenant. Jesus is called the Lamb of God because He was the final sacrifice under that first covenant. When His sinless blood was shed, that settled sacrificing for sins forever. Under the Old Covenant, the blood of animals could only "atone" for sins, or cover them up. But the blood of the Lamb of God obliterates them.

When you become a believer, the blood of Jesus does not cover up your sins, it completely redeems you. Your sins are no more. His blood washes you clean. After that, when you come before God, He sees you as clean. You don't have to sacrifice an animal to get forgiveness—or do anything else, for that matter. You simply have to repent...and the blood of Jesus will cleanse you. He paid the price for your sin. You don't have to pay any price. You can't! There's nothing you can do to be forgiven, except ask for forgiveness and have faith in the blood.

FOR FURTHER STUDY:

1 John 1:7-9

DAILY SCRIPTURE READING:

Numbers 26; John 11

In the same way, if the devil is putting condemnation on you, don't receive it. Just plead the blood, like you would plead your case before a judge. Because of the blood, you're innocent, as though you'd never sinned. You've been redeemed. You've been reconciled. You've been bought with the blood of Jesus.

## *Speak the Word*

*Because of the blood of Jesus, God forgives my sins and cleanses me from all unrighteousness.*

*1 John 1:9*

> "Thou therefore endure hardness, as a good soldier of Jesus Christ."
> 2 TIMOTHY 2:3

# Endure Hardness

There are no "ifs" about it. Hard times are going to come in the life of every believer. There will be times when circumstances will seem dark, times when you face seemingly impossible obstacles, times when defeat seems inevitable.

In 2 Timothy 2:3, the Apostle Paul didn't tell Timothy, *"If* hard times come, endure them." He simply said, *"Endure hardness."*

Some Christians become confused when those times come. "What's happening here?" they cry. "I thought Jesus redeemed me from the curse!"

He did, but you can rest assured, Satan will challenge that redemption. He will try his best to steal it from you by pulling you off your walk of faith. Jesus warned us about that in the parable of the sower in Mark 4:14-17. He said, *"Satan cometh immediately, and taketh away the word that was sown in their hearts...."*

Satan will not sit idly by while you sail through life, effortlessly believing the Word of God. He'll pressure you with hard times. He'll attack you with sickness or lack, then he'll lie to you and tell you that God doesn't care. He'll try to convince you that God is not going to answer your prayer this time. He'll attempt to talk you into believing there's no way out and that you will end up a miserable failure.

When those hard times come, don't cave in to pressure. Don't give up. Stand on the Word and endure hardness like a good soldier until victory comes.

## *Speak the Word*

*I endure hard times as a good soldier of Jesus Christ.*
*I stand firm for God has given me the victory.*
*2 Timothy 2:3*

FOR FURTHER STUDY:

2 Timothy 2:1-7

DAILY SCRIPTURE READING:

Numbers 27-28; John 12

*Kenneth*
# From Rascal to Righteous

MARCH 12

"He is not ashamed to call them [us] brethren."
HEBREWS 2:11

All of us struggle with habits at some time or another. We work at them and work at them to change. There may be some things in your life today that are a little slow in coming around. You will have to resist the devil in those areas. But you can stand against him. You can take the Word of God and put him out.

In the meantime, do not allow yourself to be subjected to harassment or condemnation, whether it be physical or spiritual. It's dangerous.

Don't let yourself or anyone else say things like, "I'm so unworthy. I'm so bad. I'm so worthless." That's against the Word of God. If Jesus walked through the door and stood right there for the next 20 years preaching every minute of every day, He would never call you unworthy. It's proven in Hebrews 2.

Jesus is not ashamed of you...therefore, you don't have any business being ashamed of yourself!

So stop it and start believing what the Bible says. Believe that you're God's workmanship created in Christ Jesus. Start confessing that. Instead of talking about what a messed-up rascal you are, start agreeing with the Word and calling yourself the righteousness of God in Christ Jesus (2 Corinthians 5:21). Practice seeing yourself that way. Practice seeing yourself operating in the victory. After all, Jesus has already won it for you. So receive that victory by faith!

## *Speak the Word*

*Jesus is not ashamed of me, therefore, I am not ashamed.*
*Hebrews 2:11*

FOR FURTHER STUDY:

Hebrews 9:11-28

DAILY SCRIPTURE READING:

Numbers 29-31:24;
John 13-14

"To whom ye forgive any thing, I forgive also: for if I forgave any thing, to whom I forgave it, for your sakes forgave I it in the person of Christ; Lest Satan should get an advantage of us: for we are not ignorant of his devices."
2 CORINTHIANS 2:10-11

# I Will Walk in Love!

Love is the real secret of our success. That's why Satan is working furiously day in, day out to deceive and pressure us into stepping out of love. He is constantly sending situations our way to tempt us to stop yielding to love and to yield to the "enemies of love."

It's vitally important that we not be ignorant of the devil's devices, because when we're ignorant or unaware, we're more likely to fall prey to them.

It is important for us to study the Word to know what love is and what it is *not.* We need to study the enemies of love so that when the devil tempts us with them, we can quickly recognize his strategies and say, "No, devil! I refuse to do that. It's unloving, and I choose to walk in love!"

Some people don't realize that resisting temptation is that simple. (Notice, I didn't say *easy.* I said *simple.*) But it is! Temptation is nothing more than *a solicitation to do evil.* In times of temptation, the devil comes to you like a solicitor or a salesman and makes you a presentation. He brings an influence into your life and puts an opportunity in front of you to sin. One reason we fail to reject the devil's solicitations at times is because we don't recognize temptation for what it is. We buy the devil's line before we even realize he's selling something to us.

So we have to learn his devices.

The enemies of love are things such as *envy,* which the dictionary defines as "a feeling of discontent and ill will because of another's advantages, possessions or success." Jealousy, which is a little stronger than envy, is also an enemy of love. To be *jealous* is to be "suspicious, apprehensive of rivalry or resentfully envious." Proverbs 6:34 says, *"Jealousy is the rage of a man."*

Pride, too, is listed in 1 Corinthians 13 as an enemy of love. It is an overly high opinion of one's self, exaggerated self-esteem, or conceit—and it shows itself through haughty or arrogant behavior. Pride is something we have to watch for in our lives. The moment we start to think more highly of ourselves than we ought, we need to humble ourselves before God and repent of pride.

Other enemies of love include bitterness, resentment and unforgiveness. Those three things are among the biggest obstacles to walking in love, especially among people who have truly been hurt or abused.

Examine your heart. Listen to your mouth. Are you walking in love, or in the enemies of love? Love is the real secret to your success in relationships, on the job, in your marriage, everywhere. Make a quality decision today: I will walk in love!

## Speak the Word

*I am not ignorant of Satan's devices. I determine to walk in love and refuse to allow him to take advantage of me.*

*2 Corinthians 2:10-11*

FOR FURTHER STUDY:

Romans 13:8-10;
1 Corinthians 13:1-8

DAILY SCRIPTURE READING:

Numbers 31:25-54, 32;
John 15

*Kenneth*

# Make the Distinction

*"I know I'm supposed to use my faith to be healed. But wait a minute. I went to a miracle service the other night, and I saw a great many people get healed who'd never exercised that kind of faith. Why can't I just get my blessings that way? Why do I have to work so hard?"*

Have you ever heard someone say something like that? It's a very good question, one that often leaves many people confused during times of great outpouring like we're experiencing in the Church right now.

Even ministers can get drawn off course when they step into a meeting and God simply drops the gift of faith upon them. Suddenly they find themselves operating in power beyond anything they've ever experienced and they say to themselves, *I didn't do anything to exercise that kind of faith. God just sovereignly gave it to me. So I suppose I should quit trying to develop faith and just let God give it as He wills.*

The reason people start thinking that way is because they fail to make the distinction between the kind of faith God gives every believer, and the special manifestation of faith that is described in 1 Corinthians 12.

It is a wonderful, glorious thing when the gifts of the Spirit begin to flow. It is marvelous when God moves in on the scene with His own faith and, by the operation of His own Spirit, accomplishes things that none of us are well enough developed in faith to accomplish. But never lose sight of this fact: Those special manifestations of faith were not given to us to live by each day. It's our own faith that is to be developed and used for that purpose.

Why then does God sometimes choose to meet those day-to-day type needs, such as the need for healing, through the ministry gifts? I wondered that myself some years ago. I saw it happen in Kathryn Kuhlman's ministry, so I asked the Lord about it.

*Miss Kuhlman is My nursery attendant,* He explained. *I have sick spiritual babies all over the world. They don't know to walk in the Word. They don't know what you know about living by faith. Some of them are so lazy they will never know it. But I want them well anyway.*

So learn to make the distinction between the faith you are developing and the gift of faith. Both are needed. You're not developing your faith just for yourself. The Master is training you to help with the little ones who are coming into the kingdom of God in this end-time outpouring by the thousands.

> "Now concerning spiritual gifts, brethren, I would not have you ignorant.... There are diversities of gifts, but the same Spirit.... For to one is given by the Spirit the word of wisdom; to another the word of knowledge by the same Spirit; To another faith."
>
> 1 CORINTHIANS 12:1-9

FOR FURTHER STUDY:

1 Corinthians 12:1-11

DAILY SCRIPTURE READING:

Numbers 33; John 16

## *Speak the Word*

*I walk by faith and not by sight. I allow God to move in my life by faith.*

*2 Corinthians 5:7*

> "For thou,
> Lord, wilt
> bless the
> righteous;
> with favour
> wilt thou
> compass him
> as with
> a shield."
> PSALM 5:12

# You're One of God's Favorites!

What would life be like if you were one of God's favorite people? Stop and think about that for a moment. How would it be to have His supernatural favor wrapped around you like a shield all the time, covering you from head to toe?

It would relieve all your anxieties. It would calm all your fears. In short, it would save your life. I know it would because the Bible says so. Ephesians 2:8 puts it this way: *"By grace are ye saved through faith."*

Now, *grace* is a word many people use and don't understand. But what it means is "favor." Unconditional favor. God's favor saves you. If you'll look up the word *save* in Greek, you'll find it doesn't just refer to going to heaven when you die, though that's included in its meaning. To be *saved* actually means "to be delivered, preserved, healed and made sound and whole."

If you are a believer, you know that God's grace at work in your life enabled you to be born again. But did you know that grace did not stop working the moment you made Jesus the Lord of your life? That was just the beginning! God will minister grace to you every day if you'll let Him. Psalm 5:12 ensures that.

If you're born again, Psalm 5:12 is talking about you. You've been made righteous by Jesus' blood so God's favor is available to you constantly. Whatever you need today to be delivered, preserved, healed, made whole, sound and complete...call upon God's favor by faith. Say, "Surely, O Lord, You bless the righteous! You surround me with Your favor as with a shield! Thank You for Your continual supernatural favor. I am favored by God!"

## *Speak the Word*

*God surrounds me with favor as with a shield. I am one of God's favorites!*
*Psalm 5:12*

FOR FURTHER STUDY:

Psalm 5

DAILY SCRIPTURE READING:

Numbers 34-35;
John 17

*Kenneth*
# No Shades of Gray

Oftentimes people associate forgiveness only with those major resentments they've been carrying against someone. But true forgiveness is also for all those "little" hurts and offenses that cause you to go out of your way to avoid someone. It's those memories that cause you to treat someone with less warmth and love because they have injured you in some way.

I'm talking about any attitude you have that falls short of the full light and love of God Himself.

Some people don't want to give up those kinds of things. They'll say, "I love God. Glory! Hallelujah! My fellowship with Him is fine. I'm just having a tough time fellowshiping with Sister So-and-So. But after what she did to me, I just can't help it."

According to the Bible, people who say things like that are lying. They're trying to walk in darkness and light at the same time, and 1 John tells us it can't be done. Notice in the above verse, he didn't stutter. He didn't say, "Well, bless your heart. Unforgiveness is a sin, but I know how hard these things can be sometimes."

No, he said bluntly: "If you walk in darkness and say you have partnership with God, you're lying about it."

The sad thing is, many Christians who are walking in unforgiveness don't know they're in darkness. They think that because they read their Bibles and say "Amen" at church, they're in fellowship with God. But 1 John 2:11 says, *"He that hateth his brother is in darkness, and walketh in darkness, and knoweth not whither he goeth, because that darkness hath blinded his eyes."* A man who does not forgive is hating his brother.

"I don't hate him," you may say. "I just don't like him very much!"

How far outside of love do you have to go before it can be called hate? As far as God is concerned, just one step outside of love is hate. To Him there are no shades of gray. In His eyes, anything less than love is sin.

So make the decision today to forgive...every little hurt.

> "This then is the message which we have heard of him, and declare unto you, that God is light, and in him is no darkness at all. If we say that we have fellowship with him, and walk in darkness, we lie, and do not the truth."
> 1 JOHN 1:5-6

FOR FURTHER STUDY:

1 John 2:7-11

DAILY SCRIPTURE READING:

Numbers 36;
Deuteronomy 1;
John 18

## *Speak the Word*

*I determine to walk in love and to forgive others,
even as God for Christ's sake has forgiven me.*
*Ephesians 4:32*

> "I have set before you life and death, blessing and cursing: therefore choose life."
> DEUTERONOMY 30:19

# Don't Look Back!

"Oh, God, please...give me more faith...make me a better Christian...take these cigarettes away from me! Oh, God, help me walk in love!"

How many times have you heard (or prayed) prayers like that? Plenty, I'd guess. Everyone, including me, has prayed that way at one time or another. But these prayers are very ineffective. You can pray them all day and all night and end up just as faithless, just as hooked on cigarettes, and just as unloving as you were when you started.

You see, there's a crucial element missing in prayers like that. An element that, if present, will hook you up to the supernatural, overcoming power of Almighty God—and, if absent, will leave you as helpless as can be.

The element I'm talking about is what I call the *Quality Decision*.

A quality decision is a rock-solid decision—one from which there is no retreat and about which there is no argument. It's a deliberate act of your will. What's more, it's the one thing God will not do for you. He has provided everything else. He's even gone as far as to say, *"I have set before you life and death, blessing and cursing: therefore choose life."* But the actual choosing, the decision, is up to you.

If you don't use this powerful decision-making ability according to the Word of God, you'll end up bound to and dominated by the circumstances of this world.

If you make a quality decision that you will walk by faith and live by the Word of God, that you will be delivered from cigarettes, that you will walk in love, then you will...because you've hooked up to the power of God. You aren't making a decision that you'll have to carry out in your own human strength. God will back you up and enable you to be an overcomer. So whatever your battle is today, in whatever area you want victory, make a quality decision. And don't look back!

## Speak the Word

*God has set before me life and death, blessing and cursing.*
*I choose life. I choose God's blessings.*
*Deuteronomy 30:19*

FOR FURTHER STUDY:

Joshua 24:14-18

DAILY SCRIPTURE READING:

Deuteronomy 2-3; John 19

*Kenneth*

# Start Your Own Healing Revival!

There was a time not so very long ago when it was just as tough to get people born again as it is to get them healed today. Religious tradition had convinced people that salvation just couldn't be obtained by the average person. But then, praise God, people like Dwight L. Moody came on the scene and started preaching the new birth. They started telling people that Jesus bore their sins and if they'd receive the gift of salvation in simple faith, they'd be born again!

Whole denominations like the Baptists preached that message to everything that stood still. You'd hear it in every church service. If you walked in the door and admitted you weren't saved, somebody would grab you and say, "Jesus died for your sins, man! Trust Him, receive Him as your Lord and He'll save you right now."

Now what do you think would happen if everyone picked up on the truth about healing in the same way?

I can tell you what would happen. Healing would become as easily received as the new birth, and we'd wonder why we had so much trouble with it for so long!

What's more, in that environment, if someone prayed for healing and then said, "I don't think I got anything. I don't feel any better," do you know what they'd be told? The same thing people are told today when they doubt their salvation because they don't "feel" saved. Some mature believer would pull them aside and say, "Now listen here. You can't go by feelings. You have to do this by faith. If you wait until you feel something to believe you're saved (or healed), you'll never be able to receive!"

If you're sitting there right now wishing such a healing revival would begin, stop wishing and start your own! Dig into the Word. Study and meditate the truth about healing and the redemption. Listen to tapes of men and women of God who have the revelation of it.

Then start preaching. Preach it to yourself. Preach it to your children. Preach it to your dog if he's the only one who will listen. It probably won't do much for him, but it will help you—and that's what matters.

### FOR FURTHER STUDY:

1 Peter 2:21-24

### DAILY SCRIPTURE READING:

Deuteronomy 4-5; John 20

If you'll do that, you'll eventually get to the point where you'll fight sickness and disease the same as you do sin. You'll be just as tough on Satan when it comes to standing for the redemption of your body as you are when it comes to the redemption of your spirit.

I'm not saying all this will be easy. It won't be. Not in this life. Not in this world. Just as you don't live in victory over sin without putting forth an effort, you can't bumble along in life and have God just drop healing in your lap. No, you'll have to stand for it. You'll have to fight the good fight of faith. But you will win...and the healing revival will have begun!

## *Speak the Word*

*Jesus took my infirmities and bore my sicknesses. By His stripes I am healed!*
*Matthew 8:17; 1 Peter 2:24*

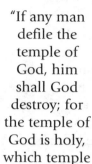

> "If any man defile the temple of God, him shall God destroy; for the temple of God is holy, which temple ye are."
> 1 CORINTHIANS 3:17

# Walk in Holiness

"Nobody could be as holy as God is."

Have you ever heard people say that? It could be that you think that way. Well, if so, it's time to change your thinking.

If you are born again, God has called you to be holy. That's your destiny. That's where you're headed. Romans 8:29 says He predestined us to be conformed to the image of His Son.

If you are born again, you have been made holy. Now you are being called to walk out what you are on the inside. To be like the Father, you have to give yourself to Him. How much you give of yourself to God is how much He reveals Himself to you. That's how you become conformed to His image.

Being conformed to His image is a process. Your spirit man has been completely changed. In it dwells the Holy Spirit. But your soul—your mind, will and emotions—and your body are conformed to His image over time. You grow up spiritually the same as you grow up naturally.

You are on a journey. The Bible says you are changed from Glory to Glory even into the image of the Spirit of the Lord, as you continue to behold in the Word of God as in a mirror the Glory of the Lord (2 Corinthians 3:18, AMP). As you look at Him in the Word, you are changed by the Holy Spirit into His image.

If you are living separated unto God, disconnected from darkness, you will stand out and be distinguished.

Many people are born again, but they never disconnect from their old life. They never spend enough time hearing from God, reading the Word for themselves, spending time in prayer or learning how to listen to the Holy Spirit within them, teaching them how to separate from the world. As a result, they never change on the outside.

But the change on the outside is what enables you to walk free. It's when you change on the outside that you experience the blessings of God. When you change on the outside, you experience all that God provided for you when He saved you.

That's when you will walk in holiness.

## Speak the Word

*I do not defile the temple of God. I walk in holiness.*
*1 Corinthians 3:17*

FOR FURTHER STUDY:

Leviticus 20:7;
2 Corinthians 6:14-7:1;
Hebrews 12:14

DAILY SCRIPTURE READING:

Deuteronomy 6-8;
John 21;
Acts 1

*Kenneth*

# That's Heavy, Man

The Glory of God is hard to put into words. But God gives glimpses of it all throughout the Bible. The first time the Glory is mentioned is in Genesis, and it's referring to the wealth of God. So, God's Glory includes His wealth, but it's much, much more than that.

In the book of Exodus, God's Glory could be seen going before the Israelites in a pillar of cloud by day and in a pillar of fire by night. Habakkuk saw God's Glory and described it as lightning-like shafts of splendor that streamed from His hands (Habakkuk 3:4, AMP).

But the word *glory* actually means "heavyweight." God is *heavy* with everything you could ever want or need. He is so heavy with healing, that if everyone in the whole world believed Him for healing at once, no one would have to wait until tomorrow to be healed because God was tired.

In Acts 5:15, this heavy, weighty Glory was flowing out of Peter. As he walked by, people were healed: *"Insomuch that they brought forth the sick into the streets, and laid them on beds and couches, that at the least the shadow of Peter passing by might overshadow some of them."*

It wasn't Peter's shadow that healed them. It was that field of Glory that surrounded him. It was the very manifested presence of God.

If you need healing today, expect the Glory. If you need finances, expect the Glory. If you need relationships restored, expect the Glory. It's heavy, man, and it's all you'll ever need.

> "And the Lord went before them by day in a pillar of a cloud, to lead them the way; and by night in a pillar of fire, to give them light; to go by day and night."
> EXODUS 13:21

## *Speak the Word*

*My God supplies all my needs according to His riches in Glory.*
*Philippians 4:19*

FOR FURTHER STUDY:

Exodus 13:15-22

DAILY SCRIPTURE READING:

Deuteronomy 9-10;
Acts 2

> "For the battle is the Lord's, and he will give you into our hands."
> 1 SAMUEL 17:47

# Enjoy the Fight!

I've seen it happen more times than I can count. Someone hears the faith message. They find out that if they'll base their prayers on the Word, they can have anything they ask from God.

They read Mark 11:24 where Jesus said, *"What things soever ye desire, when ye pray, believe that ye receive them, and ye shall have them,"* and they're quick to obey. They pray, believe that they receive, shout the victory...and then the devil comes and knocks them flat on their backs.

Why? Because they weren't properly prepared to defend themselves against his attacks. The moment you take a faith stand, he gets more aggressive than ever. But don't let that bother you. You can whip him every time if you'll use these four steps in defeating Satan's attack.

1) *Make the decision.* It takes a decision of your will to take a faith stand. The dictionary defines *will* as "strong purpose, intention or determination." When you go to the Lord in prayer and believe you receive, you must have a strong purpose and determination not to waver until your answer comes. You must make an irrevocable decision to continue in your confession of faith—no matter what.

2) *Resist the devil.* When he comes at you with images of failure or lack or sickness—rebuke those images instantly in the Name of Jesus. Then jerk your mind back to the Word of God and begin to say the scriptures out loud that apply to your situations.

3) *Attend to the Word.* Spend time in the Word of God every day. I know it sounds simple. Yet this is where so many believers miss it.

4) *Speak faith only.* The devil can't do anything to you if you won't open the door to him with your words. Satan doesn't have any authority over you. Jesus Christ is your Lord. Satan can't rob you unless you authorize that robbery yourself! Satan comes to get your words! That's how he gets a foothold.

That's the four-point victory plan. If you follow it, it will work for you every time. I like what Ken says, "A good fight is the one you win." So go ahead, enjoy the fight—the victory is already won!

## *Speak the Word*

*I fight the good fight of faith. It's a good fight because
Jesus has already won it for me.*
*1 Timothy 6:12*

FOR FURTHER STUDY:

2 Chronicles 20:14-17

DAILY SCRIPTURE READING:

Deuteronomy 11-12;
Acts 3

*Kenneth*

# Overcoming the Bungadeeshu Rash

Over and over, beginners in faith have come to me and said, "Brother Copeland, I know it's right to walk by faith, and I've made a decision to believe the Word. But every time I take a step, all hell breaks loose.

"I start believing God for healing and I break out in the Bungadeeshu rash. I get healed of that and my eyes cross! I believe for prosperity, get my car paid off and the engine blows up. Then the washing machine breaks and I lose my job. It seems like I get over one wall only to hit the mountain behind it!"

No, it doesn't *seem* like that. It *is* like that!

When you're just taking off on a life of faith, you have more problems and less spiritual skill than you will a few years down the road. And because you're just getting started, obstacles that one day won't be any threat at all can send you sprawling.

How do you get through all these things and keep going? How do you "keep the power on" in your faith walk? You *consider* the right things. You change the focus of your attention. Abraham considered not his own body in believing for a son. You must not consider the things in this natural world that appear to contradict the Word of God. You can't consider your circumstances. What you must consider is Jesus. What does considering Jesus really mean?

1) To consider Jesus, you must consider His Word. The Holy Spirit will paint an accurate picture of Jesus in your heart as you study the Word.

2) The second way to consider Jesus is to act on Hebrews 3 and consider Jesus as the Apostle—the "Sent One." Believe that He is sent to you to give you life continually.

3) Consider Jesus the High Priest of our profession. He continually watches over your words and actions of faith to see to it that they come to pass.

4) Consider Jesus to be faithful. Be confident He will do what He has said.

God is upholding all things by the Word of His power (Hebrews 1:3). If you want to be upheld, get over on His Word. It will see you through to victory. It will give you power to consider Jesus...and the strength to consider not those things which surround you.

So keep the power coming—keep considering Jesus—and eventually you'll never have to be bothered by the likes of the Bungadeeshu rash!

> "And being not weak in faith, he considered not his own body now dead, when he was about an hundred years old, neither yet the deadness of Sarah's womb: He staggered not at the promise of God through unbelief; but was strong in faith, giving glory to God; And being fully persuaded that, what he [God] had promised, he was able also to perform."
> ROMANS 4:19-21

FOR FURTHER STUDY:

Hebrews 3:1-6

DAILY SCRIPTURE READING:

Deuteronomy 13-14; Acts 4

## *Speak the Word*

*I am not weak in faith, considering my own body.*
*I consider Jesus. I believe the promise of God.*
*Romans 4:19-21*

> "[The Father] has delivered and drawn us to Himself out of the control and the dominion of darkness and has transferred us into the kingdom of the Son of His love."
> COLOSSIANS 1:13, AMP

# Be Kingdom of God-Minded

Where do you live? I realize that's a simple question, but I want you to stop and think about your answer for a moment. Your immediate response might be to think of the spot on this earth where you wake up each morning.

But if you're a believer, you need to think more deeply than that. You need to become aware that although you are in this world, you do not belong to its natural order. You are a citizen of heaven. You are, even here and now, privileged to live in that kingdom.

That statement would startle many Christians. Religion has taught them that they won't reach God's kingdom until they die and go to heaven. But Colossians 1:13 says we've already made the transfer.

Because God dwells in us and among us, His kingdom is present with us right now. Jesus said it this way: *"For behold, the kingdom of God is within you (in your hearts) and among you (surrounding you)"* (Luke 17:21, AMP).

Certainly we will go on to the place called heaven when our bodies die or when Jesus catches us away. But, thank God, since we're already citizens of the kingdom now, we can enjoy many of the benefits of heaven right here on earth. We can live our lives in love, peace, joy, prosperity, health and victory. We can also bring those kingdom blessings to others who are still under the dominion of darkness.

"If Christians can do that," you may ask, "why don't they?"

Mostly it's because they haven't been very aware of the kingdom of God. They have been so absorbed in the kingdom of this world—the world that they can see and touch—they haven't given much thought to God's kingdom.

But we can change that! We can obey the instruction of the Apostle Paul who wrote: *"Aim at and seek the [rich, eternal treasures] that are above, where Christ [the Anointed One] is, seated at the right hand of God. And set your minds and keep them set on what is above—the higher things—not on the things that are on the earth"* (Colossians 3:1-2, AMP).

By studying and meditating on what the Word has to say about the kingdom of God, we can become more and more kingdom of God-minded. There is so much revelation in the Word about the kingdom of God. I challenge you to study on your own. Get out your concordance and look up all the references to the kingdom of God or the kingdom of heaven. Let the reality of that kingdom get down in your heart so that you become kingdom of God-minded!

## *Speak the Word*

*God has delivered me out of the kingdom of darkness and transferred me into the kingdom of the Son of His love.*
*Colossians 1:13, AMP*

FOR FURTHER STUDY:

Matthew 6:33, AMP;
Luke 17:20-21;
John 3:3-21

DAILY SCRIPTURE READING:

Deuteronomy 15-16;
Acts 5

*Kenneth*

# Fear Not

The fear of death is the parent of all fears. Every fear that exists springs from that one basic fear. Satan was the author of it.

But the Bible says that Jesus destroyed Satan's authority over death. Jesus pulled the plug on fear forever. It doesn't have any authority over you at all. If you allow fear in your life, it will unhook you from faith and the supernatural every time. Fear will cut you off from God's power and put you back in bondage to the natural realm.

"Well, Brother Copeland, sometimes I just can't help being afraid."

Yes, you can! Sure, Satan is still a killer. He's still roaming around as a spiritual outlaw, killing, stealing and destroying (John 10:10). But he doesn't have any right to just come storming in anywhere he wants. In fact, it's outright impossible for him to do it apart from fear, because fear plays the same role in this twisted world of darkness as faith does in the supernatural world of light.

If you just stay with God, and stay on the Word, you can stop the fear.

That's what Jesus told Jairus to do, isn't it? Jairus had run into an impossible situation in the natural. His little daughter was at the point of death and there was nothing he could do to save her. So, by faith, he hooked into the supernatural. He came to Jesus and said, "If You'll lay Your hands on her, she shall live."

But before Jesus reached the little girl, the devil took a shot and killed her. Someone came and told Jairus, *"Thy daughter is dead: why troublest thou the Master any further?"* (Mark 5:35).

Do you know what Jesus said to him? *"Be not afraid, only believe"* (verse 36). In other words, *Don't let fear unhook you, Jairus. Just keep the faith, stay connected to the supernatural and everything will turn out all right.*

Now if Jesus told Jairus to fear not, that meant Jairus had the ability to fear not. And if he could cast off fear in the face of his own daughter's death, you can do it in your situation.

In fact, you *must* do it. Jesus gave us "Fear not" as a command, not a suggestion. In essence, He said, "Thou shalt not fear!" To act on fear is to act as though Satan is bigger than God. But he isn't! Besides all that, you have God on your side. Think about that. Of what in the world do you have to be afraid?

> "Forasmuch then as the children are partakers of flesh and blood, he [Jesus] also himself likewise took part of the same; that through death he might destroy him that had the power of death, that is, the devil; And deliver them who through fear of death were all their lifetime subject to bondage."
> HEBREWS 2:14-15

FOR FURTHER STUDY:

Mark 5:21-24, 35-43

DAILY SCRIPTURE READING:

Deuteronomy 17-18; Acts 6

## Speak the Word

*Jesus has destroyed him that had the power of death.*
*Therefore, I do not have to live in bondage to the fear of death.*
*Hebrews 2:14-15*

> "The eyes of the Lord run to and fro throughout the whole earth, to show himself strong in the behalf of them whose heart is perfect toward him."
> 2 CHRONICLES 16:9

# He's Waiting on You

"I'm just waiting on God...waiting on Him to prosper me...waiting on Him to heal me...waiting on Him to deliver me."

Have you ever heard anyone make statements like that? They sound good, don't they? They sound very spiritual. But the truth is, the people who make those kinds of statements don't know much about God.

I know they don't because the Bible clearly teaches that when it comes to the blessings of God—we're not waiting on Him. He is waiting on us!

What is He waiting on? Obedience.

You know, the world tries to convince us it's more exciting to sin than to obey God. But Jesus proved that it's not. He lived the most exciting life in history.

Obeying God isn't going to doom you to a life of boredom. Obeying God isn't going to cheat you out of the good things in life. No! Obedience will lead you into the most thrilling life of victory and blessing you could ever imagine.

How do you fulfill that kind of obedience? One day at a time. You don't sit around for years waiting for God to tell you to go to Africa as a missionary. You learn to do the little things He tells you to do. You learn to follow His directions on a daily basis—just going about your day doing what pleases Him.

God primarily provides those directions through His written Word, by the inward witness and by the voice of His Spirit. Many believers get very excited about the voice of God. They're eager for Him to tell them what to do about various situations in their lives. But they don't want to take time to study the written Word or be quiet enough to listen to the inward witness—which is the voice of their own spirit enlightened by the Holy Spirit.

Even Jesus, Who was more sensitive to the voice of God than any man had ever been, studied the written Word. In fact, He was so skilled in it that at the age of 12, the Jewish teachers in the Temple *"were astonished at his understanding and answers"* (Luke 2:47).

If you'll simply believe the written Word, you'll find it much easier to follow the inward witness of the voice of the Spirit. The written Word will retrain your mind to think like God thinks so that you recognize His directions. When He speaks, you'll know it's Him because what you are hearing is right in line with His written Word. And then you can walk in obedience with nothing to hinder your receiving what you need.

Remember, you're not waiting on God. He's waiting on you!

## *Speak the Word*

*I obey God and keep my heart perfect toward Him.*
*The Lord shows Himself strong in my behalf.*
*2 Chronicles 16:9*

FOR FURTHER STUDY:

Genesis 12:1-4, 13:1-4

DAILY SCRIPTURE READING:

Deuteronomy 19-20;
Acts 7

*Kenneth*

# God Is Not Mad at You!

I have six simple words for you today. Six words that run contrary to religion, rumor and popular belief. Six words of good news...GOD IS NOT MAD AT YOU!

I remember the first time I found that out. I was shocked. I hadn't been saved very long, and I had heard all my life about the terrible things God would do to you. He would make you sick and keep you poor. He would bring you crises to make you strong. Not only would He do those bad things to you, but also it was all right for Him to do them because He was God.

I don't remember anyone ever saying those exact words to me, but, as a child, that's what I heard.

Then one day I was reading the Bible and I came across Isaiah 54. It literally changed my thinking. God is not mad at us! Now that's earthshaking good news, yet religion hasn't given it much publicity.

That's such good news that some people have a hard time believing it. They start thinking of all the sin they've allowed into their lives, all the wrongs they've done. "There's no way God is going to overlook all that!" they say. "Surely He's going to do something about it."

He already did. He sent Jesus to the cross.

Read Isaiah 52. All of us have seen paintings of the Crucifixion. But none of them come close to the horror of what happened to Jesus that day. When He took the sins and sicknesses of mankind into Himself, His body became so marred, He didn't even look like a human being.

Yet it was this very event that bought us our covenant of peace and freed us forever from the wrath of God. Isaiah 53:10-11 tells us that God is satisfied! The sacrifice of Jesus' death on the cross was enough to pay for your sins and mine. Sin has no authority over you. As far as God is concerned, it's all over.

All that is left to be done on this earth is the preaching and praising and the accepting of what He has done.

So study it out. Read Isaiah 52, 53 and 54. And let that good news sink into you. Let it renew your mind. God isn't mad at you! He loves you! Just the way you are right where you are!

FOR FURTHER STUDY:

John 3:9-17

❧

DAILY SCRIPTURE READING:

Deuteronomy 21-23; Acts 8-9

## *Speak the Word*

*The mountains shall depart, and the hills be removed; but God's mercy and kindness do not depart from me. Neither is the covenant of His peace removed from me.*
*Isaiah 54:10*

"In a little wrath I hid my face from thee for a moment; but with everlasting kindness will I have mercy on thee, saith the Lord thy Redeemer. For this is as the waters of Noah unto me: for as I have sworn that the waters of Noah should no more go over the earth; so have I sworn that I would not be wroth with thee, nor rebuke thee. For the mountains shall depart, and the hills be removed; but my kindness shall not depart from thee, neither shall the covenant of my peace be removed, saith the Lord that hath mercy on thee."
ISAIAH 54:8-10

> "Is any among you afflicted [or in trouble]? let him pray."
> JAMES 5:13

# He Wants to Hear *You!*

It's wonderful to have a good pastor, and it's wonderful to know people who can pray with power—and I certainly do ask for prayer from others occasionally—but it's a believer's own prayers that are most important.

James 5:13 doesn't say, "If anyone is in trouble, he should ask his pastor to pray." No, it says if there is trouble in your life, *you* need to pray.

That's because prayer is more than just asking for something. When you pray, you fellowship with your Father. You talk to Him. He talks to you. That interaction strengthens you.

I was reminded of that at a family gathering once. One of our family members had gone to be with the Lord unexpectedly and it was a challenging time. After we had shared together and praised the Lord, one of my cousins said, "It just strengthens my faith to be around this family."

I knew exactly what she meant. I know people who are more mature in faith, and have been walking with the Lord longer than I have. And when I fellowship with those people, it makes me stronger too.

As I thought about that, it struck me. *If a person who is full of faith can strengthen me, how much more does it strengthen me to fellowship with God Himself every day in prayer?* Think about that!

You have the privilege any time, day or night, to draw near to God and come into His presence. You can keep a running dialogue going with the Lord all day long. You can continually be drawing strength from the Author and Finisher of your faith.

He is always ready to listen and respond to you. It's perfectly fine to have your pastor or other mature believers pray. But it's more important that you pray...that you have the intimate fellowship with your Father. Call on Him. He is always available and He's waiting to hear from *you!*

## *Speak the Word*

*When I am afflicted or in trouble, I pray.*
*The Lord delivers me out of all my afflictions.*
*James 5:13; Psalm 34:19*

FOR FURTHER STUDY:

1 John 5:13-15

DAILY SCRIPTURE READING:

Deuteronomy 24-25;
Acts 10

*Kenneth*
# Like a Fur Coat

God is not holding back anything that will set us free and assure us total overcoming victory in life. That's what I finally realized in 1967 when, as a young believer, I saw His Word as a love letter to me—a letter filled with promises He had made to me. I began to see that God was honorable, His Word had integrity and He was committed to doing those things He had promised—to make me the spiritually, emotionally, physically, financially and relationally successful person He had created me to be.

I found out He'd do anything in the world for me when I started living in love and acting in love. You start telling Him you love Him and start keeping His commandment of love, and He'll get all over you like a fur coat!

I remember one afternoon, I was driving down the road when my new-found awareness of God's love came all over me. I had to pull my car over and stop. It was the first time in my life I had come to God without a bunch of begging and wanting and trying to get.

> "[God] hath given unto us *all* things that pertain unto life and godliness, through the knowledge of him that hath called us to glory and virtue."
> 2 PETER 1:3

"I just can't stand to drive this car any farther," I cried out to God. "I just had to stop in order to raise my hands and tell You how much I love You, worship You and care for You! Heavenly Father, my needs are met according to Your riches in Glory by Christ Jesus.

"It just dawned on me a few days ago, that the whole world is running against You," I said. "I want to run with You! I want to do something to give You a good day. I want to do everything I can for You in a big way. Your slightest whim is my command. Just tell me what You want. Just tell me what You want me to do!"

But He wouldn't tell me! Instead, He said, *Son, what do you want Me to do for you? Is there anything?*

That's God's heart toward you. He's given you everything you need to succeed. He's given you every edge in His Word. Receive it. Take hold of it. Be all He created you to be. Read His love letter to you...start telling Him how much you love Him...and let Him get all over you just like a fur coat!

FOR FURTHER STUDY:

Psalm 36:7-10;
Proverbs 8:17-21

DAILY SCRIPTURE READING:

Deuteronomy 26-27;
Acts 11

## *Speak the Word*

*God has given me all things that pertain to life and godliness.*
*2 Peter 1:3*

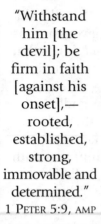

> "Withstand him [the devil]; be firm in faith [against his onset],— rooted, established, strong, immovable and determined."
>
> 1 PETER 5:9, AMP

# Put Hell on the Run

We live in an evil day. Actually, the days have been evil ever since Adam committed high treason in the Garden of Eden. But in this hour, that evil is intensifying because the end of the age is near. Jesus is coming soon, and the devil is doing everything he can to stop Him. He is killing, stealing and destroying as fiercely and as rapidly as he can.

The world around us is getting darker in these last days. And to triumph in the midst of that darkness is no stroll in the park.

Never in my life have I seen a time when it was so absolutely necessary to walk circumspectly before the Lord. Never have I seen a day when it was more crucial for us to heed the instructions God gives us in 1 Peter 5:8-9.

But we can do it, if we'll just be vigilant and alert to the dangers. (*To be vigilant* means "to be watchful and alert to danger." A vigil is an act or time of keeping awake.)

We can do it if we'll obey the instructions God gives us in Romans 12:21 and *"Be not overcome of evil, but overcome evil with good."* After all, God has given us so many good things, so much super-natural power and ability that no matter what happens in this dark world, we can emerge from it an overcomer. He has given us weapons of warfare that are not carnal, but mighty through God, to the pulling down of strongholds (2 Corinthians 10:4).

In fact, if we'll shake off the slothfulness of daily living and start walking in the spirit, we can blaze a path through life a mile wide. We can not only make it through this shadowy place to the light of Glory, we can take millions of others with us!

We can put hell itself on the run if we'll just wake up! Wake up to the Word, to prayer and to the guidance of the Holy Spirit. For in all those things, God has given us all the power, strength and wisdom we need to overcome!

## *Speak the Word*

*I am firm in faith. I am rooted, established, strong, immovable and determined. I am determined to triumph over the devil.*

*1 Peter 5:9*

FOR FURTHER STUDY:

Titus 2:11-15

DAILY SCRIPTURE READING:

Deuteronomy 28-29; Acts 12

*Gloria*

# Simplify Your Life!

In the years I have lived by faith, I've noticed that it's easy to become entangled in the affairs of this life. In fact, it sometimes seems as though this world is like an octopus always trying to grab you with its tentacles. If you don't watch out, it will wrap itself around you until you're completely caught up in the mundane, trivial things of this world.

If you let them, those trivial pursuits will hold you down and keep you from soaring on into the eternal things of God. They will choke out the Word that has been planted in your heart and leave you without faith and without power. That's what Mark 4:18-19 is talking about.

Here in the United States, we must be especially vigilant against such entanglements because we have such an abundance of material possessions! We can easily end up spending all our time just taking care of them.

As the Lord told a friend of mine in prayer one day, this nation has become a nation of maintenance men. We maintain our house. We maintain our yard. We maintain our car and our hair, our nails and our clothes. The problem is, by the time we've done what it takes to maintain all the natural things in our lives, we often don't have any time left to maintain the spirit man who lives on the inside of us.

There's only one thing to do: *Simplify your life.*

"But Gloria," you say, "the things I do are important. I can't just cut them out of my life!"

Listen, there's nothing more important than spending time with God in prayer and in the Word. So make whatever adjustments you must to spend time with God. Whenever you take on anything new, count the cost—not just in money, but in time. Ask yourself, *Can I afford this spiritually? Can I spare the precious hours and minutes this project (possession, hobby, etc.) will require and still have plenty of time to fellowship with the Lord?*

> "The ones sown among the thorns are others who hear the Word, Then the cares and anxieties of the world, and distractions of the age, and the pleasure and delight and false glamour and deceitfulness of riches, and the craving and passionate desire for other things creep in and choke and suffocate the Word, and it becomes fruitless."
> Mark 4:18-19, AMP

For Further Study:

Luke 12:22-31

Daily Scripture Reading:

Deuteronomy 30-31; Acts 13

If the answer is no, then set that project aside. I realize that may mean passing up some things you enjoy, but remember, your aim is not to please yourself. It's to please the One Who enlisted you. And believe me, when you make sacrifices for Him, He always makes sure you're well-rewarded—not only in this age, but in the age to come. Walking in obedience and fellowship with God is "the good life."

## Speak the Word

*I lay aside every weight which so easily besets me.*
*Hebrews 12:1*

*Kenneth*

> "Seek ye the Lord while he may be found, call ye upon him while he is near: Let the wicked forsake his way, and the unrighteous man his thoughts: and let him return unto the Lord; and he will have mercy upon him; and to our God, for he will abundantly pardon."
>
> ISAIAH 55:6-7

# It's Never as Hard as It Looks

There's a spiritual law all of us would do well to remember: *When hard times come, they're never as hard as they look.* That's important. Hard times are not as hard as they look—unless you are looking in the wrong place, through the wrong eyes, thinking the wrong thoughts, and imitating the wrong people.

At the onset, some problems look absolutely hopeless and insurmountable. But with a little changing of your thinking, they'll shrink back to a realistic size.

You see, wrong thoughts will paint the wrong pictures in your mind. They'll tell you things are worse than they are. They'll tell you that you don't have what it takes to succeed in life, or that the right opportunity won't come to you. But I'm here to tell you, you can succeed!

It doesn't matter how bad the economy is. People who understand money aren't afraid of hard times. In fact, it's the ungodly people who are money-minded who actually wish for hard times. Such people made great fortunes back during the Depression years. They bought up goods at about 10 cents on the dollar and ended up rich while others went broke.

But, of course, as believers, that's not our motive for prospering during hard times. We want to prosper in order to help others get back on top. We want to say, "Hey friend, let me teach you how to prosper. Come on over here in the kingdom of God. Get over here in my house. No flood of recession or depression is going to tear it down. It's built on the Rock!" (Matthew 7:24-26).

If people are sick, we can say to them, "Don't let sickness and disease knock your feet out from under you, friend. Come on over here to my house. It's a healing house. By the power of God, we can show you how to be well!"

That's what the good news is really all about.

So how do we change our thinking? Isaiah 55:6-11 tells us. We're to take up God's thoughts and God's ways. If we want to live the kind of life God has in mind for us, we must exchange our thoughts for His thoughts. We must lay down the perspectives we've gained through past experiences and instead pick up the wisdom of God—His Word. Through the Word of God we'll learn what reality is. We'll learn what is really going on in the world. And we'll learn His plan for getting through it in victory.

So the answer to every problem is in the Word. Let the Word change your thinking. Remember, times are not as hard as they look when you look from God's viewpoint!

## *Speak the Word*

*I live the kind of life God intends for me to live by exchanging my thoughts and ways for His.*
*Isaiah 55:6-11*

FOR FURTHER STUDY:

Isaiah 55:9-11

DAILY SCRIPTURE READING:

Deuteronomy 32-33;
Acts 14

*Kenneth*

# You're ANOINTED!

If you are born again and baptized in the Holy Ghost, I want you to pay close attention because I have some good news for you. So good it will cause you to shout and jump and praise God. So good it will inspire you to jump out of bed in the morning, grin real big and holler, "Look out, devil. I'm up again, and I'm going to whip you all day long!"

What news could produce that kind of joy and confidence? The news that *you* are anointed!

I can almost hear someone's religious mind working now. "Well, Brother Copeland, I'm just an old sinner saved by grace. I would never presume I was anointed."

You mean you aren't a Christian?

"Why certainly I'm a Christian!" Well, if you're a Christian, then you're anointed because the very word *Christian* is derived from the Greek word *Christ* which means "the Anointed One." Translate the word *Christian* and you'll find out it means to be anointed like Him!

In fact, to say you're anything less than anointed is to reject the inheritance Jesus purchased for you with His precious blood. Jesus didn't pay the price for sin just so you could sail to heaven in the sweet by-and-by. He did it so you could be cleansed and be the temple of the Holy Spirit Who is the Anointing (2 Corinthians 6:16). Jesus suffered, died and rose again so that He could give birth to a new race of reborn men and women who would be equipped with His own Anointing. Jesus laid down His life so that He could raise up a race of believers who would walk this earth, not only doing the same works that He did, but even greater works! (John 14:12).

> "The Spirit of the Lord is upon me, because he hath anointed me to preach the gospel to the poor; he hath sent me to heal the brokenhearted, to preach deliverance to the captives, and recovering of sight to the blind, to set at liberty them that are bruised, To preach the acceptable year of the Lord."
> LUKE 4:18-19

The very thought of doing the works of Jesus staggers the minds of most Christians today. When we think about being witnesses for "Christ," we usually think about passing out tracts and telling people the four spiritual laws. As wonderful as those things are, there is more to doing the works of Jesus. You're to preach the gospel to the poor, heal the brokenhearted, preach deliverance to the captives, recovery of sight to the blind, to set at liberty the bruised and preach the acceptable year of the Lord. Why? Because He said so, and has anointed you to do it! You can do it! You're ANOINTED!

FOR FURTHER STUDY:

Ephesians 1:17-23

DAILY SCRIPTURE READING:

Deuteronomy 34;
Joshua 1;
Acts 15

## *Speak the Word*

*The Spirit of the Lord is upon me. He has anointed me!*
*Luke 4:18*

# The Unchangeable Word of God

"In the beginning God created the heaven and the earth. And the earth was without form, and void; and darkness was upon the face of the deep. And the Spirit of God moved upon the face of the waters. And God said, Let there be light: and there was light."

GENESIS 1:1-3

God is all-powerful, therefore His Word is all-powerful. He can and does back up everything He says. Since He is Creator, His Words contain the power to create. You can see that truth borne out in the very first three verses of the Bible. You'll notice in those verses that the Spirit of God was moving before God spoke, but nothing happened until *God said*. Creation did not take place until God released words of faith.

Everything in this material creation, everything you can see, touch, taste or smell came into existence as a result of the Word of God. That means God's Word is the parent substance of all matter. Think of if! The paper this devotional is made of came from a tree that can be traced from tree to seed to tree to seed, all the way back to God's Word "Let it be."

In light of that fact, do you think His Word still has the power to change this natural, physical world? Do you think the Word that created the dirt your physical body was made from has enough power to heal that body? Do you think the Word that brought into being all the silver and gold, all the wealth of this entire earth, has enough power to supply you with the resources to pay your electric bill?

Of course! God's Word is eternal. It is sovereign. It cannot be changed. (People try to change it by saying it doesn't really mean what it says. But, thank God, it does mean what it says and there's nothing that can alter that fact.) Psalm 119:89 says, *"For ever, O Lord, thy word is settled in heaven."*

This material universe, on the other hand, is temporal. It can and does change. If you take something that is unchangeable and use it to apply pressure to something that is changeable, it's obvious which one of them will yield. *The changeable one!* Therefore, whenever you take the Word of God and apply it in faith to this temporal realm, that realm must give in and conform to the Word.

Jesus understood this truth. He lived His life by it. He had such faith in God's Word that when He spoke it, this material creation bowed its knee and obeyed Him. Demons fled. Diseases disappeared. Death gave up its grip. Bread multiplied. Winds stopped blowing. Waves ceased.

In fact, by the power of God's Word, Jesus was able to live and minister on this death-bound planet, and yet be completely free from all its bondages. And you can too!

You can speak the Word in faith to disease and it will leave. You can speak to your electric bill and it will be paid. You can speak to any circumstance, and know that the Word spoken and acted on in faith will release His power and change the changeable...all because you are standing on the *unchangeable* Word of God.

## *Speak the Word*

*God's Word is forever settled in heaven. It will never change.*
*Psalm 119:89*

FOR FURTHER STUDY:

Genesis 1

DAILY SCRIPTURE READING:

Joshua 2-4;
Acts 16-17

*Kenneth*

# He's Given You Peace

Some people have the idea that if you live by faith, you can float through life with no problems at all. Forget that right now. It will never happen this side of the rapture.

Just look at Jesus. If anyone should have been able to float through life, it was Jesus. He had perfect faith. But He had the toughest time of any man who ever walked on earth. He was persecuted, criticized and plotted against. What's more, He was tempted with every sin mankind has ever known. Yet He resisted it all.

If you think that's easy, think again. There's nothing tougher than feeling the pressure of sin, sickness, lack or grief, and yet refusing to let it dominate you. There's nothing tougher than standing up at those times and saying, "No! I'll not receive this sickness on my body. I'll not yield to this circumstance! I've been set free from the curse by the blood of Jesus, and I will live free by faith in Him!"

If you want to see just how much pressure such a stand of faith can bring, look at Jesus in the Garden of Gethsemane before He went to the cross. The pressure of the temptation He faced there put such a strain on His physical body that drops of blood poured through His skin like perspiration. But even then, sin could not conquer Him.

None of us will ever face that much trouble. We'll never have to stand against that much pressure. Yet we have available to us the same power and peace that took Him not just through the pressure at Gethsemane, but through the whipping, the mocking and the Crucifixion. We have the peace that took Him all the way through the Resurrection!

*"Peace I leave with you,"* He said. *"My peace I give unto you.... Let not your heart be troubled, neither let it be afraid."*

But, praise God, He didn't stop there. He told us how to gain access to that peace. He told us how to stand in faith when frightening things are happening all around us.

> *"If ye abide in me, and my words abide in you, ye shall ask what ye will, and it shall be done unto you"* (John 15:7).

He's given you His peace...far more than you'll probably ever need to tap into...and He's shown you how to access that peace and walk in it. So stop rehearsing the problem...and receive that abundant peace He provided for a day like today.

> "Peace I leave with you, my peace I give unto you: not as the world giveth, give I unto you. Let not your heart be troubled, neither let it be afraid."
> JOHN 14:27

FOR FURTHER STUDY:

John 16:29-33

DAILY SCRIPTURE READING:

Joshua 5-6;
Acts 18

## *Speak the Word*

*Jesus has given me His peace.*
*I do not let my heart be troubled, neither am I afraid.*
*John 14:27*

> "Of that day and hour knoweth no man, no, not the angels of heaven, but my Father only."
> MATTHEW 24:36

# Sooner Than We Think

Some time back, the Spirit of the Lord spoke to Ken and said, *I am coming sooner than you think.*

"But, Lord," Ken exclaimed, "I think You are coming soon!"

*Well, I am coming sooner than you think!* He answered.

There are many people on the earth today who don't believe that. Just as the scripture prophesies, they scoff: *"Walking after their own lusts, And saying, Where is the promise of his coming? for since the fathers fell asleep, all things continue as they were from the beginning of the creation"* (2 Peter 3:3-4).

But those people are mistaken. Jesus is coming back. There's a day and an hour appointed for His return. We know that's true because Jesus spoke of it in Matthew 24:36. At that appointed time, He will catch away those of us who are prepared for His coming and take us to heaven with Him to celebrate for seven years. Then He'll bring us back with Him when He comes to reign over the earth.

My, what a day that will be!

It's coming. There's no doubt about it. The only question is, *Will you be ready?*

If you're not ready, the thought of the Lord's return may not excite you like it does me. It may even fill you with dread and anxiety. If so, you need to make some changes.

First, you need to be born again by making Jesus the Lord of your life. Then you need to focus your attention and your affection on the things of God instead of the things of this world (Colossians 3:2).

After all, this world is not our home. It's not our final destination. We're just sojourning here, looking forward to the time when we're in the Glory and at home with the Lord. We need to constantly remember that, so we don't get entangled in this world's affairs. We need to constantly look toward heaven so when the time comes to depart, we'll be ready.

So get your thinking right. Set your heart on things that are above. Look forward to His coming. Look forward to the Marriage Supper of the Lamb. It really will happen, sooner than we think!

## *Speak the Word*

*I will be ready when Jesus comes. Therefore, I set my affection on things above, not on things of the earth.*
*Colossians 3:2*

FOR FURTHER STUDY:

2 Peter 3:1-14

DAILY SCRIPTURE READING:

Joshua 7-8;
Acts 19

*Kenneth*

# Walk in the Glory

Within the spirit of every born-again child of God, there is a divine hunger. That hunger cannot be satisfied either by the things of this world or by the theologies of religion. It is not a desire that fades with time. On the contrary, the longer we walk with God, the stronger it grows.

The Apostle Paul walked in more revelation knowledge than any man except Jesus, yet when he wrote his Philippian partners, he expressed a spiritual hunger that was so powerful it completely overshadowed everything else in his life: *"I count all things but loss for the excellency of the knowledge of Christ [the Anointed] Jesus my Lord [and His Anointing]...That I may know him, and the power of his resurrection"* (Philippians 3:8-10).

When you read those words, you can see exactly what Paul desired...a deeper revelation of the Anointed One and His Anointing...and to know the power of His Resurrection. What is the power of His Resurrection?

According to Romans 6:3-4, Jesus was raised from the dead by the Glory of God. So the power of the Resurrection is actually the Glory. Paul's burning desire was to know Jesus, the Anointed One and His Anointing...and to know the Glory of God!

The Glory is the most awe-inspiring subject in the Bible. It's so big you have to read the Old and New Testaments front to back to begin to get insight into it. In Exodus 33:18, Moses cried out to God to show him His Glory. God replied, *"I will make all my goodness pass before thee"* (verse 19). God's Glory is also His goodness. God's Glory is Himself!

Jesus is filled with and surrounded by the Glory and all that it is. All life. All goodness. He is untouchable by death ever again. He walks in all authority both spiritually and physically in heaven and in earth.

Everything man has and everything God has all rolled up into one Being with the Glory of God flowing in His veins—that's Jesus. And we are destined to be conformed to His image. We're headed toward the same fullness of Glory! That's why Jesus died for us. That's why He was raised again—so He could bring many sons unto Glory! (Hebrews 2:10).

Romans 3:23 says, *"For all have sinned, and come short of the Glory of God."* But praise God, Jesus took our sin and bore the penalty of it. Therefore we can know the Glory. We can partake of the Glory. We can let it permeate our lives and change everything! Get in on it. Get an understanding of it. Walk in the Glory!

SCRIPTURE READING:

Romans 6:3-4

✍

DAILY SCRIPTURE READING:

Joshua 9-10; Acts 20

## *Speak the Word*

*I am determined to know Jesus and the power of His resurrection.*
*Philippians 3:10*

# You're Sure to Please Him

> "Let them shout for joy, and be glad, that favour my righteous cause: yea, let them say continually, Let the Lord be magnified, *which hath pleasure in the prosperity of his servant.*"
> PSALM 35:27

If you're like me—and many other believers—you want to please God every day. And what's so wonderful is that God has told us exactly how to do this. Hebrews 11:6 tells us that it is impossible to please God without faith.

Faith pleases God because it gives Him access into your life. He needs access in order to remove burdens, destroy yokes and make of you a living demonstration of His desire to bless people and prosper them. But He has it only when we both *1) believe that He is,* and *2) believe that He is the rewarder of those who diligently seek Him* (Hebrews 11:6).

Acting on His Word is acting in faith. It gives Him the opportunity to heal your body, to prosper you, to save your children, to deliver your children from drugs—whatever it is you want and need. Faith not only gives Him access into your life, but it gives you access into His grace—His divine favor and blessings.

Third John 2 says, *"Beloved, I wish above all things that thou mayest prosper and be in health, even as thy soul prospereth."*

Look at what His prosperity includes. *To prosper,* by the definition in the dictionary, means "to excel in something desirable, to go forward." You desire to be well. You desire to be born again. You desire to go to heaven. You desire to please your Heavenly Father. You desire to feed your family. You desire to excel in whatever it takes to preach the gospel. That's prospering.

God wants you to excel in the entire realm of human existence: spirit, soul, body, financial and social. He wants you to be born again, baptized in the Holy Ghost, learning about faith, and walking by faith. He wants your mind renewed to the Word of God and walking in His wisdom—the God-given ability to use knowledge. His desire is that you know His healing power and walk in divine health. He delights when you have your financial needs met and have an abundance to give to every good work. In every relationship, He wants you to be a strong witness and lighthouse of His love, His way, His will and His power, helping others to prosper and know the Word of God.

God has committed Himself to your success in every area of life. Meditate that. Keep this thought in your mind all the time: *My God receives pleasure from my excelling by faith in every area of my life.* Think on this all day today and live it! You'll be sure to please Him!

## *Speak the Word*

*The Lord has pleasure in my prosperity. I prosper in every area of my life.*
*Psalm 35:27*

FOR FURTHER STUDY:

Galatians 3:6-11;
Hebrews 10:38;
1 John 3:22

DAILY SCRIPTURE READING:

Joshua 11-12;
Acts 21

*Kenneth*

# Preach the Word

> "And by the hands of the apostles were many signs and wonders wrought among the people....(And believers were the more added to the Lord)."
>
> Acts 5:12, 14

If the Church today would get a revelation of what happened when Jesus was raised from the dead, if we'd find out about the grace of God and how it works, the same thing would happen to us that happened to the congregation in Acts 5. We'd get bold. Not with the faking-it kind of boldness that falls flat on its face, but with the Holy Ghost-inspired, God-generated kind of boldness that brings miracles on the scene.

If you want to see what can take place when that kind of boldness is present, read the entire chapter of Acts 5. There in the midst of the apostles were many signs and wonders, people saved, the sick healed and others delivered.

For years I read this passage of Scripture and thought only the apostles were involved in this great, miraculous move of God. But that wasn't the case. It was the whole multitude of believers. Great grace was upon them all! They were all filled with the Holy Ghost and spoke the Word of God with boldness.

This group preached the Resurrection all over town until there were multitudes added to the Church. Then those multitudes began taking everyone who was sick into the streets to be healed. There were so many, the streets were full!

You can have that kind of boldness. Your church can have that kind of boldness. It's available to all believers. You have to get it by faith. The believers in Acts 4 and 5 got it by praying and believing God...and they wound up filling the entire town with the message of God's grace!

Want to turn your community upside down for God? Then get hold of the Word. Dare to believe it. Then preach it in faith with boldness. Soon, people will be pouring into the streets, running to your house, because they know that's where they can be saved, healed and delivered.

## *Speak the Word*

*I open my mouth boldly and make known the gospel of Jesus Christ.*
*Ephesians 6:19*

FOR FURTHER STUDY:

Acts 5:12-16

DAILY SCRIPTURE READING:

Joshua 13-14;
Acts 22

> "If you are willing and obedient, you shall eat the good of the land."
> ISAIAH 1:19, AMP

# Get Aggressive!

God has always promised that if you are willing and obedient, you will eat the good of the land. Understand though, that being willing means more than just saying, "Well, Lord, if You want me to prosper, I'll prosper." Being willing means that you apply the force of your will and determine to receive by faith what God has promised, no matter how impossible the circumstances may seem to be.

That's what Ken and I had to do. When we saw in God's Word that prosperity belonged to us, we were so deep in debt it looked like we would never get out. But we applied our will anyway. We became willing. We said, "We will prosper in the Name of Jesus, and we resist the curse of poverty. God says He has provided abundance so abundance belongs to us. We receive it now!"

That's the kind of aggressive stand you need to establish God's prosperity in your life. I didn't understand that for years so, without realizing it, I allowed the devil to come in and give me a hard time over finances. Then one day God revealed to me that I needed to use the same kind of stand for finances as for healing.

I had learned early on to be aggressive about healing. Once Ken and I found out that Jesus bore our sickness, we refused to put up with it anymore. We absolutely wouldn't tolerate it. We considered sickness an enemy and when it would try to come into our house, we'd stand against it.

We'd tell it, "No! You get out of here. I've been redeemed from the curse of the Law and that includes every sickness and disease. So get out!"

One day God said to me, *Why don't you treat lack the same way? Why do you put up with it? You say you've been redeemed from it, but you haven't resisted it like you do sickness and disease.*

When I heard that, I determined to make a change. I began to actively, aggressively resist lack with the same tenacity I resisted sickness and disease. And I can tell you, it made a big difference in my life.

I must warn you though, it wasn't easy. It takes effort and perseverance in the Word of God to develop that kind of resistance. If you are believing for divine prosperity, you'll need to keep a constant dose of the Word of God in your heart. You'll need to meditate on what God says about it all the time. You'll need to refuse and resist the curse of lack and poverty. You'll need to get aggressive!

## *Speak the Word*

*I am willing and obedient. I always eat the good of the land.*
*Isaiah 1:19*

FOR FURTHER STUDY:

Galatians 3:13-14

DAILY SCRIPTURE READING:

Joshua 15;
Acts 23

*Kenneth*

# Walk by Faith, Not by Sight

> "Reach hither thy finger, and behold my hands; and reach hither thy hand, and thrust it into my side: and be not faithless, but believing."
> JOHN 20:27

Eight days before Jesus said these words to Thomas the Apostle, Thomas had refused to believe the report of the other disciples—that they had seen the Lord. When they told Thomas, he said, "Unless I see and feel, I will not believe."

Jesus said that kind of believing has no faith in it. Faith is of the heart—the spirit—not the mind. To activate the believing equipment God has given every person, one must believe something he cannot see or feel—the Word of God.

Many Christians today don't realize that. They think if Jesus would appear to them in the flesh, their faith would skyrocket. But that's not so. If you're prone to depend more on sense-knowledge faith than you are on the Word of God, seeing some astounding manifestation in this natural realm can actually set your faith back. That's why Jesus did what He did on the road to Emmaus.

Two of His disciples were walking down the Emmaus road talking sadly about Jesus. So Jesus, coming alongside them said, "What's the matter with you boys?" (This is West Texas paraphrase.)

They thought He was a stranger. So Jesus began to preach to them (Luke 24:27-32). They took in all that He said, and suddenly they knew Him. But the moment they recognized Him, He disappeared. Why?

He did it because He wanted them to be blessed or empowered. He wanted to keep their spirits activated by believing the Word, instead of shutting down their spirits and simply believing He was alive because they had seen Him. He didn't want to set their faith back.

Some years ago, when I didn't understand that principle, I used to pester God to appear to me. "Lord, You appeared to Kenneth Hagin. You appeared to Oral Roberts. You appeared to T. L. Osborn ... and I want You to appear to me!"

I kept after Him about it for so long that He finally spoke to me by the Spirit and said, *Kenneth, if you keep asking Me to appear to you, I'm going to have to do it. But I'm warning you, it will set your faith back five years.*

FOR FURTHER
STUDY:

Luke 24:27-32

DAILY SCRIPTURE
READING:

Joshua 16-18;
Acts 24-25

At that point in my spiritual development, I would have come to rely on sense-knowledge faith, rather than on the faith that comes by the hearing of God's Word.

The fact is, Jesus would like to appear to every one of us. It would delight Him to just walk into the room and sit down with us. But He's had to restrain Himself, because He is training us to govern our lives by the God kind of faith. He's teaching us to walk by faith—not by sight (2 Corinthians 5:7).

## Speak the Word

*I walk by faith and not by sight.*
*2 Corinthians 5:7*

> "Have faith in God."
> MARK 11:22

*Kenneth*

# Fact vs. Truth

Jesus commanded us to operate in the same God kind of faith He has. He also told us that anyone who did it would have the same results. After all, it's His faith that's in us. He put it there.

That being the case, how do we deal with the fact that so many Christians are being defeated by sickness, poverty and every other kind of problem? By understanding that those defeats are "fact," but they are not "truth."

You see, facts can be changed. Truth can't. Truth supersedes fact. Spiritual law supersedes natural, physical law.

The law of gravity, for example, is a fact. But there is a higher law than the law of gravity. Those in the aeronautical industry know it as the law of lift. If you do certain things—make an airplane, build the wing right and engine powerful enough and so on—you'll be able to put the law of lift into motion and make an airplane fly.

How does that happen? Does gravity cease to be a fact? No. The law of lift simply supersedes it.

In the same way, sickness and disease are facts. But those facts can be superseded by the truth in Isaiah 53:5, *"With his [Jesus'] stripes we are healed."* It's a truth that can never be changed. What's more, if you'll apply that truth, it will overcome sickness every time! Truth applied changes facts.

Applying it. That's the key. You can put on your finest traveling clothes, pack your luggage and go sit down in a perfectly good airplane...but you won't get six inches off the ground unless somebody turns on the engines and begins to put the law of lift into motion.

What we need to do is apply our faith just like Jesus did. We need to learn to supersede our natural circumstances by activating the supernatural law of faith. So apply the truth to your facts today. Speak Isaiah 53:5 to your body. Speak Philippians 4:19 to your needs. Speak Isaiah 54:13 over your children. And watch the truth change the facts!

## *Speak the Word*

*I have faith in God. I walk and live by faith.*
*Mark 11:22; 2 Corinthians 5:7*

FOR FURTHER STUDY:

Matthew 21:17-22

DAILY SCRIPTURE READING:

Joshua 19-20;
Acts 26

*Gloria*

# God Will Get It to You!

> "My God shall supply all your need according to his riches in glory by Christ Jesus."
> PHILIPPIANS 4:19

Whatever you need today, God is your source. He is your supplier. Whether you need a new car or a place to live, He has it to give to you. All you have to do is access it by faith. You don't have to figure out in your natural mind how He's going to get it to you. All you have to do is believe and receive.

Let me give you an example. Remember in the Old Testament when Moses and the children of Israel were wandering in the desert? Remember how God supplied them manna to eat? In the account of that, the people of Israel began to complain and murmur. They grew tired of manna. They decided they wanted some meat (Numbers 11). Well, on they went, complaining about manna and talking about how good it was in Egypt.

Oh, how quickly we forget.

Well, Moses began to try to figure out how and where God was going to get enough to feed all of the people. Moses began reasoning with God. He said, *"Shall the flocks and the herds be slain for them?... Shall all the fish of the sea be gathered together for them?"* (verse 22).

And God said to Moses, *"Is the Lord's hand waxed short?"* (verse 23).

God did not appreciate Moses' line of questioning. Moses was saying, "Lord, it will take all the cattle we've got to feed this bunch for 30 days. It can't be done."

Not only did God not appreciate Moses' questions and attitude, God got hot! *"Is the Lord's hand waxed short?"*

You need to remember that when you have a need in your life. You have no business reasoning in your own mind how God is going to get something to you. *Well, I wonder if He's going to have someone in the church give it to me. I wonder if somebody's gonna die and leave me a bunch of money.*

God is not limited by your natural reasoning. His hand is not waxed short. He has ways that you've never even considered (Ephesians 3:20). He knows how to get it to you. That's His business. He is your source. He dropped quail on the Israelites that lasted for 30 days, right there in the camp.

God might just drop a house next door to you. He might leave a brand new car in your driveway one night. He can. He's God! He can do it however He wants to. So stop reasoning and start believing. Release your faith and receive. God will get it to you!

FOR FURTHER STUDY:

Numbers 11:18-23

DAILY SCRIPTURE READING:

Joshua 21-22;
Acts 27

## Speak the Word

*My God supplies all my need according to*
*His riches in glory by Christ Jesus.*
*Philippians 4:19*

*Kenneth*

> "In whom
> we have
> redemption
> through his
> blood, the
> forgiveness of
> sins, according
> to the riches
> of his grace."
> EPHESIANS 1:7

# "I Plead the Blood"

I went for years not knowing anything about the blood. I heard Pentecostal people plead the blood. You'd hear them all the time: "I plead the blood." I could tell it was powerful, and I could tell they knew what they were doing. But I didn't have the foggiest notion what pleading the blood actually meant.

I don't know why I didn't make the connection based on my background being American Indian. I should have. Indian life is based around blood covenants. They cut covenant. But when I finally did realize that God Almighty, in the blood of Jesus, has covenanted Himself to us...Man! I knew what those old-timers were saying and doing.

The devil has to respect the blood. When you say, "I plead the blood of Jesus in this situation," that's the blood by which the covenant was ratified, and the devil can't touch it. There's protection in the blood. There's deliverance in the blood.

When you plead the blood, you have laid down your case and put your entire confidence on an oath that is covenant-sworn by Almighty God.

When Jesus took the Communion cup in the upper room, He said, "Take this and drink it. This is the New Covenant in My blood, ratified for you."

That blood guarantees certain things. It guarantees that every word in the written Word of God is a blood-sworn oath. That blood-sworn oath is an anchor to your soul. It becomes an inner strength on the inside of you. God is your Father and Jesus is your blood brother. Everything that's His is yours and everything that's yours is His.

To be afraid to act or speak before you can see or feel something is to doubt God's sworn oath, the Name of Jesus, and the blood of the Lamb.

Jesus' blood shed for you obliterated your sin on the cross. When you received Jesus as your Lord, you took your place in your part of the New Covenant and you activated your freedom. And every time you repent of sin, it is destroyed forever and you are cleansed of its effect. That's why you can walk free of condemnation.

If the devil acuses you, don't walk in guilt. Guilt isn't yours. You've been given freedom. When you feel like you're in front of a judge and he asks, "How do you plead?" say, "I plead the blood! I'm innocent of that."

"Case dismissed—lack of evidence!"

Hallelujah! The devil has to honor that blood.

## *Speak the Word*

*In Christ I have redemption through His blood and the forgiveness of sins.*
*Ephesians 1:7*

FOR FURTHER
STUDY:

Hebrews 9:11-
10:23

DAILY SCRIPTURE
READING:

Joshua 23-24;
Acts 28

*Gloria*

# Live a Holy Life

Your body is not your own. Therefore what you do with it is not solely up to you. You've been bought with a price. You've been paid for by the sacrifice of the Son of God. Your body belongs to God. It is the temple of the Holy Spirit (1 Corinthians 6:19). *The Amplified Bible* says it is the sanctuary of the Holy Spirit.

God gave us this gift of the Holy Spirit to help us live separated unto Him—to walk in holiness. It is the Holy Spirit within you Who prompts you to do the will of God.

What would you expect if you received a spirit of unbelief? What would you expect that spirit to promote? Unbelief. If you received a spirit of lust, what would you expect that spirit to promote? Lust.

> "For ye are bought with a price: therefore glorify God in your body, and in your spirit, which are God's."
> 1 Corinthians 6:20

You haven't been given the spirit of unbelief or lust. You have been given the Holy Spirit of God Himself. God's own holiness. His own Spirit came into us when we were born again. To do what? To promote holiness and separation of our lives, our hearts, our very lifestyles and every action unto God.

Some people say not doing certain things will make you holy...like you can't wear certain clothes, you can't wear your hairstyle a certain way, or you can't wear makeup, and so on. None of those things will make you holy. They all only affect the outer man. Those kinds of things are of the Law, and the Law won't make you holy.

Only God's Spirit will make you holy. Our being united to the Lord in such a way that the Holy Spirit of God is leading us, guiding us and directing us in life is holiness. God loves you. He paid a high price for you. So glorify Him in your body. Honor Him with your lifestyle. Obey the promptings of the Spirit of God within you. Choose to live a holy life.

## *Speak the Word*

*I am bought with a price, therefore I glorify God*
*in my body and in my spirit, which are His.*
*1 Corinthians 6:20*

FOR FURTHER
STUDY:

1 Corinthians
6:9-20

DAILY SCRIPTURE
READING:

Judges 1-2;
Romans 1

> "If two of
> you agree on
> earth about
> anything that
> they may ask,
> it shall be
> done for them
> by My Father
> who is
> in heaven."
> MATTHEW
> 18:19, NAS

# Run a Harmony Check

The word *agree* Jesus uses in Matthew 18:19 can also be translated "to harmonize or to make a symphony." A symphony is composed of many instruments which, when played together, seem to be a single voice.

If you've ever heard a symphony, you know that when the individual instruments are tuning up, each one playing separately from the other, it's not much to hear. But when the conductor raises his baton and all those instruments begin to harmonize, the sound they make is tremendously powerful.

The same thing is true in prayer. Believers agreeing together in the Holy Spirit are a powerful, unstoppable force. That's why Satan fights Christian families. That's why he doesn't want men and women unified in marriage. He wants us fighting and fussing all the time because he knows it will hinder our prayers (1 Peter 3:7).

Any time you fail to get results from the prayer of agreement, run a harmony check. Ask the Holy Spirit to show you if you're in strife with your spouse (or anyone else). Then follow the instructions in Mark 11:25 where Jesus tells us, *"When ye stand praying, forgive, if ye have ought against any: that your Father also which is in heaven may forgive you."*

It is not sufficient for you and your spouse simply to agree on the particular issue you are praying about. You must also be in harmony in other areas as well. So run a harmony check!

## *Speak the Word*

*When I agree with another in prayer about anything that we ask,*
*it shall be done for us by our Father in heaven.*
*Matthew 18:19, NAS*

FOR FURTHER
STUDY:

1 Peter 3:7-12

DAILY SCRIPTURE
READING:

Judges 3-4;
Romans 2

*Gloria*
# Check Your Affections

Separating yourself from the ways of the world doesn't always mean just leaving destructive activities behind. It often means simply getting rid of those things that don't build you up spiritually.

Hebrews 12:1 says as we run the race that is set before us, we are to lay aside weights. You may have weights in your life that are slowing you down spiritually. They may not be bad things in themselves, yet they are draining you of spiritual power. You may be so wrapped up in your occupation, for instance, that you spend all your time thinking and talking about it. Or you may have a hobby that has become the center of your attention.

The problem with things like that is not that they are sinful, it's that they've captured your affection. It's time to check your affections. The Bible says in Colossians 3 that we're to set our affection on things above, not on things on the earth.

God wants you to set the affection of your heart on Him. Why? So that He can pour out His affection on you!

You can't give anything to God without His giving you much more in return. When you set your affection on Him, He will bless you, and bless you, and bless you!

> "If ye then be risen with Christ, seek those things which are above, where Christ sitteth on the right hand of God. Set your affection on things above, not on things on the earth."
> COLOSSIANS 3:1-2

## Speak the Word

*I seek those things which are above.*
*I set my affection on things above, not on things on earth.*
*Colossians 3:1-2*

FOR FURTHER STUDY:

Hebrews 12:1-4

DAILY SCRIPTURE READING:

Judges 5-6;
Romans 3

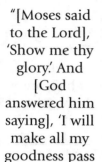

> "[Moses said to the Lord], 'Show me thy glory.' And [God answered him saying], 'I will make all my goodness pass before thee.'"
>
> EXODUS 33:18-19

# Repent—And Receive the Glory!

Good overwhelms evil—and God's goodness and Glory are one and the same. That's why God made all His goodness pass in front of Moses. It was the Glory Moses was wanting to see.

If you'll read the entire passage in Exodus 33, you'll also find that God told Moses He would have to hide him from that Glory, because if he saw God's face, he would die.

Why? Because as an un-born-again man, Moses had sin in him. His heart had never been born again. Sin is darkness. God doesn't have to try to kill darkness. He doesn't have to lift His mighty right arm and bash it in the head. When God walks on the scene and His goodness is released in its full force, it is so powerful, it just blasts evil into nothingness.

That's the reason God and man had to be separated after the Fall. He had to protect man from the power of His Glory.

But I want you to know, God isn't separated from us any longer. He is dwelling inside our reborn, human spirit—and, in these last days, He will break forth and overflow from that dwelling place to touch once again the flesh of men.

*The Holy Ghost on flesh!* Think about that. The flesh is the domain the devil thought he had locked up for himself. He's dominated that area for himself. He's dominated that area for thousands of years and because of it, we've learned how to walk by faith and not by sight or by manifestations of the flesh. We've learned how to ignore the flesh and control it, walking by faith in Almighty God's Word.

But the time at hand is one in which God will start affecting people's flesh. You'll still have to walk by faith, but you need to be prepared for physical manifestations. Because when this fire of God's Glory starts affecting the flesh, some people won't know whether to run or hide, or jump and shout.

They'll quickly realize that you just can't play around with this Glory. It is sure power. It is the kind of power that forces sickness and disease to disappear from human bodies. It's the kind of power that makes the devil pack his bag and flee!

It's the kind of power that will bring in the end-time harvest, and God is ready to pour it out in fullness. That's the reason He is calling on us to get the sin out of our lives. That's why He is saying, *Repent, so I can manifest the Glory!*

If He pours out the fullness of that Glory and you're hanging on to sin, it will destroy your flesh. So get the sin out! Cleanse the temple! The fire of God wants to come forth!

## *Speak the Word*

*The Lord shows me His Glory. He makes all of His goodness pass before me.*
*Exodus 33:18-19*

FOR FURTHER STUDY:

Exodus 33:12-23

DAILY SCRIPTURE READING:

Judges 7-9;
Romans 4-5

*Gloria*

# Love to Tithe!

*"Behold, what a drudgery and weariness this is!"* (Malachi 1:13, AMP).

Have you ever had that thought when you were writing out your tithe check? Have you ever wanted to hide your pocketbook from God so you wouldn't have to give? If so, you need to change your attitude, or it will prevent you from receiving your financial harvest. It will stop your increase.

Refuse to harbor such dishonorable thoughts toward God in your heart. Rebuke them and say, "No! I will not have that attitude. I love God and I love to tithe my tithe!"

Actually, we ought to be like a little child when it comes to giving. Have you ever noticed how excited children get when their parents give them some money to put in the offering? They can hardly wait to give it.

We ought to be the same way. We ought to look forward to giving our tithes and offerings all week long.

You see, just as tithing opens the door to increase and the blessings of God, stealing God's tithe and using it on yourself opens the door to decrease and the financial destruction the devil brings. You'll never come out ahead by keeping the tithe.

Ken and I know that from personal experience. Right after we were born again, before we had much revelation of the Word, we would try tithing for a few months. Then we'd decide we needed the money more than God did so we'd stop. As a result, we just kept on decreasing financially. We kept on getting deeper in debt.

When we began to learn and obey God's Word, we made a quality decision to tithe first, no matter what. That's when our finances turned around. We began to increase and we've been increasing ever since! Our increase increases continually!

> "No thing that a man shall devote to the Lord of all that he has, whether of man or beast or of the field of his possession, shall be sold or redeemed; every devoted thing is most holy to the Lord.... And all the tithe of the land, whether of the seed of the land or of the fruit of the tree, is the Lord's; it is holy to the Lord."
> LEVITICUS 27:28, 30, AMP

If you're not experiencing the kind of supernatural increase the Bible says belongs to a tither, then check your attitude. Check your heart. When your heart is right, you'll have a hard time *not* getting excited about it! You'll want to jump and shout and praise God every time you think about it. You won't begrudge God His 10 percent. You'll thank Him for letting it flow through your hands. You'll just love to tithe!

FOR FURTHER STUDY:

2 Corinthians 9:6-11

DAILY SCRIPTURE READING:

Judges 10-11; Romans 6

## *Speak the Word*

*I honor the Lord with my substance and with the firstfruits of all my increase. My barns are filled with plenty and my presses burst out with new wine.*
*Proverbs 3:9-10*

# God Loves You Because He Wants To!

"The Lord
shall cause
thine enemies
that rise up
against thee to
be smitten
before thy
face: they
shall come
out against
thee one way,
and flee
before thee
seven ways."
DEUTERONOMY
28:7

Do you know what the Ten Commandments mean? To the Western mind, they mean "Don't you dare steal, or kill, or covet." But to a covenant-minded person who understands God's *hesed,* they mean something entirely different.

*Hesed* is a covenant word. It means "God's mercy, kindness, tender mercies, His lovingkindness and fidelity." It's His unconditional love for you.

To the covenant man, God is saying in the Ten Commandments, *"Listen, son, there isn't any need for you to covet that fellow's wife. I have one prepared just for you. There's no need for you to murder anyone. Bring the problem to Me. I'll repay. You have a covenant with Me.*

*"There's no need for you to become a thief. I'll meet your needs according to My riches in Glory. All you need to do is live in love and faith. I'll take care of the rest."*

If you'll develop the kind of heart and mind that thinks and acts like this, it will make you fearless. Love...mercy...*hesed* casts out fear. (See 1 John 4:18.)

I can just hear your mind working. *Oh, Brother Copeland, that sounds great. But I've done some rotten things since I've been a Christian. I've messed up my part of the covenant pretty bad.*

No, you haven't. You can't mess up this covenant because it's not between you and God. It's between God and Jesus.

You can't break it. You can get out of fellowship with it, turn your back on it and refuse to receive its benefits. It will always still be there when you repent.

"Yeah, but I just don't understand how God could still love me after all I've done."

Listen, the *agape-hesed* of God isn't affected by what you do or don't do. It is an unconditional act of His will. God loves you because He *wants* to love you. He loves you because you and He are connected by the pure covenant blood of Jesus—and there's nothing you can do to change that. That's what *agape-hesed* is!

So don't let the devil deceive you one more moment. You are worthy to receive God's unconditional love. The blood of Jesus has provided you this love. Receive it. It's yours. Remember: He loves you because He *wants* to!

## Speak the Word

*The blood of Jesus makes me worthy to receive God's unconditional love.*
*I will receive and walk in that love today.*
*1 John 4:16-21*

FOR FURTHER
STUDY:

1 John 4:16-21

DAILY SCRIPTURE
READING:

Judges 12-13;
Romans 7

*Gloria*

# Give the Holy Spirit Something to Help!

God has made mighty provisions for your continued success. That's a powerful statement. But it's true. He has given you MUCH! He has given you everything you need to succeed in this life. He's given you His Word, the blood of Jesus, and the power of the Holy Spirit...to name just some of them.

But for them to work, you have to do your part. Some people who don't understand this waste a great deal of time. When they find themselves in a hard situation, they often sit back and wait for God to rescue them.

You won't get anywhere by just waiting for God to do everything. As one minister says, "The Holy Spirit is your Helper, and if you don't do what you're supposed to, He doesn't have anything to help!"

So don't just sit there—do something!

Fight the good fight of faith. Put the Word of God in your heart and in your mouth and get aggressive about it. I know it's hard to speak words of faith when you're facing an impossible situation. But you were born again to be able to accomplish hard things!

I think it was a great blessing that Ken and I were in an impossible situation financially when we first began to hear the Word of faith. (I didn't think it was a blessing then, of course, but I do now!) Our finances were minus zero at that point in our lives. We didn't have anything but our debts!

We were so desperate we had to believe God. It was the hardest believing we ever did too, because we didn't know very much in those days. But we got aggressive with our faith. We got aggressive with the Word.

The fact is, if you want to lay hold of the authority of God and walk in the supernatural, you aren't going to do it from your spiritual easy chair. You have to press yourself. As Jesus said, *"The law and the prophets were until John: since that time the kingdom of God is preached, and every man presseth into it"* (Luke 16:16).

Press. That is such an important word today. If there ever was a generation that needed to press in to God, it's ours. So take what God has given you. Get the Word in your heart and in your mouth. Plead the blood of Jesus over your circumstances and your family members. Get aggressive. And give the Holy Spirit something to help!

> "I will pray the Father, and he shall give you another Comforter, that he may abide with you for ever; Even the Spirit of truth; whom the world cannot receive, because it seeth him not, neither knoweth him: but ye know him; for he dwelleth with you, and shall be in you."
> JOHN 14:16-17

FOR FURTHER STUDY:

2 Kings 7

DAILY SCRIPTURE READING:

Judges 14-15; Romans 8

## Speak the Word

*As I do my part to press forward and lay hold of God's promises for my life, the Holy Spirit helps me.*
*John 14:26*

> "Let the weak
> say, I am
> strong."
> JOEL 3:10

# Watch Him Move!

Your confession is what you say—not just with your lips, but with your actions. Jesus is the High Priest of your confession. That means He has the authority to bring to pass anything you confess by faith that's in line with His Word. That's what He was sent by God to do. The Apostle and High Priest of our confession literally means the One God sent to watch over our words and actions of faith and see to it that they come to pass.

That means when you're broke and you confess by faith, "My God supplies all my needs according to His riches in Glory by Christ Jesus" (Philippians 4:19), Jesus has the authority to deliver to you the necessary finances. Or, when you are sick and you confess by faith, "I'm healed by the stripes of Jesus," you put yourself in a position to receive that healing from Him.

Some people say, "Oh, I couldn't confess I was healed when I was actually sick. That would be lying!"

Really? Then the prophet Joel told people to lie because he said, *"Let the weak say, I am strong."*

Joel wasn't telling people to lie. He was delivering a spiritual principle. He was telling God's people they should say what God says about them, instead of what their circumstances say about them.

The reason that seems strange to most people is they're so selfish. They see everything from their own viewpoint. But when you confess the Word instead of your circumstances, you're laying down your own viewpoint and speaking from God's viewpoint instead. When you understand that, it won't seem strange.

So speak God's Words over your circumstances today. Speak His Words in faith...and watch Him move!

## Speak the Word

*I am strong in the Lord and in the power of His might.*
*Ephesians 6:10*

FOR FURTHER
STUDY:

Proverbs 18:20-21

DAILY SCRIPTURE
READING:

Judges 16-17;
Romans 9

*Gloria*

# Get on the Road to Increase

Are you ready to take the limits off your income? I am. And the Lord has been showing me how we can do it. I'm excited about it because this is the day when we as believers need to prosper. We need to have enough not just to meet our own needs, but to see to it that the gospel is preached around the world.

Jesus is coming back soon! We don't have time to sit around wishing we had enough money to go through doors God is opening before us. We don't have time to say, "Well, one day when finances aren't so tight, I'll give to this ministry or that one so they can buy television time in Russia, or print books in Spanish." We need to increase so we can give—and we need to do it now!

How do we get on that road to increase? Through tithing. Tithing is the covenant transaction that opens the door for God to be directly involved in our increase. It is a two-way exchange in which we honor God by giving Him 10 percent of our income and He, in return, provides us with a *"surplus of prosperity"* (Deuteronomy 28:11, AMP).

"But Gloria," you may say, "I know Christians who have been tithing for years and they are not wealthy!"

Actually, you don't. You just know people who have put 10 percent of their income into the offering bucket. They went through the motions, but they weren't doing all Bible tithing requires.

You see, tithing isn't just a matter of the pocketbook. It is a matter of the heart. That's the way it is with everything as far as God is concerned. He always looks on the heart. So when we tithe as a religious routine, not in faith, just because we're supposed to, and not as a genuine expression of our love for God, we miss out on the blessings of it.

That's what happened to the people in Malachi's day. They were bringing sacrifices to the Lord. They were going through the motions of tithing. But they were not being blessed. In fact, they were living under a financial curse because the attitude of their heart was not right. (You can read about it in Malachi 1:6-8.)

What they were missing was honor! They weren't giving God their best. Because they didn't love and reverence God in their hearts, they were offering Him their leftovers. They were fulfilling religious requirements by keeping a formula with no worship.

So are you ready? Ready to take the limits off? Then tithe. But when you tithe, do it the right way. Remember to honor God with your tithe...honor Him from your heart. Soon, you'll enjoy the supernatural increase God has promised you!

> "Bring all the tithes...into the storehouse, that there may be food in My house, and prove Me now by it, says the Lord of hosts, if I will not open the windows of Heaven for you and pour you out a blessing, that there shall not be room enough to receive it."
> MALACHI 3:10, AMP

FOR FURTHER STUDY:

Malachi 3:8-12

DAILY SCRIPTURE READING:

Judges 18-19; Romans 10

## *Speak the Word*

*I bring my tithes into the storehouse. The Lord opens the windows of heaven and pours me out a blessing so great that there is not room enough to receive it.*
*Malachi 3:10*

*Kenneth*

# Ashes Under Our Feet

> "But unto you that fear my name shall the Sun of righteousness arise with healing in his wings; and ye shall go forth, and grow up as calves of the stall. And ye shall tread down the wicked; for they shall be ashes under the soles of your feet in the day that I shall do this, saith the Lord of hosts."
>
> MALACHI 4:2-3

I imagine you are probably just as tired of having the devil get in the middle of your affairs as the next guy. But, it doesn't have to be that way, you know. Read Malachi 4:2-3 again.

Notice that this scripture says *"S-U-N of righteousness,"* and not the *"S-O-N of righteousness."* That's not a mistake. Malachi was talking about a bright, blazing Glory. The wings he refers to aren't bird's wings, they're flames of fire that are shaped like wings.

But most exciting of all is the fact Malachi didn't say that "He shall go forth." He said, *"You* shall go forth."

You and I are the ones who will ensure the devil's defeat in our lives. We have all the power we need to destroy the works of the devil, and to kick him out of our affairs.

Your confession of faith and your expectancy are going to pull the Glory out of you, and you will walk in that Glory right in the face of hell and everything it has to offer.

You are the one who will go forth with this blazing Glory...the same Glory that appeared as a pillar of fire by night and cloud by day...the same Glory that filled the Temple with such power till the priests couldn't approach the altar without being knocked backward...the same Glory that raised Jesus from the dead (Jesus is the Head of the Body. We are His feet. His Glory is flowing from Him through us)...the same Glory that God said would fill the whole earth...that same Glory is what you'll use to tread on the devil as ashes under your feet!

## *Speak the Word*

*I go forth, and grow up as a calf of the stall. I tread on*
*the wicked one and he is ashes under the soles of my feet.*
*Malachi 4:2-3*

FOR FURTHER
STUDY:

Mark 16:14-19

DAILY SCRIPTURE
READING:

Judges 20-21;
Romans 11

*Gloria*
# Strife Will Keep You Carnal

It's bad enough that strife opens the door of our lives to confusion and every evil work (James 3:14-16). That alone should make us resist it with all our might. But that's not all the Bible has to say about it.

In his letter to the Corinthians, the Apostle Paul gave us even more information about the damaging effects of strife. He wrote:

*"And I, brethren, could not speak unto you as unto spiritual, but as unto carnal, even as unto babes in Christ. I have fed you with milk, and not with meat: for hitherto ye were not able to bear it, neither yet now are ye able. For ye are yet carnal: for whereas there is among you envying, and strife, and divisions, are ye not carnal, and walk as men?"* (1 Corinthians 3:1-3).

Carnal Christians are miserable people. They're born again and they know enough about God not to enjoy sin, but they aren't committed enough to stay out of sin.

If you don't want to find yourself trapped in that condition (and I know you don't) then stay out of strife, because strife will keep you carnal! It will inhibit your ability to digest the meat of the Word, and without that meat you won't be able to grow into a strong, victorious Christian. If you fuss and bicker with others, your spiritual growth will be stunted. You'll remain in a perpetual state of spiritual infancy and the devil will run over you regularly!

So grow up. Don't stay a baby. Get out of strife and into the Word. Soon you'll be the overcomer the Word says you are!

> "For ye are yet carnal: for whereas there is among you envying, and strife, and divisions, are ye not carnal, and walk as men?"
> 1 CORINTHIANS 3:3

## Speak the Word
*I walk in love and grow up in every way and in all things.*
Ephesians 4:15, AMP

FOR FURTHER STUDY:

2 Timothy 2:24-26;
1 John 5:4-5

DAILY SCRIPTURE READING:

Ruth 1-3;
Romans 12-13

> "The word of God is quick [or alive], and powerful, and sharper than any two-edged sword, piercing even to the dividing asunder of soul and spirit."
>
> HEBREWS 4:12

# His Word Is as Good as His Bond

The Word of God is not just a book! It is not just a black leather book you wag to church on Sunday and then leave on the coffee table the rest of the week. His Word has been recorded in a book...but the Word itself is what God has said and is saying to you personally!

That's powerful. That means the Word of God is ALIVE...and working every time you put it to work. That's because God's Word is His bond.

You've heard people say that about others: "A man's word is his bond." That means a person's word is the measure of his character. If a man honors his word by keeping it, then he is an honorable man. If he dishonors his word by breaking it, he is a dishonorable man. Like it or not, everyone's integrity—including God's—is judged on the basis of whether or not he keeps his word.

No doubt, that statement would ruffle the feathers of a few religious people. "Who do you think you are," they'd say, "to set up a criterion by which to judge God?"

I didn't set it up! God did. He is the One Who taught us to judge integrity on that basis. He invented the integrity of words. He set the standard.

God and His Word are one—not because we say so, but because He said so. He has made it clear that we cannot separate Him from His Word. Just as He never changes, His Word never changes. They are both the same—yesterday, today and forever.

That means that if you've been believing God for something based on His Word, you can rest assured He is faithful to keep His Word. He won't fail you. His Word is alive...it is working for you every time you speak it and act on it in faith. So stand up strong today. Put your trust in Him. Don't cave in to doubt...or despair. Remember, His Word is as good as His bond.

## *Speak the Word*

*God's Word is alive and full of power. It is active, operative, energizing and effective in my life.*
*Hebrews 4:12, AMP*

FOR FURTHER STUDY:

John 17:1-6

DAILY SCRIPTURE READING:

Ruth 4;
1 Samuel 1;
Romans 14

*Kenneth*

# From the Roots Up

You can't wipe out a weed simply by mowing it down. If you want to get rid of a weed—you must destroy its roots. That's elementary information. Even people like me who avoid yardwork at every opportunity know it.

But did you know that same basic fact is true in every other area of life? If you want to change a situation permanently, you must tackle it at its root. You can lose thousands of pounds, for example, and you'll regain every one of them (and probably more) if you don't solve that weight problem at the root.

You can get out of debt a dozen times...but you'll get right back in before you know it if you don't deal with the root of the matter.

That's what's so awesomely powerful about faith. If it's founded on the living Word of God, it will change things in your life from the roots up.

Read Mark 11 and you'll see what I mean. Jesus is walking from Bethany to Jerusalem with His disciples. He's hungry, and according to verse 13, He sees a fig tree. Seeing that it has leaves, He checks it for figs. When He sees it doesn't have any, He *"answered and said unto it, No man eat fruit of thee hereafter for ever. And his disciples heard it."* He cursed it at the root, and He answered it.

> "And Jesus answered and said unto it [the fig tree], No man eat fruit of thee hereafter for ever. And his disciples heard it.... And in the morning, as they passed by, they saw the fig tree dried up from the roots."
> MARK 11:14, 20

Jesus *answered* the fig tree because it spoke to Him first! By the very fact that it had no fruit, that tree was saying to Jesus, "Forget it, fellow. You aren't getting anything to eat here."

Your circumstances talk to you in the same way. Do you realize that? If you're standing against sickness, that sickness is talking to you every day. When you get up in the morning, it says, *You haven't received your healing. You're hurting all over. Can't you feel it? This faith stuff isn't working. You might as well go back to bed.*

Poverty will talk to you the same way. It will interrupt your every thought if you'll allow it. Its biggest lie is, *You can't afford it!*

FOR FURTHER STUDY:

2 Corinthians 4:13-18

DAILY SCRIPTURE READING:

1 Samuel 2-3; Romans 15

Those situations will talk to you all the time. So do what Jesus did. Answer them! Curse them at the root. Answer them with the Word, "By His stripes I was healed! My God meets ALL my needs according to His riches in Glory! I am more than a conqueror in Christ Jesus. I overcome by the blood of the Lamb and the WORD of my testimony! Great is the peace of my children!"

Speaking words like that in faith will change things for sure. Jesus cursed the fig tree at the root...and it made a permanent change. You have the same power where your circumstances are concerned. If you'll release your faith, you can hit even the most stubborn problem and dry it up at the source. You can get rid of it from the roots up!

## Speak the Word

*I have the same spirit of faith as Jesus. I believe, and therefore I speak.*
*2 Corinthians 4:13*

> "Having begun in the Spirit, are ye now made perfect by the flesh?"
> GALATIANS 3:3

# Just Keep the Line Open

Wouldn't life be wonderfully simple if there were only one thing that truly mattered? Wouldn't it be great if only one factor determined your success? All the confusion and complexity that clutters your life would suddenly disappear. Instead of constantly juggling priorities, you'd always know what to put first.

Well, here's a bit of news that may surprise you. There is, in fact, only one real key to victory in life. That's right. Just one. *A living connection with God.*

In years past, I used to say, "If you're not walking in victory, check your love walk." Or sometimes I'd tell people, "If you're not getting your prayers answered, make sure you aren't harboring any unforgiveness...make sure your flesh is under control...make sure you're flowing in the joy of the Lord." I had learned that by checking those spiritual gauges, you could track down the causes for failure.

But even though such gauges are very helpful, after more than 30 years of living by faith, I've come to realize that ultimately our success stems solely from our vital, continual contact with God. That one factor governs all others.

If you're in contact with the Lord, those other qualities will flow naturally from your heart. If you maintain a living connection with God, you will walk in love and joy. You will walk in forgiveness. You will keep your flesh in subjection to your spirit.

So what exactly is a living connection with God? It simply means keeping the lines of communication open between the two of you. It means going about your daily activities in such a way that you're always available to hear from heaven.

Just think, the real key to consistent victory is just one thing! You don't have to memorize a list of dos and don'ts. All you have to do is keep that flow of continual living contact with God. He's continually speaking words to our hearts by the Holy Spirit Who lives within us. Keep your ear tuned to His frequency. Keep your heart lined up with His Word. Just keep the line open!

## *Speak the Word*

*Having begun in the Spirit, I stay in the Spirit and I am made perfect.*
*Galatians 3:3*

FOR FURTHER STUDY:

1 John 1:1-7

DAILY SCRIPTURE READING:

1 Samuel 4-5;
Romans 16

*Kenneth*

# Winning the Battle of the Flesh

Do you know what it is like to be in a losing battle with your own body? I do...and I can tell you, it's miserable.

There have been times in my life as a believer when I wanted with all my heart to behave one way, and my body seemed absolutely intent on doing exactly the opposite. Times when I desperately wanted to lose excess weight, yet kept on stuffing myself with every kind of unhealthy food I could get my hands on. Times, years ago, when I so longed to quit smoking that I threw my cigarettes out the car window...then turned the car around to go back and get them.

> "And they that are Christ's have crucified the flesh with the affections and lusts."
> GALATIANS 5:24

You know what I'm talking about. You've been there too. We call it the battle of the flesh.

"Oh yes, Brother Copeland. We have to fight our flesh constantly. It has an evil nature, the nature of the old man, you know, and it opposes the nature of God in us."

Please excuse me for being blunt, but that is the most schizophrenic thing I've ever heard in my life. When we're born again, we're not half God and half devil. Jesus paid the price for our whole being on the cross—spirit, soul and body.

It bothers me when I hear a believer talk about his old, wicked, sinful, terrible flesh. We shouldn't talk like that! Jesus allowed stripes to be laid on His back so that our flesh could be healed. Ephesians 5:29 says, *"No man ever yet hated his own flesh; but nourisheth and cherisheth it."* You're doing something unscriptural and unnatural in the sight of God when you begin to hate your own body.

We do have to crucify our flesh, or take dominion over it. And we train our flesh to obey God by practice (Hebrews 5:14). We practice training our flesh by obeying the Spirit and walking in the light of God's Word. Galatians 5:16 reveals the key. It says when we walk in the spirit, we do not fulfill the lust of the flesh. It does not say to hate our flesh enough, and someday maybe it will settle down.

If you're led by your spirit, there won't be any need to impose law on your flesh because your spirit man has been reborn. He has no desire to break the law of God. He has been made the righteousness of God.

If you'll develop your spirit man and put him in charge of your body, instead of being dominated by your body, eventually you'll train that body to work with your spirit instead of against it. That's the good news!

FOR FURTHER STUDY:

Galatians 5:16-18

DAILY SCRIPTURE READING:

1 Samuel 6-7; 1 Corinthians 1

## *Speak the Word*

*I am Christ's. I crucify my flesh with its affections and lusts.*
*Galatians 5:24*

*Kenneth*

# Give...in Faith

> "Charge them that are rich in this world, that they be not highminded, nor trust in uncertain riches, but in the living God, who giveth us richly all things to enjoy; That they do good, that they be rich in good works, ready to distribute, willing to communicate."
>
> 1 TIMOTHY 6:17-18

God created us in His image. We have His very likeness branded inside of us. We have His giving image planted deep within us, and because of that, giving is one of the most basic spiritual needs we have. We need to give—and this need to give that's inside us is far greater than the need to keep.

You see, the key to enjoying all things God has given us as mentioned in 1 Timothy is being *"ready to distribute"* at all times, and *"willing to communicate."*

To be like those people who hold on to what they accumulate on this earth in order to provide for their own security, their own retirement, their own "cushion" or whatever you want to call it, is to be earthly minded. While people like this have put themselves in a position of being what the Bible calls earthly rich, Jesus says that those riches are uncertain. They are corruptible.

Obviously, Jesus is not condemning savings accounts, or the like. The point is, the "holding-on-to-everything-I've-got" mentality does not factor in faith. It does not factor in Philippians 4:19 that says *"my God shall supply all your need according to his riches in glory by Christ Jesus."*

In the world's way of thinking, money has no value unless fear is applied to it. Think about this...

Fear says, "I've worked hard for this. I may not have another opportunity to have this much again, so I'd better hold on to it as long as I can...'cause you never know."

So fear does not give because the need to give is overridden by the need to keep, and this is because faith was placed in uncertain riches. You have never had so little in all your life as to have a lot of money that you are afraid to spend.

Faith, on the other hand, says, "I received all these riches by believing God, and as long as God is around, there is always more where this came from."

Faith doesn't have to hold on to everything it gets. Faith freely gives... because faith is not in a mind-set of expecting to do without.

So how are you handling your money? In faith, or fear? Give in faith. Give freely. Give of yourself, your time, your talent and your money. Give as an expression of who you really are...someone created in the very image of God...the greatest giver of all!

## *Speak the Word*

*I trust in the living God, who gives me richly all things to enjoy.*
*1 Timothy 6:17*

FOR FURTHER STUDY:

Matthew 6:19-20

DAILY SCRIPTURE READING:

1 Samuel 8-9;
1 Corinthians 2

*Gloria*

# Put Your Reputation on the Line

God is a good God. In most circles, that's still shocking news. Do you remember what Jesus told the madman from Gadara after He cast out the demons that had possessed him? Mark 5:19 says Jesus told him to tell his friends the great things the Lord had done for him.

Jesus was concerned about God's reputation. He wanted it corrected. Everywhere He went He taught people that God was not what they had thought He was. He taught them that God is a good God. And that's the job He gave us when He left the earth (Mark 16:15).

Mark 5:25-34 tells of a woman with an issue of blood, who put her reputation on the line. It was against the Jewish Law for a woman with an issue of blood to be seen in public. But she risked public humiliation, even arrest, and fought her way through the crowd to touch the hem of Jesus' garment.

Why? Because she was more interested in Jesus' reputation than her own. She knew she couldn't get healed by staying at home doing what the religious community of her day said she should do. To receive her healing, she had to hang on to Jesus' reputation—and let go of hers. She wanted healing so desperately and believed in Jesus' goodness so fully that she was willing to risk it all.

That's how you have to be if you're going to see God work miracles in your life. You have to become so confident about how good He is that you'll dare to lay everything on the line. Choose His reputation over yours every single time.

If you've been dominated by the rumors Satan has used to smudge God's reputation, let His message from heaven set you free. It was written 2,000 years ago on a hill called Calvary. It says, "God is good." And it's signed in blood, "Jesus."

## Speak the Word

*The Lord does great things for me. He has compassion and mercy on me.*
*Mark 5:19*

> "Go home to thy friends, and tell them how great things the Lord hath done for thee, and hath had compassion on thee."
> MARK 5:19

FOR FURTHER STUDY:

Luke 8:43-48

DAILY SCRIPTURE READING:

1 Samuel 10-11;
1 Corinthians 3

> "But in a great house there are not only vessels of gold and of silver, but also of wood and of earth; and some to honour, and some to dishonor. If a man therefore purge himself from these, he shall be a vessel unto honour, sanctified, and meet for the master's use, and prepared unto every good work."
>
> 2 TIMOTHY 2:20-21

# Destined for Greatness

You are destined for greatness! God's plan and desire is for you to be so full of His Anointing, that it overflows to others, changing their lives forever!

"Well, now, Brother Copeland, you know not everyone is destined for greatness in the kingdom of God. As the Bible says, some vessels are gold and silver... others are soil and earth. I guess I'm just one of those little mud vessels."

If you are, it's your own fault! God isn't the one who decides if we're to be vessels of honor or not. We make the decision ourselves.

If you want to be a vessel of honor in the house of God, you can be. According to 2 Timothy 2:19-21, you simply have to purge yourself from iniquity and dishonor. Notice I said purge *yourself*. God won't do it for you. He cleansed you from sin the moment you were born again, but it's your responsibility to keep yourself pure. It's up to you to confess your sins and walk in holiness day by day. God will give you power, certainly, but you're the one who must put that power to work.

The Bible doesn't say Jesus will drag you away from iniquity, it says you are to *depart* from it. You are to cleanse yourself from sin as well as to cleanse yourself from the phony faith tactics and other subtle dishonorable practices many believers use.

Don't ever be like the fellow who went down to the altar and knelt down right next to the richest man in the church and began praying in his finest Elizabethan English: "Oh, God, Thou knowest how we've suffered in our house with no washing machine. You know, Lord, how my little babies have to wear dirty diapers because I don't have any way to wash them. Oh, God, You know I've given away all I have for You..."

When the rich man yielded to the pressure and gave him a washing machine, that fellow said he got it by faith. That wasn't faith! It was a religious con and that's the worst kind of con there is.

We must back away from such dishonorable ways. We need to be a people of honor who would rather wash our clothes out by hand than do something like that. We need to be the kind of people who get off in a corner where no one can hear us and pray to our Heavenly Father in secret, believing He will reward us openly!

Then, we can fulfill all of His plans for greatness...plans for us to overflow into other people's lives with the fullness of His Anointing!

## *Speak the Word*

*I am a vessel of honor, sanctified, and fit for the Master's use.*
*2 Timothy 2:21*

FOR FURTHER STUDY:

Matthew 6:5-8

DAILY SCRIPTURE READING:

1 Samuel 12-14;
1 Corinthians 4-5

*Gloria*

# An Act of Courage

MAY 1

❧

"Only be thou strong and very courageous."
JOSHUA 1:7

Do you know that obeying the Word is an act of courage? It really is, because when you obey the Word and believe God in a situation, you're swimming upstream. You're going against the current of the world.

Whether you're persevering while waiting for a better job, or working toward getting out of debt, all acts of obedience require courage. It takes courage, stamina and determination to stay with something, especially when the world has what seems to be an easier, quicker way to get there.

When most of the people and all the circumstances around you are screaming unbelief in your ears, it takes courage to stand on God's Word and not be moved.

But once you make the decision to stand and be courageous, you'll be in position and ready to activate God's three-part formula for success.

You'll find it spelled out in Joshua 1:8:

1) *"This book of the law shall not depart out of your mouth...*

2) *"But you shall meditate on it day and night...*

3) *"That you may observe and do according to all that is written in it; for then you shall make your way prosperous, and then you shall deal wisely and have good success" (The Amplified Bible).*

There they are. Three simple steps directly from the mouth of God. They are the steps that enabled Joshua to conquer the land of Canaan and bring the Israelites into their inheritance.

They are also the steps that will enable you to live like the conqueror God designed you to be. So don't give up. That better job will come. You'll be debt free. Your circumstances will change...as long as you persevere and continue to be courageous.

## *Speak the Word*

*I am strong and very courageous.*
*Joshua 1:7*

FOR FURTHER STUDY:

Joshua 23:1-11

❧

DAILY SCRIPTURE READING:

1 Samuel 15-16;
1 Corinthians 6

Kenneth

> "You are
> a chosen
> generation,
> a royal
> priesthood, a
> holy nation,
> His own
> special people,
> that you may
> proclaim the
> praises of Him
> who called
> you out of
> darkness into
> His marvelous
> light."
> 1 PETER 2:9, NKJV

# Jesus Isn't the Only One!

The anointing is increasing in believers everywhere. They are flowing in the anointing—ministering to others, and signs and wonders are following. But despite the awesomeness of God's Glory we're seeing in the Body of Christ, there's still a bunch of religious folk who say, "Oh, no. I'm not anointed. I'm nothing more than an unworthy sinner saved by grace. Jesus was the only One truly anointed."

That's an ungodly lie! Jesus isn't the only one anointed anymore! It was never God's intention to simply anoint Jesus with His power and leave it at that. God on one man was not enough!

That's why He sent Jesus to the cross and then raised Him from the dead. He wanted to open the way for us to become born again and to become a whole race of anointed men and women. He sent Jesus to be the anointed Head over an anointed Body of people who would take God's devil-busting, yoke-annihilating power to every corner of the earth.

That's been God's plan from the beginning. Through Jesus the Anointed One, He raised up a whole nation of kings and priests and called them His Church.

That's who we are! We are a chosen generation, a royal priesthood! We are anointed with the Anointing of the Anointed One!

We are to be living proof that Jesus is alive and anointed with yoke-destroying power because His Anointing is on us.

In His Name, we lay hands on the sick and they recover. We cast out devils. We speak the Word of God in faith and set the captive free! We're not unworthy sinners. The Word of God says we are joint heirs with Christ, sons of the Most High God. We're the Body of Christ—the Anointed One and His Anointing!

If someone asks you, "Do you mean to tell me you have the power to heal?" We should answer them boldly and say, "Yes, thank God, because greater is He that is in me than he that is in the world. I have the Anointing of Almighty God, and the Father within me, He doeth the works!"

Allow His Anointing to do His work. Walk in it! Stir it up! Remember: Jesus ISN'T the only one!

## Speak the Word

*I am part of a chosen generation, a royal priesthood, a holy nation.*
*I proclaim the praises of Him who called me out of darkness*
*into His marvelous light.*
*1 Peter 2:9*

FOR FURTHER
STUDY:

Acts 10:38-39

DAILY SCRIPTURE
READING:

1 Samuel 17-18;
1 Corinthians 7

*Gloria*

# Rich Rewards

Holiness is living unto God. Unlike the world's way of living, holiness isn't easy. You can't just coast along doing what everybody else is doing and be holy. It takes determination. It takes effort. It takes submitting yourself to God when, naturally speaking, you might want to do something else.

But the rewards are tremendous.

Hebrews says that without holiness, no man shall see the Lord. Does that mean if you're holy, you will see Him? Yes!

Jesus Himself said, *"He that hath my commandments, and keepeth them, he it is that loveth me: and he that loveth me shall be loved of my Father, and I will love him, and will manifest myself to him"* (John 14:21).

In other words, if you live the way I'm talking about right now—doing things that are pleasing to God—Jesus will reveal Himself to you. He can become so real to you through the Word, that it will be as if He's standing right in front of you. You can be closer to Him than you are to your best friend.

That, in itself, would be reason enough to live a holy lifestyle. But the Bible promises even more rewards!

According to 1 John 5:18, the devil can't touch you. Can you imagine what life would be like if the devil couldn't touch you? Well, that's the way God wants your life to be. He wants you so free that Satan can't hurt you in any way.

First John 3:21-22 says that if our hearts condemn us not, then we have confidence before God.

Do you know why so many people's prayers fail to be answered? It's not because God doesn't do His part. It's because the people had no confidence when they went before God in prayer. They couldn't ask in faith because their hearts condemned them.

Deep inside, you know whether or not you're giving God top priority—whether or not you're living a holy lifestyle. Make a decision today to be holy. Make a decision to live unto God. The rewards will be rich.

FOR FURTHER STUDY:

1 John 3:21-24

DAILY SCRIPTURE READING:

1 Samuel 19-20;
1 Corinthians 8

## Speak the Word

*I follow peace with all men, and holiness, and I shall see the Lord.*
*Hebrews 12:14*

> "He who by charging excessive interest and by unjust efforts to get gain increases his material possession, gathers it for him [to spend] who is kind and generous to the poor."
>
> PROVERBS 28:8, AMP

# It's Laid Up for You!

As I've studied the subject of prosperity, one point is always clear: God is a God of justice as well as mercy. He is fair in all His dealings.

His mercy is evident by His giving us the handbook—His Word—on how to live a godly life, which is the foundation for prosperity. When we are obedient to follow His commands, He takes care of us and blesses us.

His justice is evident in the outcome for those who don't live according to His Word: *"The Lord delights in justice and forsakes not His saints; they are preserved for ever, but the offspring of the wicked [in time] shall be cut off"* (Psalm 37:28, AMP).

Now, some people may feel that God is neither just nor merciful in taking a long time to fulfill some of His promises. But He's actually both! *"The Lord does not delay and be tardy or slow about what He promises, according to some people's conception of slowness, but He is long-suffering (extraordinarily patient) toward you, not desiring that any should perish, but that all should turn to repentance"* (2 Peter 3:9, AMP).

God is giving the unrighteous plenty of time to repent; however, He is well aware of what they are doing in the meantime (Proverbs 5:21, 15:3). They may appear to prosper through evildoing, but their success will be short-lived (James 5:1-4; Psalm 37:7-9). The Word of God indicates that in the last days, there will be a transfer of wealth from the hands of the wicked to the hands of the just (Proverbs 13:22). The sinners actually have the job of storing up wealth for the righteous (Ecclesiastes 2:26).

That wealth will be transferred into the kingdom of God in different ways. Those who become believers will bring their resources with them. For those who already are believers, they'll increase in faith and the Word of God operating in their lives—such as through the hundredfold return.

People who increase their giving will see ever-increasing returns. The reservoirs that have held riches from unjust gain will be tapped by their faith. The wicked rich who refuse to obey God will begin to see their wealth dwindle. And the riches will be placed into the hands of the givers.

I'm determined to be one of those givers. I'm ready to receive the riches of the wicked in my hands, to be used to reach souls and change lives. I'm ready for more prosperity.

You need to be ready too. Get your words in line with God's Word. Believe for the hundredfold return. Release your faith. Learn to give. And watch for the wealth of the wicked to come into your hands, because it's laid up for you!

## *Speak the Word*

*The wealth of the sinner is laid up for me. It finds its way into my hands.*
*Proverbs 13:22, AMP*

FOR FURTHER STUDY:

Proverbs 13:22;
Ecclesiastes 2:26;
Mark 10:30

DAILY SCRIPTURE READING:

1 Samuel 21-22;
1 Corinthians 9

*Gloria*

# "Lord, Bless Me!"

Have you ever wanted God to bless you? Well, sure you have! But the fact is, God has already treated us with overwhelming kindness. He has already given us all more than we ever dreamed possible. He has saved us. He has provided healing for us. He has blessed us in a thousand different ways. And that's what we should remember every time we tithe. We should come before the Lord and thank Him for bringing us into our promised land. Tithe with an attitude of gratitude.

If you'll read Deuteronomy 26, you'll see that's what He instructed the Israelites to do. He didn't want them to simply plunk their tithe into the offering plate without putting their hearts into it. He commanded them to come very purposefully and worship Him with it.

We would do well to do much the same thing each time we tithe. We should worship the Lord and say, "Father, once I was lost, a prisoner of sin with no hope and no covenant with You. But You sent Jesus to redeem me. You sent Him to shed His precious blood so I could be free. Thank You, Lord, for delivering me out of the kingdom of darkness and translating me into the kingdom of Your dear Son. Thank You for receiving the tithe as an expression of worship to You."

But we shouldn't stop with that. We should also say as the Israelites did, "Now, Lord, I have brought the tithe out of my house. I haven't kept it for myself. But I've given it just as You have commanded. So look down from Your holy habitation, from heaven, and bless me!" (Refer to verses 13-15 of Deuteronomy 26.)

Does that kind of talk make you nervous? Do you think God will be offended if you tell Him to bless you? He won't! He'll be delighted. After all, blessing us was His idea. It's what He has wanted to do all along.

So don't be shy. Tithe boldly! Tithe gladly! Give God the 10 percent of your income that belongs to Him, and give Him 100 percent of your heart. Then rejoice in faith and say continually, "Let the Lord be magnified, Who takes pleasure in the prosperity of His servant!" (Psalm 35:27). Begin to expect! Take the limits off God and let Him have a good time blessing YOU!

> "Honour the Lord with thy substance, and with the firstfruits of all thine increase: So shall thy barns be filled with plenty, and thy presses shall burst out with new wine."
> PROVERBS 3:9-10

FOR FURTHER STUDY:

Deuteronomy 26

DAILY SCRIPTURE READING:

1 Samuel 23-24;
1 Corinthians 10

## *Speak the Word*

*I honor the Lord with my substance and with the firstfruits of all my increase. My barns are filled with plenty and my presses burst out with new wine.*
*Proverbs 3:9-10*

> "Till we all come in the unity of the faith, and of the knowledge of the Son of God, unto a perfect man, unto the measure of the stature of the fulness of Christ."
>
> EPHESIANS 4:13

# Faith Is Here to Stay

Some years ago, in the midst of all the moves of the Spirit, God began to awaken people to the subject of faith. My first thought was, *Boy, here we go again. This is another wave.* People called it that. They called it the Faith Movement.

Some people still do. They talk about faith like it's a theological fad passing through the Christian community.

But I'll tell you something. After living the faith life for more than 30 years, I've become convinced that faith is not just a movement. It's not simply a spiritual phase sweeping through the Body of Christ. It's much more than that.

The awakening of faith we've seen over the past years has come as a result of the call of God. He is calling people from all denominations to move into a life of power. He is revealing to us a way to live victoriously—day in and day out, in good times and bad times. And isn't that what we want? Isn't that what we need?

He is teaching us that faith in His Word works, even when nothing else works. He is calling us to live by faith, not just temporarily, but as Ephesians 4:13 says, *"Till we all come in the unity of the faith, and of the knowledge of the Son of God, unto a perfect man, unto the measure of the stature of the fulness of Christ."*

If God is calling you to live a life of faith, and you've been tiptoeing around it...wondering if the movement thing is real or not...jump in now! Faith is not a movement. Faith is how God operates and lives...it's how He wants you to live.

Faith will open the door to the kingdom of God for you. And once you're in, it will keep you there—safe and healed and prosperous. Faith in the Word will keep you armed and dangerous to the devil. It will keep you free from sin and enable you to grow in the fruit of the spirit. Faith will enable you to please God. Faith is a permanent way of life for the people of God. It's a way that works when nothing else does. Faith is here to stay.

## *Speak the Word*

*I develop and attain oneness in faith with the believers.*
*I am perfect and complete in Christ.*
*Ephesians 4:13, AMP*

FOR FURTHER
STUDY:

Colossians 2:6-7

DAILY SCRIPTURE
READING:

1 Samuel 25-26;
1 Corinthians 11

*Gloria*

# Keep Your Eyes on the Light

Do you know what the most important thing in your life is? It's not where you work. It's not even your family. The most important thing in your life is keeping your heart full of the light of God's Word.

You *can* have faith strong enough to change circumstances in your life. You can live in victory instead of defeat. But you'll only do it continually by spending time in God's Word.

Proverbs 4:20-23 spells out this key to success in no uncertain terms: *"My son, attend to my words; incline thine ear unto my sayings. Let them not depart from thine eyes; keep them in the midst of thine heart. For they are life unto those that find them, and health to all their flesh. Keep thy heart with all diligence; for out of it are the issues of life."*

If your heart is full of the Word, you can get a good job—the best job! You can pray your family into line. And the way to get the Word in your heart is through your ears and your eyes. That's how you keep the Word in the midst of your heart. That's why you put God's Word first place in your life. It's the answer to everything. When you give your attention to the Word of God, every other area in your life will be successful.

You see, God's Word shows you how to live victoriously, even in a dark world. When you walk according to the Word, it shines a light on your pathway.

The Apostle Peter talks about that Light of the Word. He says to pay close attention to it like you would a lamp shining in a dark place.

Continually focus your attention on the Word of God, and you can fight the good fight of faith and win even when negative circumstances surround you. Keep your eyes on the light, and you will have light. It will bring you through to victory!

> "You will do well to pay close attention to it as to a lamp shining in a dismal (squalid and dark) place, until the day breaks through [the gloom] and the Morning Star rises (comes into being) in your hearts."
> 2 PETER 1:19, AMP

## Speak the Word

*I attend to the Word of God. I keep it in the midst of my heart.*
*It is life to me and health to all my flesh.*
*Proverbs 4:20-22*

FOR FURTHER STUDY:

Psalm 91:9-10, 14-16

DAILY SCRIPTURE READING:

1 Samuel 27-29;
1 Corinthians 12-13

> "There is no truth in him [the devil]."
> JOHN 8:44

# When Mouth Speaks, Mind Listens

You might as well face it. As long as you are on this earth, the devil is going to talk to you. He has a right to test your faith by bringing you circumstances and lies to see if you'll receive them.

But when he does, refuse them. Cast down those fearful imaginations and every thought that is contrary to the promise of God (2 Corinthians 10:5). Say, "The Lord is on my side. I WILL NOT FEAR!"

Then open your mouth and speak the Word of God. Use it to contradict the devil's lies. If he tells you, *You won't have enough money for your house payment this month,* don't just struggle silently with that thought. Speak up. Say right out loud, "I will have the money for my house payment. I know I will because my God supplies all my needs according to His riches in Glory by Christ Jesus!"

I found out a long time ago that when my mouth speaks, my mind has to stop and listen to what it's saying. Maybe you won't fully believe that confession the first time you make it. But if you'll keep saying it, you'll keep hearing it. And what you hear, you'll believe. Eventually your faith will be so strong and your heart will be so full, you'll start speaking with total confidence.

That's when the devil will run for cover because fear has no chance when faith comes on the scene. Faith is the original. Fear is the counterfeit. And the real overcomes the phony every time.

### *Speak the Word*

*The Lord is on my side. I do not fear!*
*Psalm 118:6*

FOR FURTHER STUDY:

1 Peter 5:6-9

DAILY SCRIPTURE READING:

1 Samuel 30-31;
1 Corinthians 14

*Gloria*

# Become a Candidate for Increase

❧

"Keep out of debt and owe no man anything, except to love one another."
ROMANS 13:8, AMP

I remember back before Ken and I knew we could trust God to take care of us financially, I thought it was my job to worry about how we were going to pay our bills. I spent a great deal of my time thinking things like, *What are we going to do about this or that bill?* I think I felt obligated to worry!

Then I found out it wasn't God's will for me to worry! His will is for us to believe Him to care for us. I also learned that as believers, we're not to seek after material riches. We're not to pursue money like people do who are without God. They have to pursue it. They don't have a covenant with God, so if they don't seek material goods, they won't get them!

But we're not like those people. We're not in the world without God and without a covenant (Ephesians 2:12-13). We have God's promise of provision. He has assured us in His Word that He will not only meet our needs, but give us abundance.

It's important for us to remember, however, that a covenant is always between two parties. It has two sides to it. A covenant says, *If you'll do this, then I'll do that.*

God's part of the covenant is to prosper us—spirit, soul and body, as well as financially. Our part is not to seek after prosperity, but to seek first His kingdom, His way of doing and being right! Our part is to say, "Lord, I'll do whatever You tell me to do. I'll obey Your Word and do what is right in Your sight—even if it looks like it will cost me."

Of course, obeying God's Word NEVER costs in the long run. It PAYS! You always put yourself in a position for increase when you seek after God and do things His way.

I'll be honest with you though, there will be times when you can't see how that increase is going to come. Ken and I know. We've been there.

When we first read Romans 13:8, we weren't too excited about it. At that time in our lives, it looked to us like we'd never be able to do anything financial without borrowing money. We thought, *How will we ever buy a car? How will we get a home? How will we finance our ministry? We're doomed!*

But we had already decided to obey God no matter what the cost, so we committed to Him to get out of debt even though we thought it would be to our disadvantage. Of course, that decision has since turned out to be one of the wisest financial decisions we've ever made.

That's the way it always is. Obeying God always works to your advantage in the end! So start today putting yourself in a position to increase. Give His Word first place in your life. Commit to getting out of debt and living debt free. Make the adjustments the Holy Spirit tells you to make. Make yourself a candidate for increase!

FOR FURTHER STUDY:

Psalm 37:21-40

❧

DAILY SCRIPTURE READING:

2 Samuel 1-2; 1 Corinthians 15

## Speak the Word

*I keep out of debt and owe no man anything, except to love him.*
*Romans 13:8, AMP*

> "Their [Our]
> hearts...are
> knit together
> in love."
> COLOSSIANS 2:2,
> AMP

# Love Your Way to Success

Our hearts are knit together in love. That's what God says about believers. The word translated "love" in this verse is *agape*. *Agape* never means "I will love you if..." *Agape* means "I will to love you regardless." That's the unconditional love of God that's brought to life when a blood-covenant relationship has been established. We are covenanted together by the blood of Jesus. We are in Him and He is in us.

Now, you may know some people with whom you don't want to be knit together. They may make some things a significant challenge for you. But you are commanded to walk in love. So do it. Start releasing the love *(agape)* that's been shed abroad in your heart by the Holy Spirit. Throw fear out. Throw worry out. Bring in the joy. "It is my will to love you."

LOVE, LOVE, LOVE! Love is beyond defeat. The Bible says love NEVER fails. When you release love into a situation, you have released God. Think about that. When you release love into a situation, you have released God into that situation. And then Jesus becomes responsible for its success.

The Word of God is love.

The Name of Jesus is love.

The gifts of the Spirit are love.

The blood of Jesus is love.

We are born of the Holy Spirit Who is love.

Heaven is love.

Love is heaven.

The person who refuses to love is missing out on the very best God has to offer. Don't YOU miss out on any of it. Release love every moment into every situation, every prayer and every thought, until it totally consumes your life.

GO FOR IT! It will strengthen you and cast out every fear that has robbed you of God's greater blessings. It'll drive the devil out of your affairs and set you free from every torment of darkness.

Be still before the Lord and sense the flow of *agape,* mercy, blessed love of Jesus coming up like a fountain from the Holy Spirit into your spirit. Then love others with the love of God. If it seems too hard, remember, once you start releasing love into a situation, Jesus becomes responsible for its success. Love never fails, and Jesus never fails! So love your way to success!

## *Speak the Word*

*I walk in love and I never fail because love never fails!*
*1 Corinthians 13:8, AMP*

FOR FURTHER
STUDY:

John 13:34-35

DAILY SCRIPTURE
READING:

2 Samuel 3-4;
1 Corinthians 16

*Gloria*

# Mature in Love

Strife has many dangers. But one serious consequence to walking in strife is that it will hinder your prayers by robbing you of one of the greatest promises ever given to us. You can find that promise in Matthew 18:19.

The devil hates agreement between believers. Agreement opens the windows of heaven to us, and it closes the door on every destructive thing he can do. So he will continually try to disrupt that agreement by causing strife and division in the two places where believers come together in the most powerful way: the family and the church.

Until now, you may not have thought of your family as a powerful force for God, but it is if you're in agreement with one another. So make it your goal to stay out of strife and walk in love at home.

Oddly enough, home is often the most difficult place to be loving. I think that's because we don't have our guard up when we're at home. We're not worrying about our reputation or trying to impress anyone. At home, nothing will stop you from being selfish—except your commitment to walk in the love of God.

> "Again I say unto you, That if two of you shall agree on earth as touching any thing that they shall ask, it shall be done for them of my Father which is in heaven."
> MATTHEW 18:19

But don't be fooled into thinking it doesn't matter how you act at home. It matters a great deal. In fact, years ago, the Lord said this to me and I have never forgotten it: *If you allow Satan to stop you with strife at your front door, you'll be no threat to him anywhere else.*

So make the commitment to keep strife out of your home. Learn to live a lifestyle of agreement with your spouse and your children. See to it that your prayers prevail by being in harmony with the members of your family. The moment you mess up and get in strife, make it right. Say to the other person, "Please forgive me. I love you. I don't want to be in strife with you." Then say to the Lord, "Father, I repent of that. I'm not going to be a strife person. I refuse to yield to strife. I choose to walk in love."

You may have to repent quite a bit at first because you've probably developed habits that will take awhile to change. But don't get disgusted with yourself and give up. Just keep acting on the Word, and you'll continue to mature in love.

FOR FURTHER STUDY:

Proverbs 17:1;
Mark 11:25-26;
1 Peter 3:7

DAILY SCRIPTURE READING:

2 Samuel 5-6;
2 Corinthians 1

## Speak the Word

*I keep strife out of my life by acting on the Word.*
*My prayers are effective and not hindered.*
*1 Peter 3:7*

> "And the floors shall be full of wheat, and the fats shall overflow with wine and oil. And I will restore to you the years that the locust hath eaten.... And it shall come to pass afterward, that I will pour out my spirit upon all flesh."
> JOEL 2:24-25, 28

# It's Beginning to Rain

If you're like me, right now you're thinking, *Oh man, I want to be in on this move of God in the last days. I don't want to be on the fringes of it either—I want to be right in the middle!*

You can be—if you'll get yourself ready. How? Primarily by doing these three things...

First, prepare yourself for the greatest criticism you've ever experienced. There's never been a move of God that's avoided criticism, and this outpouring will be no exception. If Jesus couldn't avoid it, neither can you. Be determined to pay no mind to any criticism.

Second, get the sin out of your life. You know how. Just repent! And make a change. There must be a new fire of holiness burning and sweeping through the people of faith in this land. We're free people, made free by the Son of the living God. But we are never free from obeying the Word and the ways of God. That's where our freedom lies.

Third, pray for the rain. Zechariah 10:1 tells us to pray for the rain in the time of the latter rain. Well, the time is here. So we need to pray for the fullness of it.

We must get in our prayer closets. Go before God and turn off the pleasures of this world. Turn off the loud noise the devil is making out there. All that entertainment is only meant to do one thing and that's to distract you away from prayer and the things of God's Word.

Don't let it succeed. Instead start praying and using your faith. It's time to pray and intercede until this outpouring bursts fully upon our land and the lands around the world.

What a sight it will be when it does! Years ago when I was praying about this final rain, the Lord said to me, *I've been manifested as the rain. I've been manifested as the fire or as lightning. I've been manifested as the wind. But I've never been manifested as all four at the same time. Now, in the time of the former and latter rain, you're going to see all of Me for the first time ever.*

Think of it! A spiritual storm of the power of the living God. And it's not coming in another century or two. Or even another decade or two. It's coming now, so get ready for it! Glory to God, it's beginning to rain!

## *Speak the Word*

*It's beginning to rain! The Lord is pouring out His Spirit on all flesh!*
*Joel 2:28*

FOR FURTHER STUDY:

2 Chronicles 5:11-14

DAILY SCRIPTURE READING:

2 Samuel 7-8; 2 Corinthians 2

*Gloria*

# Your Future Is Bright!

Your future is stored up in your heart! It's not dictated by your history, or your current circumstances. Your future is determined by you!

In the Scripture verses above, Jesus said that what was in your heart is what comes forth. So consider this: Who stored up the evil things that were in the evil man's heart? Obviously, the man himself did it. Who stored up the good things in the good man's heart? Again, the man himself did.

In the same way, you're the only one who can make deposits of God's Word into your heart. Your spouse can't do it for you. Your pastor can't do it for you. Even God can't do it for you.

God has already done His part to help you. He's the One Who made your heart to be a depository for His Word. He's the One Who opened the account for you when you were a spiritual baby. As the Scripture says, *"God hath dealt to every man the measure of faith"* (Romans 12:3). The moment you were born again, He put the initial measure of faith in your heart—but you're the only one who can make that measure increase.

And you can do that by taking the Word of God and putting it into your heart. Each time you make a deposit of the Word, your faith balance grows, and your future gets brighter. Isn't that exciting? And there is no limit to the size of deposit you can make into your heart!

The more you deposit, the better things are, because that is where you will draw from to change the circumstances in your life. Your heart holds the faith you'll need to cover any bill the devil tries to send your way. If he tries to put sickness and disease on you, you can draw from the Word of God about healing and it will give you victory in that area. If you've just been released from prison, you can draw from the Word of God about God's plans for your welfare and have peace that you can make it just fine.

Your future really is bright! The Lord says in Jeremiah 29:11 (NIV), *"For I know the plans I have for you...plans to prosper you and not to harm you, plans to give you hope and a future."* Put the Word in your heart. Speak it out in faith, and watch your circumstances change.

> "Out of the abundance of the heart the mouth speaketh. A good man out of the good treasure of the heart bringeth forth good things: and an evil man out of the evil treasure bringeth forth evil things."
> MATTHEW 12:34-35

FOR FURTHER STUDY:

Psalm 119:33-40

❧

DAILY SCRIPTURE READING:

2 Samuel 9-10;
2 Corinthians 3

## Speak the Word

*Out of the abundance of my heart, my mouth speaks.*
*I bring forth good things out of the treasure of my heart.*
*Matthew 12:34-35*

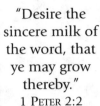

# Overcome Your Flesh

One time a fellow came up to me and said, "Brother Copeland, I'll tell you what my problem is. It's my flesh."

I said, "Well, overcome it."

"But, you don't understand!"

"No, but Jesus does," I answered. "And He said He's already overcome the world. So go get in the Word, pray, believe God and walk away from that problem. The power is within you to do it."

Suddenly it hit him what I was saying. He stopped being hung up on the problem and started focusing on the answer.

That's what you need to do. Quit seeing yourself defeated by your flesh and start seeing yourself like the Word says you are—raised up together with Jesus and seated with Him in heavenly places! (See Ephesians 2:6.) Get your perspective on things from that heavenly position with Him.

Meditate in the Word and give your spirit man something to grow on. As 1 Peter 2:2 says, desire the sincere milk of the Word that you may grow. Then move on to the *"strong meat [of the Word which] belongeth to them that are of full age, even those who by reason of use have their senses exercised to discern both good and evil"* (Hebrews 5:14).

Bring your spirit man into ascendancy over your mind and your body. You'll still have to fight the fight of faith to keep them in line. But if you're walking in the spirit, you'll win every time. With a healthy, Word-controlled, obedient body, you'll be glad you did.

## *Speak the Word*

*I overcome the flesh by seeing myself as the Word says I am—*
*raised up together with Jesus and seated with Him in heavenly places.*
*Ephesians 2:6*

FOR FURTHER
STUDY:

Ephesians 2:1-7

DAILY SCRIPTURE
READING:

2 Samuel 11-13;
2 Corinthians 4-5

# God's Servants and Handmaidens

MAY 15

❧

"Tarry ye in
the city of
Jerusalem,
until ye be
endued with
power from
on high."
LUKE 24:49

On the Day of Pentecost, about 120 of God's servants and handmaidens were gathered in the upper room continuing in one accord in prayer and supplication (Acts 1:14-15). They were in place, ready to move into the streets as soon as God's Spirit was poured out upon them. They were doing exactly what Jesus told them to do.

The shameful part of it was, only about a fourth of those who had been instructed to be there were present. Jesus had appeared to more than 500 of them and told them all the same thing...to tarry until they were endued with power.

Apparently 380 of them decided to stay home!

What's the difference between the 380 who didn't follow Jesus' instructions and the 120 who did?

Those in the first group were merely Christians. Those in the second group were God's *servants and handmaidens.*

The Word translated "servants and handmaidens" in Acts 2:18 is the Greek word *doulos.* It is the same word used twice, once in the feminine form and once in the masculine form.

In this particular instance, *doulos* refers to someone who has voluntarily subjected himself to another person's will. It describes a bondslave who could be free if he wanted to be, but chooses instead to be wholly subservient to another because of his love for that person.

If you are a servant or handmaiden, you will be committed to the Lord Jesus. It is not a commitment He forces upon you. It is one you make by choice, because you love Him.

You see, when you were born again, you did not become a hired servant of God. You became a child of God, a son or daughter of the Almighty. You were made free and *"if the Son therefore shall make you free, ye shall be free indeed"* (John 8:36).

But if you truly love the One Who set you free, you will trade that freedom for a life of service to Him. That's what the Apostle Paul did, for in Romans 1:1 (AMP), he calls himself *"a bond servant of Jesus Christ."*

Choose today to be a bondslave...one who longs to stay close to the Master's side...serving Him wholeheartedly from a heart of love and devotion. Choose to be one of God's servants and handmaidens.

FOR FURTHER
STUDY:

Luke 10:38-42

❧

DAILY SCRIPTURE
READING:

2 Samuel 14-15;
2 Corinthians 6

## Speak the Word

*I am not enslaved by sin. I am free to be a servant of Jesus Christ.
I choose His will above my own.*
John 8:34-36

# You Shall See the Glory of God

There is coming a time when the Glory of God won't just radiate out from God, it will radiate from us! It will burn within us and upon us with such power that the devil and all his hordes will be like ashes under the soles of our feet!

It is almost unthinkable to them that such Glory and power could reside in and flow through the flesh-and-blood bodies of men and women. Yet the Bible tells us that's what will happen.

We've seen the beginning of this...on the Day of Pentecost. To grasp the impact of that day, you have to forget those Sunday school pictures depicting tiny flames hovering over the heads of the disciples. You need to get the images of God as described in Habakkuk 3:3-4, Ezekiel 1:1-28 and Malachi 4:1-3...you need the images of God's Glory as seen in His fire, His light, His magnificent brightness.

Go through these passages of Scripture and think about His blazing fire of Glory! Think on Ezekiel's description of God's Glory being a fire from the loins up and a fire from the loins down...and then you will realize what happened in the upper room in Acts 2.

God Himself came in!

Everything was shaken with such a great sound of wind that it sounded like a freight train coming through a tunnel. It was the Glory! It roared in and filled the whole room. Then a blazing fire appeared, and He sat on, or enveloped, each disciple one by one!

On that day, God was able to at last embrace His people. They'd been washed in the blood of Jesus. Sin had been defeated at Calvary. They'd been reborn and made righteous with God's own righteousness. So He could come to them without any cloud, without any covering of any kind. He could come to them as His own Glorious Self! He came on them and into them.

Now it is our time to walk in that brighter-than-sunlight, radiating, fiery power that is so pure and full of the presence of God that the devil can't withstand it. It is God's plan for us to walk in the light as He is in the light, to walk in the Glory as He is in the Glory (1 John 1:5-7). It is time for us to shine! He's equipped us to do it here and now. So stretch your capacity to conceive and to believe. Study what the Word says about the Glory. Make it your aim to walk in the light as God is in the light. Believe...and you shall surely see the Glory of God.

## Speak the Word

*I walk in the light, as He is in the light.*
*I walk in the Glory, as He is in the Glory.*
*1 John 1:7*

*Gloria*

# Count It All What?

Usually, when you're in the midst of a trial, the last thing you feel like doing is counting it all joy. Naturally speaking, you're not in the mood to jump and sing and rejoice over this opportunity to develop patience.

But the truth is, you should. If you'll let patience have her perfect work, you'll obtain perfect health. If you're in financial trouble, you'll have all your needs met. It means you will receive whatever the Word of God has promised you!

Hebrews 10 confirms that. Addressing a group of people who had been through an extremely fiery trial, it says: *"Call to remembrance the former days, in which, after ye were illuminated, ye endured a great fight of afflictions; Partly, whilst ye were made a gazingstock both by reproaches and afflictions; and partly, whilst ye became companions of them that were so used. For ye had compassion of me in my bonds, and took joyfully the spoiling of your goods, knowing in yourselves that ye have in heaven a better and an enduring substance. Cast not away therefore your confidence, which hath great recompence of reward. For ye have need of patience, that, after ye have done the will of God, ye might receive the promise"* (verses 32-36).

You might as well know right now that if you want to enjoy the health, deliverance and prosperity God has promised you, you'll have to let patience work. You'll have to believe God when it's hard to do. You'll have to keep walking in faith when your flesh just wants to quit.

That may sound negative, but it's not. It's just the truth. And if you know that truth, you can prepare yourself in advance for those hard times by deciding that when they come, you won't give up. You can train yourself for victory by starting right now to develop the force of patience you'll need to make it through when the going gets tough. In the end, you might just surprise yourself. You'll be counting it all joy without giving it a second thought!

> "My brethren, count it all joy when ye fall into divers temptations; Knowing this, that the trying of your faith worketh patience. But let patience have her perfect work, that ye may be perfect and entire, wanting nothing."
> JAMES 1:2-4

## Speak the Word

*I count it all joy while I am in the midst of my trials.*
*I let patience have her perfect work in me that I may be perfect and entire.*
James 1:2-4

FOR FURTHER
STUDY:

Romans 5:1-5

DAILY SCRIPTURE
READING:

2 Samuel 18-19;
2 Corinthians 8

# Talk to the Mountain

"Have faith in God. For verily I say unto you, That whosoever shall say unto this mountain, Be thou removed, and be thou cast into the sea; and shall not doubt in his heart, but shall believe that those things which he saith shall come to pass; he shall have whatsoever he saith."

MARK 11:22-23

*"I just don't know what we're going to do. This situation is just a mess...."*

That is a classic example of speaking *about* the problem and not *to* the problem...and it will get you nowhere except deeper into unbelief and into more problems!

Speaking out loud to your problems may sound strange to you, but God instructed us to in Mark 11:22-23. He said to speak *to* the mountain. The mountain represents any problem or adversity in your life. You can change your circumstances by speaking to them.

Romans 4:17 refers to such faith talk as *calling "things which be not as though they were,"* and both God Himself and Abraham (the father of our faith) did it.

It's important to note that *calling things that be not as though they were* is quite different from *calling things that are as though they are not.* When I declare that my needs are met according to God's riches in Glory, I am not denying the existence of any financial problems I might be experiencing. I'm not pretending they aren't there. I am calling forth the provision and declaring by faith that those needs are met. I am speaking to that financial mountain and commanding it to be removed and cast into the sea.

I remember one Sunday morning many years ago when I had to speak to a mountain of sickness that was trying to prevent me from preaching. I was so sick that as I stood behind the pulpit and started to read the Word, I began to pass out.

Now, I had already gone to God earlier that morning on the basis of His provision and by faith believed I received my healing. But the manifestation had not yet come. So I told the congregation I would be right back, went to another room and started speaking to that mountain.

I ranted and raved and jumped all over the devil. I told him that I was healed by the stripes of Jesus. I told him his power over me had been destroyed, and I commanded him in Jesus' Name to get his filthy hand of sickness off me. When I walked out of that room, I didn't feel any better physically, but I knew I'd done what the Word instructed me to do, so I went right back in and started preaching on healing.

At first my voice sounded bad. My body ached from my toenails to my hair. But as I was preaching, suddenly the power of God hit me, healed me and gave me so much strength, I was able to preach all morning long! I had spoken to the mountain in faith, believing, and it had been cast into the sea!

## *Speak the Word*

*I believe those things which I say shall come to pass and
I do not doubt in my heart. I shall have what I say.*
*Mark 11:23*

FOR FURTHER
STUDY:

Mark 11:22-26

DAILY SCRIPTURE
READING:

2 Samuel 20-21;
2 Corinthians 9

*Gloria*

# Identify the REAL Enemy

Persecution comes through people...sometimes through those we love the most and are closest to. But despite what you're tempted to believe, those people are not the source of your problem.

According to Mark 4, it's the devil himself who stirs up persecution. It's one of the strategies he uses to steal the Word out of your heart.

So when persecution comes your way, don't get sidetracked by getting angry with the people involved. They aren't operating on their own, they're being driven by the devil's influence.

Use the power and authority Jesus has given you and bind that persecuting devil. Then break the power of deception over the people he has been using, and pray that they'll be free to know the truth.

Once you understand who the real enemy is, and pray accordingly, the next thing God instructs you to do is to continue in your well-doing. *"For so is the will of God, that with well doing ye may put to silence the ignorance of foolish men"* (1 Peter 2:15).

You're not called to argue. You're not called to defend your position or your name when men speak evil about you. Just leave all that in the hands of the Lord and continue doing what God has called you to do.

That's what Jesus did. He didn't quit. When He was reviled, He reviled not. He just kept right on preaching the gospel, healing the sick and delivering all who were oppressed of the devil. He just kept right on walking in victory!

I know it's tough to be quiet in times of persecution, but you can do it if you're confident that God will ultimately deliver you. That's why Paul was able to live so triumphantly. In 2 Timothy 3:11, he said God delivered him from ALL of his persecutions!

Glory to God, we're not in this alone! When we're in the midst of persecution, God is right there with us. So rely upon Him. Spend time in prayer. Listen to what He says. Obey His instructions when it seems like all of hell has broken loose upon you. He'll deliver you out of those persecutions—not just once in a while, but *every* time!

> "But thou hast fully known my doctrine, manner of life, purpose, faith, longsuffering, charity, patience, Persecutions, afflictions, which came unto me at Antioch, at Iconium, at Lystra; what persecutions I endured: BUT OUT OF THEM ALL THE LORD DELIVERED ME."
> 2 TIMOTHY 3:10-11

FOR FURTHER STUDY:

Matthew 5:10-16

DAILY SCRIPTURE READING:

2 Samuel 22-23; 2 Corinthians 10

## Speak the Word

*The Lord delivers me out of all my persecutions.*
*2 Timothy 3:11*

> "Then Peter came to Jesus and asked, 'Lord, how many times shall I forgive my brother when he sins against me? Up to seven times?' Jesus answered, 'I tell you, not seven times, but seventy-seven times.'"
>
> MATTHEW 18:21-22, NIV

# No Whining, Please

We need to face the fact that we can't walk with God and be even a little unforgiving or a little offended. If we're going to walk with God, we must allow His love to drive out every trace of any kind of unforgiveness.

"But you just don't know how badly they treated me!"

Has God forgiven your sin?

"Yes."

Then you forgive them. Period. End of discussion.

Quit crying and whining about how hurt you are. Maybe you have been mistreated, but if so—get over it! Everybody has been mistreated in some form or another.

The reason I can talk so straight to you about this is that God has already said these things to me. I remember one day when I was moping around at home. I'd just come in from preaching on the road and it seemed that as soon as I got there, I had to start fighting the devil. I was whining about it when Gloria said something to me I didn't like.

"Oh, she doesn't care about me anyway," I muttered in self-pity.

Right then, the Lord spoke up in my heart and said, *It isn't any of your business whether she cares for you or not. It's your business to care for her.*

Then He added something I'll never forget. He said, *I'm the One Who cares whether you hurt or not. Your hurts mean everything in the world to Me, but they ought to mean little or nothing to you.*

As the Church, we need to learn that today. We need to quit paying so much attention to our own hurts and cast them over on God. We need to take a lesson from the pioneers of the faith.

People like Peter and John and those Pentecostal old-timers years ago would walk into the very jaws of hell. They'd go through persecutions that make the things we face look like child's play. They didn't come out crying about how they'd been hurt either. They came out saying, "Glory to God! We're getting an opportunity to suffer for His Name. What a privilege!"

When you have that attitude, it's not hard to forgive because your focus isn't on yourself. It's on God and His purposes, God and His love.

If you want to discover the secret to real forgiveness, that's where your focus has to be—on God. We are instructed to forgive others in the same way, or on the same basis, that God has forgiven us.

## *Speak the Word*

*I forgive others, as God for Christ's sake has forgiven me.*
*Ephesians 4:32*

FOR FURTHER STUDY:

Matthew 18:21-35

DAILY SCRIPTURE READING:

2 Samuel 24;
1 Kings 1;
2 Corinthians 11

*Gloria*

# Fulfilling Your Destiny

"What's God's plan for my life?" We've all asked that question at some point in our lives. Christians everywhere are longing to answer God's call. They're eager to fulfill the divine purpose for which they were created. But they need direction in finding out what that plan is...

God never intended for us to be in the dark about His plan for our lives. He left us clear, written instructions concerning His will for us. What's more, He gave us a pattern to follow so we could see how to carry out those instructions.

The pattern is Jesus. You've been sent forth into the world to continue His ministry. I know that sounds like a tall order, but it's true. He said so Himself in John 17:18.

> "As thou [the Father] hast sent me into the world, even so have I also sent them [those who believe on me] into the world."
> JOHN 17:18

Once we realize Jesus is the pattern, we need to find out exactly what Jesus was sent to do: *"For this purpose the Son of God was manifested, that he might destroy the works of the devil"* (1 John 3:8).

Think about that. You're called to finish what Jesus began: to destroy, undo and bring to naught the works of the devil on earth. That is the job God wants us to do.

"That's a big job, Gloria! How on earth am I ever going to do that?"

The same way Jesus did. After all, He promised, *"He that believeth on me, the works that I do shall he do also; and greater works than these shall he do; because I go unto my Father"* (John 14:12).

In short, the works, or ministry of Jesus was threefold: 1) He healed the sick, 2) He cast out demons, and 3) He preached the good news of the kingdom of God.

Now, I know it's easy to do the preaching and not the other two works. But the gospel was never designed to be preached without proof that Jesus is alive today. Jesus didn't just say, "The kingdom of God is here." He demonstrated it. He proved the truth of what He was saying by operating in the supernatural power of God.

And He expects us to do the same. *That's* God's plan for your life!

God's program is still the same. It didn't change when Jesus went to sit at the right hand of the Father. He's still expecting us to do the things He did and finish what He started. He is sitting at the right hand of God this very minute, waiting for us. He is waiting for us to rise up by the Spirit of God and make His enemies His footstool. So what are you waiting for? Fulfill God's plan in the earth. Fulfill your calling. Fulfill your destiny.

FOR FURTHER STUDY:

Matthew 8:16, 9:35

DAILY SCRIPTURE READING:

1 Kings 2-4; 2 Corinthians 12-13

## *Speak the Word*

*I believe in Jesus. I am sent by Him. I fulfill my destiny.*
*John 17:18*

# A Frog-Strangler Is Coming

> "He that believeth on me, as the scripture hath said, out of his belly shall flow rivers of living water. (But this spake he of the Spirit, which they that believe on him should receive.)"
> JOHN 7:38-39

A spiritual flood is coming! As we would say in West Texas, we are in for a frog-strangler rain of the Holy Ghost, and it has already begun to fall!

The prophets of God have been prophesying about this rain for thousands of years. Of course, they don't call it a frog-strangler like I do. They call it "the former and latter rain," an outpouring of the Spirit that combines the power of the Old Covenant with the power of the New Covenant manifesting, all at the same time.

As a believer, you are a vessel that contains God's power and Glory. A vessel is a pitcher that you pour from. That means *you're* the spout where the Glory comes out!

Now, let me ask you this...According to John 7:38-39, where did Jesus say the rivers of the Spirit would flow? *From inside the belly (or heart) of believers.* Where does the Holy Spirit reside? *Inside believers.*

So where will this final dynamic supernatural flood of power come from in these last days?

You've got it—*it will flow forth from the spirit of believers. From Holy Ghost-filled people like you and me!*

"But, wait a minute," you say. "We're talking about signs and wonders of global proportions here. We're talking about a flood that will cover the whole earth with God's Glory. How could something of that magnitude come from one person like me?"

It won't. It will come from all of us together. It will come as the Holy Spirit river flowing out of you joins up with the Holy Spirit river flowing out of me. Then our rivers will come together with the rivers of millions of other believers.

It will come when, like those disciples in the upper room, we start praying in one accord—when we stop fussing with one another and begin to agree with one another and come into unity of faith.

Your natural mind might have a hard time grasping that such a thing is even possible. But it is. What's more, it will happen because the Bible says so (Ephesians 4:13). And when it does, we'll see the same things the early Church saw when they were in one accord—and greater things.

Signs and wonders will start following us. Some crippled fellow sitting outside the church building will get healed because a believer jerked him up by the hand and said, "In the Name of Jesus, rise and walk!" Then he'll start jumping up and down, and running through town telling how he's been healed—and 5,000 people will get saved in a day. I'm telling you...it will be a frog-strangler rain of the Holy Ghost!

FOR FURTHER STUDY:

Jeremiah 17:7-13

DAILY SCRIPTURE READING:

1 Kings 5-6; Galatians 1

## *Speak the Word*

*I believe in Jesus and in the Spirit of God.*
*Therefore, out of my belly flow rivers of living water.*
*John 7:38-39*

*Gloria*

# More Than Enough

God doesn't promise just to meet your basic needs. He says He'll give you an abundance. Some religious people would argue about that. But the truth is, there's nothing to argue about because the Word makes it perfectly clear. Look back at what we just read from Deuteronomy.

Look at that for a minute. If you don't have abundance, why would you need a storehouse? A storehouse is where you put extra, the surplus, the "more-than-enough."

If that's not clear to you, verse 11 of that chapter says point-blank that *"the Lord shall make you have a surplus of prosperity"* (AMP). I want you to remember those words—*a surplus of prosperity*—because that's God's will for you. When you made Jesus Christ the Lord of your life, God's blessing came upon you, not so you could just "get by," but so you could have a surplus of prosperity.

That shouldn't really surprise you. After all, if you look at God's history with man, you'll see that when He had His way, man was abundantly supplied. Everything in the Garden of Eden, for example, was good. The temperature was just right. The food was right there on the trees. All you had to do was pull it off and eat it. Talk about fast food! There was plenty of gold in the Garden. Adam and Eve lacked nothing

In the same way, God cares just as much about your abundance. He wants you to have more than enough. He wants you to have good things, a good home, good food...everything! He's the God of more than enough!

> "The Lord shall command the blessing upon thee in thy storehouses, and in all that thou settest thine hand unto."
> DEUTERONOMY 28:8

## *Speak the Word*

*The Lord commands His blessings upon my storehouses and in all that I set my hand to do.*
*Deuteronomy 28:8*

FOR FURTHER STUDY:

Psalm 35:27;
Proverbs 3:9-10

DAILY SCRIPTURE READING:

1 Kings 7-8;
Galatians 2

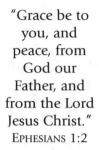
> "Grace be to you, and peace, from God our Father, and from the Lord Jesus Christ."
>
> EPHESIANS 1:2

# More Than a Greeting

Have you ever stopped to think what that phrase *"Grace be to you"* actually means? I think most people just read over it assuming it's just a greeting of sorts.

Well, it's far more powerful than that. The Apostle Paul said, "I am what I am BY THE GRACE OF GOD!" (1 Corinthians 15:10).

Acts 14:3 says that God's Word is the word of His grace. Then in Acts 20:32, it says that the word of grace is able to build you up and give you an inheritance among all them which are sanctified.

Man, that is far too powerful to just be a greeting on a letter!

Most believers have treated the subject of God's grace too lightly. For some reason, in the minds of most people, it's something vague with no real definition, other than maybe God's favor, or unmerited [undeserved] favor, as the *Amplified Bible* says.

It certainly is that, all right, but left with just that, without a vital revelation of its power, it leaves you without understanding of something Jesus died for us to stand in.

The Word says we are heirs of grace. Partakers of it. Built up by it. Justified by it. Made all sufficient by it in all things. Made to abound to all good works by it. Saved by it through faith.

The Word also says we should grow in grace (2 Peter 3:18). No one can grow in anything from God without spending time in His Word (1 Peter 2:2). God's grace is mentioned more than 120 times in the New Testament alone!

That should be enough to let us know that we should be spending a whole lot more of our time studying and meditating on it. After all, it has been deposited in the reborn spirit of every person who has accepted Jesus Christ as personal Savior and made Him Lord of his or her life (1 Corinthians 1:4).

Grace is powerful. It is God's willingness to enter into covenant with you, authorizing you to live in Him and giving you the right to authorize Him to come live in you, and live out your life through you. Read that over and over until you get understanding of it in your spirit.

Grace is a powerful force that you need to do the things God's called you to do. So dig into the Word. Let the spirit of revelation reveal it to you. Let it become far more than a greeting on a letter.

### *Speak the Word*

*Grace and peace have been given to me from God my Father, and the Lord Jesus Christ.*
*Ephesians 1:2*

FOR FURTHER STUDY:

Romans 5

DAILY SCRIPTURE READING:

1 Kings 9-10; Galatians 3

*Gloria*

# Destroy Those Incoming SCUDS

Jesus warned us that the distractions of this age, the deceitfulness of riches and the lusts of other things can creep in and choke the Word and make it fruitless (Mark 4:19). Right next to that verse in my Bible, I've written the letters S-C-U-D. They stand for the phrase, "Satan Continuously Uses Distractions." He's always sending those SCUD missiles at you to discourage you and draw you off course.

*Hey,* he'll whisper, *have you noticed you don't have any money? Have you noticed your body is in pain? Have you heard all the ugly things people are saying about you?*

How do you fight distractions like that? Just *"continue thou in the things which thou hast learned and hast been assured of, knowing of whom thou hast learned them."*

> "Continue thou in the things which thou hast learned and hast been assured of, knowing of whom thou hast learned them."
>
> 2 TIMOTHY 3:14

I'll tell you the truth: It's not the great revelation you haven't had yet that causes you defeat. It's failing to do what you already know. So whenever you reach a hard place, continue to do what you know and you'll make it through in victory.

You have everything it takes to be a winner. You have everything you need to be a part of the glorious, victorious end-time army of God. Get aggressive. Press in. Lay hold of the kingdom of God with all the force you can muster. That's the price you pay to win this race. But one thing is sure, you not only have the present victory, but also the eternal victory you gain will be worth it all.

Satan won't ever stop in his relentless efforts to distract you. But you have the power to overcome. You have the power and the knowledge to continue to do what God has already told you to do. It's that simple. Continuing will put you over. Don't quit believing and acting on God's Word. You have what it takes to destroy those incoming SCUDS!

## *Speak the Word*

*I am not distracted, but I continue in the things which I have learned.*
*2 Timothy 3:14*

FOR FURTHER
STUDY:

Mark 4:14-20

DAILY SCRIPTURE
READING:

1 Kings 11-12;
Galatians 4

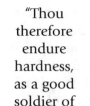

> "Thou
> therefore
> endure
> hardness,
> as a good
> soldier of
> Jesus Christ."
> 2 TIMOTHY 2:3

# Be a Good Soldier

Make no mistake about it. There are hardships involved in being a soldier of the Lord Jesus Christ. But there is no hardship, no problem, no suffering and no onslaught of persecution that can conquer you. Nothing hell can devise is powerful enough to overcome the mighty Name of Jesus and the power of the full armor of God.

You are thoroughly equipped for victory. Yet to win that victory, you will have to go to the battleground. You will have to face the fact that you are a soldier.

Some Christians whine, "I don't feel like fighting the fight of faith today. It's too hard!"

That doesn't make any difference. You don't ask a soldier if he'd like to get up and go to combat this morning. You don't say, "Sir, could I bother you for a few moments? I hate to interrupt your checker game, but we're having a war about 10 miles up the road and I just wondered if you'd like to go?"

No! You don't ask a soldier to go to the battlefield. He is under authority. He does what he is ordered. A good soldier is willing to serve.

God is looking for soldiers like that. He is looking for people who are as eager to get in on the action as the boys on my fifth-grade football team. I'll never forget that team. There were about 14 of us and every one of us was constantly hanging on the coach's arm, begging him to let us in the game.

"Put me in there, Coach. I can whip that guy. Just let me have that ball. Nobody can catch me!"

One thing about that bunch of boys, we were eager. We weren't any good, but we were ready.

If you'll be ready spiritually, if you'll be a good soldier, if you'll endure the hardness, God will put you where the action is. He'll give you more excitement than you ever dreamed you'd have. He'll help you turn tragedies into triumphs and temptations into testimonies...if you'll give Him an opportunity.

## *Speak the Word*

*I endure hardness as a good soldier of Jesus Christ.*
*2 Timothy 2:3*

FOR FURTHER
STUDY:

Romans 8:35-39

DAILY SCRIPTURE
READING:

1 Kings 13-14;
Galatians 5

*Gloria*

# Don't Be Caught by Surprise

We all know that Jesus is coming back someday. And, I believe, it's much sooner than we all think. So we need to be ready.

It's our responsibility to be prepared. God has given us everything we need. He has put His own Spirit within us. He has given us His written Word. He has given us teachers, preachers, pastors, evangelists, apostles and prophets to help us learn how to live by faith, how to live separated from the world, how to walk in the spirit, and how to operate in the power of God. But we must decide to make those things the priority in our lives.

One way to keep them a priority in our lives is by cultivating the expectancy of Jesus' soon return. We must spend time studying and meditating the scriptures about Jesus' coming.

Even though God hasn't disclosed to us the exact day or the hour, according to the Bible, if we're alert, we will know the season of His return. In fact, Jesus Himself said in Matthew 24 that His coming would be like the Flood in Noah's day.

That flood took the world by surprise, didn't it? The people were just going about their natural business, not expecting anything unusual, when suddenly they were swept away. They were completely in the dark about what was happening.

But Noah wasn't caught by surprise! He'd been building the ark for years. He'd been expecting the Flood. He didn't know the day or the hour, but he knew it was coming and he was ready. When it started to rain, Noah wasn't in the dark, he was in the ark!

That's how we're supposed to be. We're to be aware of the season (1 Thessalonians 5:1-6). If you're watching and in tune with the Spirit, you won't be in the dark. You won't be unaware at the time of Jesus' coming. You'll know in your spirit He is at the door. You won't be caught by surprise.

> "For yourselves know perfectly that the day of the Lord so cometh as a thief in the night."
> 1 THESSALONIANS 5:2

## Speak the Word

*I look up and lift up my head for my redemption is drawing near!*
*Luke 21:28*

FOR FURTHER STUDY:

Matthew 24:32-44

DAILY SCRIPTURE READING:

1 Kings 15-16;
Galatians 6

❧

"Also every
sickness, and
every plague,
which is not
written in the
book of this
law, them will
the Lord bring
upon thee,
until thou be
destroyed."
DEUTERONOMY
28:61

# Yield to Life!

Tradition has taught that God uses sicknesses, trials and tribulation to teach us. This idea, however, is not based on the Word. God has never used sickness to discipline His children and keep them in line. Sickness is of the devil, and God doesn't need the devil to straighten us out!

"But Brother Copeland, what about Deuteronomy 28:61? It says the Lord will put sickness on me." The wording of the *King James Version* of such scriptures has caused many people to draw this conclusion.

In *Young's Analytical Concordance to the Bible,* Dr. Robert Young sheds some crucial light on that. There he explains that the Hebrew language contains idioms which cannot be translated into the English language and properly understood. Also, there was little understanding of permissive and causative verbs.

In other words, according to Dr. Young's studies, Deuteronomy 28:61 should have been translated with a permissive verb and would more accurately read, *"Every sickness and every plague, which is not written in the book of the law, them will the Lord ALLOW TO ASCEND upon thee until thou be destroyed."* (You can read verse 15 and see how it confirms this.)

"But even if God is not the source of sickness," you may ask, "isn't it still true that He allows the devil to make us sick?"

Yes. Not from the standpoint of correction, but from the standpoint of authority. God allows it because we do. Why? Because He's given us the right to make our own choices, along with authority over the kingdom of darkness in Jesus' Name.

According to Deuteronomy 30:19, He has set before us life and death, blessing and cursing. He has further instructed us to choose life. The choice of what we experience is up to us. It has been that way since Creation.

You have the power to live after God's ways and resist sickness, or not to. You have the choice to let Satan run over you, or use the authority you have been given. Good and perfect gifts come from God. No matter what tradition has taught, sickness and disease simply don't fall into the category of good and perfect gifts...ever.

So make a decision today. Resist Satan's sicknesses and diseases. Cast off those old traditions. Yield to all that God has put within you. Yield to life!

## Speak the Word

*The Lord has set before me life and death, blessing and cursing.*
*I choose life!*
*Deuteronomy 30:19*

FOR FURTHER
STUDY:

James 1:12-17

❧

DAILY SCRIPTURE
READING:

1 Kings 17-19;
Ephesians 1-2

*Gloria*

# Don't Chase Success—Let It Chase You!

How much do you want to succeed in life? Enough to change what you're saying? Enough to change where your attention is focused? Enough to act on the Word of God even when the rest of the world is telling you it will never work?

If you want it that much, the Word of God guarantees you'll get your fill of success in life. Good success. Not the kind the world gives, but God's own brand of success.

> "The blessing of the Lord, it maketh rich, and he addeth no sorrow with it."
> PROVERBS 10:22

Success the world's way has a price tag of misery attached to it. But Proverbs 10:22 says God adds no sorrow to His blessings.

I will warn you of this, though. Satan won't like it if you choose the way of success. He'll try to talk you out of it, and since he knows God's success formula, he knows exactly what tactics to use.

He'll pressure you to say negative things. He'll try to distract you from the Word and get your attention on anything—it doesn't matter what it is, as long as it isn't the Word.

His goal is to stop your faith. He knows it's the only force that can cause impossible situations to change.

He also knows that it comes from the Word of God. So when he sees that Word going in your heart and hears it coming out of your mouth, he doesn't just sit there. He starts talking. Doubtful thoughts will come into your mind, thoughts that are just the opposite of what God's Word says.

But those thoughts don't become yours unless you believe them and speak them. That's what he wants you to do, of course. If the Word says you're healed, he'll say you're sick. If the Word says you're forgiven, he'll say you're still guilty. If the Word says your needs are met, he'll tell you they're not.

But if you won't let go of your faith, if you'll keep the Word in your mouth and in your heart, you can't lose. There's no force the devil can bring against you that will overcome the Word of God. It will make you a winner every time.

So if you've been wanting good success and it's been eluding you, quit wondering if you have what it takes to make it—and remember instead Who is with you and in you. Then turn to the Word of God and put God's success formula to work in your life. Start talking it. Start thinking it. Start doing it.

FOR FURTHER STUDY:

Romans 8:31-34

Before long, you won't be chasing success...it will be chasing you!

## *Speak the Word*

*The blessing of the Lord makes me rich and He adds no sorrow with it.*
*Proverbs 10:22*

DAILY SCRIPTURE READING:

1 Kings 20-21;
Ephesians 3

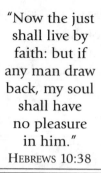

> "Now the just shall live by faith: but if any man draw back, my soul shall have no pleasure in him."
> Hebrews 10:38

# What Are You Waiting For?

Did you know God doesn't want you sitting around waiting for a thunderbolt from heaven to stir you into action? Did you know He wants you to step out in faith and power just because the Bible says we can?

"But, Brother Copeland, I'd be afraid that if I did that, it would just be me."

Well, think for a moment. Would that really be so bad? After all, you've been born again. You've been baptized in God's Spirit. The love of God has been shed abroad in your heart by the Holy Ghost. You're a joint heir with Jesus and you have a covenant in His blood.

God didn't do all that in you for nothing. He didn't re-create you so you could sit around like a puppet, afraid to take any initiative of your own.

He created you to be His partner, a worker *"together with him"* (2 Corinthians 6:1). That means you have a part to do. You have responsibilities, and to fulfill them, you must take your place as a son of God.

When people come along and say, "Do you mean to tell me you have the power to heal?" you shouldn't shake your head and say, "Oh, no. I'm just a nobody."

You should say, "Yes, because the Father is in me and He does the works! Jesus said when believers lay hands on the sick, they'll recover. And, praise God, I'm a believer!"

You see, faith is the force God has given us to govern our personal lives day in and day out. He expects us to take that spiritual force—the same force He used to create the material world—and change circumstances, heal our physical bodies, and keep our lives in line with His Word. He expects us, even in the midst of an outpouring of miraculous power, to take our stand and be *"followers of them who through faith and patience inherit the promises"* (Hebrews 6:12).

So the next time you have an opportunity to step out, do it! What are you waiting for?

## *Speak the Word*

*I live by faith. I do not draw back.*
*Hebrews 10:38*

**For Further Study:**

Hebrews 6:9-15

**Daily Scripture Reading:**

1 Kings 22;
2 Kings 1;
Ephesians 4

*Kenneth*

# Praise Him!

When you've prayed and believed God to change circumstances, based on the Word of God, then you are to begin praising and thanking Him in the midst of those circumstances while you wait for them to change.

There's power in praise—and it's a fundamental element of faith. If you praise God, you'll be able to triumph over every attack. Psalm 8:1-2 confirms that. The devil is not going to hang around listening to the praises of God. Praise shuts his mouth. So put it to work.

Praise God that the mountain is gone even while it's still standing there. Praise Him for setting you free.

Praise Him for the blood of Jesus that paid the price for your sin and delivered you from every curse.

Praise Him in the morning. Shout your way to work every day.

Praise Him at noon.

Shout your way home every evening.

Praise Him at night.

Praise Him when you don't feel like praising Him! It will make a difference.

Gloria and I have applied truths like this for more than 30 years, and God has brought us out on top every time.

> "O Lord, our Lord, how majestic is your name in all the earth! You have set your glory above the heavens. From the lips of children and infants you have ordained praise because of your enemies, to silence the foe and the avenger."
> PSALM 8:1-2, NIV

## *Speak the Word*

*My continual praise and thanksgiving to God give Him
the opportunity to intervene in my circumstances and bless me.*
Psalm 145

FOR FURTHER STUDY:

Psalm 150

DAILY SCRIPTURE READING:

2 Kings 2-3;
Ephesians 5

Kenneth

❧

"Casting down imaginations, and every high thing that exalteth itself against the knowledge of God, and bringing into captivity every thought to the obedience of Christ."

2 CORINTHIANS 10:5

# The Biggest Problem Isn't Big Enough

It absolutely doesn't matter what you are facing today...nothing is too big a problem when you factor in the anointing! Take hold of the anointing by beginning to expect. Start expecting something good to happen to you. Lay hold of the hope that's set before you in the promises of God.

Don't be a stranger to those promises. Dig into them in the Word of God. Find out what God has said about your situation. Then start saying, "I expect it because God promised it!"

Think about those promises and meditate on them. Let them build an image inside you until you can see yourself well...until you can see yourself with your bills paid...until you can see yourself blessed and prosperous in every way.

If you'll do that, you'll eventually get bigger on the inside than you are on the outside. Your hope will grow so strong that the devil himself won't be able to beat it out of you.

When we're confronted by impossible situations in this world, we have a covenant right to factor in Jesus! Factor in the power of His Word! Factor in His Anointing!

Some say, "That sounds too easy." No, it's not easy! When the devil begins to pull the noose of hopelessness around your neck with poverty or sickness or some other terrible situation, you have to fight and fight hard. And you fight hard by grabbing hold of the hope in the Word and using it to demolish every thought that would rise up against it.

*"Casting down imaginations, and every high thing that exalteth itself against the knowledge of God, and bringing into captivity every thought to the obedience of Christ."*

The battleground where hope is won or lost is not on the streets, it's in the mind. It's in the imagination where expectancy begins to take form. So take your stand on that battleground. Begin now to expect the anointing to destroy the yokes in your life. Begin now to expect God to keep His covenant promises to you.

Fight for that expectancy in the Name of Jesus. Take your hope, fill it with faith and storm the gates of hell. They will not prevail against you!

## Speak the Word

*I cast down imaginations, and every high thing that exalts itself against the knowledge of God. I bring every thought into captivity to the obedience of Christ.*
*2 Corinthians 10:5*

FOR FURTHER STUDY:

Hebrews 6:16-20

❧

DAILY SCRIPTURE READING:

2 Kings 4-5;
Ephesians 6

*Gloria*

# Consecrate Yourself

JUNE 2

❧

"I always do those things that please Him [my Father]."
JOHN 8:29, NKJV

Many years ago, before I understood much about living a holy and consecrated lifestyle, I prayed and believed God for the money to buy a house. At the time, it seemed to me like a big request. After all, Ken hadn't been in the ministry very long, and we'd never owned a house before. What's more, we'd committed to God not to borrow money, so the amount of cash we needed seemed monumental.

It took me awhile, six years to be exact, but I got it by faith. Some years later, I found another house I wanted. Once again, I prayed and believed God for it. But this time was different. I had begun to walk in the things I am teaching now, so when I prayed, I had a confidence toward God that I hadn't experienced with the first house.

Somehow I just expected Him to give me what I asked. I knew in my heart I'd been diligent to do the things He wanted me to do. I had consecrated myself to Him. I'd been faithful to Him—and I expected Him to be faithful to me.

And He was. The second house only took three weeks!

You see, it's not God Who holds out on us. Our prayers are hindered because our own lack of consecration affects our heart. It keeps us from receiving what God wants to give.

Jesus had so much confidence in the Father that His faith knew no possibility of defeat. He also always did those things that pleased His Father. Can you see the connection?

Jesus' total dedication to pleasing God caused total confidence in the Father. And total dedication in your life to the things of God will do the same for you. If you'll plant God's Word in your heart and confess it with your mouth, before long you'll see the results springing forth. Jesus will make Himself real to you. And your heart will be constantly filled with confidence toward God.

If that's not a fabulous way to live, I don't know what is!

So make those adjustments today to get your affection on God. Consecrate yourself to Him, and watch your confidence level soar!

## Speak the Word

*I always do those things that please my Father.*
John 8:29, NKJV

FOR FURTHER STUDY:

Ephesians 4:17-24

❧

DAILY SCRIPTURE READING:

2 Kings 6-7; Philippians 1

> "Who [God] satisfieth thy mouth with good things; so that thy youth is renewed like the eagle's."
> PSALM 103:5

# Conditioned Responses...of the Faith Kind

I love to talk about my youth being renewed, praise God! When someone talks to me about getting old and feeble, it's like waving a red flag in front of a bull because I've built up a conditioned faith response about that. When somebody starts the "old and feeble" routine, I'll say, "My mouth is filled with the good things of the Word of God so that my youth is renewed. You can do what you want to, Brother, but I'm not going to fall apart in my old age."

You may think that's extreme. But I'll tell you something, until you build up those kinds of conditioned faith responses, you'll just flow downstream with the rest of the world. You'll end up drifting into sickness, poverty, depression and all the rest of the devil's deadly stuff.

You can live above the rotten circumstances of the world if you'll guard your words. I have faith-building things I say every day of the year. I don't wait until I'm facing a crisis. I build my faith continually: "This is a ministry that is debt free.... Thank God, we're a family without tragedy...." I say those things every single day. I even confess Psalm 103 when I brush my teeth!

God calls that putting up *"the shield of faith, wherewith ye shall be able to quench all the fiery darts of the wicked"* (Ephesians 6:16).

Every time you do that, your spirit will get stronger. Your spiritual muscles will get in shape. If you keep on exercising those faith responses, when the devil does send some deadly situation your way, you'll be ready for it. You'll be able to deliver the knockout blow that will put Satan on his ear. You'll be able to resist him and he'll have to flee from you.

Conditioning yourself to respond in faith isn't complicated. Anyone can do it. You train yourself in the spirit just like you trained yourself to tie your shoes when you were 6 years old. By practicing.

Practice responding in faith that same way. Work on it. Do it over and over again until it becomes an automatic, conditioned response. If you'll do that, when you need it, your faith will be there for you.

## *Speak the Word*

*God satisfies my mouth with good things.*
*He renews my youth as the eagle's.*
*Psalm 103:5*

FOR FURTHER STUDY:

Isaiah 54:14-17

DAILY SCRIPTURE READING:

2 Kings 8-9;
Philippians 2

*Gloria*

# Get Out of My Garden!

Satan is an outlaw. God has given us laws to keep him in line, but he won't abide by them unless we enforce those laws.

That's not really surprising. Things work the same way in the natural realm. In the United States, for example, we have laws against selling drugs. We have laws against murder. We have laws against stealing. But if those laws aren't enforced, what happens? Thieves and murderers continue to operate. The law has to be enforced.

Once you understand that, you'll see why Satan works so hard to get you to talk about your problems instead of God's promises. He knows your authority to enforce God's law is in your words. If he can get your words going in the wrong direction, he can get authority over your life—even though it doesn't belong to him.

Satan doesn't care what belongs to him. He's a thief. He's a killer. He takes what he can get. So you have to use the Word of God on him when he tries to come into your garden and spoil it.

That's what Adam should have done when Satan showed up in *his* garden. The first time that creature opened his mouth to question the Word of God, Adam should have said, "Get out of my garden, you serpent!"

> "Be sober, be vigilant; because your adversary the devil, as a roaring lion, walketh about, seeking whom he may devour: Whom resist stedfast in the faith, knowing that the same afflictions are accomplished in your brethren that are in the world."
> 1 PETER 5:8-9

And that's what you and I should do too. The first time the devil starts trying to bring doubt and unbelief to us—*Do you really think God is going to heal you? Do you really think God is going to send you the money to pay that bill?*—we should just tell him to take his lies and get out of our lives!

How do you do that? Just say, "You Doubt, you Unbelief, you Fear—in the Name of Jesus, leave my presence. Yes, I really do believe the Word of God!" Quote that Word and don't stop. Refuse to listen to words that kill, steal and destroy (John 10:10).

FOR FURTHER STUDY:

Acts 28:1-6

❧

DAILY SCRIPTURE READING:

2 Kings 10-12; Philippians 3-4

Just keep on speaking and studying what the Word of God says about your situation until it's that Word you're hearing in your heart all day, instead of those lies of the devil. When you're walking in the authority God's given you, and speaking the Word of God, then you'll have no trouble telling the devil, "Get out of my garden!" And he'll surely flee.

## Speak the Word

*I am sober and vigilant. I resist the devil steadfastly in faith.*
*1 Peter 5:8-9*

> "The name of the Lord is a strong tower: the righteous runneth into it, and is safe."
>
> PROVERBS 18:10

# You Have a New Name!

Did you know your name has been changed? Well, if you are born again, it certainly has. When you make Jesus the Lord of your life, you are brought into a covenant relationship with Jesus and your name is changed!

To fully appreciate what that means, you'll have to think about the Blood Covenant. When a person enters covenant with another, they become absolutely one with each other. They exchange garments saying, "All that I have and all that I am is now yours."

Actually, when someone enters a covenant of blood, he is giving himself completely away. He is no longer his own. His assets and his debts, his strengths and his weaknesses belong forever to his covenant brother. In evidence of this, at the close of the covenant ceremony, the families involved exchange names with one another.

When you accepted Jesus as your Lord and Savior, He took your name. Your name was sin. Your name was weakness. Your name was whatever you inherited from Adam. Your life was ruled by fear, and hell was your home destination.

Then you decided to accept Jesus. He gave Himself away to you. You gave yourself away to Him. His life became yours. Your life became His. You turned loose of Adam as your father and received God as your Father.

You have become His heir—a joint heir with Jesus.

Ephesians 3:15 says the whole Body of Christ has been named after Him both in heaven and earth. That includes you and me! Philippians 2:9 says He has been given a name that is above every name that is named.

You've been given that Name! Its authority is yours!

You can't call yourself discouraged anymore. That's not your name. You can't answer when the devil yells, *Hey, poor boy.* That's not your name. Jesus has taken those old names of yours. They're gone. Don't answer to them anymore.

When poverty calls, don't answer "Yes." Answer "No!" When your body calls itself sick, answer "No! That's not my name. I am healed." And when the devil tries to tell you you're alone and discouraged, answer him out loud, "That's not in my covenant. I am strong in the Lord."

No matter what the devil tries to bring against you, the NAME of the Lord is your strong tower. Whatever He has called Himself in His Word is who you are now. You have a new name and it's above every other name.

## *Speak the Word*

*The name of the Lord is a strong tower. I run into it and I am safe.*
*Proverbs 18:10*

FOR FURTHER STUDY:

Hebrews 8:6-13

DAILY SCRIPTURE READING:

2 Kings 13-14;
Colossians 1

*Gloria*

# Risky Business

Several years ago, this ministry fell behind financially—nearly $6 million of television bills behind! It looked to us like the answer to that problem was very complicated. We thought about selling all our ministry property and buildings so we could use the money to pay off the deficit. But then, we wouldn't have had any place to house the ministry operations.

Things looked dark. But do you know what got us through that situation? It wasn't some new revelation from God. It wasn't some flash from heaven bringing us an instant solution.

What overcame that deficit was the same thing that put food on our table more than 30 years ago when we first began to live by faith: a patient application of the Word of God.

I had our old reel-to-reel tapes of Kenneth Hagin's messages transferred to cassettes and listened to them again. We made fresh application of the simple principles of confession he'd taught us so many years ago. We corrected ourselves in the things we had let slip. We increased our deposits of God's Word in our hearts and said the Word with our mouths.

> "Wherefore seeing we also are compassed about with so great a cloud of witnesses, let us lay aside every weight, and the sin which doth so easily beset us, and let us run with patience the race that is set before us."
> HEBREWS 12:1

In other words, we just did like James 1:4 says. We let that trial work patience in us, and when it was done, we lacked nothing. Not only was the deficit paid, but we haven't been behind financially since that time.

What's more, the testimony of that particular victory has encouraged others in similar situations.

That's the risk the devil always takes when he puts you through a trial. He takes the chance you'll come through in victory and end up stronger than you were before, instead of weaker. He takes the chance of giving you another testimony of the miracle-working power of God.

If you're facing a challenging situation, and the devil is up to risky business, just apply the foundational truths you've already learned. Do what you know to do, as you expect the Holy Spirit to teach you more, and God will take care of the rest. The devil will suffer another defeat to the glory of God!

FOR FURTHER STUDY:

James 1:1-8

❧

DAILY SCRIPTURE READING:

2 Kings 15-16; Colossians 2

## Speak the Word

*I lay aside every weight and sin which so easily besets me.*
*I run with patience the race that is set before me.*
*Hebrews 12:1*

> "By whom also we have access by faith into this grace wherein we stand, and rejoice in hope of the glory of God."
>
> ROMANS 5:2

# Faith Connects You

It is so important to develop your faith. Why? Because faith is what connects you to the blessings of God. It's the force that gives those blessings substance in your life (Hebrews 11:1). And besides that, it pleases God (Hebrews 11:6).

It's faith that reaches into the realm of the spirit, grasps the promise of God and brings forth a tangible, physical fulfillment of that promise. It brings spiritual blessings. It brings the car that you need, or the healing for your body. It brings action or manifestation in this earth.

Romans 5:2 says we have access by faith into the grace (favor) of God. Therefore, if you want grace for the new birth, you must receive it by faith. If you want God's grace in your finances or any other area of your life, you must get it by faith.

I like to think of it this way: *When you believe the Word of God, you open the window to your life and give God the opportunity to move there.*

Oddly enough, that bothers some people. They can't understand why God needs *an opportunity.* After all, He is God. Can't He do anything He wants?

Yes, He can. And He wants to respond to our faith. You see, He is not like the devil. He doesn't force Himself on you. He waits for you to give Him an opening by believing His Word. When you believe His Word, and make your stand, even in the midst of the most impossible situations, God moves in on your situation.

Remember, faith speaks! But it doesn't say just any old thing. It speaks the Word of God. When cancer attacks, faith doesn't say, "I'm dying of cancer." Faith says, "I'm healed by the stripes of Jesus. Therefore I'll live and not die, and declare the works of the Lord." That faith mixed with His Words gives God an opportunity to work...it gives Him something to work with! It gives Him an opening.

It's what you say continually that comes to pass in your life. So, if you're believing God for finances, make it a habit to say things like this: "According to Deuteronomy 28, lack is a curse of the Law. And Galatians 3:13 says Jesus has redeemed me from that curse. Therefore I'm redeemed from the curse of lack! My needs are met according to God's riches in Glory by Christ Jesus."

Then every time your bills come to mind, call them paid in the Name of Jesus. Call yourself prosperous. Call yourself debt free. Call things that be not as though they were.

Simply put, operate in faith! Because faith connects you!

## *Speak the Word*

*Jesus has given me access by faith into the grace by which I stand.*
*I rejoice in hope of the glory of God.*
*Romans 5:2*

FOR FURTHER STUDY:

Luke 17:5-6

DAILY SCRIPTURE READING:

2 Kings 17-18; Colossians 3

*Gloria*

# He Really Is Good

If God ever filed suit for defamation of character, almost everyone on the planet would be found guilty of slander. What traditional religion has taught about God would make any sane person want to run for cover. As a matter of fact, 45 years ago when Oral Roberts started preaching that God is a good God, it made most preachers mad—especially Full Gospel preachers.

But it was the revolutionary news that God is a good God that brought about the great healing revival of the late '40s. Until then, most people hadn't known God wanted to do them good. They had been told it was God Who made them sick. They had been told He put pain and disease in their bodies to teach them something. Many had been told that sometimes it simply was not God's will to heal them, and some that God never heals today.

Imagine how shocked those people were when Brother Roberts first made his bold proclamation that God is a good God and He wants you well.

As a result of that proclamation, people's attitude toward healing began to change. Faith began to rise up in their hearts. Then great miracles began to take place.

Before that time, most people were afraid of God. When you're in fear, it's impossible to open up your heart to God. It's hard to receive anything good from a God you can't trust.

But once you know the truth about Who your Father is and what kind of nature He actually has, it's easy to receive His blessings. That's why it's so important to know what God is really like.

Psalm 145 tells the truth about God. He:

- is gracious
- is full of compassion
- is slow to anger
- is of great mercy
- is good to all
- satisfies the desire of every living thing
- is nigh to all who call on Him
- fulfills the desire of them that fear Him
- hears our cries and saves us
- preserves all who love Him

"The Lord is gracious, and full of compassion; slow to anger, and of great mercy. The Lord is good to all: and his tender mercies are over all his works."
PSALM 145:8-9

That's the picture of God you should hang on the wall of your heart. When you see God as He really is, you don't have to work to have faith. You don't have to memorize formulas. You just trust Him. He really is a good God!

FOR FURTHER STUDY:

Psalm 145

DAILY SCRIPTURE READING:

Isaiah 56-57; Psalm 56

## Speak the Word

*The Lord is gracious, and full of compassion. He is slow to anger and of great mercy. The Lord is good to me and His tender mercies are over me.*
*Psalm 145:8-9*

# Your True Destiny

Did you know that right here, in the midst of the same environment that's dragging the world into defeat...right here in the midst of the same storms that are tearing the world apart...you and I and every other born-again child of God can live in victory?

We can put on the whole armor of God, walk right into the midst of the worst circumstances the world has to offer us, and none of them will be able to bring us down.

That's why God told us to put on His armor in the first place! He knew it would protect us. The Word of the living God and the full armor of God is bulletproof. It's sickness-proof, debt-proof, recession-proof. It will cause you to stand when everything around you is falling apart!

But you have to get dressed. You have to walk in it!

You can't just give it a passing nod and then go on watching what the world watches and saying what the world says. If you keep copying the world's ways, you're going to share in the world's destiny. But if you'll copy Jesus—if you'll say what He says and nothing else—you'll share His destiny. It's your choice.

Romans 12:2 says, *"Be not conformed to this world: but be ye transformed by the renewing of your mind, that ye may prove what is that good, and acceptable, and perfect, will of God."* You won't find the will of God by copying the world. You'll find it by copying Jesus. *"If ye continue in my word, then are ye my disciples indeed; And ye shall know the truth, and the truth shall make you free"* (John 8:31).

So put on the whole armor, that you will be able to stand. For victory, my friend, is your true destiny.

## Speak the Word

*I put on the whole armor of God and stand against the wiles of the devil.*
*Ephesians 6:11*

FOR FURTHER
STUDY:

Ephesians 6:11-20

❧

DAILY SCRIPTURE
READING:

2 Kings 21-22;
1 Thessalonians 1

*Gloria*

# He's Looking for You!

God is looking for you. That's right. If you'll read the Bible, you'll see that ever since the world began He's been looking for people who by faith and obedience would allow Him to bless them right here on the earth. He's been looking for people who would allow Him to demonstrate His power on their behalf—people whose supernaturally abundant lives would make them a walking advertisement of the mercy and power of God.

For example, look at the children of Israel in the Old Testament. God wanted them to be this kind of people. He prepared a marvelous land for them to enjoy. It was a land flowing with milk and honey (Exodus 3:8). It was a land of rest and abundance where no enemy could stand before them and no sickness or disease could stay on their bodies (Exodus 23:25).

In fact, as soon as they came out of slavery in Egypt, God wanted them to go to that land. It was a short journey. But they wouldn't go! Instead, they spent 40 years wandering around in the wilderness, getting nowhere.

> " For the eyes of the Lord run to and fro throughout the whole earth, to show himself strong in the behalf of them whose heart is perfect toward him."
>
> 2 CHRONICLES 16:9

All this happened thousands of years ago, but do you know what? God hasn't changed at all since then. He still wants to lead His people into a place of blessing and prosperity.

The problem is that in many ways His people haven't changed that much either. The same thing that kept the children of Israel out of the Promised Land is keeping most believers out of their personal promised land today. The problem is unbelief.

"But Gloria, that can't apply to me. I believe in God."

Israel believed in God too. But when the scouts sent into the Promised Land came back and reported there were giants there, the children of Israel became scared.

If they had believed God, it wouldn't have mattered how big those giants were, they could have marched right in there expecting God to make those giants scatter in every direction. But they didn't believe God!

So often we try to be smart and figure things out instead of just trusting God and doing what He says. And as a result, we end up in disobedience—which always leads to unbelief. But God doesn't ask us to be smart. All He asks us to do is to listen to His Word and obey His voice. Why? Because He knows that if we don't, we'll end up living out our lives on this earth in a wilderness of defeat like that generation of Israelites did.

God is looking for you. Don't let the giants in your life scare you into hiding. Don't let them defeat you. Stand up and let God see you. Let Him know you'll be faithful and obedient. Let Him know you'll trust Him and His Word no matter what the circumstances say or look like. Then worship Him knowing you'll see Him demonstrate His power and faithfulness on your behalf!

FOR FURTHER STUDY:

Numbers 13:25-33

❧

DAILY SCRIPTURE READING:

2 Kings 23-24; 1 Thessalonians 2

## Speak the Word

*I keep my heart perfect toward God so that He shows Himself strong on my behalf.*

*2 Chronicles 16:9*

❧

> "Be patient therefore, brethren, unto the coming of the Lord. Behold, the husbandman waiteth for the precious fruit of the earth, and hath long patience for it, until he receive the early and latter rain."
> JAMES 5:7

# Seek the Knowledge of His Glory

My friend, it is time for the Glory. We've reached the last of the last days. We've come to the time about which Zechariah prophesied: *"Ask of the Lord rain in the time of the latter or spring rain. It is the Lord Who makes lightnings, which usher in the rain and give men showers of it, to every one grass in the field"* (Zechariah 10:1, AMP).

In this verse, he wasn't just referring to natural rain. He wasn't just talking about natural lightnings. He was referring to that bright, shining cloud of God's Glory that would usher in the outpouring of the Spirit and open the way for the end-time harvest of souls. He was pointing to the same day James referred to in the New Testament.

Both Zechariah and James were looking ahead to the time immediately preceding the return of Jesus. That's our day! We've reached that time. The Glory is beginning to flash around us and the rain has started to fall.

It is awe-inspiring to think that God has chosen us—this generation of believers—to be alive at this moment. He has chosen us to help usher in the Glory. What a great privilege!

But with great privilege comes great responsibility. Because of the time in which we live, we cannot afford to just sit around and play church. We cannot afford to wave our hands and flippantly say as some have done in years past, "Oh, Glory!" without giving any thought to what the Glory actually is.

No, it is our responsibility to follow the example of the Apostle Paul and make it our determined purpose to know Him, the Anointed One and His Anointing, to know His burden-removing, yoke-destroying power, and to know the power of His Resurrection, which, according to Romans 6:5, is the Glory of God (Philippians 3:10). It's our responsibility to press on in to Jesus until we come to understand and experience the Glory! (2 Corinthians 4:6).

Some people shy away from that responsibility. They say, "Well, I'm not seeking the Glory, I'm just content to seek the Lord."

But you can't separate the two. You can't separate Jesus, the Anointed One and His Anointing, from the Glory. You can't separate the Holy Spirit from the Glory. You can't separate the Father from the Glory. They are all One, and They are all glorious! The Glory is the manifestation of God Himself. So seek the Lord and the knowledge of His Glory.

## *Speak the Word*

*I am patient unto the coming of the Lord,*
*for He is waiting for the precious fruit of the earth.*
*James 5:7*

FOR FURTHER STUDY:

2 Corinthians 4:6-7

❧

DAILY SCRIPTURE READING:

2 Kings 25;
1 Chronicles 1-2;
1 Thessalonians 3-4

*Gloria*

# Awake, O Sleeper!

As I was reading this scripture some time ago, that phrase, *"Awake, O sleeper,"* seemed to leap out at me. It reminded me that the "daily-ness" of life can sometimes lull us to sleep spiritually. It can cause us to doze off to sleep. But I believe the Spirit of God is sending out a wake-up call to us today.

He is saying, as He did in this verse, "Wake up, Sleeper! The day of the Lord is coming."

There are three things that will take us through these evil, end-time days in strength and Glory:

1) The Word of God

2) Prayer

3) The Guidance of the Holy Spirit

You can overcome every evil that comes against you if you'll keep your faith strong. And the simple key to keeping your faith strong is this: *Stay in the Word of God.*

By being *constant in prayer* (Romans 12:12), you can maintain fellowship with your Father. Just talk to Him throughout your day and listen. Being in touch with Him will keep you strengthened. And you'll see your prayers answered.

If you *keep your spiritual ear tuned to the Holy Spirit,* and obey those promptings in your spirit, you'll avoid the pitfalls and traps of the devil.

So wake up! Throw off those covers of laziness and indifference and take your position in Christ—the Anointed One and His Anointing. Get in the Word, in prayer and obey the Holy Spirit. Give God first place in your life and He will keep you under His shadow of protection in these last days.

FOR FURTHER STUDY:

Ephesians 5:11-20

DAILY SCRIPTURE READING:

1 Chronicles 3-4;
1 Thessalonians 5

## Speak the Word

*I live purposefully and worthily and accurately.
I live wisely and make the very most of the time,
because Jesus is coming soon.*
Ephesians 5:15-16, AMP

"Take no part in and have no fellowship with the fruitless deeds and enterprises of darkness, but instead [let your lives be so in contrast as to] expose and reprove and convict them...Awake, O sleeper, and arise from the dead, and Christ shall shine [make day dawn] upon you and give you light. Look carefully then how you walk! Live purposefully and worthily and accurately, not as the unwise and witless, but as wise—sensible, intelligent people; Making the very most of the time— buying up each opportunity— because the days are evil."
EPHESIANS 5:11, 14-16, AMP

# From a Dog to a Prince

"And David said unto him, Fear not: for I will surely shew thee kindness for Jonathan thy father's sake, and will restore thee all the land of Saul thy father; and thou shalt eat bread at my table continually."

2 SAMUEL 9:7

Most people know the story of the covenant between David and Jonathan. The Word says, *"The soul of Jonathan was knit with the soul of David, and Jonathan loved him as his own soul"* (1 Samuel 18:1). These two men, a sheep-herder and a prince, entered into a blood covenant with one another.

What most people don't know is what happened after Jonathan died. The covenant relationship continued between Jonathan's son Mephibosheth and David.

You see, David's unconditional love *(hesed)* didn't end the day Jonathan was killed. It remained within him—even though he had become king. Even though he was wealthy and powerful, his covenant with Jonathan still burned inside him. He was so compelled that years later he cried out, *"Is there yet any that is left of the house of Saul, that I may show him kindness for Jonathan's sake?"* (2 Samuel 9:1). One of Saul's former servants, Ziba, gave David his answer: *"Jonathan hath yet a son, which is lame on his feet.... Behold, he is in the house of Machir, the son of Ammiel, in Lo-debar"* (verses 3-4).

When David sent for him, Mephibosheth was afraid David would kill him. He came into the palace, threw himself at David's feet, and began to religiously bawl and squall about what an unworthy dog he was (verses 6-8). David didn't even acknowledge his unworthy dog talk. In his eyes, Mephibosheth wasn't a dog. He was a rich man. He just didn't know it. David had kept his covenant with Jonathan...and all of Jonathan's wealth had been set aside for an heir. All Mephibosheth's life he had been covenanted to David, but he didn't know it. David was as much his father as Jonathan was because of the blood covenant between them.

That's the message of God's prosperity. Mephibosheth didn't do anything to become prosperous. Somebody sent for him, picked him up, and placed him in the middle of the most prosperous situation he'd ever seen in his life. Somebody loved him—not because of anything he had done, but because he was the heir of a blood covenant.

Once you grasp that, you won't ever believe you don't deserve to be healed, blessed or delivered. You didn't do anything to get where you are except receive Jesus. Once you did that, the Holy Spirit "fetched" you and placed you in the middle of the abundance of God Himself. You are surrounded by His blood. You are filled with His Spirit. You are crowned with His crown. And you wear the robe of His righteousness. Receive who you are in Christ Jesus today. Live like the son or daughter of the King. You're a prince... destined to live in abundance in your spirit, soul and body.

FOR FURTHER STUDY:

2 Samuel 9

DAILY SCRIPTURE READING:

1 Chronicles 5-6;
2 Thessalonians 1

## *Speak the Word*

*God has made me a king and priest and I reign on the earth.*
*Revelation 5:10*

*Gloria*

# God Has More Than Enough!

JUNE 14

> "My God shall supply all your need according to his riches in glory by Christ Jesus."
> PHILIPPIANS 4:19

Do you remember the elder brother in the story of the prodigal son? His younger brother had asked for his share of the inheritance, so the boys' father divided his estate between them. The younger brother ran off and squandered his share of the estate on a sinful lifestyle. The elder brother stayed home and faithfully served his father. When the younger brother repented and returned home, asking only to be treated as a servant in his father's house, the father received him with open arms. He killed a calf for him so they could celebrate with a feast because he had come home. He put a robe on his back and a ring on his finger.

The older brother was furious and pointed out to his father that he'd always been faithful to serve him and that the father had never killed a fatted calf for him!

The father's answer to him is very important to us. We need to consider it very carefully: *"Son, thou art ever with me, and all that I have is thine"* (Luke 15:31). The father had divided his estate between his two boys. Therefore, after the younger brother had taken his goods and departed, everything that was left belonged to the elder son. Everything! He could have eaten a fatted calf every day if he'd wanted. Every animal on the estate belonged to him, but he didn't take advantage of his inheritance!

A multitude of Christians are going to find themselves in the same situation when they get to heaven. They're going to find out after they get there what belonged to them down here. They're going to realize too late that they were cheated and swindled out of their earthly inheritance by religious tradition.

They're going to find out that God has always wanted His people to live in abundance, and all He has is ours. He put every good thing in this earth for His family. He didn't put riches here for the devil and his family. He put them here for us. God wants you to live in a good house. He wants you to have the car you need. He wants you to be so blessed you don't even have to think about those things. He wants you to be able to think about Him instead of thinking about how you're going to buy your next tank of gas!

Listen, God isn't anywhere near broke! He has enough wealth to richly supply ALL of His children. Lack is not His problem. His problem has been getting His people to believe what He says about their prosperity in His Word. His problem has been getting us to be kingdom of God-minded in our finances.

So go beyond what you can figure out...and just trust Him to do what He has promised. Base your actions, your prayers and your faith on what the Word says, and not your circumstances. Get kingdom of God-minded!

FOR FURTHER STUDY:

Luke 15:11-32

DAILY SCRIPTURE READING:

1 Chronicles 7-8;
2 Thessalonians 2

## Speak the Word

*My God supplies all my needs according to His riches in glory by Christ Jesus.*
*Philippians 4:19*

# Everyone Has Children

Years ago, I was like any parent. I was facing an awesome responsibility with little to no training! So I did what I've learned to do about everything. I sought the Lord.

As I sought the Lord regarding them, God gave me two very important instructions that have literally changed the lives of my children. I have carried them through with my grandchildren and it is amazing how powerful they are.

1) *Don't magnify their sin.* Remember, they are not just your children, they are your brothers and sisters in Jesus. The Word says where you see a brother sin, ask or pray and God will give you life for them (1 John 5:16). In Galatians 6:1, the Word says, *"Brethren, if a man be overtaken in a fault, ye which are spiritual, restore such an one in the spirit of meekness; considering thyself, lest thou also be tempted."*

Restore! That means work to put back together. We must magnify the Word, the love of God and pray. Bind the devil and let him know he cannot have your children.

2) *Treat them with respect.* Remember to confess Isaiah 54:13, that they are taught of the Lord and great is His Anointing on them...and then act in faith on that Word promise. Treat them like they are God's anointed even when they act like the very devil.

Now this does not mean you don't correct, and it doesn't mean you ignore wrong conduct, but you do the correcting with respect and in love. If you desire and demand respect from them, then demand respect from yourself for them.

"Brother Copeland, I don't have any children."

Yes, you do. Everyone has children. They are all around you. They are on the streets. They are in your church. They are such a large part of our society that they affect everything we do. Begin to pray for the outpouring of God on the children around you. This is God's time for the children. This is harvest time among the young people. Every time you hear of violence on TV about children, say out loud, "Our children are taught of the Lord and great is the peace and anointing that's on them." AMEN!

## *Speak the Word*

*My children are taught of the Lord and great is their peace.*
*Isaiah 54:13*

FOR FURTHER
STUDY:

Psalm 127

DAILY SCRIPTURE
READING:

1 Chronicles 9-10;
2 Thessalonians 3

*Gloria*

# He'll Lead You to Holiness

If we want to enjoy the grace and power of God in one area of our lives, we need to be willing to have it in other areas. We can't selectively obey God in certain areas and not in others. We can't be holy in one area and not another. We have to give Him our entire lives.

If we want to enjoy the blessing and favor of God in our midst, then we'll have to receive the grace of God that teaches us to deny ungodliness everywhere.

The Apostle Paul says, *"If ye live after the flesh, ye shall die: but if ye through the Spirit do mortify the deeds of the body, ye shall live. For as many as are led by the Spirit of God, they are the sons of God"* (Romans 8:13-14).

Paul is telling us that although grace has freed us from the Law, it has obligated us to walk in obedience to the Holy Spirit. And the Holy Spirit will never condone sin in our lives. On the contrary, He will lead us to put to death immoral desires and activities.

If you will fellowship with God and stay in living contact with Him, the Holy Spirit will lead you into holiness. He will say to you, for example, *Stop using that profane language. Use words that glorify the Lord.* Or *Stop reading those worldly novels and read more of the Word.*

> "For the grace of God that bringeth salvation hath appeared to all men, Teaching us that, denying ungodliness and worldly lusts, we should live soberly, righteously, and godly, in this present world."
>
> TITUS 2:11-12

Now that may sound like a legalistic requirement, but it's not. Here's why: It's the favor of God that He corrects us. He is teaching us how to live free.

Another part of that grace is that you don't have to do it in your own strength. Whatever the Holy Ghost asks us to do, He also empowers us to do. The Bible says in 1 Corinthians 10:13 that He gives us the strength to overcome every temptation.

That's why the New Testament speaks to us in such strong terms about holiness. Nowhere does it say, "Well, I know you Christians have been sinning a lot lately. But, hey, I understand. Life is tough and at least you're trying."

No! It just says, *"Be ye holy"* (1 Peter 1:15). We have no excuse for living unholy lives. Because by grace, God not only tells us what we need to do to be holy—He gives us the ability to do it!

FOR FURTHER STUDY:

Romans 6:1-22

And, I'm telling you, it is high time we started using that ability. We've reached the end of this age. Jesus is coming sooner than we think. It is time to get the slack out of our lives and become absolutely focused on God. It's time to drop everything that pulls us away from Him. It's time to get our flesh under control and yield only to the Holy Spirit.

Don't yield to the temptation that it's impossible to live holy before Him. That's a lie! He's empowered you and enabled you to succeed. He's given you His grace to see you through. Yield to obedience in every area. Yield to His Spirit. He'll lead you to holiness. He is doing you a favor.

DAILY SCRIPTURE READING:

1 Chronicles 11-12; 1 Timothy 1

## *Speak the Word*

*I live soberly, righteously and godly, in this present age.*

*Titus 2:12*

# Just Laugh at the Devil

"The kings of the earth set themselves, and the rulers take counsel together, against the Lord, and against his anointed, saying, Let us break their bands asunder, and cast away their cords from us. He that sitteth in the heavens shall laugh."
PSALM 2:2-4

God is pouring out His Spirit like never before. We are in the midst of the greatest harvest of souls, the likes we've never before seen. But with all that anointing He's placed in and on us, He's also given us great responsibility as the end-time Church.

Psalm 2:2-4 helps us to catch hold of what God is telling His people today. And Psalm 37:12-13 says, *"The wicked plotteth against the just, and gnasheth upon him with his teeth. The Lord shall laugh at him: for he seeth that his day is coming."*

As this age draws to a close, I'm hearing the Lord say, *Hey! Give Me a couple of days here. There are a lot of things I've been wanting to do, but My hands have been tied. But now that they're untied, let's have some fun. Let's have a good time—and win billions of souls before we go!*

What do you think all this laughing in the spirit is about, anyway?

Well, we just read it in the Psalms. Satan's time is up, and God is laughing at him! God is having one *BIG* time of it. He is laughing at the devil all over the world. He's laughing at him in churches. He's laughing at him in meetings. He even has preachers going around preaching and teaching laughing.

The bottom line is, you can go ahead and laugh at the devil too. He's through! He's finished!

Hebrews 10:12-13 tells us that Jesus, *"after he had offered one sacrifice for sins for ever, sat down on the right hand of God; From henceforth expecting till his enemies be made his footstool."*

Notice that Jesus didn't sit down to do nothing. No, He sat down *expecting* till His enemies be made His footstool. He sat down, or He entered into God's rest.

Would you please tell me how in the world will Jesus defeat His enemies sitting down? It's simple: He has already defeated the enemy. What's more, He gave you and me authority over the enemy, with the command to go into all the world and preach the gospel and tread on His enemy.

So go ahead, laugh. God is. Jesus is. But do it *expecting*. Do it expecting, until your financial enemies, until your physical enemies, until your family's enemies—or whatever enemies—be made your footstool.

## *Speak the Word*

*The Lord sits in the heavens and laughs at the devil.*
*I join in with God and laugh at the devil, too!*
*Psalm 2:4*

FOR FURTHER STUDY:

Psalm 3

DAILY SCRIPTURE READING:

1 Chronicles 13-14;
1 Timothy 2

*Gloria*

# Enough for Every Good Work

When Ken and I were first learning to walk in faith for prosperity, about 30 years ago, we didn't know very much of God's Word yet. We received our revelation piece by piece. Every time we'd learn something new, we'd put it into practice.

Actually, it's much easier for us now to walk in prosperity than it was back then. Today, we have to believe for millions of dollars just to pay our TV bills. But that's not nearly as challenging as it was to believe God back then for food on the table. During those days I often had to pray in the spirit just to pay my way out at the grocery store. That was the hardest time of all because we were just learning.

You have to grow in these things. If you're just now hearing that God wants you to prosper, you probably won't be able to get a million dollars in cash by this time next week.

Why? Because your faith isn't up to that yet. What you need to do is start right where you are. Start believing God for rent money. Start believing God to buy groceries. Start believing and then increase.

That's what we did. We just kept growing. We kept listening to God and walking in the faith that we had, and it grew bigger. And we kept tithing and giving!

What's important is to start now. Don't wait until next month. If you want a change, make a change. Start believing God for the things you need today. Start thanking Him for them. Tell the devil you're out from under his curse. Grab hold of the Word of God and don't let go.

If you'll do that and stay with it, and continue to do what God tells you, you'll eventually have a surplus of prosperity so that not only can you pay your bills, but you can also have the capacity to give into every good work!

> "And God is able to make all grace abound toward you; that ye, always having all sufficiency in all things, may abound to every good work."
> 2 CORINTHIANS 9:8

## Speak the Word

*God makes all grace abound toward me. I always have all sufficiency in all things. I abound to every good work.*
*2 Corinthians 9:8*

FOR FURTHER STUDY:

Philippians 4:15-19

DAILY SCRIPTURE READING:

1 Chronicles 15-17;
1 Timothy 3-4

> "Jesus took him by the hand, and lifted him up; and he arose."
> MARK 9:27

# Someone Is Waiting on You!

Mark 9 recounts the story of a father who brought his demon-possessed son to Jesus and asked for help. According to the scripture, Jesus rebuked the spirit and commanded it to come out.

*Simple enough,* we think. But in verse 26, Jesus was in a position to undo everything with unbelief...or simply trust. *"And the spirit cried, and rent him sore, and came out of him: and he was as one dead; insomuch that many said, He is dead."*

What a situation! The man brings his son to Jesus for help. Jesus rebukes the spirit, casts it out, and now the boy looks dead! From a purely natural perspective, it looked as though Jesus had just made the situation worse.

You've probably felt the same way where laying hands on the sick is concerned. Maybe you've laid hands on someone, and they haven't looked healed. Or, maybe you're not even willing to risk laying hands on someone because you aren't sure they'll be healed.

Well, settle the issue here and now and forevermore.

When Jesus was faced with what was happening to that little boy, He had more faith in the Word of God than He had in his natural senses. He wasn't moved by physical appearances. He simply trusted that what He had said was done. In verse 27, *"Jesus took him by the hand, and lifted him up; and he arose."* He arose!

If you've laid hands on someone, and they haven't look healed, don't let that tempt you into believing that healing didn't come. Healing always comes. Your responsibility is to be obedient to the Word of God and lay hands on the sick.

Now, not everyone may be healed. Sometimes people won't receive the healing. Sometimes they're full of fear or doubt or unforgiveness, and they can't receive what God is giving them.

But when that happens, the last thing you want to do is withdraw your faith and say, "Well, I guess it didn't work this time." Don't do that! Your faith may be the only hope that person has! Keep believing God. Act like Jesus did. Trust. Don't be moved by what you see with your natural eyes. Say, "Lord, I did what Your Word said. I laid hands on the sick and as far as I'm concerned, every person I've laid hands on is recovering. I'm standing in faith for that recovery. God, open the eyes of their understanding, so they can fully receive their healing."

Once you do that, never back off again. Go forward in faith. Boldly lay hands on the sick. Expect God to do exactly what He promised. And just like the little boy, there are people out there right now who need someone with enough faith to deliver their miracle—people who are waiting for someone just like you!

## *Speak the Word*

*In Jesus' Name I lay hands on the sick and they recover.*
*Mark 16:18*

FOR FURTHER STUDY:

Mark 9:14-29

DAILY SCRIPTURE READING:

1 Chronicles 18-19;
1 Timothy 5

*Gloria*

# A Word to the Wise

For years now I've been telling people to spend time in the Word. Almost everywhere I preach, no matter what topic I'm talking about, it seems I always get back to the importance of putting the Word first place in my life.

You may have heard me say it a hundred times. But you know, hearing it isn't enough. It's doing it that will give you success.

Jesus taught us that principle in Matthew 7. There He told about two men. Both of them had heard the Word, yet Jesus said one of the men was foolish and the other wise. What made the difference between the two? The wise man acted on what he heard and the foolish man didn't.

You may know full well that you need to spend time in the Word. But unless you act on that knowledge, it won't do you any good when the storms of life come.

So take action! Begin now to set aside time for the Word each day. Begin now making it the number one priority on your schedule. Don't wait until you're faced with some terrible situation or some storm of life to do it.

Have you ever tried to build a house in a storm? Ken has been through several hurricanes, and he has seen the wind blow so hard that coconuts shot through the air like cannonballs. Just think about some poor fellow out there trying to build his house with the wind blowing at 120 mph!

Don't do that. Don't wait until you're desperate to make time for the Word. Make the decision and start today.

Then, when the storms of life come against your house, you'll be sitting inside in front of the fireplace just rocking and praising God. You'll be glad that you didn't let the devil talk you into being too busy for the Word.

"Therefore whosoever heareth these sayings of mine, and doeth them, I will liken him unto a wise man, which built his house upon a rock: And the rain descended, and the floods came, and the winds blew, and beat upon that house; and it fell not: for it was founded upon a rock."
MATTHEW 7:24-25

## Speak the Word

*I am a wise man because I hear God's words and I do them.*
*Matthew 7:24*

FOR FURTHER STUDY:

Proverbs 1:1-9

DAILY SCRIPTURE READING:

1 Chronicles 20-21; 1 Timothy 6

# Don't Miss the Move!

The word *weeping* in this passage represents the Old Covenant form of repentance. The New Covenant word for *repentance* means "to turn around, to change the way you're going." But in the Old Covenant, to weep for your sin and to mourn for it was really all you could do. You couldn't get born again. But, praise God, in New Testament times, not only can you have godly sorrow for it (see 2 Corinthians 7:10), but you can also get rid of it by the blood of the Lamb!

But, Old Covenant or New, one thing remains the same—repentance is mandatory for anyone who wants to be in on the move of God.

*Well, there's certainly no hope for my church,* you may be thinking. *There's so much junk going on in it, we'd never get it all repented. Sister So-and-So is mad at Brother Such-and-Such. This group is cross with that group. And everybody is upset with the preacher! I guess we'll just miss out on the end-time Glory.*

Don't be so sure. If the bunch that was gathered in the upper room on the Day of Pentecost could repent and get in unity in just a few days, then your church can too, if you'll just keep praying and believing God for it.

"Brother Copeland, are you saying Peter and John, and Mary, the mother of Jesus, and all the rest of the disciples had to repent before the Holy Spirit could fall on them?"

I certainly am. There was *trouble* in this ministry! The treasurer had been stealing and ended up committing suicide...the rest of the disciples argued about who would be top guy...there was so much strife, John and James' mother got involved...Peter denied the Lord...just to name a few of the troubles.

But somehow in that upper room, they dropped their differences. Jesus' mother was there. James and his brothers were there. Peter and John were there. All those who had been cross with each other were there...and they were all right with one another. In fact, the Bible says they *"were all with one accord"* (Acts 2:1).

I'm telling you, some repenting had gone on! And God Almighty came on the scene. The Glory was poured out.

*"And suddenly there came a sound from heaven as of a rushing mighty wind, and it filled all the house where they were sitting. And there appeared unto them cloven tongues like as of fire, and it sat upon each of them. And they were all filled with the Holy Ghost, and began to speak with other tongues, as the Spirit gave them utterance"* (Acts 2:2-4).

## Speak the Word

*I turn to the Lord with all my heart. He is gracious, merciful, slow to anger and of great kindness.*
*Joel 2:12-13*

---

"Therefore also now, saith the Lord, turn ye even to me with all your heart, and with fasting, and with weeping, and with mourning: And rend your heart, and not your garments, and turn unto the Lord your God: for he is gracious and merciful, slow to anger, and of great kindness."
JOEL 2:12-13

---

FOR FURTHER STUDY:

2 Corinthians 7:9-10

DAILY SCRIPTURE READING:

1 Chronicles 22-23; 2 Timothy 1

*Gloria*

# Tell "Dignity" Goodbye

Some years ago, when I first began to catch sight of the supernatural power of joy, I did a study on it. During that study, I discovered that one of the biblical words for *joy* is translated "to shine." Another word means "to leap." Another means "to delight." But in every case, joy is more than an attitude, it is an action.

As I studied, I also found out that, as Psalm 149 says, joyful praise gives God pleasure. It doesn't offend God when we boisterously praise Him. He likes it. It gives Him pleasure to see us shine and leap and express our delight in Him.

*"Let the saints be joyful in glory...Let the high praises of God be in their mouth, and a twoedged sword in their hand"* (verses 5-6).

I know that by natural standards, that kind of exuberant praise doesn't look very dignified. I looked up the word *dignified* once. It meant a lot of things, including "self-possession" or "self-respect." I do not want to be self-possessed. I want to be Holy Spirit-controlled. But I am sure that my idea of dignity had kept me from being as free as I should be with the Lord.

As believers, we need to get past the point where we care about that. We need to focus instead on pleasing God. We should have such a desire to please Him that we don't care how we look to other people.

*"But Gloria, that's easy for you to say. You're comfortable with expressing yourself to God in praise."*

I haven't always been. I was so conservative when I first began to walk with God that it took me a long time to even begin to lift my hands in praise. But I broke through that "dignity" and so can you!

> "Praise ye the Lord. Sing unto the Lord a new song, and his praise in the congregation of saints. Let Israel rejoice in him that made him: let the children of Zion be joyful in their King. Let them praise his name in the dance: let them sing praises unto him with the timbrel and harp. For the Lord taketh pleasure in his people."
>
> Psalm 149:1-4

## Speak the Word

*I praise the Lord. I praise the Lord in the dance.*
*I sing praises to Him with musical instruments.*
*For the Lord takes pleasure in me.*
*Psalm 149:1-4*

For Further Study:

Psalm 149

Daily Scripture Reading:

1 Chronicles 24-25;
2 Timothy 2

# Rain Is on the Way

> "And it shall come to pass, if ye shall hearken diligently unto my command- ments...to love the Lord your God, and to serve him with all your heart and with all your soul, That I will give you the rain of your land in his due season, the first rain and the latter rain, that thou mayest gather in thy corn, and thy wine, and thine oil."
> DEUTERONOMY 11:13-14

God Himself says He is coming to us as rain (Hosea 6:3). Not just as rain, but specifically as the *former and the latter rain.*

What is the former and latter rain? In natural terms, the Israelites knew the former rain as the fall rain that prepared the soil for planting, and the latter rain as the spring rain that moisturized the soil to bring forth a good harvest.

In spiritual terms, the former and latter rains represent the move of God's Spirit under the Old and New Covenants.

The Bible calls the former, Old Covenant rain of the Spirit, a "moderate" rain. Under that covenant, people would go hundreds of years without hearing the voice of God in the earth and without seeing someone anointed of the Holy Ghost. If there was anyone in the land who was anointed with the Spirit of the living God, it would be some prayer warriors somewhere who didn't draw much attention to themselves so people didn't see them.

Eventually, however, a little rain would fall. Then, a prophet of God, a great priest or king would be raised up in the land. The Spirit of God would be upon that person and the Anointing and miracles of God would flow through them. If you could get under the ministry of such a person, you could be healed, have your needs met supernaturally and hear the voice of God.

To understand how powerful even that "moderate" rain was, you have to realize that even Jesus' ministry was under the Old Covenant. He was the Lamb of God sacrificed under the Old Abrahamic Covenant. So, as powerful as the ministry of Jesus was, it did not show the fullness of the rain of the Holy Spirit.

He said it didn't! Just before He went to the Cross, He told His disciples, *"He that believeth on me, the works that I do shall he do also; and greater works than these shall he do; because I go unto my Father"* (John 14:12).

How could Jesus say such an astounding thing? He knew the latter rain was on the way!

## *Speak the Word*

*I expect the Anointing and the miracle power of Jesus
to flow through me because Jesus sent the latter rain of
the Holy Spirit when He returned to the Father.*
*John 14:12*

FOR FURTHER STUDY:

Hosea 6:1-3

DAILY SCRIPTURE READING:

1 Chronicles 26-27; 2 Timothy 3

# The Word Is Truth

Notice that this verse doesn't say, "Thy Word is fact." Truth goes beyond facts. The fact may be that you don't have any money. The fact may be that the doctor said you have an incurable disease. But what does the truth have to say about it?

You see, the truth is absolute. Truth doesn't yield. Truth doesn't change. Thus, facts are subject to truth.

It can be a fact that you are sick as can be, but God says you were healed by the stripes of Jesus when He died on the cross. That's the truth. Now you have a choice. You can apply the truth of God's Word to the fact that you're sick and the fact will change—or you can agree with the facts and things will stay like they are.

I'll tell you right now, it will be much easier just to agree with the facts, because facts scream a lot louder than the Word of God does. God's Word will be quiet—until it starts coming out of your mouth.

But once that Word begins to come out of your mouth in faith, it will be the final word. If it's God's Word about healing, you'll be healed. If it's His Word about prosperity, you'll be prosperous. If it's His Word about deliverance, you'll be delivered.

God has given you His contract. When you do your part by believing, speaking and acting on a heart full of faith, God's Word will come to pass. No circumstance on earth and no demon in hell can stop it.

So forget all those stories you have heard about so-and-so who believed the Word and it didn't work for him. Quit asking questions and settle it once and for all. God's Word is truth.

## *Speak the Word*

*God's Word is truth. I believe His Word and not my circumstances.*
*John 17:17*

FOR FURTHER STUDY:

Psalm 119:
151-152, 160

❧

DAILY SCRIPTURE READING:

1 Chronicles 28-29;
2 Timothy 4

# Break Through the Wall

"Wherefore remember, that ye being in time past Gentiles in the flesh...ye were without Christ [the Anointed One], being aliens from the common-wealth of Israel and strangers from the covenants of promise, having no hope, and without God in the world: But now in Christ [the Anointed One] Jesus ye who sometimes were far off are made nigh by the blood of Christ [the Anointed One]."
EPHESIANS 2:11-13

Have you ever hit a brick wall? No, not a physical one, but an emotional one. The kind that comes when you've chased every lead you knew to get a job, or get the money to pay a bill, or learn a new skill to get a better job. You know the feeling. It's frustrating, and it usually drives even a weak believer to cry out to God.

Well, there's one sure way to punch a good-size hole in that wall and watch it start to crumble until it is totally obliterated! I call it factoring in the anointing.

According to the Scriptures, before you were born again, you were without the Anointed One (Jesus). Well, if you were without the Anointed One, you were also without the anointing, right? But now, you are in the Anointing of Jesus. That anointing is available to you in every situation you face to destroy (obliterate completely!) every yoke of bondage. The Anointing of God is God on flesh doing those things only God can do.

That's why you can have hope in the most hopeless situations. It doesn't matter who you are or what color your skin is. It doesn't matter where you live or if you never made it past the sixth grade. You can break out of that hopeless situation if you'll factor in the anointing.

The anointing factor is what the world always forgets. They say, "We'll build this wall so big nobody will ever get through it. We'll build it big enough to block out the gospel and keep the people under our thumb." But they fail to consider the anointing factor. It destroys walls. If you don't believe it, ask the believers in Berlin!

So whatever wall you are facing today, begin factoring in the anointing in your life. If someone says to you, "Well Brother, you can't expect to succeed. You can't expect to prosper. You can't expect to be healed..." ask yourself, *Is there a yoke holding me back?* Maybe your yoke is a lack of education, the need for a better job, or a sickness.

If a yoke is holding you back, then rejoice! Because the anointing will destroy it!

## *Speak the Word*

*The anointing factor removes every burden and breaks through every yoke and wall that may try to hold me back.*
*Isaiah 10:27*

FOR FURTHER STUDY:

Isaiah 10:24-27

DAILY SCRIPTURE READING:

2 Chronicles 1-3;
Titus 1-2

*Gloria*

# No Deposit—No Return

Everything we could ever need is waiting for us in the realm of the spirit with our name on it. All we need to do is get it from there to here.

How do we do that? With faith.

Faith is the "currency" we use to transfer God's provision for us from the unseen realm of the spirit to this natural, earthly realm. Or, as Hebrews 11:1 says, *"Faith is the substance of things hoped for, the evidence of things not seen."*

Spiritual currency works the same way as natural currency. If you have an abundance in your natural bank account, you can enjoy plenty of material things. If you have an abundance of faith in your spiritual account, you can enjoy plenty of *every-thing*—wealth, health, good relationships, peace, success—because the Bible says God *"giveth us richly all things to enjoy"* (1 Timothy 6:17).

The problem is, many believers don't have a clue where faith actually comes from, where it's stored or how to get it out when they need it. That's crucial information. In fact, without it, you're spiritually broke. So let's study these a moment:

Where does faith come from? Romans 10:17 says, *"Faith cometh by hearing, and hearing by the word of God."*

Where is faith stored? *"The word is nigh thee, even in thy mouth, and in thy heart: that is, the word of faith, which we preach.... For with the heart man believeth unto righteousness; and with the mouth con-fession is made unto salvation"* (Romans 10:8, 10). Your faith is stored up in your heart—and since your faith (or lack of it) determines your future, the truth is, your future is stored up in your heart as well.

How do you get it out? When you want to make a withdrawal from your faith account, speak the Word of faith. Don't talk the circumstances. Don't "tell it the way it is" (or looks, in other words). Speak the end result. Say what God says the outcome is going to be. But don't put it in the future. Faith calls things as though they were.

Let me ask you this: How much faith do you have in your heart account right now? Is it enough to handle your current situation? Is it enough to produce victory every day of your life? If not, you'd better start making some big deposits of God's Word. Remember: No deposit—no return.

> "The word is nigh thee, even in thy mouth, and in thy heart: that is, the word of faith, which we preach."
> ROMANS 10:8

**FOR FURTHER STUDY:**

Matthew 12:35-36

**DAILY SCRIPTURE READING:**

2 Chronicles 4-5; Titus 3

## *Speak the Word*

*The Word of God is near me. It is in my mouth and in my heart.*
*Romans 10:8*

## Joy COMETH

❧

"Weeping may
endure for a
night, but joy
cometh in the
morning."
PSALM 30:5

Many believers drag around in defeat day after day, month after month, year after year. You've heard them. They sound something like this: "I just can't figure it out. I believe the Bible. I believe Jesus has set me free from this sickness. I believe He has set me free from this sin...I believe He has set me free from this lifestyle of lack. But I still can't get the victory."

The problem is, those people are too spiritually weak to receive what Jesus has given them. They need a tonic that will put some muscle back in their believing. They need something to put a sparkle in their eye, a spring in their step, and give them the spiritual might they need to knock the devil in the head and take back what belongs to them.

And that's exactly what the joy of the Lord will do. Nehemiah 8:10 says the joy of the Lord is our strength. That verse is literally true. To understand why, you must realize that joy is not happiness. Happiness is a fleeting, temporal condition that depends on the comfort of your flesh. Joy, on the other hand, is a vital spiritual force. It is not based on outward circumstances, but upon the condition of your heart.

Happiness is wimpy. It disappears every time there's trouble. But joy is tough. If you'll let it, it will keep flowing in the midst of the most miserable situation. It will enable you to stand as solid as a stump until the time of trouble is over.

I realize if you're sitting there right now in the midst of trouble, you probably feel like it will never be over. But, believe me, it will! "Weeping may endure for a night, but joy *cometh* in the morning."

If you are a person of faith, it doesn't matter how dark conditions may seem to be right now, you can rest assured, a brighter day is on the way. That's because the devil cannot sustain an attack. He doesn't have the power. So if you'll let the force of joy keep you strong, you will outlast him and he'll eventually have to give up and admit defeat!

Remember, the Word promises that joy COMETH! And joy is your strength. It's tough. It will enable you to overcome...and it's inside of you. Yield to it and your trouble will be over soon enough.

### *Speak the Word*
*The joy of the Lord is my strength. Joy comes to me!*
*Nehemiah 8:10*

FOR FURTHER
STUDY:

Psalm 30

❧

DAILY SCRIPTURE
READING:

2 Chronicles 6-7;
Philemon

*Gloria*

# From Trouble to Triumph

If you're in trouble right now, you're not by yourself. At some time or another, everyone faces trouble. Believers face trouble...and unbelievers face trouble. It's just a part of living in the earth.

But here's something you need to know: If you're a believer, you can expect to come out of that trouble in triumph. That's right. God brings His people out of trouble—any kind of trouble. In fact, if you're a born-again child of God, coming out of trouble is one of the benefits of your salvation.

Maybe you didn't know that. But the word *salvation* includes a whole lot more than being born again and going to heaven when you die. It actually means "material and temporal deliverance from danger and apprehension; preservation, pardon, restoration, healing, wholeness and soundness."

Look at those first few words again: material and temporal deliverance from danger. They leave no doubt about the fact that coming out of trouble is part of our salvation package.

"But the trouble I'm facing is of my own making," you say. "Will God deliver me from this mess even though it's my own fault?"

Yes! And it's a good thing, because that's usually the way it is. We get into trouble by ourselves and then we turn to Him for help. But, even so, He is always there. We can't wear out His mercy and patience. (If we could have, we already would have!)

Second Chronicles 15:4 tells of a time when the people of Israel turned away from God and got themselves in trouble...and God found them.

The same will be true for you. When you turn to the Lord and seek Him, you will find Him. God won't say to you, "Why are you coming to Me now? Why didn't you talk to Me before you got into this situation?"

That's what we deserve to hear, but—THANK GOD!—He is the God of all mercy. He will always receive you. He will always listen to you. And He will always take you from trouble to triumph!

> "But when they in their trouble did turn unto the Lord God of Israel, and sought him, he was found of them."
> 2 CHRONICLES 15:4

## *Speak the Word*

*When I am in trouble, I turn to the Lord and seek Him, and I find Him.*
*2 Chronicles 15:4*

FOR FURTHER STUDY:

2 Chronicles 15

DAILY SCRIPTURE READING:

2 Chronicles 8-9;
Hebrews 1

"Thou [God]
madest him
[man] to have
dominion
over the works
of thy hands;
thou hast
put all
things under
his feet."
PSALM 8:6

# You're in Charge

There is a particular phrase I've heard spoken countless times over the years, and I like it less every time I hear it. No doubt, you've heard it too, usually in drawn out, religious-sounding tones—when circumstances seem to fall short of what God has promised us in His Word.

"Well, Brother, you have to remember...God is sovereign."

As spiritual as that phrase might sound, it really bothers me. It's not that I don't believe God is sovereign. Certainly He is. According to *Webster's Dictionary*, *sovereign* means "above or superior to all others; supreme in power, rank or authority." Without question, God is all those things.

But all too often, when people refer to the sovereignty of God, what they're actually saying is, "You never know what God will do. After all, He's all-powerful and totally independent, so He does *whatever* He wants *whenever* He wants."

The problem with that view of sovereignty is it releases us of all responsibility. After all, if God is sovereign, He will do what He wants anyway, so we might as well go watch television and forget about it, right?

Wrong. After 30 years of studying the Word and preaching the gospel, I've come to realize that God does very few things—if any—in this earth without man's cooperation. Even though it belongs to God—it is His creation and He owns it.

According to Psalm 8:6, God Himself put mankind in charge. He doesn't intervene in the affairs of earth whenever He wants. He respects the dominion and authority He has given us. So, until man's lease on this planet expires, God restricts His power on the earth, taking action only when He is asked to do so.

Since the people who do the asking (the intercessors) are often very quiet people who do their praying in secret, it may appear at times that God simply acts on His own. But regardless of appearances, the Bible teaches from cover to cover that God's connection with man is a prayer and faith connection. When you see Him act in a mighty way, you can be sure there was someone somewhere praying and interceding to bring Him on the scene.

## Speak the Word

*God has given me dominion over all the works of His hands.*
*He has put all things under my feet.*
*Psalm 8:6*

FOR FURTHER
STUDY:

James 5:13-18

DAILY SCRIPTURE
READING:

2 Chronicles 10-11;
Hebrews 2

*Kenneth*

# Find the Promise

If you're facing a faith challenge, the very first thing you should do is go to the Word and find the promise of God that covers your situation. Second Peter 1:3-4 is our assurance that there is such a promise for everything.

Once you have found the promise, and have settled it in your heart, focus your attention on it. Keep it in the forefront of your thinking. My children proved the power of this principle years ago when they were very young.

They came to me and told me they wanted a boat, so we could go out on the lake as a family and have some time to ourselves. "That sounds great to me," I said. "But your mother and I will not use our faith to get it. We'll agree with you, but you kids will have to get it by using your own faith."

So, off they went. They opened the Bible and found promises that applied to them. (John was too young to read. He just listened and agreed.) Then they wrote out an agreement, signed it and taped it to the refrigerator door. From that day forward, every time they walked past the refrigerator, they would slap that agreement and say, "Thank God it is done!" In other words, they kept it constantly before their eyes and in their heart.

Every once in a while John would get mad at Kellie and I'd say, "Son, you'd better watch out. You can't operate in faith without operating in love. And it will take faith to get that boat."

"Oh!" he'd say. "I repent! I repent!"

To make a long story short, 10 days later, a fellow called me and gave me a fishing boat. Then, another fellow called me and gave me a light cabin cruiser.

"Why *two* boats?" I asked the Lord.

*Go read their agreement,* He answered.

Those kids had agreed on the "perfect boat." To them that meant a boat we could use to fish, water ski and carry the entire family. It took two boats to fill the bill!

Finding the promise of God made faith easy for John and Kellie, and it will make it easy for you too. It's easy to believe someone will do something for you if you know they've already said they would—especially when it's someone like our loving Heavenly Father.

**FOR FURTHER STUDY:**

Proverbs 4:20-27

**DAILY SCRIPTURE READING:**

2 Chronicles 12-13; Hebrews 3

> "According to his divine power [God] hath given unto us all things that pertain unto life and godliness, through the knowledge of him that hath called us to glory and virtue: Whereby are given unto us exceeding great and precious promises: that by these ye might be partakers of the divine nature, having escaped the corruption that is in the world through lust."
>
> 2 PETER 1:3-4

## Speak the Word

*God has given me everything that pertains to life and godliness.*
*2 Peter 1:3*

> "Faith cometh
> by hearing,
> and hearing
> by the word
> of God."
> ROMANS 10:17

# Faith Cometh by Hearing

One of the greatest healing evangelists I've ever known once said to me, "I don't understand it. I have laid hands on more than 2 million people. I've seen miracles of every description. But I'm the last guy in the world to ever get healed."

Just think, that evangelist had seen Jesus face to face more than once. His hand had been set on fire with the healing touch of God. But he couldn't live on those experiences. He had to learn, just like you and I do, to walk one step at a time confessing, believing and standing on the Word of God.

"Well, maybe that's true," you say, "but I still think I would have more faith if Jesus would appear to me like He did to that evangelist."

No, you wouldn't. Jesus said, *"Blessed are they that have not seen, and yet have believed"* (John 20:29). *Blessed* means "empowered." So, according to Jesus, you'll have more power if you'll believe before seeing a physical manifestation.

Why is that true? It's because for you to believe something you don't see with your physical eyes, you have to turn inward. You have to activate your spirit being. When you do that, the part of you that is like God rises up and gets stronger.

Am I saying you should avoid the spectacular manifestations and displays of God's power that are occurring around us in these final days?

Absolutely not! Enjoy them to the fullest. Go to every meeting you possibly can. Be a part of the move of God. But don't lay down your faith in the process.

Keep standing on the Word, first and foremost. The Word will work when the gifts are flowing and when they're not. The Word will work in the daytime and in the dark. The Word will work for any man, woman or child who will put it to work. It is eternal, settled in heaven and earth forever.

Remember this: Faith—the everyday kind of faith you use for living—doesn't come from moving in the gifts of the Spirit. It doesn't come from seeing Jesus or having special visitations and experiences with God. It comes by hearing and hearing and hearing the Word of God.

## *Speak the Word*

*As I hear the Word of God, faith comes to me.*
*Romans 10:17*

FOR FURTHER
STUDY:

John 20:24-29

DAILY SCRIPTURE
READING:

2 Chronicles
14-15;
Hebrews 4

*Gloria*

# Don't Be a Sippin' Saint

JULY 2

❧

"Now I have written unto you not to keep company, if any man that is called a brother be a fornicator, or covetous, or an idolator, or a railer, or a drunkard, or an extortioner."
1 CORINTHIANS 5:11

Honestly, I'm shocked at how some Christians live. When I see believers who go to church on Sunday, then live like the world the rest of the week, it disturbs me. Ken and I haven't been raised spiritually like that. Our spiritual parents did not train us that way. They live what they preach. The people we run with act the same all the time. When we take off on our motorcycles, we might look like the world with our helmets and our leathers on, but we praise God, talk faith and act in love just like we do when we're preaching at a convention.

If your friends don't do that, you need to find some new friends. If your friends are worldly, you need to separate yourself from them because they'll pull you down to their level.

Now it's good to go to sinners and bring them the gospel. But the Scriptures tell us not to have ongoing fellowship with them. They'll start influencing you toward their unholy way of thinking. Pretty soon, you'll be talking the way they talk and watching the television shows and the movies they watch. Next thing you know, you'll be doing everything else they're doing too.

We've been set apart for God's sacred use! We don't need to be watching television sitcoms that make light of immorality. Those programs are intended to desensitize people to sin. Satan takes his best shots in the entertainment industry.

I realize some people will argue about that. But the Bible warns us that we're not to be like the children of Israel when they indulged in the sinful ways of the world (1 Corinthians 10).

Don't play around like the people in the world do. It will get you in trouble. (They are already in trouble.) You might start out doing something on a small scale. You might indulge in just a little glass of wine after dinner now and then. You might become a "sippin' saint."

"Well, Gloria, I don't think it will lead to anything else."

Maybe not, but you have to admit that it is certainly an open door. What's more, compromising ourselves for something as silly as a drink is foolishness. Why would we want something like that in our way when we can walk in the Glory of God?

FOR FURTHER STUDY:

1 Corinthians 5:11;
2 Corinthians 6:14-18, 7:1

❧

DAILY SCRIPTURE READING:

2 Chronicles 16-18;
Hebrews 5-6

If you think I'm begin legalistic, think again. There is nothing legalistic about holiness. In fact, under the Law, holiness is totally unattainable. That's because holiness doesn't come by simply observing outward rules or laws. Holiness comes as the result of the work of grace God does in our hearts! It manifests in our lives as we live out what, by grace, God has put within us.

So don't be a sippin' saint. Be a doer of the Word. Live a life of holiness.

## *Speak the Word*

*I walk in holiness, not in compromise with the world.*
*1 Corinthians 5:11*

❦

"And it shall come to pass, if thou shalt hearken diligently unto the voice of the Lord thy God, to observe and to do all his command-ments which I command thee this day, that the Lord thy God will set thee on high above all nations of the earth: And all these blessings shall come on thee, and overtake thee."

DEUTERONOMY 28:1-2

# Overtaken—For Better or Worse

God promised Abraham that He would be his shield and his exceeding great reward (Genesis 15:1). No question about it, that promise caused Abraham to be extremely prosperous in every way and it will do the same for you, if you're a born-again child of God. What is it like to be blessed in every way?

Deuteronomy 28:1-9 tells us. It lists that you can be blessed in the city, in the field, in the fruit of your body, the fruit of your ground, the fruit of your cattle, the increase of your kine, the flocks of your sheep...it says you shall be blessed when you come in and when you go out. It says your enemies will be smitten before you, and on and on it goes. You'll just be blessed in every area, from your job to your family to your possessions to your everyday comings and goings.

Does all that sound too good to be true? Well, it's not. That's the blessing Jesus bought for you on the cross. And it will begin to operate in your life if you'll "hearken unto the voice of the Lord your God."

Notice I didn't say it will operate just because you are a Christian. Ken and I were Christians for five years before we began to listen to God's Word about prosperity. So, during that time, the curse continued to run loose in our lives. It didn't just creep up quietly. It jumped on us and overtook us. No matter how hard we tried, we couldn't outrun it or get away from it.

Then we began to believe God's Word about prosperity—to be willing and obedient—and good things started to happen. First a few. Then a few more. The longer we obeyed God and walked in faith about finances, the more those good things increased.

Just like the curse once overtook us, now the blessings of God overtake us. I like that much better.

The same thing will happen to you if you'll follow the instructions in Deuteronomy 28...hearken diligently unto the voice of the Lord, observe His command-ments...and all these blessings will overtake you.

## *Speak the Word*

*I hearken diligently to the voice of the Lord and obey all His commandments. All of His blessings come on me and overtake me!*
*Deuteronomy 28:1-2*

FOR FURTHER STUDY:

Deuteronomy 28:1-9

❦

DAILY SCRIPTURE READING:

2 Chronicles 19-20; Hebrews 7

*Kenneth*
# Put the Devil on the Run!

Jesus is the Christ. The Greek word *Christ* means "the Anointed One." And since Isaiah 10:27 tells us the yoke of the devil is destroyed by the anointing, we don't have to run scared when the devil comes against us, our loved ones or our nation. We can put him to flight with the blood of the Lamb, the Word of our testimony and the yoke-destroying Anointing of Jesus Christ Himself!

That's what Jesus expects us to do. He has already taken care of every kind of trouble that could ever come to the human family when He was put on the Cross, raised from the dead, and glorified at the right hand of the Father. He spoiled the principalities and powers of darkness. He triumphed over them and made an open show of them (Colossians 2:15). He stripped the devil of every last vestige of power.

Jesus has done His part. He has taken back the devil's authority over the earth and He has given it to us. Just before He ascended to heaven He said, *"All power is given unto me in heaven and in earth. Go ye therefore..."* (Matthew 28:18-19). He delegated His power and authority to us—His Church—then *"after he had offered one sacrifice for sins for ever, [he] sat down on the right hand of God; From henceforth expecting till his enemies be made his footstool"* (Hebrews 10:12-13).

He expects us to stand up in the midst of the storms of life and dominate those storms with faith-filled words. He expects us to look sickness and lack and terror in the face and say, "You get under my feet in the Name of Jesus!"

I realize you may not feel like you can do that today. You may be facing the greatest struggle of your life. It may really be hard right now. But, regardless of how you feel, if you're a born-again child of God, you can do it because the Bible says, *"Whatsoever is born of God overcometh the world: and this is the victory that overcometh the world, even our faith"* (1 John 5:4).

You are destined to overcome. You have that anointing—the Anointed One—residing on the inside of you if you are born again. Stir up that anointing. Stand up in the midst of the storm. Speak to it with all the power and authority that's been given to you. If you'll do that, you'll dominate the storm and put the devil on the run!

> "And it shall come to pass in that day, that his burden shall be taken away from off thy shoulder, and his yoke from off thy neck, and the yoke shall be destroyed because of the anointing."
> ISAIAH 10:27

FOR FURTHER STUDY:

Matthew 14:22-33

DAILY SCRIPTURE READING:

2 Chronicles 21-22; Hebrews 8

## *Speak the Word*

*Jesus has taken the burden from off my shoulder and the yoke from off my neck. His anointing has destroyed the yoke.*
*Isaiah 10:27*

# God Is Able!

Can you imagine what it would be like to have the richest measure of the divine presence, and become a body wholly filled and flooded with God Himself? I can! That's the Glory. That's the fullness of God's manifest presence in the earth and I want it!

I want not just my own life, but the whole earth to be filled with the Glory of God. In fact, I believe, as the Church, that we're falling short if we're satisfied with anything less.

We're not only cheating ourselves, we're cheating the world when we don't live in God's Glory. For when God's presence is manifested, the world is changed. Sinners get saved. Lives are forever altered.

Some people say we can't have revival now because people are just too calloused. They don't care about God anymore. But the greatest revivals in the world have come in the past, during the darkest of days. They've come when men's hearts were the coldest.

Well, our world is dark and it's getting darker. Men are belligerent against the things of God and openly show disrespect for Him. But that just tells me we're primed and ready for the manifest presence of God to fill the Church. It tells me we're ready for the Glory!

You may not feel like God can manifest His Glory through someone as unglorious as you. But let me assure you, He can. For in the closing words of Paul's prayer in Ephesians 3 he says, *"Now unto him that is able to do exceeding abundantly above all that we ask or think, according to the power that worketh in us, Unto him be glory in the church by Christ Jesus throughout all ages, world without end"* (verses 20-21).

That verse plainly says, GOD IS ABLE! He not only wants to manifest His fullness through you and me, He is *able!* You couldn't do it. I couldn't do it. Even if the whole Church got together and we all tried to fill ourselves with the Glory of God, we couldn't do it.

But God is able!

## Speak the Word

*God grants me out of the rich treasury of His glory to be strengthened and reinforced with mighty power in my inner man.*
*Ephesians 3:16, AMP*

"May He [God] grant you out of the rich treasury of His glory to be strengthened and reinforced with mighty power in the inner man by the (Holy) Spirit [Himself]— indwelling your innermost being and personality.... that you may be filled (through all your being) unto all the fullness of God—[that is] may have the richest measure of the divine Presence, and become a body wholly filled and flooded with God Himself!"
EPHESIANS 3:16, 19, AMP

FOR FURTHER STUDY:

Philippians 3:7-11

DAILY SCRIPTURE READING:

2 Chronicles 23-24; Hebrews 9

*Gloria*

# Live a Life of Power!

To live a life pleasing to God, you must have the spiritual strength to lay aside natural pursuits at times. How do you develop that strength? First and foremost by spending time in the Word and in prayer. As you spend time in His Word, by the power of that Word, the Holy Spirit will separate you not only from sin, but also from the unnecessary things in life. He will impart to you the spiritual might and grace you need to obey the instructions in Ephesians 4:22-24.

Those verses tell us that righteousness and holiness are two different things. Righteousness is the right-standing with God you gained when you were born again. The only thing you did to be made righteous was to make Jesus Christ the Lord of your life.

Holiness is another matter. You are not *made* holy. Holiness is the result of your choices. It's what you do with your time and your actions. It's your conduct. It comes when you make a decision of your will to live according to the precepts of the Lord. In short, holiness is doing those things that please the Father. To be *holy* is to be *"sanctified, and meet for the master's use"* (2 Timothy 2:21). *Sanctified* means "set apart." Set apart from what? From the world! God wants us to be so caught up in spiritual things that we lose interest in carnal activities and pursue Him with all our heart.

According to Romans 12:1-2, being wholly dedicated to God is your reasonable service. God expects us all to live holy. He says, *"Be ye holy; for I am holy"* (1 Peter 1:16).

When you see the power and Glory of God start to flow in greater measure through you, you won't regret you made those sacrifices. When you lay hands on a crippled person and see him made whole instantly, you'll be glad you turned down that carnal movie your friends went to see.

You may think I'm being overly dramatic, but I'm not. Those things are happening—not just at the hands of famous preachers or full-time ministers, but at the hands of everyday believers. They can happen in your life.

Determine to be a part of it all. Make up your mind not to be sidelined by doing petty things that please yourself. Dedicate yourself wholly to the Father. Choose to live holy. Choose to live a life of power! Choose to live for God!

> "Strip yourselves of your former nature...And be constantly renewed in the spirit of your mind...put on the new nature...created in....true righteousness and holiness."
> EPHESIANS 4:22-24, AMP

FOR FURTHER STUDY:

Romans 12:1-2

DAILY SCRIPTURE READING:

2 Chronicles 25-26;
Hebrews 10

## Speak the Word

*I strip myself of my former nature. I am constantly renewed in the spirit of my mind. I put on the new nature that is created in righteousness and true holiness.*
*Ephesians 4:22-24, AMP*

"Walk by faith,
not by sight."
2 CORINTHIANS
5:7

*Kenneth*

# Work Harder!

*"We just need to get out of the way and let God work. After all, we can't do anything anyway. He's the One Who is in control."*

Have you ever heard anyone say things like that?

I'm sure you have. In fact, if you're like most of us, you've said them yourself. At the time, they probably sounded very good. Very religious. Very humble.

But let me warn you, that kind of attitude can also be very dangerous. It can leave you sitting passively while the devil tears up everything around you. It can leave you in tears, begging God to fix a situation for you when He was saying all along, "Take care of it yourself! I'll back you. I've given you My Name. I've given you My authority. I've given you My own faith. Now, use it!"

Right now, especially, we must be on guard against such spiritual passivity, because we are on the edge of a great outpouring of God's Glory. It has already begun, and it will become much stronger. During times like these, even believers who know better can get lazy. They can look around them at the signs and wonders God is working and say, "I guess I don't need faith anymore. It looks like God is taking care of everything Himself now."

Don't make that mistake. Even though God is moving mightily in end-time manifestations, He still expects His people to walk by faith (2 Corinthians 5:7) and live by faith (Hebrews 10:38).

Don't get lazy just because the Glory is here. Work harder! Spend more time in the Word and develop your faith to a greater measure than ever before. Then, as Smith Wigglesworth once said, stretch your faith as far as it will go, knowing that the Holy Ghost has nine manifestations of His own to add to it if you need them.

Get yourself ready so that when someone falls to the floor under the healing gift of the Spirit, you'll be there beside them with your Bible, helping them up and saying, "Now, friend, let me show you how to stay well."

We've come to the last of the last days. God's schedule demands that He pour out His Spirit in great manifestations of power now. You'll see them everywhere. In churches all over the world, the cloud of God's Glory will get so thick at times, the people won't be able to see one another.

God's manifest presence will fall as rain—on the just and the unjust. It will fall on those who have learned to walk by faith and those who haven't. But that rain will remain, not on those who are sitting passively waiting on God to take control, but on those who have dared to believe and behave as joint heirs of Jesus. It will abide on the household of faith!

**FOR FURTHER STUDY:**

Hebrews 10:32-39

## *Speak the Word*

*I am just, and I live by faith.*
*Hebrews 10:38*

**DAILY SCRIPTURE READING:**

2 Chronicles 27-28;
Hebrews 11

*Gloria*

# Be Confident in His Medicine

JULY 8

❦

"Having done all, to stand. Stand...."
EPHESIANS 6:13-14

As you put God's prescription for health (Proverbs 4:20-24) to work in your life, don't be discouraged if you don't see immediate results. Although many times healing comes instantly, there also are times when it takes place more gradually.

So don't let lingering symptoms cause you to doubt. After all, when you go to the doctor, you don't always feel better right away. The medication he gives you often takes some time before it begins to work. But you don't allow the delay to discourage you.

When you take God's medicine you are really "treating" your spirit, which is the source of supernatural life and health for your physical body.

So release that same kind of confidence in God's medicine. Realize that the moment you begin to take it, the healing process begins. Keep your expectancy high and make up your mind to continue standing on the Word until you can see and feel the total physical effects of God's healing power.

When the devil whispers words of doubt and unbelief to you, when he suggests that the Word is not working, deal with those thoughts immediately. Cast them down (2 Corinthians 10:5). Speak out loud if necessary and say, "Devil, I rebuke you. I bind you from my mind. I will not believe your lies." Then say for your own hearing and benefit something to confirm your faith like, "God has sent His Word to heal me, and His Word never fails. That Word went to work in my body the instant I believed it. So as far as I am concerned, my days of sickness are over. I declare that Jesus bore my sickness, weakness and pain, and I am forever free."

Then, *"having done all, to stand. Stand"* until your healing is fully manifested (Ephesians 6:12-14). Steadfastly hold your ground. Remember, your confidence is in God's Word, His medicine...not in your symptoms.

## *Speak the Word*

*When I have done all to stand, I continue to stand.*
*Ephesians 6:13-14*

FOR FURTHER STUDY:

Psalm 107:1-20

❦

DAILY SCRIPTURE READING:

2 Chronicles 29-30;
Hebrews 12

❧

"You hold
a sacred
appointment,
you have been
given an
unction—you
have been
anointed
by the
Holy One."
1 JOHN
2:20, AMP

# You Are an "Anointed!"

We've thrown around the word *anointing* in religious circles for years without really understanding what it means. But if we're to walk in the power of the gospel, we must let it become a reality to us.

The anointing is God's presence, His essence. It's the thing that makes God be God. The anointing is God on flesh enabling flesh (you and me) to do those things that are impossible for flesh to do.

For instance, flesh can't heal anyone. Even Jesus' flesh couldn't heal anyone. His flesh came from Mary. It was as human as hers. Yet His perfect, sinless flesh speaking the Words of a perfect, sinless God, caused God's Anointing to be upon Him without measure (see John 3:34).

It's not hard for our minds to grasp the fact that the anointing was upon Jesus. What's tough to comprehend is that the same burden-removing, yoke-destroying anointing that was on Him is available to us.

"Oh, Brother Copeland, that can't be. After all, our flesh is not sinless."

No, but God counts it that way if we'll stay under the blood. That's what grace is all about—*giving us the anointing when we don't deserve it!* Our very name, *Christians,* means "the anointeds."

Just like Jesus couldn't heal in His own flesh, neither can you. But in the anointing, Jesus did bring healing, and so can you. You see, everything you need to do today can be done in the Anointed One and His Anointing.

His Anointing is on you, in you and all over you. Because of it, you have been enabled to do things you couldn't normally do...whether it's day-to-day responsibilities, or laying hands on someone and releasing the healing power of God. You can be and do everything God created you to be and do in His Anointing. You *are* an anointed!

## *Speak the Word*

*I have been anointed and given an unction by the Holy One.*
*1 John 2:20, AMP*

FOR FURTHER
STUDY:

Acts 8:5-8

❧

DAILY SCRIPTURE
READING:

2 Chronicles 31-33;
Hebrews 13;
James 1

*Gloria*

# Your Natural *Supernatural* Disposition

The fruit of the spirit are so vital and so powerful that if I had to choose between the fruit and the gifts of the Spirit (which, thank the Lord, I don't!)—I'd choose the fruit. Why? Because it's possible to have spectacular gifts of the Spirit manifesting in your life, yet still get so far off-course you end up shipwrecked, a spiritual failure.

When you have the fruit of the spirit flowing in your life, however, you can be assured you will never fall!

That may sound extreme—but it's true. I know it is because the Bible makes that very promise in 2 Peter 1. Yet we've all discovered that walking according to our new nature is not a stroll in the park. There's a struggle involved. Galatians 5:17 tells us the desires of the flesh are opposed to the desires of the spirit. So when we decide to obey the desires and promptings of our reborn spirit, our flesh still wants control.

The way to keep from losing that battle is found in Galatians 5:16: We're to walk and live habitually in the spirit. Hebrews 5:14 reveals that our flesh is trained by practice.

Sometimes when I tell people that walking in the spirit is the secret to having the fruit in their life, people think I'm telling them to do something mysterious and difficult. But actually, walking in the spirit is quite simple. You do it by putting God first place in your life. You do it by maintaining fellowship with Him through His Word and through prayer—yielding in obedience to Him in everything.

As you yield to the fruit of the spirit within you, something happens to your character. It is transformed. You are transformed. You develop what I call your natural *supernatural* disposition. It's the disposition of character that you were originally created to have. It's what God intended for you all along...not what you've developed in life through the world's input.

But it won't come automatically. You'll have to spend time in the Word and in prayer. You'll have to choose to yield to love, and joy and peace, and so on. And when you do, you'll be yielding to the best you've ever been. You'll be yielding to your natural *supernatural* disposition!

For Further Study:

Galatians 5:22-26

❧

Daily Scripture Reading:

2 Chronicles 34-35; James 2

## *Speak the Word*

*I give diligence to make my calling and election sure by walking in the fruit of the spirit. Therefore, I never fall.*
*2 Peter 1:5-8,10*

❧

"Giving all diligence, add to your faith virtue; and to virtue knowledge; And to knowledge temperance; and to temperance patience; and to patience godliness; And to godliness brotherly kindness; and to brotherly kindness charity. For if these things be in you, and abound, they make you that ye shall neither be barren nor unfruitful in the knowledge of our Lord Jesus Christ.... Give diligence to make your calling and election sure: for if ye do these things, ye shall never fall."

2 Peter
1:5-8, 10

> "Your sins are forgiven you for his name's sake."
>
> 1 JOHN 2:12

# Because of the Blood

Just what is the basis for the forgiveness God has extended to us? First John 2:12 tells us the answer..."*for his name's sake.*" In other words, God has put His Name on an agreement. He has given us His oath that, because Jesus poured out His blood and paid the price for sin, all men are forgiven in His sight. He has put His Name to a document which says He has reconciled the whole world to Himself by Jesus the Anointed, and He is no longer holding anyone's sin against them. (Read 2 Corinthians 5:18-19.)

Why did God put His Name on that document? Because of the blood of Jesus. God forgives our sin because *He honors the blood.* He has said, *I will accept any man, any woman, any child from any place in the world regardless of any sin they have committed. I swore it in the blood and I will do it because of My Name.*

Considering our sin, it would be just for God to say to us, "Get out of My sight. What are you doing walking in here wanting to be a part of My family? Look at your mean, ugly self! Who do you think you are wanting to come into My heaven?"

But, praise God, He doesn't consider our sin. He considers the blood of Jesus. He administers justice based on His blood-sworn oath of forgiveness and, because He honors that blood, He justifies us by wiping out all our sin. The Bible says He remembers our sins no more!

Let me tell you, when I sin there is no way in this world I would go before the throne of grace asking God to forgive me on the basis of how many years I've been in the ministry. I wouldn't pull a dumb stunt like that. I'll just go in and plead the blood of Jesus, because I know God honors the blood.

That's where my faith rests. I don't have to wonder what God is going to do. I don't have to wonder if He will forgive me. I know He will because He swore it in the blood of His own Son.

## *Speak the Word*

*My sins are forgiven because of the blood of Jesus
and for His Name's sake.*
*1 John 2:12*

FOR FURTHER STUDY:

Romans 3:19-26

❧

DAILY SCRIPTURE READING:

2 Chronicles 36;
Ezra 1;
James 3

*Gloria*

# Walk in Love

How much do we really know about love? We've talked about it. We're familiar with all the scriptures about it. And we've heard so many sermons about it that, if we're not careful, we'll just let them flow in one ear and out the other.

But in spite of all that, most of us don't know the first thing about the real power of love. For instance, researchers have found that hostility and the stress it causes are physically damaging, but walking in love is good for your health. And the benefits don't end there.

*Agape* love, God's love, is a new kind of power. It makes you the master of every situation. As long as you walk in love, you cannot be hurt and you cannot fail. No weapon that is formed against you will prosper. No one even has the power to hurt your feelings, because you are not ruled by feelings but by God's love. You are loving as He loves.

E. W. Kenyon accurately tagged this *agape* love "a new kind of selfishness." You no longer seek your own success, yet your success is guaranteed!

This love is revolutionary. If we fully understood the great return from living in God's love, we'd probably be competing with each other, each of us trying to love the other more. And without a doubt, everyone would emerge from that competition a winner!

Think about that. When you're yielding to love, you'll be enjoying the best God has to offer. Love. Joy. Peace. The whole world is chasing after those things. People are trying to reach out and get them through drugs and alcohol and immorality. But they can't. The things that are against God only draw you further from a life of peace and well-being.

The only way to achieve that kind of life is to receive Jesus as your Lord and Savior...and learn to yield to the love of God placed inside of you. It's really rather simple. You can live in hostility and be stressed out...or you can walk in love...and have supernatural peace.

FOR FURTHER STUDY:

John 14:27-31

DAILY SCRIPTURE READING:

Ezra 2-3;
James 4

## Speak the Word

*Above all I put on love and enfold myself with the bond of perfectness which binds everything together in harmony.*
*Colossians 3:14, AMP*

"Therefore, as God's chosen people, holy and dearly loved, clothe yourselves with compassion, kindness, humility, gentleness and patience. Bear with each other and forgive whatever grievances you may have against one another. Forgive as the Lord forgave you. And over all these virtues put on love, which binds them all together in perfect unity. Let the peace of Christ rule in your hearts, since as members of one body you were called to peace."
COLOSSIANS 3:12-15, NIV

> "For every one that useth milk is unskilful in the word of righteousness: for he is a babe. But strong meat belongeth to them that are of full age, even those who by reason of use have their senses exercised to discern both good and evil."
>
> HEBREWS 5:13-14

# Never Play Fair!

Look at those verses again. How do they say to bring your senses in line? First by becoming skillful in the word of righteousness, and second, by reason of use, or practice.

You have to practice walking in the things of the Spirit. Practice walking by faith. Practice walking in love. Practice, practice, practice!

At first, your flesh will rebel against it. Since it's not been trained that way, it will be contrary for a while. Some people don't realize that, therefore, they get discouraged when they stumble around and fall the first few times they try to walk by the Spirit in some area.

Don't be that way. Keep practicing. Pick out someone who is nearly impossible to love and start practicing on them. If you strike out the first time at bat, don't worry about it. There are more than three strikes in this game. You just keep swinging until you hit.

Somebody once asked me, "Don't you ever have any failures?"

No, I don't...because I don't play nine-inning games. I play until I win. I will have a lot of opportunities to fail if I receive failure. My shortcomings are many. I've fallen on my face many times. But I don't count that as failure. I just count that as practice. But when I win, praise God, that's for real!

"But Brother Copeland, that's not playing fair."

You show me in the Word of God where it says we have to play fair with the devil. I don't play fair with him. I go in with a stacked deck. I go in with the Name of Jesus that's above every name. There's nothing fair about that. But that's OK, because the devil is already whipped. We don't have to play fair with him anymore, we just go in and exercise the victory.

## *Speak the Word*

*I train myself to win as I practice walking in the things of the Spirit.*
*Hebrews 5:13-14*

FOR FURTHER STUDY:

Hebrews 5:12-14

DAILY SCRIPTURE READING:

Ezra 4-5;
James 5

*Gloria*
# Take the High Way

If you want to accurately understand the leading of God, then get better acquainted with His high ways than you are with the world's low ways. Focus your time and attention on Him and His Word.

Jesus operated that way. The Bible says He got up long before daylight to pray. Sometimes He spent the entire night communicating with God.

Jesus made spending time with God the number one priority in His life. That's how He knew what God wanted Him to do. That's how He perfectly pleased Him. He spent time with Him.

Jesus' disciples knew by watching His lifestyle that His power was connected to the time He spent praying. That's why they asked Him, *"Lord, teach us to pray"* (Luke 11:1).

The instructions Jesus received in those times with God weren't always easy. In the Garden of Gethsemane, He sweated blood and said, *"O my Father, if it be possible, let this cup pass from me: nevertheless not as I will, but as thou wilt"* (Matthew 26:39).

> "My thoughts are not your thoughts, neither are your ways my ways, saith the Lord. For as the heavens are higher than the earth, so are my ways higher than your ways, and my thoughts than your thoughts."
> ISAIAH 55:8-9

You may be in a type of Garden of Gethsemane right now. God may be telling you to do something your flesh just doesn't want to do. He may have been telling you for months to get up earlier every morning so you can spend more time in prayer or in the Word. And you've been thinking for months, *Yes, I really ought to do that*...and then hitting the snooze button on your alarm and going back to sleep.

Perhaps God has been speaking to you about other adjustments you need to make in your life. He may be saying, *This is what you can do about this situation. Here's what you need to change.*

No matter how insignificant God's instructions may seem to you right now, you need to take them seriously. You need to obey them. What may seem of little significance now, may cause you to avoid serious consequences later. God's directions are always in your best interest.

If you'll spend time with Him, you'll learn His ways—and you can forget the world's low ways. You'll learn to take the high way!

FOR FURTHER STUDY:

Matthew 26:36-46

DAILY SCRIPTURE READING:

Ezra 6-7;
1 Peter 1

## *Speak the Word*

*As I spend time in the presence of God, His thoughts become my thoughts and His ways become my ways.*
*Isaiah 55:8-9*

> "Christ was raised up from the dead by the glory of the Father, even so [or by that same glory] we also should walk in newness of life."
> ROMANS 6:4

# Expect the Glory

When Ezekiel saw God in His Glory, he said He was a fire from the loins up and from the loins down (Ezekiel 8:2). The fire of God is called the Glory. The wind of God is called the Glory. The smoke of God is called the Glory. The fullness of God is called the Glory.

It is all the Glory because the Glory of God refers to the supernatural life and essence of God...the very presence of God manifested—seen or heard.

"Well, Brother Copeland, that kind of awesome Glory is reserved for God and God alone."

Not according to the Bible. In fact, Psalm 8:5 tells us that in the beginning man was crowned with that Glory.

That's right! In the Garden of Eden, man and woman weren't walking around unclothed. God had crowned them with the same fire and flame of beauty that was on God Himself.

Do you know what it means to crown? It means to anoint! God put His hands on their heads and crowned them with His own presence and Glory so that they began to shine just like God shines.

They weren't standing out there vulnerable to the elements. They were surrounded and protected by a shimmering force field of Glory.

That Glory was lost to mankind when Adam sinned. Most people know that. But what they don't realize is that the Glory was restored when Jesus was resurrected! Romans 6:4 says so.

According to the Word of God, you and I are supposed to be walking in the Glory. We are anointed with the Glory of God. And everything we need is in the Glory. Your healing and more are in the Glory. Your finances and more are in the Glory. Your heart's desire and more are in the Glory. So expect the Glory! Expect God's presence to be manifested in your life. Lift your expectations to expect it. In His presence is fullness of joy!

## Speak the Word

*I walk in newness of life by the same glory that raised up Christ from the dead.*
*Romans 6:4*

FOR FURTHER STUDY:

Psalm 8;
Ezekiel 8:1-4

DAILY SCRIPTURE READING:

Ezra 8-9;
1 Peter 2

*Gloria*

# Build Your Foundation First

JULY 16

"Beloved, I wish above all things that thou mayest prosper and be in health, even as thy soul prospereth."
3 JOHN 2

Never try to build a house without first laying a foundation. I don't care how eager you are to get it finished, how excited you are about filling it with furniture and decorating it all just right—take time to put down a solid foundation first. If you don't, that house will be so unstable, it will soon come tumbling down.

That's simple advice, isn't it? Everyone with any sense at all knows it. Yet, in the spiritual realm, people make that mistake all the time. They see a blessing God has promised them in His Word, and they are so eager to have it, they ignore the foundational basics of godly living and pursue just that one thing.

That's especially true in the area of prosperity. Often, people are so desperate for a quick financial fix, they just pull a few prosperity promises out of the Bible and try to believe them—without allowing God to change anything else in their lives. Of course, it doesn't work and those people end up disappointed.

It's important to truly grasp what the Apostle John was saying in 3 John 2. Notice, he didn't just say, "I want you to prosper." He said, "I want you to prosper as your soul prospers." He tied financial prosperity to the prosperity of our mind, will and emotions.

God's plan is for us to grow financially as we grow spiritually. He knows it is dangerous to put great wealth into the hands of someone who is too spiritually immature to handle it.

You can see dramatic evidence of that fact in the lives of people who have acquired financial riches through this world's system, apart from God. In most cases, such riches just help people to die younger and in more misery than they would have if they'd been poorer.

In light of that, it's easy to see why God wants us to increase financially at the same rate we increase spiritually. He wants us to outgrow our fleshly foolishness so our prosperity will bring us blessing and not harm.

"But, Gloria," you say, "I need financial help fast!"

Then get busy growing. Get busy building your foundation for prosperity. How? By finding out what God says in His Word and doing it.

Keep in mind that the foundation of prosperity is a continual lifestyle built on the Word of God. It is doing whatever God tells you to do, thinking whatever He tells you to think, and saying whatever He tells you to say. Godly prosperity is the result of putting God's Word first place in your life—both to hear it and do it. So start building now!

FOR FURTHER STUDY:

Luke 6:47-49

DAILY SCRIPTURE READING:

Ezra 10;
Nehemiah 1-2;
1 Peter 3-4

## Speak the Word

*As my soul prospers, I prosper in my finances and in my health.*
*3 John 2*

∽

"Now, Lord,
behold their
threatenings:
and grant
unto thy
servants, that
with all
boldness they
may speak thy
word."
ACTS 4:29

# Preach...With True Boldness!

Have you ever noticed that miracles most often occur among people who are bold about God?

Boldness and the miraculous are so closely tied together that some people "try" to act bold just to get things to happen. Of course, it doesn't work. I've seen people pray just as loud as they could in a restaurant just to prove they were bold about God, and all they did was irritate everybody in the place.

Yet someone with true boldness can do the same thing and great power will be released. Smith Wigglesworth had that kind of boldness. I have a friend who was with him one day in London in a cafeteria. Before Mr. Wigglesworth sat down to eat, he looked around and in his powerful, booming voice he said, "I didn't notice anybody praying over this meal and giving God thanks." Then he began to pray.

Everybody in there dropped their fork and bowed their head. When he got through, people all over the room said, "Amen!" Mr. Wigglesworth's prayer brought that whole cafeteria to a standstill because he had boldness from God.

Most people hear that and say, "Oh, I could never be that bold."

But let me tell you, if you're a believer and you have a Bible—you can be! To find out the secret behind real spiritual boldness, read Acts 4. In that chapter, the boldness of God came on an entire congregation of believers. It didn't happen by chance. It wasn't an unexplainable "faith accident." Boldness came on those people for a specific reason because of a specific thing, and it came in answer to a specific prayer.

Here's the situation. Peter and John had ministered healing to the cripple at the gate called Beautiful. That miracle had so stirred the city that the Jewish religious leaders had taken them into custody and threatened them severely, charging them never to preach in the Name of Jesus again in Jerusalem.

And the first thing the congregation did was start praising God. They'd just been threatened by the local authorities, but they went to the Higher Authority. They went straight to the King of kings and Lord of lords!

Then, in verse 29 they asked for boldness to speak the Word!

These believers didn't major on the threats. They majored on the Word. Every word they prayed came from the written Word.

We can learn something from that. When there's a threat, preach the Word. When there is sickness, preach the Word. When there is lack, preach the Word. When the devil comes on the scene, preach the Word! Preach the Word in season and out! And when you preach it, preach it with boldness!

## Speak the Word

*God grants me boldness so that I can speak His Word.*
*Acts 4:29*

FOR FURTHER
STUDY:

Acts 4:23-33

∽

DAILY SCRIPTURE
READING:

Nehemiah 3-4;
1 Peter 5

# Growing in the Grocery Store

Contrary to what you might think, you don't have to wait for a major trial to develop patience. We have wonderful opportunities in all those small but irritating situations we encounter every day.

In fact, developing your patience a little at a time, in all those everyday situations, is what will build a foundation for you to stand on when major trials come.

I ran into one such situation once in the grocery store. I was in a hurry, so I chose the express line. There were only a couple of people in line and they just had a few items to buy, so I didn't think it would take long.

But that clerk was so slow! As my frustration mounted I thought, *They ought to put a sign here that says "Slow-Motion Line"!*

What was that? An opportunity to exercise patience.

Such opportunities are important, because when you exercise patience, it grows. If you'll use it in small things, it will be strong enough to handle the bigger things when they come along. Every fruit of the spirit increases in you as you exercise it.

Remember that the next time some little aggravation is about to make you lose your temper. Instead of saying, "I've had it," say, "No, in Jesus' Name, I choose to yield to the force of patience God has put within me. I believe I'll just count this slow grocery line to be a joy and use it as an opportunity to grow!"

> "For ye have need of patience, that, after ye have done the will of God, ye might receive the promise."
> HEBREWS 10:36

## Speak the Word

*I let patience have her perfect work, that I may be perfect and entire, wanting nothing.*
*James 1:4*

FOR FURTHER STUDY:

2 Peter 1:3-8

DAILY SCRIPTURE READING:

Nehemiah 5-6;
2 Peter 1

> "For God hath
> not given
> us the spirit
> of fear; but of
> power, and of
> love, and of a
> sound mind."
> 2 TIMOTHY 1:7

# Get the Right Perspective

When the Israelites came out of Egypt, they had just seen a marvelous display of God's miraculous power. Yet, as they faced the Red Sea with the Egyptian army at their backs, they turned on Moses and said, "Is it because there were no graves in Egypt that thou hast taken us away to die in the wilderness?" (Exodus 14:11).

What could possibly have caused these people to doubt God and make such a traitorous statement after all He had already done for them? Fear.

They began to fear what the enemy could do to them, and they were overwhelmed by the drive toward self-preservation.

That apparently innocent desire you have to protect yourself will cost you dearly when it comes to walking with God. It infected the Israelites to such a degree that they forgot the signs and wonders. Suddenly they saw themselves as just people again—not people with whom God dwells, but just people.

If you don't watch out, Satan will try to give you that perspective too. When you start believing the promises of God and marching toward victory over sickness or sin or lack, Satan will tell you that you're just a natural person.

He'll tell you that you can't trust the supernatural power of God to pull you through. He'll get you into a natural rather than a supernatural perspective. Instead of walking in the fear of God, you'll walk in the fear of the devil and his work. You'll walk in the fear of death or the fear of sickness or the fear of poverty or something else. And those fears will keep you from listening to and obeying the Word of God.

That's why you need to learn to think with the mind of Christ. You need to live with your thoughts on the things of God instead of the things of the world, to come to a place where you're resting in the power of God.

God wants us to rest in His power. He wants us to know Him so well and trust Him so much that when Satan tries to threaten us, when he tells us we're going to go broke or we're going to die or whatever manipulation he uses, we just laugh at him.

You and I need to come to a place in this world where we trust God with every detail of our lives. Start practicing that today. Believe His Word. Speak it to your problems...and watch faith rise up. Then you'll have the right perspective and victory will be yours!

## *Speak the Word*

*God has not given me the spirit of fear, but of power, and of love, and of a sound mind.*
*2 Timothy 1:7*

FOR FURTHER
STUDY:

Exodus 14:8-14

DAILY SCRIPTURE
READING:

Nehemiah 7-8;
2 Peter 2

# Usher In His Presence

❧

"Let us offer the sacrifice of praise to God continually, that is, the fruit of our lips giving thanks to his name."
HEBREWS 13:15

Oftentimes we think about praising God, but because we don't feel like it, we shrug off that prompting in our spirit, and don't do it. But God is worthy of our praise—whether we feel like praising Him or not. We must realize that praise is not governed by our emotions. Hebrews 13:15 says we are to praise Him continually.

Under the Old Covenant, when the people had problems, they went to the priest and he would offer a sacrifice to God. That would bring God on the scene.

Today, under the New Covenant, we are to do the same. Only we are the priests under God (Revelation 5:10). As we offer up the sacrifices of praise before our Most High Priest, Jesus, our communication with God is great.

Psalm 22:3 says God inhabits the praises of His people. Our praise brings God personally on the scene. At times of high praise, the *shekinah* Glory of God will fill an entire place with His sweet presence.

When Solomon finished building the house of the Lord, the trumpeters and singers lifted their voices as one, and with trumpets, cymbals and instruments of music, they praised the Lord saying, *"For he is good; for his mercy endureth for ever."* The Glory of God filled the house so that the priests could not even minister because of the cloud (2 Chronicles 5:13-14). God Himself inhabited the praises of His people.

So usher His presence into your situation. Praise Him in the midst of your needs. Praise Him, regardless of your feelings. Obey the Word and praise Him continually. He is worthy to be praised! To praise when you don't feel like it is an act of honor. God said, "He that honors Me, him will I honor."

## *Speak the Word*

*I offer the sacrifice of praise to God continually.*
*The fruit of my lips gives thanks to His Name.*
*Hebrews 13:15*

FOR FURTHER
STUDY:

Revelation 5:7-10

❧

DAILY SCRIPTURE
READING:

Nehemiah 9-10;
2 Peter 3

JULY 21

❧

"Be strong in
the grace that
is in Christ
Jesus."
2 TIMOTHY 2:1

# Be Strong in Grace

Paul instructs us to be strong in grace. But what is grace? And what does it do? Titus 2 tells us, *"For the grace of God that bringeth salvation hath appeared to all men, Teaching us that, denying ungodliness and wordly lusts, we should live soberly, righteously, and godly, in this present world"* (verses 11-12).

Grace teaches us. It teaches us how to live in freedom in this world.

Whenever the Spirit of God corrects you, whenever He points out a mistake you're making or speaks to you about something you're doing that is grieving Him, don't be mad. Be glad! It's the grace of God teaching you something to make your life better.

Grow strong in that grace by spending time every day in prayer. Live each day expecting the Spirit of God to counsel and instruct you about the things in your life—big and small.

*Expect* to hear from Him. If you don't, you won't listen for Him, and you're not likely to hear Him because He speaks in a still, small voice. As a rule, His words are quiet words. They're not overwhelming words. If you don't have a spiritual ear tuned to heaven, you'll miss them.

So, every morning of your life spend time praying in the spirit, talking to the Father and reminding yourself that the Holy Ghost is inside you, constantly teaching and guiding you. Become strong in the grace of God.

## *Speak the Word*

*I am strong in the grace that is in Christ Jesus.*
*2 Timothy 2:1*

FOR FURTHER
STUDY:

Psalm 32

❧

DAILY SCRIPTURE
READING:

Nehemiah 11-12;
1 John 1

*Kenneth*

# The Word Is Alive

How can God's Word become one thing for one person and something else for another?

Because it is alive! The Word of God is full of life. Full! Therefore, it administers life wherever it is applied. It doesn't matter how dark and deadly your circumstances may be. There is enough life in God's Word to totally over-whelm all the death that the world, the devil or circumstances can bring you.

The Bible likens the Word to a natural seed. Every seed has within it all the DNA required to produce whatever kind of seed it is. If it's a peach seed, all that is required to be a peach tree is in the seed.

In the same way, the Word of God has the supernatural life within it to fulfill the promises of God in your life. You plant it in your heart as a seed, but when it comes up, it produces salvation, prosperity, healing, deliverance—whatever God has said belongs to you!

If you have a need in your life today, go to the Word of God. Find a promise to stand on regarding your need...begin planting that seed in your heart. Say it aloud over and over as you let that Word take root inside of you. Let that Word become real to you. And then watch it come alive!

"For the word of God is quick, and powerful, and sharper than any twoedged sword, piercing even to the dividing asunder of soul and spirit, and of the joints and marrow, and is a discerner of the thoughts and intents of the heart."

HEBREWS 4:12

## *Speak the Word*

*The Word of God is alive and powerful. It discerns
the thoughts and intents of my heart.*

*Hebrews 4:12*

FOR FURTHER STUDY:

Psalm 119:50, 93

DAILY SCRIPTURE READING:

Nehemiah 13;
Esther 1;
1 John 2

> ❧
>
> "And he gave
> heed unto
> them,
> expecting
> to receive
> something
> of them."
> ACTS 3:5

# Stick Your Neck Out

Real Bible hope is not "wishing." It is earnest, intense expectation that what God has said will come to pass.

How do you develop that kind of hope? You stay in the Word until your neck stretches out!

"Till my what stretches where?"

You read right...till your neck stretches out! I particularly like this definition of hope because I know what it means to have my neck stretched.

When I was a little boy, my grandfather was my hero. He was a full-blooded Cherokee Indian and I wanted to act like him, look like him, curse like him and spit like him—much to my mother's chagrin. When my mother would tell me that he and my grandmother were coming to see us, I would get so excited I could hardly wait.

Every minute or two, I'd run to the window to see if they had arrived. Every noise sent me running for the door. I tell you, my neck was stretched out in anticipation. My Pawpaw was coming and I expected him any moment.

That may sound like a simple example, but the Lord once told me if people would just expect Him to move as much as a child expects his grandparents to arrive, He could move on their situation and change things drastically by the power of His Spirit.

That's what happened in Acts 3 to the crippled man at the gate Beautiful. He had been sitting by that gate begging, his head down and his eyes to the ground. But when Peter and John walked by and said, *"Look on us!"* that man lifted his head and began to expect. Hope rose up in him because he was *"expecting to receive something of them."*

What are you hoping for? Life? Health? Something you know you're called to do? What you're hoping for is what you're thinking, speaking and meditating. Line up your thoughts and words with your faith, with your hope. Begin to expect God to move on your situation and change things drastically. Expect him to do something. Expect Him to come on the scene...just like a little child expects his grandparents to arrive.

## Speak the Word

*I give heed to God, expecting to receive from Him.*
*Acts 3:5*

FOR FURTHER
STUDY:

Acts 3:1-11

❧

DAILY SCRIPTURE
READING:

Esther 2-4;
1 John 3-4

*Gloria*
# Who Is a Wise and Faithful Servant?

We are living in an exciting time. Jesus' return is soon! But it's also a sobering time. It is not the time to be lazy about spiritual things. This is not the time to ride the fence...there won't be anybody on the fence much longer anyway. A separation of light and darkness is coming, and either you're going to go on with God or you're going back.

In the story of the 10 virgins in Matthew 25, it wasn't until the foolish five actually heard the shout that they decided to get ready. *"And while they went to buy,"* it says, *"the bridegroom came"* (verse 10).

Have you ever noticed with some people that their timing is always off? But if you listen to the Spirit of God, your timing is good. You'll be at the right place at the right time. *"While they went to buy, the bridegroom came; and they that were ready went in with him to the marriage: and the door was shut."*

Are you ready...or not? Not only are you and I in a place where we've never been before, but the world has never been where it is now. We're coming to the end of the age.

We must get to the place where we hear from God and do what He says—where we stay ready to be used. It won't work to wait until the last moment and then try to get ready. We are the Church. We have a job to do before He comes.

Matthew 24:44-45 says, *"Therefore be ye also ready: for in such an hour as ye think not the Son of man cometh. Who then is a faithful and wise servant, whom his lord hath made ruler over his household, to give them meat in due season?"*

Right there in my Bible beside that question, *"Who then is a faithful and wise servant?"* I've written in my Bible margin, *"Gloria!"* You do the same thing. You are the only one who can make that decision in your life. Write your name by that verse and say, "Lord, I'm going to be a faithful and wise servant. I'm going to be ready!"

> "Now it is high time to awake out of sleep: for now is our salvation nearer than when we believed. The night is far spent, the day is at hand: let us therefore cast off the works of darkness, and let us put on the armour of light."
> ROMANS 13:11-12

## *Speak the Word*

*I am a faithful and wise servant of the Lord Jesus Christ.*
*Matthew 24:45*

FOR FURTHER STUDY:

Matthew 25:1-13

DAILY SCRIPTURE READING:

Esther 5-6;
1 John 5

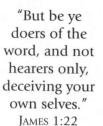

> "But be ye doers of the word, and not hearers only, deceiving your own selves."
>
> JAMES 1:22

*Gloria*

# More Than Mental Assent

One of the greatest enemies of real faith is what's called "mental assent." People who operate in mental assent read the Word and think they believe it. But when pressure comes, they don't act on it.

Mental assenters say, "I believe the Bible from cover to cover. I believe I'm healed by the stripes of Jesus because the Bible says so."

But when sickness actually comes and attacks their bodies, they stop saying, "By His stripes I'm healed" and start saying, "I'm sick."

Real faith believes what the Word says even though your eyes and your feelings tell you something different. Faith doesn't care what the symptoms are. It doesn't care how the circumstances look. It's not moved by what the banker says, or the doctor, or the lawyer, or the bill collector.

Faith in God's Word will change the symptoms. It will change the bank. It will bring the money to get the bills paid. Faith will turn every defeat into victory. It is God's success formula!

But you have to give that faith an opportunity to work. You have to keep God's Word in your mouth and meditate on it in your heart *"that you may observe and do according to all that is written in it; for then you shall make your way prosperous, and then shall you deal wisely and have good success"* (Joshua 1:8, AMP).

So determine in your heart today to speak God's Word out your mouth and to speak nothing contrary to that Word. Don't be a mental assenter. Be a mighty person of faith. Be a doer of the Word!

## Speak the Word

*I am a doer of the Word of God, and not just a hearer only.*

*James 1:22*

FOR FURTHER STUDY:

Matthew 7:24-29

DAILY SCRIPTURE READING:

Esther 7-8;
2 John

*Gloria*

# Jesus Lives in You!

I'm always looking for revelations from God that will change my life, aren't you? Divine insights that will take me to new levels of life and Glory.

A few years ago, God gave me just such a revelation. It was so vast that I've been meditating on it ever since. I can tell it to you in five words: *Jesus Christ lives in me.*

"But, Gloria," you say, "that's no big revelation. All Christians know that!"

No, they don't. Oh, they may know it with their heads, but not with their hearts. If they did, the Church today would be an entirely different Church, so full of the Glory of God that sinners would be beating down our doors to get in and get saved. We would be a Church where miracles and healings were not unusual, but commonplace. A Church so full of the grace of God that even worldly people would wonder at the power of God in our lives.

Paul describes in Ephesians 5:27, *"a glorious church, not having spot, or wrinkle, or any such thing; but...holy and without blemish."*

Praise God, as born-again believers, we have the hope of Glory! That means we can confidently expect the fullness of God's manifest presence in our lives. We don't have to just wish for it or read about other people who have experienced it. We can live in God's Glory ourselves. We can do this because Jesus, the Anointed One, the Lord of Glory Himself, lives inside every one of us!

I want you to think about it. Let the thrilling reality of it start to sink into your heart. Let it begin to dawn on you that Jesus, the Anointed One—not just Jesus as He was when He walked on the earth 2,000 years ago, but the glorified, resurrected Jesus—really lives inside you!

> "Even the mystery which hath been hid from ages and from generations, but now is made manifest to his [God's] saints: To whom God would make known what is the riches of the glory of this mystery among the Gentiles; which is Christ in you, the hope of glory."
> COLOSSIANS 1:26-27

## Speak the Word

*The Anointed One and His Anointing lives in me.*
*He is my hope and expectation of Glory!*
*Colossians 1:27*

FOR FURTHER
STUDY:

2 Corinthians
2:14-17

DAILY SCRIPTURE
READING:

Esther 9-10;
3 John

> "For he that cometh to God must believe that he is, and that he is a rewarder of them that diligently seek him."
>
> HEBREWS 11:6

# The Key to Pleasing Is Receiving

As a teenager and young adult, there were many times before I left home that I came to my earthly father, A.W. Copeland, with things that seemed messed up beyond hope in my life. What a relief it was to hear him say, "Well now, this thing is not as bad as it looks."

"Boy, that's good, because I thought I'd messed up for life," I'd say.

"No," he'd reply, "now let's think about this a little bit."

As we would talk about the situation, my father would bring up things that I hadn't considered and didn't know. Soon relief and peace would begin to settle into my spirit, and I would think, *Whew, I'm going to get out of this. Thank God...and thank Daddy!*

Why did that happen? I became comfortable in the midst of my circumstances when I'd listen to him. I put my confidence in his desire for my success. My willingness to make decisions that honored Daddy's word and his commitments to me gave him the opportunity to do what was always in his heart for me.

If I had continued to walk in it as I grew older, instead of thinking I was smarter than Daddy, I could have enjoyed even more benefits in that father-son relationship. But I didn't. I rebelled. I began to think I knew more than Daddy did—and I continually got deeper into trouble.

That was so stupid. Daddy already knew how to get me out, but I wouldn't listen to him. Without faith in someone who knew better, I made decisions that continually worsened my situations.

The atmosphere this created drove a wedge between my daddy and me. Did his love for me change? No. Had my actions made him less willing to do everything he could to help me? Not at all. The choices I was making hurt him because eventually he could no longer reach me, and I couldn't reach him. But none of it was his fault—it was mine.

God is the same way. No matter what we do, His love for us never changes. When we get into a mess, He wants to help us get out. He rewards those who diligently seek Him. Pleasing God is as simple as getting in a position to receive all that is in His heart to give. He is a loving Daddy Who wants to help us. He delights in our prosperity and well-being (Psalm 35:27).

So go to Him. Tell Him about your mess...trust Him with your life...and then watch Him unravel it all...and give you His perfect peace.

## *Speak the Word*

*God is my rewarder as I diligently seek Him.*
*Hebrews 11:6*

FOR FURTHER STUDY:

Psalm 46;
Psalm 125:1-2

DAILY SCRIPTURE READING:

Job 1-2;
Jude

*Gloria*

# Walking With a Whole Heart

If you are in trouble today, take heart. There is definitely a way out.

Second Chronicles 6:14 says God shows mercy to those who walk before Him with all their hearts. So, if you're in trouble today, take an honest look at your relationship with God.

Ask yourself, *Am I walking before God with all my heart? Is there any area of my life that I'm withholding from God? Is there any area I want to control and keep for myself?*

Let me tell you why that's important. It's not that God is holding out on you and begrudging you His deliverance when you aren't living before Him whole-heartedly like you know you should. But your personal faith level is affected.

If you look at 1 John 3:20-22, you can see what I mean: *"For if our heart condemn us, God is greater than our heart, and knoweth all things. Beloved, if our heart condemn us not, then have we confidence toward God. And whatsoever we ask, we receive of him, because we keep his commandments, and do those things that are pleasing in his sight."*

You see, it's not what God knows about you that keeps your prayers from being answered. When you know you're not living for God and doing what you know to do, it causes you not to have confidence toward Him.

So check your heart today. If you're following Him with your whole heart, there's a great and mighty confidence that comes up within you. No devil can shake that confidence. No one can talk you out of it. And no distress—no matter how great—can pressure you into letting go. No matter what happens, you remain certain that God will deliver you!

## *Speak the Word*

*I walk before the Lord with all my heart. He keeps His covenant with me and shows me mercy.*
*2 Chronicles 6:14*

> "O Lord God of Israel, there is no God like thee in the heaven, nor in the earth; which keepest covenant, and shewest mercy unto thy servants, that walk before thee with all their hearts."
> 2 CHRONICLES 6:14

FOR FURTHER STUDY:

Psalm 37:3-11

DAILY SCRIPTURE READING:

Job 3-4;
Revelation 1

> "That at the name of Jesus every knee should bow, of things in heaven, and things in earth, and things under the earth."
>
> PHILIPPIANS 2:10

# Have Faith in the Name

If you've been born again, you belong to the Lord Jesus Christ. You are a joint heir with Him. You are covenanted together with Almighty God by the blood of Jesus. You've been given Jesus' own Name—the Name that is higher in authority than any other name, the Name at which every knee must bow.

But for you to effectively use the Name of Jesus, you need to develop your faith in that Name.

Think about it this way. Gloria and I belong to one another. We are covenanted together in the blood of Jesus by holy matrimony. She has my name. She writes it on a check without reservation. She has as much right to sign that name as I do.

It's her name. It has been given to her. When somebody asks her who she is, she doesn't say, "I'm Gloria Neece operating in the name of Kenneth Copeland."

No, she says, "I'm Gloria Copeland."

That's the kind of confidence you need to have about the Name of Jesus. You need to know you've been named after Him. Know that when you speak, you're speaking with His authority.

You need to have faith in that Name. Many times people start using the Name of Jesus, trying to work up their faith. But faith doesn't come from the Name. Faith comes from hearing and hearing by the Word of God (see Romans 10:17).

So, if you're having trouble in that area, go back to the Word and study the Name. Then when you use it, you'll have that sense of authority on the inside that is founded on the living Word.

## *Speak the Word*

*At the Name of Jesus every knee shall bow. I have confidence in that Name.*
*Philippians 2:10*

FOR FURTHER STUDY:

Acts 3:12-16

DAILY SCRIPTURE READING:

Job 5-6; Revelation 2

*Gloria*

# When God's on Your Side

When we yield to love, which is God's very nature (He is love!), we begin to look and act like Jesus Himself would if He were living in our bodies—which, of course, He is! Instead of acting like carnal Christian babies, we do what Ephesians 4:15 says and grow up enfolded in love.

It's love that causes us to grow up! It's love that will bring us to our ultimate goal of being *"the completeness of personality which is nothing less than the standard height of Christ's own perfection—the measure of the stature of the fullness of the Christ, and the completeness found in Him!"* (Ephesians 4:13, AMP).

I'll warn you though, if you decide to take the path of love, there will be times when it seems as though love will make you the underdog instead of the victor. There will be times when you're wrongly treated, and you'll feel like it would be to your disadvantage to be patient, kind and long-suffering. Your flesh will rise up and say, "Now wait a minute! If I just keep on being kind and loving, people will run right over me."

> "Enfolded in love, [we] grow up in every way and in all things into Him, Who is the Head, [even] Christ, the Messiah, the Anointed One."
>
> EPHESIANS 4:15, AMP

But that's not true. You see, when you walk in love, you put yourself in a position where God Himself can protect you. When you quit seeking your own, He seeks your own *for* you. And He is a great One to have on your side, because when He is for you, no one can stand against you (Romans 8:31-39).

You can see that in the life of Jesus. He always walked in love—not just when people were praising Him and honoring His ministry, but also when He was being bitterly rejected and mistreated (1 Peter 2:23).

As a result, no man or demon could touch Him. When the people at Nazareth tried to throw Him off a cliff, He just walked through the midst of them. When the soldiers came to arrest Him in the Garden, He just said, *"I am He,"* and they all fell to the ground under the power of God (John 18:1-6). If Jesus had not given Himself up willingly, He never could have been crucified, for He alone had the power to lay down His life. No one could take it from Him because He lived the life of love.

**FOR FURTHER STUDY:**

Luke 4:24-32

❧

**DAILY SCRIPTURE READING:**

Job 7-9; Revelation 3

Love is powerful! If you're being mistreated, or if someone has hurt you deeply, yield to that powerful force of love on the inside of you. Let it rise up strong in you and overtake that hurt. When you do, not only will you be healed on the inside, you will be victorious over the schemes of the devil on the outside. When you walk in love, God is on your side. And when God is on your side, you can't help but succeed. Love never fails.

## *Speak the Word*

*Enfolded in love, I grow up in every way and in all things into Christ.*
*Ephesians 4:15, AMP*

# Don't Wait for the Doughnuts!

There was a time in my life when I made a decision that I was going to live by faith. I didn't know anything about faith at the time. I just made the decision that I was going to live by it because the Word of God said, *"The just shall live by faith"* (Hebrews 10:38). From that time on, I had to begin making decisions based on the Word of God rather than on my circumstances.

But let me tell you something, I didn't just go charging into life expecting those decisions to come easily. I began to establish myself in what the Word says, so I'd know what to do when faced with a difficult situation.

I listened to teaching tapes on faith for hours upon hours, day after day. I meditated through situations in the Bible in my own prayer time. I'd think through what I was going to do if faced with those situations. Then sure enough, I'd go right out and run smack into exactly what I'd been meditating about just hours earlier.

When that happened, there wasn't any question about what to do. I just took the faith route. Why? The decision was already made in the time of meditation, prayer and praise!

That's how I conquered the food problem I once had. I made a quality decision to put sugar out of my life. I could do it because I made the decision once and for all in a time of prayer and fasting.

From that decision on, I refused to consider my body. When someone would hand me a piece of pie and my body would say, *Well, maybe we ought to think about this a moment,* I'd just say, "You hush, body."

Certainly my flesh moaned and groaned for a while, but before long, it just lined up with my will and, of course, my faith. Now it doesn't bother me at all.

You see, my faith took control of my flesh once I made that quality decision.

Look at the things in your life that you want to change. It may not be food, but if it is, waiting until they pass you the doughnuts to decide won't get you delivered. Making a quality decision ahead of time will ensure your success.

## *Speak the Word*

*I am not conformed to this world. I am transformed as I renew my mind.*
*And I prove what is the good and acceptable and perfect will of God.*
*Romans 12:2*

FOR FURTHER STUDY:

Romans 8:9-13

DAILY SCRIPTURE READING:

Job 10-11;
Revelation 4

*Gloria*

# Don't Judge Another Man's Servant

If you've made a commitment to keep strife out of your home, you may have noticed a new front-line battle: more pressure than ever to get in strife in your church!

Maybe the devil has provoked someone to be rude to you and hurt your feelings. Or maybe he made sure you found out about something someone else did wrong, and then you talked about it to others.

When he presents you with that opportunity, turn him down—*fast!* Treat that temptation to gossip and stir up strife like you would a poisonous snake, because in the eyes of God, participating in strife in the Church is one of the most serious of sins (Proverbs 6:16-19).

God considers stirring up strife such a grave sin that He lists it alongside murder and lying. So stay away from it. Ask God to reveal to you if you've entered into strife inadvertently. He may remind you of a time you passed along some gossip or criticized the pastor. If He does, repent, and be more conscious of those things in the future. Determine in your heart that from now on, if you see your brother sin, you'll believe God for him and pray for him instead of perpetuating that brother's problem by talking to everyone about it.

I realize sometimes that seems extremely difficult to do. But here's something that will help you. When you're tempted to get in strife by judging a fellow believer, remember Romans 14:4 and ask yourself, *"Who art thou that judgest another man's servant?"*

The devil will try to push you into making a decision about that person, to say whether he's guilty or not guilty. But don't give in to that pressure. It's not your job to judge others. (Isn't that a relief?) First Corinthians 4:5 says, *"Judge nothing before the time, until the Lord come, who both will bring to light the hidden things of darkness, and will make manifest the counsels of the hearts: and then shall every man have praise of God."*

> "These six things doth the Lord hate: yea, seven are an abomination unto him: A proud look, a lying tongue, and hands that shed innocent blood, An heart that deviseth wicked imaginations, feet that be swift in running to mischief, A false witness that speaketh lies, and he that soweth discord among brethren."
>
> PROVERBS 6:16-19

If you're in a church where the pastor has done wrong, and you feel you don't want to follow him, that's fine. I don't blame you. Leave that church and go to one with a pastor you can trust and respect. But do it quietly. Don't sow discord before you go. Most important of all, wherever you go, be sure to go in love. Go in love and guard diligently against strife. When you do, you will keep your faith strong and your blessings out of the devil's hands. Walk in love and you will always live in victory!

FOR FURTHER STUDY:

Proverbs 26:20-21; Romans 14

DAILY SCRIPTURE READING:

Job 12-13;

## *Speak the Word*

*I determine to walk in love. I do not sow discord among the brethren for that is an abomination to God.*
*Proverbs 6:16,19*

"Wisdom is the principal thing; therefore get wisdom: and with all thy getting get understanding. Exalt her, and she shall promote thee.... She shall give to thine head an ornament of grace: a crown of glory shall she deliver to thee."
Proverbs 4:7-9

# Get the Principal Thing

How many times have you prayed and failed to receive your answer? I can tell you it wasn't because God missed it! The Word of God says you ask and receive not because you ask amiss (James 4:3). You need wisdom to ask for the right thing. That means you need God's thoughts about the situation before you can pray effectively.

You may be crying out to God for healing when what you actually need is a miracle. You may be praying about a money shortage when what you have is a giving shortage. You may even be causing the problem yourself without knowing it.

You need God's wisdom! How do you get it?

Jesus shows us in Luke 11:49. He began speaking, *"Therefore...said the wisdom of God...,"* then He began to quote Scripture. He called the written Word of God the wisdom of God. God's wisdom is His Word.

So let the Word of God, the wisdom of God, begin to influence your thinking. Soak your mind in it. Don't just scan it lightly. Dig in it. Learn it. Take it seriously.

Then begin to pray in the spirit. Let the Spirit of God start a process of spiritual insight in your heart as you pray and worship in the spirit. After a while, you'll begin to understand things in a new way. You'll begin to have a whole new interpretation of the problem.

You may suddenly have a realization, a deep conviction, an inner knowing. Someone may call you on the telephone and say, "I just got a word from the Lord this morning and I'm so excited about it...." And what they say is exactly what you need to hear.

However you get it, remember, wisdom is the principal thing. God's way of thinking will save your life, pull you out of debt, and put you on the road to prosperity. It will introduce you to possibilities you have never seen before and get you out of any trouble.

## *Speak the Word*

*Wisdom is the principal thing; therefore I get wisdom!*
*Proverbs 4:7*

For Further Study:

1 Corinthians 2:6-9

Daily Scripture Reading:

Job 14-15;
Revelation 6

*Gloria*

# Abraham, Moses, Joshua...and You!

Do you need more faith in your heart account? Well, put some in there! You can have as much as you want. How much Word you put in your heart determines how much faith you're going to have available when you need it.

It's up to you. No one else can keep you from making that deposit either. If you can get a Bible, you can make a deposit every day. In fact, you'd better make a deposit every day, because chances are you'll need to make a withdrawal sometime during the day. And withdrawals without deposits can leave you stranded without sufficient spiritual resources to get the job done.

> "Seek ye first the kingdom of God, and his righteousness; and all these things shall be added unto you."
>
> MATTHEW 6:33

Some people want to float through life without putting out the effort to build up their spiritual account. They want to enjoy the heavenly blessings, but they don't want to develop the faith it takes to bring those blessings down to earth!

Don't be one of those people! Don't expect to get something from God without faith. It's not going to happen.

Abraham had to act in faith to get Isaac. Moses had to act in faith to get the Israelites to the Promised Land. Joshua had to act in faith to get the walls of Jericho to come down. Rahab had to act in faith to keep her part of the wall around Jericho *from* falling down. And if Abraham, Moses, Joshua and Rahab had to have faith, then you have to have faith too. All of the great victories written in Hebrews 11 were manifested in the earth by and through faith! That's just the way it is.

That's why the most important thing you have to do in this life is to keep your heart full of the Word of God—because everything else can be taken care of if that account is full. That's what Jesus meant in Matthew 6:33.

When you put the Word first, all things will come to you...including more faith. So don't wait any longer! Get into the Word, put it in your heart, and watch your faith account grow!

## Speak the Word

*I seek first the kingdom of God and His righteousness,*
*and all that I have need of is added to me.*
*Matthew 6:33*

FOR FURTHER
STUDY:

Romans 10:14-17

DAILY SCRIPTURE
READING:

Job 16-17;
Revelation 7

*Kenneth*

# YOU Can Do It All

When Jesus asked, *"Whom say ye that I am?"* Peter blurted out, *"Thou art the Christ [the Anointed One], the Son of the living God" (Matthew 16:15-16).*

Peter, perhaps better than anyone, knew what that anointing could do. As a fisherman, he'd seen Jesus draw every fish in the river of Galilee around his boat. Even though Peter had fished all the night before without catching a thing, when Jesus stepped on board, he finished the day with a net-breaking, boat-sinking load!

Peter had watched Jesus feed thousands with just a few loaves and fishes. He'd seen Him heal multitudes and deliver them from demonic oppression. Peter had pulled money for taxes from a fish's mouth at Jesus' instruction. He'd walked on water at Jesus' word.

Peter knew why Jesus could do those things—He had the Anointing of God on Him. He had the burden-removing, yoke-destroying, world-changing, devil-chasing, healing, delivering, explosive, supernatural, universe-creating power of the Holy Spirit flowing through His flesh, enabling Him to do what flesh cannot do!

So when Peter heard Jesus say, "You will be baptized with the Holy Ghost and receive power to be My witnesses" (Acts 1:5, 8), he knew what Jesus was talking about...*My God, we've got it! We've got that anointing. The power that was on Jesus is on me now! The fish will come to my boat now! I'll be able to walk on the water if I have to, to get this gospel out!*

That had to be what Peter was thinking. He didn't know anything else. He'd never been to seminary. There were no theologians to calm him down and tell him God's miracle-working power had passed away. All he knew was, *Jesus is the Anointed of God, the Son of the living God, and His Anointing is on us!*

In light of that, why are believers today not as excited about the Baptism in the Holy Spirit? Why, instead of charging out into the world and turning it upside down with the power of God like those first disciples did, do most modern-day believers do little more with the anointing than talk in tongues now and then?

Because we have a limited revelation of what can actually happen when the Anointing of Jesus operates through us. That needs to change. The fact is, there is an anointing through Jesus by the Holy Spirit, that the Father has sent in His Name, to do any and every righteous act on the face of this earth, by any person who knows Him as Lord. And that includes you. You are anointed to do all that Peter imagined and more. You are anointed to do all that you dream. You are anointed to be mighty, to be world-overcoming, to change the world you live in today. You can do it all!

## *Speak the Word*

*The manifestation of the Spirit is given to me for my profit.*
*1 Corinthians 12:7*

FOR FURTHER STUDY:

Matthew 16:13-19

DAILY SCRIPTURE READING:

Job 18-19;
Revelation 8

*Gloria*

# Go Ahead. Laugh!

AUGUST 5

❧

"The joy of the Lord is your strength."
NEHEMIAH 8:10

Something peculiar has been happening to believers these last few years. They're beginning to rejoice! God is pouring out a spirit of joy so strong, it causes people to laugh for hours. Some of them literally end up on the floor, doubled over laughing with the joy of the Lord.

I've seen Ken so filled he could hardly minister. The next day, however, he could not only stand and preach, he felt stronger than he had in 10 years.

I have to tell you though, when God's people start to praise Him and rejoice with that kind of abandon, it makes some Christians nervous. As a result, many of them are folding their arms, sitting back and saying, "I'm not going to be caught acting like that!"...and as a result, they are missing out on a powerful move of God.

Before *you* fold your arms and sit back, know this. When we become like Jesus and desire God so intently that we're willing to cast aside our desire to please men, and praise Him without reservation, we'll truly see the Glory of God.

Why? Because God manifests Himself where He's wanted. He shows up where hearts are hungry. He's not going to reveal Himself to a great degree among people whose hearts are only partially turned toward Him.

Consequently, He's finding people who want Him more than anything else life has to offer. He's finding people who want His presence more than they want to be respected by their neighborhood.

If you are one of those people, you've probably already found out that some of your friends (or family) don't like it. The Glory of God offends them, and they don't want to be around you—especially when you're laughing! You have probably found that it's most often the religious people who have criticized this rejoicing the most harshly.

Or, you may be in the other group...you're not too sure about all this laughing. You're not sure you have the strength to face the criticism of the religious people. I have good news for you. You can get that strength by rejoicing because the Bible says, *"The joy of the Lord is your strength!"*

So go ahead. Laugh!

## Speak the Word

*The joy of the Lord is my strength.*
*Nehemiah 8:10*

FOR FURTHER STUDY:

Psalm 126

❧

DAILY SCRIPTURE READING:

Job 20-21;
Revelation 9

> "These signs shall follow them that believe; In my [Jesus'] name shall they cast out devils...they shall lay hands on the sick, and they shall recover."
>
> MARK 16:17-18

# Healing Always Comes

They *shall* recover.

Not, they might recover.

But, they *shall* recover.

Have you ever just sat and let that sink in? It's a very definite promise. And as believers, our responsibility is to believe it—no matter what our senses tell us. That's because our physical senses frequently give us an inaccurate picture of what is really happening. They're limited. They can't relay to us what is happening in the realm of the spirit.

For example, have you ever laid hands on someone and then had the devil say you'd just made the mistake of your life? I have.

Years ago I was in a church service when some people brought in a young girl and asked me to minister to her. She suffered from epileptic seizures. The minute I walked up to her, the Lord told me the seizures were caused by a spirit. So I stood in front of her and said, "In the Name of Jesus, you'll have to take your hands off this girl, you foul devil. Leave her now!"

Wham! She hit the floor with one of the worst seizures I had ever seen. Four or five people picked her up and carried her out. As they were leaving, I heard the Holy Spirit say, *No!*

So that's what I said too. I hollered, "No, no, no!" the entire time they were carrying her out.

I never did hear from the girl or her family, so, of course, the devil would harass me and say, *Boy, she sure didn't get delivered, did she? She went out worse than she came in!*

But I'd rebuke him and say, "No, devil. The Word says when I tell you to flee, you flee. So as far as I'm concerned, you fled that day."

Years passed. Then one day someone gave me a tape of a Full Gospel Business Men's Fellowship meeting. Do you know what was on that tape? The mother of that little girl giving her testimony of how God delivered her daughter from epilepsy the night I laid hands on her.

I'm so glad I didn't withdraw my faith because she didn't look healed!

God always does His part. He said when we lay hands on the sick, they shall recover. Whether someone receives healing is not our judgment call. Our assignment is to lay our hands on them, believe the Word, pray or whatever else we're instructed to do by the Word. We can rest assured that when we obey Him in faith, healing always comes.

## *Speak the Word*

*I believe and these signs follow me: In Jesus' Name I cast out devils, I lay hands on the sick, and they shall recover.*

*Mark 16:17-18*

FOR FURTHER
STUDY:

Mark 16:15-20

DAILY SCRIPTURE
READING:

Job 22-24;
Revelation 10-11

*Gloria*

# Sober Up!

> "Follow...holiness, without which no man shall see the Lord."
> Hebrews 12:14

Jesus is coming soon! I know some people scoff at that idea. (That's no surprise; the Bible says they would.) But I don't care what those people say. The signs are clear. We are at the end of the end!

The final outpourings of the Holy Spirit have already begun. Reports of miracles, signs and wonders, dreams and visions like those prophesied in Acts 2 are coming in from around the world. And we are going to see more of the power of God, more signs, more wonders and more Glory than anyone has ever seen before. God is going to manifest Himself among us in marvelous ways!

Actually, our situation today is much like the one the Israelites found themselves in after Moses led them out of Egypt. When they reached the foot of Mount Sinai, God spoke and told them He was about to manifest Himself in their midst (Exodus 19:9-11). Right now, God is saying much the same thing to us, *Get ready! I'm about to manifest Myself in your midst!* He's telling us to sanctify ourselves, to get our lives cleaned up.

We need our robes of righteousness bright and spotless. When His power comes in its fullness, it will bring life to what's good and death to what's bad. It's time we realize that when God manifests Himself in great measure among us, His Glory will destroy sin in a moment's time. So those who are clinging to sin will be in trouble.

"Now wait a minute, that sounds like Old Testament theology to me."

No, it isn't. Do you remember what happened to Ananias and Sapphira in Acts 5? As far as I know, they were members in good standing of the New Testament Church. But they conspired together to lie to the Holy Ghost and, as a result, they both died in church on the same day!

We haven't seen anything like that in recent times, because the power of God hasn't been in manifestation as powerfully among us as it was in the early Church. When there's just a little power being manifested, then people get away with more. But when there's a lot of the power of God being manifested, people get away with things for a shorter period of time.

**For Further Study:**

1 Peter 1:13-16

**Daily Scripture Reading:**

Job 25-26; Revelation 12

Sin was dealt with quickly in Ananias and Sapphira that day. Of course, it didn't have to be dealt with in that way. They could have repented on the spot. They could have said, "I was wrong. Forgive me!" But they didn't. They clung to their sin. So when the power of God extinguished that sin, their lives were extinguished too.

I realize that's a sobering thought. But the Bible instructs us to be sober in these last days. It says we should be serious about sanctifying ourselves. So examine your heart and sober up! Jesus is coming soon.

## Speak the Word

*I follow holiness so that I shall see the Lord.*
*Hebrews 12:14*

> "And David spake to the men that stood by him, saying, What shall be done to the man that killeth this Philistine, and taketh away the reproach from Israel? for who is this uncircumcised Philistine, that he should defy the armies of the living God?"
>
> 1 Samuel 17:26

# How to Kill a Giant—Step 1

How do you kill a giant? How do you handle a problem that's so big, you can't see beyond it—and so stubborn it just won't go away?

You stand on your covenant with Almighty God! That's how.

When David stood before men in the army of Israel, and called the giant the *uncircumcised Philistine,* he knew what he was saying. Circumcision was the mark of the covenant between the Israelites and Jehovah God. As the seed of Abraham, David knew he had covenant promises from God that covered the situation. In Deuteronomy 28:7, God had said, *"They [your enemies] shall come out against thee one way, and flee before thee seven ways."*

David believed that promise. It didn't matter whether his enemy was a lion or a bear or some man who had defied God. David knew he would defeat him. He was aware of the covenant he had with God through Abraham—and it altered his perspective.

David started talking about the victories of God. He kept on saying, "This giant is no problem. I can take him down for you." David was operating by faith in his covenant with God.

That covenant promised him protection from man, beast and enemy. It promised him protection of his flock and of his person. Because of the covenant of God, that giant was dead the moment David declared he was. As he talked about the victory, David grew stronger and the picture in his mind grew clearer. Before the day was over, the image of faith that was on the inside of him had become a physical reality that everyone could see.

You too have a blood covenant with God. It's a covenant ratified by the blood of Jesus, and the Bible says it's a better covenant with better promises than David had (Hebrews 8:6). If you have a problem as big as a giant staring you in the face, and all you feel is defeat, you need to check your focus. Where have you been looking lately? Are you looking at the size of the problem—or are you looking at your covenant and the power of God?

When you focus your attention on your covenant with God, everything changes. It's an opportunity for God Almighty to receive more glory in your life than ever before. Not only that, it's an opportunity for you to come out proclaiming the power of the gospel more boldly than ever before!

So there you have it. The way to kill a giant in your life...and the way to experience the thrill of victory through your covenant with God.

## Speak the Word

*God always causes me to triumph in Christ.*
*2 Corinthians 2:14*

For Further Study:

1 Samuel 17:26-50

Daily Scripture Reading:

Job 27-28;
Revelation 13

*Gloria*

# Decide, in Advance!

There's no question about it, if you are a born-again believer, you want to walk in love...you can't help it, it's part of your new nature. But wanting to do it isn't enough. You have to go a step further and make a quality decision to *do* it!

You must make up your mind in advance to obey the instruction in Ephesians 5:2 and constantly order your behavior within the sphere of love. Notice I said *in advance*. If you wait until you're facing a tough situation to decide how you want to respond, you'll almost certainly make the wrong choice. Rather than ordering your behavior by the law of love, you'll end up allowing circumstances or even the devil to order your behavior instead.

So prepare yourself now for what's ahead. If there's a person in your life who is particularly difficult to love, make them a special project. (That kind of person usually needs love even more than anyone else.) Make plans not just to "put up with them," but to go out of your way to be kind and loving toward them.

"But Gloria," you may say, "You just don't know this person like I do. It would be too hard to love them. I can't do it."

> "Be ordering your behavior within the sphere of love, even as Christ also loved you and gave himself up in our behalf and in our stead as an offering and a sacrifice to God for an aroma of a sweet smell."
> EPHESIANS 5:2, Wuest

Yes, you can! You're a disciple of the Lord Jesus Christ. You are filled with His Holy Spirit and power. And God has planted in your heart His very own love—the love that never fails. So make a decision to give over to that love and let it flow.

Then start strengthening your spirit by feeding on what the Word of God says about love. As you meditate on that Word, it will energize and create within you the power and desire to will and to work for God's good pleasure. It will increase your ability to walk in love.

Keep yourself on a steady diet of God's Word. Counteract the worldly voices and fleshly desires that pull away from love by filling your ears and your eyes with scriptures like 1 Corinthians 13. Read them at night before you go to bed. Read them in the morning when you wake up. Write them out on note cards and tape them to your bathroom mirror so you can meditate on them while you're brushing your teeth.

FOR FURTHER STUDY:

Romans 12:9-21

❧

DAILY SCRIPTURE READING:

Job 29-30;
Revelation 14

If you do that, I guarantee you, that Word will come alive in you. It will talk to you and help you stick with your decision to walk in love. When you get fed up with someone, and you're about to tell them off, it will speak up and remind you that love is not touchy, fretful or resentful.

Then, instead of giving that person a piece of your mind, you'll give him the love of God, and he'll be blessed. God will be pleased. And you'll have the victory!

## *Speak the Word*

*I walk in love, even as Christ has loved me.*
*Ephesians 5:2*

*Kenneth*

# Surviving the Counterattack

It's the moment we love more than any other—the moment of victory. It's the moment when our healing manifests and the symptoms of sickness finally disappear. It's the moment when Satan's attack against our finances or our family is defeated and the breakthrough comes at last.

What do you do when that moment comes?

I'll tell you what most Christians do. They kick up their heels in celebration. Then, breathing a sigh of relief, they put away their Bible, turn on the television and say, "Thank heavens, that battle's over! Now I can relax."

Big mistake.

You see, while they're taking a spiritual vacation, Satan is planning his counterattack, plotting to snatch the victory from under their very nose.

I first began to notice the effectiveness of such counterattacks years ago. Someone I knew, who had been studying a well-known healing evangelist, came to me and said, "I believe the Lord has taken His hand off Brother So-and-So."

"Really?" I asked in surprise.

"Oh, yes," he answered. "People are truly healed in his meetings, but when I follow up with them later, many of them aren't healed anymore."

Although I couldn't agree with his conclusions, I knew *something* was wrong.

People came to this minister's meetings, heard the Word of God, and experienced God's presence. In that atmosphere of faith, it was easy for them to receive their healing.

But when they left the meeting, they didn't take that atmosphere with them. They stepped back into their old, unbelieving lifestyle that had made them vulnerable to sickness in the first place. So when the devil launched his counterattack with a few symptoms, these people just yielded to him. They said, "Oh my, I thought I was healed, but I guess I wasn't."

"What's wrong with that?" you ask. "What else could they say?"

I'll tell you what! They could have said, "Look here, devil. According to the Word, I am healed by the stripes of Jesus. I received that healing at the meeting, and I don't intend for you to steal it. So pack up your symptoms and go!"

If those people had spoken words like that in faith, and refused to give in to the devil, they could have kept their healing. If they had resisted the devil as it says to in James 4:7, they could have defeated the counterattack.

Stop being surprised by the counterattacks—and start being prepared for them. Lay a foundation of faith in your life, so when the devil comes like an old windbag and blows some lies, pains and adverse circumstances your way, your victory will not come tumbling down.

## *Speak the Word*

*I resist the devil and he flees from me.*

*James 4:7*

FOR FURTHER STUDY:

1 John 5:1-4

DAILY SCRIPTURE READING:

Job 31-32; Revelation 15

*Gloria*

# Living the Good Life!

Every day it just blesses me how good God is to us. He blesses us all the time. Ken and I have such a wonderful life, we just can't help but be thankful. And the more thankful we are and the more we expect those blessings, the more of them come flooding in on us.

God favors us. But let me tell you, you're one of His favorites too! I know you are because God's mercy and favor are over all His works (Psalm 145:9)—and Ephesians 2:10 says we are all His workmanship!

Psalm 145:8-9 says, *"The Lord is gracious, and full of compassion; slow to anger, and of great mercy. The Lord is good to all: and his tender mercies are over all his works."*

God is gracious. Do you know what that means? It means He is disposed to show favors. It's just His nature to bless people. He is also *"full of compassion."* The word *compassion* there is not just a passive word like *pity*. It is a force that stirs one to action. One definition of compassion is "eager yearning."

Isn't that wonderful? God is eagerly yearning to do you good! In fact, the Bible says that God is looking for someone to bless. He is not satisfied unless He can do someone good (2 Chronicles 16:9).

I remember the day I realized that, I was desperate for help. I picked up the Bible and read in Matthew 6:26 that God cared for the birds of the air. What a revelation that was to me! No one had ever told me God was good. They had never told me He loved me. They just told me a lot of "do nots."

When I read that scripture I thought, *Well, if God cares for birds, He cares for me!* I gave God my life and asked Him to do something with it. And that's all it took. I gave God an opening and His love flooded through it.

*Flooded* is a good word to use to describe the mercy of God, because when we give Him the slightest opening, His mercy rushes in upon us.

> "For we are God's [own] handiwork (His workmanship), recreated in Christ Jesus, [born anew] that we may do those good works which God predestined (planned beforehand) for us, (taking paths which He prepared ahead of time) that we should walk in them—*living the good life* which He prearranged and made ready for us to live."
> EPHESIANS 2:10, AMP

You see, God wants to do you good. He wants you to live the good life! So, the next time someone tells you God's will is for you to be sick or downtrodden, just remember that. God has a good life planned for you even in this dark world. A life of health. A life of joy. A life of ministering and helping people. A life of abundance. That good life has been prearranged and made ready for you to live. Everything you need in the natural realm—a home, a car, a family, a mate—has all been stored up with your name on it. So go for it! Receive your destiny! Live the good life!

FOR FURTHER STUDY:

Matthew 6:25-34

DAILY SCRIPTURE READING:

Job 33-34; Revelation 16

## *Speak the Word*

*I live the good life which God has prearranged and made ready for me to live.*
*Ephesians 2:10, AMP*

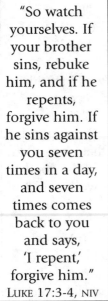

> "So watch yourselves. If your brother sins, rebuke him, and if he repents, forgive him. If he sins against you seven times in a day, and seven times comes back to you and says, 'I repent,' forgive him."
>
> Luke 17:3-4, NIV

# Serious Business

My forgiving someone doesn't have anything to do with what that person did or didn't do to me. I forgive them because of the blood. God honored the blood and forgave me in the face of my sin, so even as He has forgiven me, I forgive you.

For me not to forgive would be to dishonor that blood.

This is serious business we're talking about here! When you dishonor the blood of Jesus, you're stepping out from under its protective covering into the devil's territory. You're stepping out into darkness where he can get a shot at you.

I don't know about you, but I don't want to go out there. I don't care what anyone may do to me, I won't let their mistreatment of me push me out into darkness. No, I'll just honor the blood, forgive them and keep right on walking in the light. If somebody hits me on the cheek, I'll just do what Jesus said: forgive and turn the other cheek.

Some people think if you do that, you'll get the daylights beaten out of you. But they're wrong. If you keep your faith up, when you turn the other cheek, God will protect you from the one who's trying to hit you.

I know of a preacher who experienced that. He was witnessing to a member of a New York street gang who was threatening him with a knife. Instead of fighting back, the preacher just kept telling him Jesus loved him. The guy kept swinging that knife, trying to cut that preacher, but every time he tried, a force he couldn't see would stop him. He literally couldn't touch him.

As a result, that gang member fell down on his knees, received Jesus and today he is one of the most outstanding evangelists in the world!

Listen, my friend, forgiveness is one of the most powerful forces in existence! To walk in forgiveness is to walk in victory.

## *Speak the Word*

*I honor the blood of Jesus by choosing to forgive;*
*therefore, I walk in victory and power.*
*Luke 17:3-4; Revelation 1:5*

For Further
Study:

Colossians 1:9-14

Daily Scripture
Reading:

Job 35-36;
Revelation 17

*Gloria*

# Burn, Brother, Burn!

Never underestimate the drawing power of joy. It's like a blazing fire that captures the attention of people in darkness. In fact, in a dream I had many years ago, God called it "spontaneous combustion."

I didn't even know what the term meant until the next day. When I looked it up in a dictionary, here's what I found: *Spontaneous combustion*—"the process of catching fire and burning as a result of heat generated by an internal chemical reaction."

That's it! Joy—the process of catching fire and burning as a result of heat which comes from the Holy Ghost!

It's time to rejoice, to rise up out of our exhaustion and implement the power of praise. When you do, you'll enter a domain of power, freedom and the joy of the Lord. It's a domain that's alive and shining with the presence of God.

So throw off those old inhibitions. Take God at His Word. Leap. Shout. Sing. Be ready to obey the Spirit of God. Let yourself catch fire in the Spirit and never stop burning!

> "Be glad in the Lord, and rejoice, ye righteous: and shout for joy.... Rejoice in the Lord, O ye righteous: for praise is comely for the upright."
> PSALM 32:11-33:1

## Speak the Word

*I am glad in the Lord and I rejoice. I shout for joy because praise is becoming and appropriate for those who are upright in heart.*
*Psalm 32:11-33:1, AMP*

FOR FURTHER STUDY:

Psalm 100

DAILY SCRIPTURE READING:

Job 37-39;
Revelation 18-19

❧

"And now abideth faith, hope, charity [or love], these three."
1 CORINTHIANS 13:13

# The Three Most Powerful Elements

Wishing won't accomplish anything in the kingdom of God. But hoping will, especially when you couple it with faith and love!

Hope is one of the three most powerful elements in the universe. It is one of the three eternal and living substances that run the entire kingdom of God. I preach a lot about faith. I'm constantly teaching believers that they can't get anything done in the kingdom of God without faith. But do you want to know something? Faith can't get anything done without hope—intense expectation!

Hebrews 11:1 says, *"Now faith is the substance of things hoped for...."* In natural terms you might say faith is the building material and hope is the blueprint. You have to have hope before faith can begin building anything in your life.

For instance, someone who has liver cancer might say to me, "I fully expect to be healed of this liver condition." I might say to them, "What makes you believe that, when the doctor just declared your condition incurable?"

If he has Bible hope, he'll say, "I'm going to be delivered from this liver condition because God's Word says every sickness and every disease is under the curse of the Law, and Galatians 3:13 says Jesus has redeemed us from the curse of the Law, being made a curse for us. In other words, Jesus has already redeemed me from the curse of this liver condition. *That's* why I fully expect to be delivered from it."

When you have that kind of clear, Word-based image inside you, you have real Bible hope—and it's an absolute must for anyone who wants to live by faith.

So put hope to work in your life today...and couple it with faith and love. Then you will have the three most powerful elements in the universe working for you!

## *Speak the Word*

*I hope and expect in the mercy and love of God
and He takes pleasure in me.
Psalm 147:11*

FOR FURTHER STUDY:

Colossians 1:21-24

❧

DAILY SCRIPTURE READING:

Job 40-41;
Revelation 20

*Gloria*

# Your Heavenly Account

Have you ever read anywhere in the Bible where God said, "Since you might forget Me if you get rich, I'm going to keep you poor"?

I sure haven't. I don't believe you have either because it's not in there! But He did say to "always remember that I'm the One Who gives you the power to get wealth" (Deuteronomy 8:18). In other words, Remember where you got it!

As born-again believers, you and I are God's people just as the Israelites were. Since we are Christ's, then we are *"Abraham's seed, and heirs according to the promise"* (Galatians 3:29). Therefore, we can expect God to anoint the work of our hands. We can expect Him to bless us and give us the power to get wealth!

"But Gloria," you may say, "I know people who have served God and put Him first all their lives, yet they were always broke. God didn't give them the power to get wealth!"

Yes, He did. They just didn't know how to use it.

You see, God's abundance doesn't just fall out of heaven and hit us on the head. He has designated ways for us to receive it. If we don't know how to operate in those ways, we will miss out on what is ours.

That's really not surprising when you think about it. Even things on earth work that way. For example, you can have a million dollars in a bank account, but if you don't know it's there or if you don't know how to make a withdrawal on your account, you won't be able to enjoy that money.

The same is true in the kingdom of God. The Bible says you have a heavenly account. The Apostle Paul referred to it when he wrote to his partners and thanked them for giving into his ministry (Philippians 4:17).

Your heavenly account is much like an earthly bank account in that you can make deposits into it. Not only is it possible to make deposits there, but according to Matthew 6:19-21, Jesus told us it is very important for us to do so.

> "Lay not up for yourselves treasures upon earth, where moth and rust doth corrupt, and where thieves break through and steal: But lay up for yourselves treasures in heaven...For where your treasure is, there will your heart be also."
> MATTHEW 6:19-21

FOR FURTHER STUDY:

Matthew 6:19-21

DAILY SCRIPTURE READING:

Job 42;
Proverbs 1;
Revelation 21

So sow to the spirit. Sow to your heavenly account. Give to others. Meet their needs. Give to the work of God through ministries and outreaches—this is above your tithe. And when you give to these, release your faith. Name your seed. Tell God what you are believing for. It's a wonderful thing to have an account in heaven! It's a wonderful thing to know as Paul's partners did, that *"God will liberally supply (fill to the full) your every need according to His riches in glory in Christ Jesus"* (Philippians 4:19, AMP).

## Speak the Word

*I lay up for myself treasures in heaven, for where my treasure is, there will my heart be also.*
*Matthew 6:19-21*

> "My son, attend to my words; incline thine ear unto my sayings. Let them [the Words of God] not depart from thine eyes; keep them in the midst of thine heart.... Keep thy heart with all diligence; for out of it are the issues of life."
>
> PROVERBS
> 4:20-21, 23

# Change Your Routine

So many people walk around saying things like, "Well, I'm just so tired...I'm so weak...Things are looking so bad." Then suddenly, they think they're going to jerk their faith out from under the table and raise the dead with it.

Well, they're not going to do it because spiritual things don't work that way. Faith needs to be taken out from under the table, all right, but not to just use it to get out of a jam and then toss it aside again. Keep it in action every day so it can grow.

According to Proverbs 4, God says you must keep His Word constantly in your ears and in your heart. He says to guard your heart diligently. To be *diligent* means to be "hard-working, industrious, persevering."

Why do you have to be so diligent with the Word? Because the devil is diligent with his junk. He's constantly throwing fiery darts at you. He works diligently to make sure the world is surrounding you with fear and sickness and poverty and every other kind of garbage he can use to destroy you.

But you can protect your spirit from those things by conditioning yourself to respond to every one of them with the Word of God. Change your routine, and make a decision right now to begin that spiritual conditioning. Start today and make speaking the Word part of your daily life.

## *Speak the Word*

*The Word of God is near to me. It is in my mouth and in my heart.*
*Romans 10:8*

FOR FURTHER
STUDY:

Proverbs
15:1-7, 23

DAILY SCRIPTURE
READING:

Proverbs 2-3;
Revelation 22

*Gloria*
# Shout for Joy!

Matthew 5:10-12 is the secret to overcoming persecution. At the very moment when persecution comes, you are not to be depressed. You're not to be angry or discouraged. You are to rejoice and be glad! Not just glad, but exceedingly glad!

Luke 6:23 takes that command even further. It says, *"Rejoice ye in that day [of persecution], and leap for joy: for, behold, your reward is great in heaven."*

A few days after I first noticed that instruction in the Scripture, someone came into my office and told me of something critical that had been written about us. So I just took that verse literally. I got up and began to leap for joy. "Glory to God! Joy, joy, joy!" I shouted.

I'm sure the person sitting on the other side of my desk was surprised, but I didn't care because the Word worked. I found out you can't jump for joy and shout praises to God and be depressed at the same time.

Remember that the next time persecution comes your way. It will ruin the devil's whole scheme. He thinks he has figured out what that persecution will do to you. He thinks it will discourage you and stop your ministry.

But if you'll immediately begin to leap and jump for joy...if you'll believe what Jesus said, and shout, "Praise God, I'm blessed!" the tables will be turned. The devil will end up being the one who's discouraged. He sent that persecution to stop you, not to bless you. Just think how frustrated he'll be!

## *Speak the Word*

*I rejoice and am exceedingly glad when I am persecuted*
*for righteousness' sake, for the kingdom of heaven is mine.*
*Matthew 5:10-12*

> "Blessed are they which are persecuted for righteousness' sake: for theirs is the kingdom of heaven. Blessed are ye, when men shall revile you, and persecute you, and shall say all manner of evil against you falsely, for my sake. Rejoice, and be exceeding glad: for great is your reward in heaven: for so persecuted they the prophets which were before you."
> MATTHEW 5:10-12

FOR FURTHER STUDY:

John 15:16-27

DAILY SCRIPTURE READING:

Proverbs 4-5;
Psalm 1

# Time Has Culminated in Jesus!

> "Behold, the days come, saith the Lord, that the plowman shall overtake the reaper, and the treader of grapes him that soweth seed; and the mountains shall drop sweet wine, and all the hills shall melt."
>
> AMOS 9:13

Time as we have known it is over. These are *different* times now. And what I'm about to tell you is almost unthinkable, not from a bad standpoint, but from a good one.

You and I have entered into a sliver of time, a little, narrow band of time, which is the biggest and perhaps the most important block of time since the creation of Adam. We have stepped over—in the spiritual realm *and* the natural—into exceeding, abundantly above all that we can ask or think (Ephesians 3:20).

John 6:5-13 records the event where Jesus took the basket of five loaves and two fish and fed thousands of people. Now if there was ever a picture of exceeding, abundantly above all that we can ask or think, this is it. There were thousands of people eating until they were full, and 12 baskets filled with leftovers.

People today would say, "My, what a wonderful miracle!" And they're right, it was a miracle. But this was more than a miracle. On that day, *time* culminated in Jesus. It was compressed, or tightly compacted, within a short space. The growing time for the seed the little boy planted in Jesus' ministry was instant.

The disciples told Jesus, "There's a boy here with some bread and a couple of fish." Jesus asked for the food, and they got it for Him. He took it, looked toward heaven, gave thanks for it, blessed it, broke it and distributed it among His disciples. They, in turn, took the food and distributed it among the people...and they distributed it...and distributed it—to approximately 20,000 people. Then, they went back and picked up all the leftovers. There were 12 baskets full!

What I want you to see is that this whole process of Jesus' taking the loaves and fish into His hands, blessing it, breaking it and distributing it, is the whole sowing and reaping process condensed into a matter of moments.

That lad sowed his five barley loaves and two small fish into the ministry of Jesus. Jesus received the boy's seed—planting it in fertile soil. He watered it, then *immediately* there was a harvest. Not only was there enough to feed everyone until they were full, there was also plenty left over for the storehouse. Whose storehouse? That little boy's storehouse! He was the one who planted, wasn't he?

So what happened? The reaper caught up with the sower. Amos 9:13 prophesies that there is a time coming when seed time and harvest time will run together. That young fellow sowed his bread and fish into Jesus' ministry that morning, and went home later that afternoon with 12 baskets full—all because time culminated in Jesus. And that, my brother and sister, is the kind of time we're living in today.

## *Speak the Word*

*Because of Jesus, time has culminated. The time has come when the plowman has overtaken the reaper. Seed time and harvest time are running together.*
*Amos 9:13*

FOR FURTHER STUDY:

John 6:5-13

DAILY SCRIPTURE READING:

Proverbs 6-7;
Psalm 2

*Gloria*

# The Counsel of the Lord

Many Christians have a counseling mentality today. They think that Scripture says, "If there's any troubled among you, let him go for counseling and get the pastor to pray." But that's not what it says.

Let me tell you Whose counsel will bring you out of trouble—the counsel of the Lord. Ken and I know that from experience. Some years ago, for instance, this ministry faced serious financial trouble. We were a million dollars in the red and no matter what we did, we just couldn't seem to shake that deficit.

So Ken began to seek the wisdom of God. He prayed and said, "What is the problem here, Lord?"

Then he got still and listened for the counsel of God. Sure enough, that counsel came.

God said, *Give the top 10 percent of the ministry's gross income away.*

Now, those instructions made no sense to the natural mind. They seemed like foolishness. But we were just "foolish" enough to follow them. And, of course, when we did, God brought us out of that deficit.

Let me warn you. You're never going to figure out the counsel of the Lord with your mind. He is so much smarter than we are that sometimes His wise counsel sounds foolish to us. We have to come to a place of faith where we simply say, "God, I realize that You're smarter than I am, so I'll do whatever You say."

Remember though, God isn't going to interrupt your life with His wisdom. He will wait on you to turn to Him, to seek after Him. You must do as Psalm 34:4 says: *"I sought the Lord, and he heard me, and delivered me from all my fears."*

## Speak the Word

*I seek the Lord and He hears me.*
*He delivers me from all my fears.*
*Psalm 34:4*

FOR FURTHER
STUDY:

Psalm 34

DAILY SCRIPTURE
READING:

Proverbs 8-9;
Psalm 3

# Jesus, Bartimaeus and You

> "For I say, through the grace given unto me, to every man that is among you, not to think of himself more highly than he ought to think; but to think soberly, according as God hath dealt to every man the measure of faith."
>
> ROMANS 12:3

In my years of ministry, I've seen people who will learn a little about faith and put it into practice. But when they don't get instant results, they sometimes get discouraged. They begin to think they just don't have the kind of faith that people in the Bible had. If that's happened to you, let me assure you, God hasn't shortchanged you. You have everything it takes to live by faith!

The Word says God has given every man *"among you"*—or every believer—the measure of faith. That means He deposited the same measure of faith inside you that He deposited in me—and every believer on earth. It's a force inside your spirit that's just as much a part of you as the juices in your stomach that digest your food. It's as real inside your spirit as your brain is inside your head.

No new creature was ever created with half a faith. Someone might have some kind of deformity in his or her body, but no one has any deformity in his born-again spirit. Everybody's newborn spirit has faith in it. And that faith increases as it hears and receives the Word of God.

It doesn't matter who you are, where you are or what you are. If you have made Jesus Lord of your life, you have more faith capacity in you than Jairus had when he directed Jesus toward his daughter (Mark 5).

You have more faith capacity in you than the woman with the issue of blood had when her touch brought Jesus to a halt in the middle of the road. Your faith is the very same faith Jesus has. He is the Author of your faith.

Has God changed? No. Never has. Never will. So if Jairus...and the woman on the road...and Bartimaeus...and the leper...and the two blind men could receive from the Anointing of Jesus, so can you. You already have in you all the faith you'll ever need. If there is weakness, it is in the development and the release of that faith.

## *Speak the Word*

*God has dealt to me the measure of faith.*
*My faith grows more and more as I hear the Word.*
*Romans 12:3; 10:17*

FOR FURTHER STUDY:

Mark 10:46-52

DAILY SCRIPTURE READING:

Proverbs 10-12;
Psalms 4-5

*Kenneth*

# The Only Thing

With all the Glory and power God is pouring out right now, you'd think every believer on earth would be happy as a pig in the sunshine. You'd think every one of us would be healed and delivered and shouting God's praises all day long. You'd think we'd all be free of every bondage of the devil.

But, quite frankly, many believers are more frustrated today than they've ever been in their lives. God's miracle-working power is falling around them like rain...yet no matter where they go, they can't seem to get wet! These baffled believers go from one meeting to the next, hoping God will heal them of some sickness, or free them from some habit or sin that has ensnared them.

When they get to the service, they shout and holler and praise God. They run up and down the aisle and have a great time. They fall on the floor under the power of God.

Yet, as wonderful as all those things are, by the time they get home, they're hurting again. So they sadly say, "Well, I guess I didn't get anything tonight either."

If that has happened to you, I want you to pay close attention. If you've been walking around thinking, *I just don't understand it. In times past, anybody could pray for me and I'd get healed. But now even the most anointed ministers can pray for me and nothing happens,* I want you to know something: God is not neglecting you. He is not ignoring your need. He is telling you it's time to grow up.

Don't cry over this. It's good news! God is letting you know that you're mature enough in Him that you don't need baby food anymore. You don't need anybody to feed you healing and deliverance. You don't have to run around from one meeting to another trying to get in on a miracle. You've grown to the point where He expects you to pick up your Bible and get what you need by faith.

You're not alone either. There are many other believers who have reached this same stage of spiritual growth. From now on, if they're going to walk in freedom—from sickness, sin, disease, poverty and all the rest of the devil's junk—they'll have to get it from the Word.

Jesus is saying to them, as He has said to me, *"Ye shall know the truth, and the truth shall make you free"* (John 8:32). What's more, it is the only thing that will make you free!

"Sanctify them—purify, consecrate, separate them for Yourself, make them holy—by the Truth. Your Word is Truth."
JOHN 17:17, AMP

FOR FURTHER STUDY:

John 8:31-38

DAILY SCRIPTURE READING:

Proverbs 13-14; Psalm 6

## Speak the Word

*I know the truth and it makes me free.*
*John 8:32*

# Continue DAILY

> "They were pricked in their heart, and said unto Peter and to the rest of the apostles, Men and brethren, what shall we do? Then Peter said unto them, Repent, and be baptized every one of you in the name of Jesus Christ for the remission of sins, and ye shall receive the gift of the Holy Ghost."
> ACTS 2:37-38

When the disciples all got in one accord and were baptized in the upper room, a multitude of people gathered in Jerusalem to see what all the noise was about. Peter went out and told them to do the same thing he and the rest of the disciples had been doing for days—"Repent!" In essence he said, "Do what we've been doing, man. Repent! Repent and you'll be baptized in the Holy Ghost just like we were!"

Sure enough, they did and the Spirit was poured out on them.

"Well now, Brother Copeland, our church had a repentance service back about six years ago. Everybody went down to the altar and cried. It was really great."

I'm sure it was, but the repenting you did six years ago won't put you in the place of Glory today. If we are in the midst of this outpouring, we have to do like the early Church did. Acts 2:46 says they continued daily with one accord, in the Temple, and having Communion from house to house.

They didn't stop praying and repenting when the outpouring hit one glorious day. They didn't just have a great meeting and then go back to watching TV and fussing with one another. They stayed in the Word. They stayed in agreement.

When a disagreement cropped up, the disciples picked out seven men of good report, full of the Holy Ghost and power, and went down and straightened things out (see Acts 6:1-8). When they did, the Glory of God fell.

What does that mean for you and me? It means that if we'll keep ourselves in a state of repentance, if we'll continue daily to get sin out of our lives and get right with our brothers and sisters in Christ, then in this day of Glory, God will work wonders through us. Not just in church, but at work! At the Parent-Teacher Organization meeting! At the grocery store!

The Glory will make us more alive. It will turn us into carriers of the healing, transforming, miracle-working power of God.

God will use us to bring rivers of His presence to the dry places. He'll use us to stir up those who have fallen asleep, to shake them to the very soles of their feet...and the dead will come alive on every corner in this earth!

## *Speak the Word*

*I continue in the Word; therefore, I am Jesus' disciple.*
*John 8:31*

FOR FURTHER STUDY:

Acts 2:37-47

DAILY SCRIPTURE READING:

Proverbs 15-16; Psalm 7

*Gloria*

# Receive His LIFE

The Word of God and its power to heal your body is more than just good information. It actually has LIFE in it! Jesus said so in John 6:63.

Every time you take the Word into your heart, believe it and act on it, that life of which Jesus spoke, the very LIFE of God Himself, is released in you. You may have read the healing scriptures over and over again. You may know them as well as you know your own name. Yet, every time you read them or hear them preached, they bring you a fresh dose of God's healing power. Each time, they bring life to you and deliver God's medicine to your flesh.

That's because the Word is like a seed. Hebrews 4:12 (AMP) says it is *"alive and full of power—making it active, operative, energizing and effective...."* It actually carries within it the power to fulfill itself!

> "It is the spirit that quickeneth [or makes alive]; the flesh profiteth nothing: the words that I speak unto you, they are spirit, and they are life."
> JOHN 6:63

When you planted the Word about the new birth in your heart, then believed and acted on it, that Word released within you the power to be born again. By the same token, when you plant the Word about healing in your heart, believe and act on it, that Word will release God's healing power in you.

When you read the Bible, you'll see that spiritual power has been affecting this physical world ever since time began. In fact, it was spiritual power released in the form of God's Word that brought this natural world into existence in the first place. He spoke it into being.

It must become a revelation to you, that God's Word is the force that originally brought into being everything you can see and touch—including your physical body. It will then be easy to believe that the Word is still capable of changing your body today. It makes perfect sense!

So get into the Word. Speak its life-giving force aloud over your body in faith...and receive your healing! Receive His LIFE!

## Speak the Word

*The Spirit quickens me. The words that Jesus speaks to me are spirit and life.*

John 6:63

FOR FURTHER STUDY:

Hebrews 4:1-12

DAILY SCRIPTURE READING:

Proverbs 17-18; Psalm 8

> "The god of this world [the devil] hath blinded the minds of them which believe not, lest the light of the glorious gospel of Christ, who is the image of God, should shine unto them."
>
> 2 CORINTHIANS 4:4

# Praying Brother In

Do you know how to pray your family into the kingdom of God with skill? I have found that many Christians don't. They throw prayers in every direction and hope something comes of it. That's especially true when they pray for the lost. I've met people who've prayed for 20, 30 or 40 years without results.

Knowing how to pray with skill can change that. Understand this: If you've been interceding for your brother (or anyone else), there's nothing wrong with him except the devil! No human being who truly understood the salvation Jesus offers would reject it of his own free will. No one!

Why, then, are so many people still unsaved? Second Corinthians 4:4 tells us that the devil is the one who has blinded their minds. Once you realize that it's the devil—not your brother—who's the real problem, your first prayer step becomes clear. You must get the devil out of your brother's way.

Jesus said you can't enter into a strong man's house, and spoil his goods, except you first bind the strong man (Matthew 12:29). So bind him. Say, "You spirit operating in the life of my brother, blinding him to the gospel to keep him out of the kingdom of God, I bind you now. I belong to the Lord Jesus Christ. I carry His authority and righteousness, and in His Name I command you to desist in your maneuvers. I spoil your house according to the Word of God, and I enter into it to deliver my brother from your hands."

Now, you may not be able to cast that devil entirely out of the situation, because your brother may invite him back in faster than you can cast him out. But you can bind that spirit and keep it bound. It may keep you busy for a few days, but you can do it.

You'll find your next prayer step in Matthew 9:37-38. Jesus, looking out at the multitudes who needed ministry, said to His disciples, *"Pray ye therefore the Lord of the harvest, that he will send forth labourers into his harvest."* It's the Word of God that brings faith for salvation (Romans 10:17). See to it that the Word comes across your brother's path.

"How?" you say. "He won't listen to me!" Maybe not, but God knows who he will listen to, and He'll send that person halfway around the world to talk to your brother if necessary.

Once you've prayed for your brother like that, from then on, put your faith in action by treating him like he's saved—not like he's no good. Talk to him about the good things of God the way you would if he were already born again. Then just stand back and watch how things change. You'll be amazed.

## *Speak the Word*

*I bind the spirits blinding the minds of my loved ones concerning the gospel of Jesus Christ. I obey the command of Jesus by asking the Lord of the harvest to send forth laborers into this harvest, for it is truly plenteous.*
*2 Corinthians 4:4; Matthew 9:37-38*

FOR FURTHER STUDY:

Matthew 9:37-38; 12:29

DAILY SCRIPTURE READING:

Proverbs 19-20; Psalm 9

# Be Light on Your Feet

Listen, it's just about supper time in the kingdom of God! Jesus is preparing a banquet for us in heaven and it's almost complete. So get ready. Don't be so caught up in the world's activities that you can't hear what He is telling you to do.

Now is the time to consecrate and dedicate every fiber of your being, every moment of your life and everything you do to the Lord's service. You don't want anything to hold you back in this thrilling hour. You don't want anything to keep you from walking in the spirit and experiencing the Glory God is about to manifest in the earth.

Jesus taught about this kind of readiness in Matthew 25:1-13:

*"Then shall the kingdom of heaven be likened unto ten virgins, which took their lamps, and went forth to meet the bridegroom. And five of them were wise, and five were foolish.*

*"They that were foolish took their lamps, and took no oil with them: But the wise took oil in their vessels with their lamps.*

*"While the bridegroom tarried, they all slumbered and slept. And at midnight there was a cry made, Behold, the bridegroom cometh; go ye out to meet him.*

*"Then all those virgins arose, and trimmed their lamps. And the foolish said unto the wise, Give us of your oil; for our lamps are gone out.*

*"But the wise answered, saying, Not so; lest there be not enough for us and you: but go ye rather to them that sell, and buy for yourselves. And while they went to buy, the bridegroom came; and they that were ready went in with him to the marriage: and the door was shut.*

*"Afterward came also the other virgins, saying, Lord, Lord, open to us. But he answered and said, Verily I say unto you, I know you not.*

*"Watch therefore, for ye know neither the day nor the hour wherein the Son of man cometh."*

The point this parable makes very clear is this: When it comes to being ready and dedicating yourself to the Lord, you're the one who has to do it. You must go and buy oil for yourself—ahead of time. You must see to it that you're ready for God. You must make sure there's nothing in your life that would cause you to shrink back from His presence.

So prepare yourself! Consecrate yourself to God and keep yourself full of the Word and the Holy Spirit so that when you hear the blast of the trumpet announcing Jesus' return, you'll be so light on your feet that you'll just lift right out of here!

FOR FURTHER STUDY:

Colossians 3:1-10

◀

DAILY SCRIPTURE READING:

Proverbs 21-22; Psalm 10

## *Speak the Word*

*I do not know the day nor the hour when Jesus will return; therefore I will continue to watch for Him.*
*Matthew 25:13*

*Kenneth*

"These things have I spoken unto you, that my joy might remain in you, and that your joy might be full.... Ask, and ye shall receive, that your joy may be full."
JOHN 15:11, 16:24

# Run the Devil Off With Joy!

Whatever is happening in your life today, you need to stir up the joy that is within you as a born-again child of God.

How can you do that?

For starters, you can begin by meditating on the Word of God. When you meditate on the Word and revelation begins to rise in your heart, joy comes! It comes because you begin to have a deeper and clearer knowledge of the Father. It comes because you realize you can go boldly before Him in prayer on the basis of the Word, and be confident your prayers will be answered.

If you've been sorrowing over a wayward child, for example, you can replace your sad thoughts with a revelation of God's promise in Isaiah 54:13, and joy will come into your heart. Suddenly, instead of crying over what the devil is doing to that child, start shouting about what God will do. You laugh and say, "You might as well forget it, devil. Just pack up and go home right now, because as far as I'm concerned, the victory is won. All my children shall be taught of the Lord. And great shall be the peace of my children!"

Then when the devil comes back at you and says, *Maybe so, but aren't you sorry over all the years that child has wasted?* you can shoot the Word right back at him and say, "No, I'm not sorry. I don't have to be sorry because Jesus bore my griefs and carried my sorrows (Isaiah 53:4). So I'll just go ahead and have myself a grand time rejoicing in Him!"

Proverbs 15:23 says, *"A man hath joy by the answer of his mouth."* When you start answering the troubles and trials you're facing with the Word of God, it will release joy in you and run the devil off. He can't stand the joy of the Lord!

So stir up that joy within you. Meditate the Word. Replace wrong thoughts with God's thoughts. And enjoy the victory!

## *Speak the Word*

*I ask and I receive, that my joy may be full.*
*John 16:24*

FOR FURTHER STUDY:

Isaiah 51:11-16

❧

DAILY SCRIPTURE READING:

Proverbs 23-24; Psalm 11

*Gloria*

# None of These Things Move Me

If you want to rob persecution of every last scrap of its power, adopt the attitude Paul had in 2 Corinthians 4:17-18. He wasn't concerned about the pressure he was experiencing down here on the earth. And, believe me, he was under tremendous pressure.

He'd probably laugh at us talking about persecution these days, we've had so little of it.

Paul's thoughts weren't centered on this natural life. He was thinking about that eternal weight of Glory. He was looking ahead to spending eternity in the presence of Jesus.

So he didn't grow weary. He didn't faint under persecutions, tribulations or threats. In fact, in Acts 20:24 he said, *"None of these things move me, neither count I my life dear unto myself, so that I might finish my course with joy."*

Once you adopt that attitude, the devil won't be able to control you at all. He won't be able to find any persecution that will stop you.

You'll have your eyes so fixed on running your race and finishing your course, you won't even pay any attention to his junk. Instead of fussing and fuming over all the ugly things people are saying about you, you'll be busy looking forward to the day when you will stand face to face with Jesus and hear Him say, "Well done, thou good and faithful servant."

## *Speak the Word*

*I do not look at the things which are seen, but at the things which are not seen: for the things which are seen are temporal; but the things which are not seen are eternal.*

*2 Corinthians 4:18*

"For our light affliction, which is but for a moment, worketh for us a far more exceeding and eternal weight of glory; While we look not at the things which are seen, but at the things which are not seen: for the things which are seen are temporal; but the things which are not seen are eternal."

2 CORINTHIANS 4:17-18

FOR FURTHER STUDY:

1 Corinthians 9:24-27

DAILY SCRIPTURE READING:

Proverbs 25-27;
Psalms 12-13

Kenneth

> "But this is that which was spoken by the prophet Joel; And it shall come to pass in the last days, saith God, I will pour out of my Spirit upon all flesh: and your sons and your daughters shall prophesy, and your young men shall see visions, and your old men shall dream dreams."
>
> ACTS 2:16-17

# A Glorious Outpouring

On the first day of that latter rain outpouring in the book of Acts, 3,000 people were born again. Ever since that time, we've continued to see the manifestation of that rain. We saw it all the way through the book of Acts.

Now if the glorious things we read about in Acts were only the beginning of that which was spoken of by the prophet Joel, can you imagine what lies ahead?

Think about that for a moment. This outpouring of God's Spirit on His servants and handmaidens will contain the Holy Ghost power seen in the Old Covenant, plus the power of the early Church in the New. This is the former and latter together!

Can you imagine someone walking around with the power that Elisha and Elijah had and the power that Peter and Paul had—all at the same time? It's about to happen!

If you'll get your act straightened up and get yourself moving in the Spirit of God, it will happen to you. It won't matter whether you've been to Bible school or not, my friend. If you'll dare to believe God, you can get in on this glorious event.

When I say glorious, I mean *glorious!*

## Speak the Word

*In these last days, God is pouring out His Spirit upon all flesh.*
*He is pouring out His Spirit upon me!*
*Acts 2:16-17*

FOR FURTHER STUDY:

Joel 2:21-29

DAILY SCRIPTURE READING:

Proverbs 28-29; Psalm 14

*Gloria*

# His Hand Isn't Short

AUGUST 29

"And the Lord said unto Moses, Is the Lord's hand waxed short?"
NUMBERS 11:23

We need to go beyond believing only what is reasonable to our intellect. For example, we need to stop being content just to believe God for the money to make our house payment each month. We need to start believing Him for the money to pay off the entire mortgage!

"But Gloria, I just don't know how God would ever get that kind of money to me."

So what! Moses didn't know how God was going to bring in enough meat to feed several million Israelites for a month either. So when God said He was going to do it, Moses said, "It would take all our herds and flocks to feed this bunch! It would take all the fish in the sea!" (verse 22).

*"And the Lord said unto Moses, Is the Lord's hand waxed short?"* Then He proved He was able to do what He said by raining so much quail out of heaven, the Israelites actually got sick of it—just like He said.

When you have a need in your life that seems impossible to meet, think about that. Remember the question God asked Moses, *"Is the Lord's hand waxed short?"*

No! It wasn't short then and it isn't short now. God knows how to get the job done. He knows how to get you everything you need. So look to Him as your source. Become expectant. Become miracle-minded, blessing-minded, and supernatural-increase-minded...God-minded!

God knows how to do everything. You don't have to worry about that. Just focus on your part—believe, speak the Word and walk in the ways of God. Stop limiting God just because you don't understand how He is going to do the things He has promised. If we had to depend on what we could understand, we'd be in great trouble. But we don't! All we have to understand is that God is God and He has all power. He is able to do exceeding, abundantly above all we can ask or think!

That means if you can think it, God is able to do more than that.

If you can dream it, God is able to do more that that.

If you can hope for it, God is able to do more than that!

Whatever you need, GOD IS ABLE! He is able to satisfy your needs and godly desires and much, much more. His hand is not short!

FOR FURTHER STUDY:

Numbers 11: 16-23, 31-32

DAILY SCRIPTURE READING:

Proverbs 30-31; Psalm 15

## Speak the Word

*The Lord's hand is not waxed short. He is able to meet all my needs!*
*Numbers 11:23*

*Kenneth*

> "I receive not honour from men. But I know you, that ye have not the love of God in you. I am come in my Father's name, and ye receive me not: if another shall come in his own name, him ye will receive. How can ye believe, which receive honour one of another, and seek not the honour that cometh from God only?"
>
> JOHN 5:41-44

# Don't Play the Game!

Honor. Godly honor. It's the kind of honor that keeps its word and standard of integrity no matter what. It never fails—it always succeeds.

Every day, commitments of honor are required of you. You have choices to make regarding ethics in your job, disciplining your children, keeping your marriage strong—and it's hard. It's a choice between God's honor and man's. One brings true and sure success...and one brings shallow, temporal success that ends in ultimate failure. In other words, it looks good but doesn't last.

You just can't live the Christian life without honor. You'll never be faithful without it. You can't be. Without honor, you don't have the power to be faithful. It's just not in you.

In John 5:41-44, Jesus told the Pharisees about honor that comes from God only. That's the kind of honor we must have to stand in our day. You can be a powerful force in the earth as a believer who walks by faith, but to do it, you must operate in His honor.

Man's definition of honor, however, is quite different from God's. It is a derivative of the honor of God, but it is light and shallow—it is a false honor that deceives men. The world's honor that comes from men and is given to men is what I call the "honor game." In this sport, everything is done to gain the prestige, power and authority that other men can give. It's temporal, short-lived and dishonorable in view of what some men will do to get it.

In playing the game, people will scheme, beg, swap favors, cheat and "shade the truth" to "win." You may work with people like that. These schemers may receive the same physical privileges, the same "honor" as those who are truly deserving—although they did not win with true honor. But know that in the long run, they don't win.

On the other hand, God is faithful to honor you when you act honorably. That's because you are acting in something that originated in Him! He is honorable. So don't play the game! Live honorably with the honor that comes from God alone. Your rewards will be far greater and eternal...He guarantees it.

## *Speak the Word*

*As I honor God, He honors me.*
*1 Samuel 2:30*

FOR FURTHER STUDY:

Psalm 15

DAILY SCRIPTURE READING:

Ecclesiastes 1-2;
Psalm 16

*Gloria*

# Don't Be an Unholy Tare

> "The time is come that judgment must begin at the house of God."
>
> 1 PETER 4:17

I believe we've come to the time the Apostle Peter was referring to when he wrote these words. We haven't heard a lot about that judgment in recent years. But that's not because the New Testament doesn't teach about it. It does! In fact, Jesus Himself talked about that judgment in Matthew 13. In years past, I didn't understand that chapter because I kept thinking He was referring to the rapture of the Church in the last days. But I knew that couldn't be right because He refers to the *wicked* being removed—not the righteous.

Recently, I've come to believe that He is talking about the separation of the holy from the unholy that will take place in the final days of this age.

According to Jesus, there is coming a time at the end of the world, at the harvest time, when the tares are going to be taken out. It's the time when the righteous will shine with the Glory of God. It's the time when Jesus will sanctify His Church and cleanse it so that He *"might present it to himself a glorious church, not having spot, or wrinkle, or any such thing; but that it should be holy and without blemish"* (see Ephesians 5:26-27).

If you're an unholy tare, that's a frightening thought. But if you've set your heart on being holy, it's exciting. It means that you are going to be a part of that glorious Church.

"But I don't know if I can be holy, without spot or blemish!"

Yes, you can. And so can I. By the grace of God we'll be that Church. We have to be. If this is the end, then there's nobody else to do it. We're it! We're all God has. And because He is God, He can bring it forth in us!

God *is* able! So let's believe that. Let's act on it. Let's pray for ourselves and each other the inspired words of the Apostle Paul:

*"And may the God of peace Himself sanctify you through and through—that is, separate you from profane things, make you pure and wholly consecrated to God—and may your spirit and soul and body be preserved sound and complete [and found] blameless at the coming of our Lord Jesus Christ, the Messiah. Faithful is He Who is calling you [to Himself] and utterly trustworthy, and He will also do it"* (1 Thessalonians 5:23-24, AMP).

## Speak the Word

*The God of peace sanctifies me through and through.*
*My whole spirit and soul and body are preserved blameless*
*unto the coming of my Lord Jesus Christ.*
*1 Thessalonians 5:23*

FOR FURTHER STUDY:

Matthew 13:24-30

DAILY SCRIPTURE READING:

Ecclesiastes 3-4;
Psalm 17

> "Servants, obey in everything those who are your earthly masters, not only when their eyes are on you, as pleasers of men, but in simplicity of purpose (with all your heart) because of your reverence for the Lord and as a sincere expression of your devotion to Him. "
> COLOSSIANS 3:22, AMP

# The Sure Path to Promotion

You may not realize it, but if you're a born-again believer, you have a quality within you that is in great demand in the world today. It's a quality employers prize so highly that they'll promote people who have it—and often pay top dollar for it. It's a quality so valuable it can make you a success in every area of your life.

What quality could possibly be so precious? The quality of faithfulness.

Employers are desperate for faithful people. The world is full of employees who will just do enough to keep from getting fired. It's full of people who may come to work—and may not. That's how worldly people are!

But it's a treasure for employers to find a person who works wholeheartedly at his job, who is trustworthy and dependable and honest. So when an employer finds a person like that, he's usually eager to promote him.

The fact is, every believer ought to be that kind of person. Each one of us should live a lifestyle of faithfulness. As Ken says, we should make it a lifestyle to do what's right, do it because it's right. Anything less is disobedience to God's Word.

We should follow Colossians 3:22-24. It's God's instruction for employees. Ken and I have seen some of the staff members in our ministry take that attitude and, as a result, be promoted again and again. One man started out with the job of duplicating tapes for us, but over the years he was so faithful that he eventually became the director over the business affairs of the entire ministry.

You may think, *Well, that wouldn't work in my case. My boss is an unfair man. He wouldn't reward my faithfulness.*

That's no problem. The Scripture doesn't say your reward will come from your employer. It says your reward will come from the Lord!

You see, God has established a principle of sowing and reaping in the earth—and that principle is always at work (Galatians 6:7). If you plant faithfulness in your job, you will receive blessing in return—even if that blessing means a different but better job.

So make up your mind to put your whole heart into your work, no matter how menial or unpleasant it may seem to be. Do it well. Do it with a smile and an attitude of enthusiasm and say, "Lord, You know I am believing for another job. And I am sowing faithfulness into this job as seed for a better job." I guarantee you, a better job will soon come along.

## *Speak the Word*

*I obey my earthly masters with all my heart, out of reverence for the Lord, and as a sincere expression of my devotion to Him.*
*Colossians 3:22, AMP*

FOR FURTHER STUDY:

Galatians 6:7-10

DAILY SCRIPTURE READING:

Ecclesiastes 5-6; Psalm 18

*Gloria*

# Go the Rest of the Distance

Many Christians today have come the greater part of the distance in their walk with God. They've been delivered of old habits, and have learned to give God first place in their lives. They've trained themselves to get up early and spend time with God each day. They aren't living in habitual sin and being led by their flesh all the time. They know what God wants them to do. They know His will for their lives. They have grown up to be mature believers. But they haven't arrived.

"Why, Gloria, what do you mean?"

God is calling all believers, including mature believers, to greater consecration. He wants us to spend more time in prayer, more time in the Word. There may not be sin in our lives, but there are little things holding us back spiritually. It could be natural things taking up too much of our time—things that keep us from more of God. Hebrews 12:1 calls them "weights."

The Spirit of God is faithful to tell us those adjustments we need to make. Maybe He's telling you to get up earlier like He told me at one point in my life. In fact, I'm thinking of getting up even earlier than I have been. I want more time. I want more time before I go out and live my day. For years I've gotten up as early as I needed. If I have to catch an early flight to travel overseas for example, well, I just get up at 3 a.m. or 4 a.m. Whatever it takes. I just do it.

God speaks to us about what's in our hearts. He loves us. He says, *Just put that aside. Lay it aside for a while. It's taking up too much of your thoughts, too much of your time.*

You need to ask yourself, *What makes me tick? What is it that I think of when I wake up in the morning? What is it that's the center of my attention in this life?*

If it's not God and His Word and His kingdom, then you need to make a change. You need to get God at the center of your life.

Don't divide your loyalty. Keep yourself, your attention, undivided. Seek first the kingdom of God and put first things first. Those three things right there will give you a successful spiritual life. And if you have a successful spiritual life, you'll have a successful natural life.

So pick up the pace. Go the rest of the distance. You can't win a race with weights attached to your feet! Lay aside those weights and run with patience the race God has set before you.

> "Now every athlete who goes into training conducts himself temperately and restricts himself in all things. They do it to win a wreath that will soon wither, but we [do it to receive a crown of eternal blessedness] that cannot wither."
> 1 CORINTHIANS 9:25, AMP

FOR FURTHER STUDY:

1 Corinthians 9:23-27

DAILY SCRIPTURE READING:

Ecclesiastes 7-8; Psalm 19

## Speak the Word

*I lay aside every weight and the sin which does so easily beset me.*
*I run with patience the race that is set before me.*
*Hebrews 12:1*

> "A man's belly shall be satisfied with the fruit of his mouth; and with the increase of his lips shall he be filled. Death and life are in the power of the tongue: and they that love it shall eat the fruit thereof."
>
> PROVERBS
> 18:20-21

# What Are You Becoming?

If you're not sure what you're becoming, let me give you a hint. You're going to be whatever you think about and talk about all the time.

I can listen to you talk for 30 minutes and tell you exactly what you'll become. It doesn't take a prophet to do that. It just takes someone who will listen to your words.

So listen to yourself. If you don't like what you hear, change it. Become better by beginning to think God's Word, talk God's Word and act on God's Word.

Nobody on earth can determine what you're going to become but you. Yes, you! Don't blame it on the devil. He can't change it. Don't blame it on your parents, your background or your circumstances. And certainly, don't blame God.

Forget those things which are behind...and do what Abraham did. The Bible says, *"He considered not his own body now dead, when he was about an hundred years old, neither yet the deadness of Sarah's womb"* (Romans 4:19).

He just said to himself, *Old man, you don't count. Neither do you, Granny. What counts is God's Word and I am exactly what God says I am.*

Do you want to become what God says you are? Do you want to be healed? Do you want to become free financially? Do you want to become a powerful witness in your circle of influence? What is your dream?

You can determine your outcome in life by changing your words to God's Words, and releasing your faith. You *can* become all you were meant to be.

## Speak the Word

*My belly shall be satisfied with the fruit of my mouth,*
*and with the increase of my lips, I am filled.*
*Proverbs 18:20*

FOR FURTHER
STUDY:

Matthew
12:33-37

DAILY SCRIPTURE
READING:

Ecclesiastes 9-11;
Psalms 20-21

*Gloria*

# God Wants You Healthy—Every Day!

I have some revolutionary news for you today. God wants you healthy! Every day!

*Oh, I know that,* you may quickly think, *I know God will heal me when I get sick.*

Yes, that's true. He will. But that's not what I'm saying. I'm telling you God's perfect will is for you to live continually in divine health. His will is for you to walk so fully in the power of His Word that sickness and disease are literally pushed away from you. Isn't that good news?

You've probably heard a lot about God's healing power, but there is a difference between divine healing and divine health. Years ago, the powerful preacher John G. Lake put it this way, "Divine healing is the removal by the power of God of the disease that has come upon the body. But divine health is to live day by day, hour by hour in touch with God so that the life of God flows into the body just as the life of God flows into the mind or flows into the spirit."

Proverbs 4:20-22 tells us God's Word is life to us and health to our bodies. That word *health* in Hebrew means "medicine." God's Word has life in it. It is actually spirit food. As you feed on it, you become strong spiritually and physically.

When you read the Word and meditate on it, you are actually taking God's medicine. If you will be faithful to take it continually, eventually it will be as hard for you to get sick as it was for you to get well.

But it's a process. You can't just read the healing scriptures once and then go on about your business. You must continually feed on the Word of God to keep healing in your life. When you do that, you'll be walking healed every day! You'll be walking in divine health.

> "And ye shall serve the Lord your God, and he shall bless thy bread, and thy water; and I will take sickness away from the midst of thee."
> EXODUS 23:25

## Speak the Word

*I serve the Lord my God, and He blesses my bread and my water and takes sickness away from my midst.*

*Exodus 23:25*

FOR FURTHER STUDY:

Isaiah 40:28-31

DAILY SCRIPTURE READING:

Ecclesiastes 12;
Song of
Solomon 1;
Psalm 22

*Kenneth*

"He could do
no mighty
work there,
except that He
laid His hands
on a few sick
people and
healed them.
And He
marveled
because of
their
unbelief."
MARK 6:5-6, NKJV

# Stop the Anointing Blocker

Prepare yourself. The anointing is increasing everywhere in the lives of God's people. It's flowing in greater power not only in the ministries of apostles, prophets, evangelists, pastors and teachers, but also in the lives of mechanics, homemakers, computer programmers, and sales clerks. It's increasing in the lives of believers everywhere.

In the same way, when the message of the Anointed One and His Anointing was preached in the New Testament, the same power of God fell on the people.

But just like then, there is something that can block the power of the anointing, and I want to warn you about it. I want to put you on alert so the devil can't sneak up on you and rob you of the Glory that's ahead.

What is this evil thing? It is taking offense at the message of Jesus.

"But, oh, Brother Copeland, I'd never be offended at Jesus!"

No doubt that's what the people of Nazareth thought too before Jesus came to preach at their synagogue. They would have scoffed at the idea of being offended at the Scriptures. After all, they'd been studying them all their lives. But they did become offended.

You see, these people had been expecting the anointing. They just never expected it to be the boy from down the block. In their minds, he was just Mary's son, the fellow who used to have a carpentry business! They were offended when Jesus said He was anointed (Luke 4:18), and He could do no mighty works there. Their unbelief and religious ideas short-circuited the anointing (Mark 6:5-6).

If you'll read the Gospels, you'll find that attitude of offense is the thing that successfully stopped the flow of the anointing. Sin didn't stop it. Unworthiness didn't stop it. Taking offense did.

In Jesus' teaching on the sower sowing the Word in Mark Chapter 4, He pointed out that becoming offended stops the Word from producing in one's life. Offense opens the way for Satan to steal the Word, which stops faith (Romans 10:17). Faith is our anointing connection. When that connection is broken, there is nothing working to remove burdens and destroy yokes because that's what the anointing does.

So check your heart. Make the quality decision to never, ever become offended, to never turn loose of the anointing in order to hold on to offense. These are the last days. God's Glory is filling the earth. And He's filling it through you...if you'll stop the anointing blocker!

## *Speak the Word*

*I have great peace because I love God's law, and nothing shall offend me.*
*Psalm 119:165*

FOR FURTHER STUDY:

Mark 6:1-6

DAILY SCRIPTURE READING:

Song of Solomon 2-3;
Psalm 23

*Gloria*

# Don't Settle for "Payment Faith"

"Those who seek the Lord shall not lack any good thing."
PSALM 34:10, NKJV

God has always wanted His people to live in abundance. Even in the book of Deuteronomy, He talked about His people living in a land where they would live in goodly houses and where there was no scarcity.

He has told us that all He has is ours. God put everything in His Word for you and me. And He has no shortage! He wants you to live in abundance. He wants you to live in a good house. He wants you to have the car that you need. He wants you to be so blessed that you don't even have to think about those things. That way, you can just think about Him, instead of trying to make your car go another 50 miles.

He wants His family to be abundantly supplied, to be following Him, to be walking after His ways of doing and being right.

Now, I know it costs money to live. It costs money to go places and do things. It costs money to reach people for Jesus. And God's got the money! He's not broke.

But He's had a problem...getting His people to believe what He says in His Word concerning their prosperity.

One thing that interferes with our believing and receiving is located right between our ears. It's called reason. When Jesus asked Philip how they were going to feed the 5,000, he began to reason. He began to look and see what was possible. "Lord, if we had two hundred penny worth of bread, we couldn't even begin to do it. There wouldn't be enough to feed the people."

But Jesus already knew what was to happen. He wasn't looking at anything but Father God.

That's the same God you and I are hooked up to today. That same God knows how to multiply and bless and prosper you and me now. God knows how to get things done.

What we have a tendency to do is release our faith for what we believe we can see—that, along with some help from God, might come to pass. For example, some people have "payment faith" and some people have "house faith."

"Lord, I believe to make this payment. I believe to make my car payment. I believe to make my house payment."

Why don't they just believe for a house?

Get out beyond reason. Get out beyond what's reasonable. Now, don't quit making your car payment or your house payment, but get your faith out there. Let God multiply you and be your source. Pay it off supernaturally and get the next one without payments. Base your faith and praying on what the Word says, not on what you see is possible in this realm. According to the Bible, all things are possible with God and all things are possible to the believer. God and a believer make an unbeatable pair!

Don't settle for payment faith when you can have "have it" faith!

FOR FURTHER STUDY:

Ephesians 3:20;
Hebrews 6:12-15

DAILY SCRIPTURE READING:

Song of Solomon 4-5;
Psalm 24

## Speak the Word

*I seek the Lord and I do not lack any good thing.*
*Psalm 34:10, NKJV*

> "Now he that ministereth seed to the sower both minister bread for your food, and multiply your seed sown."
>
> 2 CORINTHIANS 9:10

# The Twice-Sown Seed

Matthew 14 records the event of how Jesus took the seed—the young lad's bread and fish—gave thanks for it, blessed it, broke it and gave it to His disciples to feed thousands of people. Before Jesus did all this, however, He told the disciples, *"Bring them hither to me"* (verse 18).

Why do you suppose Jesus told the disciples to give Him the bread and fish? Why did Jesus want to *handle* that seed?

The reason was the anointing of increase. The anointing of *increase* is literally and figuratively in the hands of the minister, just as it was present in Jesus' hands that day.

God's way is for goods to come into the ministry—the minister receive it, handle it, bless it and distribute it, or sow it—then for it to go out, multiplied in greater number than when it came in.

When the boy sowed seed into Jesus' ministry—the loaves and fish—Jesus received it, applied His Anointing of increase to it, and then sowed it into His disciples and the multitude. After everyone was full, Jesus told His disciples to *"gather up the fragments that remain, that nothing be lost"* (John 6:12).

The 12 baskets full of leftovers belonged to that boy. However, those baskets were only the boy's immediate harvest from having sown directly into Jesus' ministry. The fulfillment of his harvest, the fulfillment of God's obligation to him, was the fruit from seeds multiplied and sown into the lives of 20,000 people. He fed the multitudes for Jesus and had enough seed to last a lifetime. That's twice-sown seed.

Twice-sown seed is where you and I need to learn to exercise our faith and keep our expectancy. We need to expect His Anointing in every situation. We have moved into an era of exceeding, abundantly beyond what we could ask or think, a time when God now has the opportunity for His people to have more than enough to do *all* that He wants us to do, instead of the devil stealing everything as fast as it grows in the field.

Think of all the missionaries who have gone to China, Africa, South America and all those places. They preached, shed their tears and gave their lives, and it looked like the devil had the upper hand.

Well, I have news for you: Every seed sown for the last 2,000 years—every word preached, every tear and drop of blood shed—is coming up...*Now!* All 2,000 years' worth of gospel seed planted is coming up a hundredfold, and we're the ones to bring it in. It's time for the final harvest of souls! Millions of souls! So let's get to it.

## *Speak the Word*

*God ministers seed to the sower and bread for my food.*
*He multiplies my seed sown.*
*2 Corinthians 9:10*

FOR FURTHER STUDY:

John 4:35-39

DAILY SCRIPTURE READING:

Song of Solomon 6-7;
Psalm 25

*Gloria*

# More Than a History Book

When you meditate on God's Word, you're going to do more than just read it. You're going to take it into your heart in a very personal way and apply it to your situation.

When you read a scripture about the blessing of prosperity, for example, you won't think, *Hey, that sounds nice, but I could never have it.* Instead, you'll apply it to yourself and say, "Hallelujah! That's God's Word to me. He says He'll meet my needs liberally, according to His riches in Glory by Christ Jesus (Philippians 4:19), and I'm expecting Him to do that in my situation!"

If you've been reading the Bible like a history book, make a change and begin to see it as though God is talking directly to you. Take time to meditate on it. Think about it. Digest it. Take it so personally that it moves from your head to your heart. Then it will become powerful and active in your life.

> "You shall meditate on it [the Word] day and night."
> JOSHUA 1:8, AMP

## Speak the Word

*I meditate on God's Word day and night.*
*I observe to do it and I have good success!*
*Joshua 1:8*

FOR FURTHER STUDY:

Psalm 119:73-80

DAILY SCRIPTURE READING:

Song of Solomon 8;
Isaiah 1;
Psalm 26

> "For God, who commanded the light to shine out of darkness, hath shined in our hearts, to give the light of the knowledge of the glory of God in the face of Jesus Christ [the Anointed One and His Anointing]."
>
> 2 CORINTHIANS 4:6

# Ask for It!

I have meditated and studied the scriptures concerning the Glory until I am fully expecting it to manifest in my life. I'm expecting resurrection power to accompany me wherever I go. I'm expecting the same Glory that shone like fire on the face of Jesus to shine in me and my situation.

I'm expecting my God to supply all my needs. How? ACCORDING TO HIS RICHES IN GLORY!

I'm not looking for that Glory to come floating down from heaven. I'm expecting it to come from inside me. I'm expecting it to come from inside you.

I'm expecting it to come out of us because 1 Chronicles 16:27 says, *"Glory and honour are in his [God's] presence,"* and since God Himself is present in us through the indwelling Holy Spirit, the Glory is already inside us!

Our problem up to now hasn't been a lack of Glory. It's been a lack of understanding. We haven't had a revelation of the Glory of God within us. We haven't known how to cooperate with the Glory. But God doesn't intend for us to remain ignorant.

God hasn't left us in the dark. He has commanded the light to shine and give us a working knowledge, an ability to comprehend and understand how to use the Glory of God that dwells within us. He has given us the *"mind of Christ"* (1 Corinthians 2:16). In other words, the same anointing that is on the mind of Jesus is available to us.

There's no need for you to stay tied up in knots over some problem the devil has pushed on you. There's no need for you to be stopped by some mountain of sin, sickness or poverty the devil has put in your path. You have the Glory of God on the inside of you. You have the anointing to release the manifestation of that Glory.

When you put the Word of God in your heart and in your mouth, expect your words to be filled with the same resurrection power that caused hell itself to bow its knee 2,000 years ago. Expect the all-powerful goodness of God to permeate your whole being—spirit, soul and body—until your life shines with the very light that shines from Jesus' face, the light that illumines all of heaven.

So ask for it! Ask God for the knowledge of the Glory today. James 1:5 promises He will give it to you liberally!

## *Speak the Word*

*God shines in my heart to give me the knowledge of the Glory.*
*2 Corinthians 4:6*

FOR FURTHER STUDY:

2 Chronicles 7:1-3

DAILY SCRIPTURE READING:

Isaiah 2-3;
Psalm 27

# Pulling the Plug on Your Faith

*"Where envying and strife is, there is confusion and every evil work."*
JAMES 3:16

Have you ever had everything going smoothly, seen your faith working and really seeing results, only to have something odd creep up inside you? Maybe you began to feel just a little irritated at the success of others. Or, maybe you've begun to feel a little discouraged that a circumstance hasn't yet changed.

Watch out! It could be that you've allowed envy or strife to enter in. You see, Satan knows that if he can stop your faith from working, he can disrupt everything. But he also knows he can't very well just come barreling in the front door and steal the faith right out of your heart, so he slips in the back way. He uses envy and strife to interrupt the flow of love in your life.

The minute love is disrupted, your faith stops working because "faith works by love" (Galatians 5:6).

Many Christians don't understand that principle, so they struggle along, quarreling and fussing with one another—and wondering all the while why their faith isn't producing results. They don't realize that if you want to walk in the power and blessing of God, you cannot allow envy or strife into your life. Period.

According to James 3:16, envy and strife give the devil an open door into your life.

What kinds of "evil work" will the devil bring through that open door? Everything from depression to murder. Yes, murder! That was envy's first recorded act in Genesis 4. Cain murdered Abel because he was envious.

So what should you do?

Shut the door! Stubbornly resist those fleshly pressures and temptations of the devil. Treat strife just like you'd treat a rattlesnake, or any other deadly invader. Refuse to let it in!

If you've become aware of someone around you who is being more successful than you, don't be naive enough to fall into the trap that envy is setting. Trick the devil. Turn the tables on him! Start praising God for the success of that person. Do what you can to help them be even more successful.

In other words, whatever your situation, start walking in love and laying down selfishness. If you'll do that, you'll keep the door open for the blessings of God. You'll keep the devil from pulling the plug on your faith!

FOR FURTHER
STUDY:

Genesis 4:1-15

DAILY SCRIPTURE
READING:

Isaiah 4-6;
Psalms 28-29

## Speak the Word

*I walk in love and resist envy and strife. For where envying and strife is, there is confusion and every evil work.*
*James 3:16*

> "Humble yourselves therefore under the mighty hand of God, that he may exalt you."
>
> 1 PETER 5:6

# Dare to Step Out

God can take the most simple person in the world who will dare to believe what is written in the Word, and empower him to do any job he is called to do.

I know this because God did that for me. The reason I'm so blessed today is because I am so simple that I believe God is smarter than I am. When I see something in the Bible that doesn't agree with what I think, I change what I think and believe the Word of God.

Jesus admonished us to come as little children. So do that. Humble yourself and just take the Word as it is written. If God says you'll do the works, don't argue, just agree with Him and get busy!

Say, "Father, Jesus said, *'He that believeth on me, the works that I do shall he do also'* (John 14:12). I don't know how to do the works, but Your Word says I will. So I place myself at Your disposal. I expect to do the works that Jesus did!"

Then step out boldly and act on your faith. The bolder we are, the more power there can be released through us. Did you know that? It's when we hesitate and are afraid of what people might think that nothing happens. So make up your mind now to be bold—whether you want to or not.

That's how it works. But you have to take the first step. Do what the Bible says to do whether you feel like it or not. That's called ACTING ON THE WORD! And that's called FAITH!

## *Speak the Word*

*I humble myself under the mighty hand of God so that He may exalt me.*
*1 Peter 5:6*

FOR FURTHER STUDY:

Matthew 18:1-5

DAILY SCRIPTURE READING:

Isaiah 7-8;
Psalm 30

# What You Compromise to Keep, You Lose

> "Set a watch, O Lord, before my mouth; keep the door of my lips."
> PSALM 141:3

Did you know that the devil can't do anything to you if you won't give him any place? That's right. If you won't speak words of doubt and unbelief, but instead speak words of faith, he can't sustain his attack.

You see, if you're born again, Satan doesn't have any authority over you. Jesus Christ is your Lord. Satan can't rob you unless you authorize that robbery yourself!

Satan comes to get your words! That's the only way he can get a foothold. So refuse to speak words contrary to what you believe. Speak only faith—even under pressure. No matter what Satan is saying to you in your thoughts, no matter what the people around you are saying, keep agreeing with the Word of God. Keep saying what God says.

It will be tough sometimes, I know. But you can do it! When things look hopeless, don't give up and start speaking defeat. Double up on your confession of faith.

Learn to immediately answer every doubt with God's Word. Learn to answer every fear with God's Word. Learn to do combat with the sword of the Spirit.

Refuse to allow Satan to intimidate you with threats. He can only do what you say. He has no authority over you unless you give it to him. If you won't give him any place, he won't be able to carry out even one of those threats. It's when you become timid and fearful with the words of your mouth that Satan gains the upper hand.

Don't ever allow fear to make you compromise your confession of faith. I learned this long ago: What you compromise to keep, you lose. Stand firm and keep talking faith and you'll defeat any attack.

## Speak the Word

*The Lord sets a watch before my mouth. He keeps the door of my lips.*
*Psalm 141:3*

FOR FURTHER STUDY:

Matthew 9:18-26

DAILY SCRIPTURE READING:

Isaiah 9-10;
Psalm 31

*Kenneth*

# The Muscle of God

"I tell you the truth; It is expedient for you that I go away: for if I go not away, the Comforter will not come unto you; but if I depart, I will send him unto you."

JOHN 16:7

I have found that most Christians seem to think the first time the Holy Spirit did much of anything was on the Day of Pentecost. But that's not true. The Holy Spirit has been at work on this planet ever since the beginning.

When God said "Light be!," the Spirit swung into action and slung this universe into being. He was there just waiting to create. That's how the Bible introduces the Holy Spirit!

You see, the Holy Spirit is the muscle of God. Every time you see power in manifestation, you can be sure the Holy Spirit is on the scene. When the Holy Spirit came on Samson, he single-handedly killed a thousand Philistine soldiers (Judges 15:14-16).

Some people get the idea that Samson was able to do those great exploits because he was a giant of man. But he was really just an ordinary fellow. He only became extraordinary when the Spirit of God came on him.

The prophet Elijah was the same way. On his own, he was just as normal as you and me. He was once so frightened by the threats of a woman that he hid in the wilderness and asked God to kill him so he wouldn't have to face her.

But when the Holy Spirit came on him, Elijah was a powerhouse. He once called down fire from heaven, killed 450 prophets of Baal, and outran the king's chariot (drawn, no doubt, by the fastest horses in the nation of Israel). And he did it all in one day (1 Kings 18-19).

Now don't get the idea from these examples, however, that the Holy Spirit is simply a mindless source of raw power. Far from it! When He moves in on a situation, He does it with all wisdom and understanding so vast that it staggers the mind.

"Well then, why hasn't He helped me before now? Heaven knows I've needed it!," you say.

He's been waiting for you to give Him something to work with. He's been waiting there inside you, waiting for you to speak the Word of God in faith. That's been His role since the beginning—to move on God's Word and deliver the power necessary to cause that Word to manifest in the earth. That's what He did at Creation...and that's what He is commissioned to do for you.

But remember, He's your helper, not your dominator. So decide right now to start opening that door. Develop an awareness of the reality of the Holy Spirit within you. Stop spending all your time meditating on the problems you're facing and start spending it meditating on the power of the One inside you. Release the muscle of God to work for you!

## *Speak the Word*

*I have received the Holy Spirit; therefore I have received power!*
*Acts 1:8*

FOR FURTHER STUDY:

Judges 15:14-16;
1 Kings 18

DAILY SCRIPTURE READING:

Isaiah 11-12;
Psalm 32

*Gloria*

# Keep the Union

If you remain in constant contact with God, if you are vitally united with God, all of the power of heaven is at your disposal.

Did you get that? Think about that for a moment. Think how wonderful it would be to have such harmony with God that He did everything you asked Him to do!

According to Jesus, that kind of prayer power is available to every believer. It's available to you and to me...IF we will make our union with God the most important thing in our lives.

So let's do it! Let's stop compromising and allowing the things of the world to eat away at our time with God. Let's get His Word into our hearts so deeply that no one else's opinion seems important.

Then let's start asking. Let's ask for what we need. Ask for what we want. Ask God to meet the needs of others. And, of course, believe we receive when we ask.

We won't have to be shy about it. We can be bold, knowing that when we give God priority in our lives, He gives us priority in His life. That's what Jesus meant when He said, *"Whoever [really] loves Me will be loved by My Father. And I [too] will love him and will show (reveal, manifest) Myself to him..."* (John 14:21, AMP).

The Lord explained it to Rufus Moseley—a great man of God who went to heaven some years ago—in these words: "Life in Jesus is gloriously easy. It has one responsibility: the responsibility of remaining in union. If you stay in union with Me, I'll take care of everything else."

Isn't that a delightfully simple instruction? You keep the union. He'll take care of everything else.

> "I am the Vine, you are the branches. Whoever lives in Me and I in him bears much (abundant) fruit. However, apart from Me—cut off from vital union with Me—you can do nothing. If a person does not dwell in Me, he is thrown out as a [broken-off] branch and withers."
>
> JOHN 15:5-6, AMP

## Speak the Word

*I abide in Christ and let His words abide in me.*
*I bear much fruit and glorify God.*
*John 15:7-8*

FOR FURTHER STUDY:

John 14:21-26

DAILY SCRIPTURE READING:

Isaiah 13-14;
Psalm 33

> "The Lord is on my side; I will not fear: what can man do unto me?"
> PSALM 118:6

# Stay Hooked

NO SITUATION HELL CAN BRING ABOUT IS DAMNABLE ENOUGH TO HOLD UP AGAINST THE ANOINTING OF GOD!

You don't have to be afraid! It may look as if everything is falling down around your feet, but don't ever change. Don't react to it. Don't give it any response.

Just stand your ground. Be like the little guy who came into my office some 20 years ago and said, "Brother Copeland, I've quit my job. I've decided to live by faith and preach the gospel."

I sat there and looked at him thinking, *He couldn't preach his way out of a paper sack! Lord, it won't be 90 days before this guy will be back here wanting money.*

The Lord answered and said, *Then give him some!* (That ended that right there!)

That young fellow didn't have much going for him at the time, naturally speaking. But he had dug into the Word of God and spent hours upon hours listening to tapes and studying his Bible until he hooked into the supernatural by faith.

Over the next years, some people told him he couldn't preach. (Not me. I was smart enough to keep my mouth shut.) But he wouldn't let go. Others told him he wouldn't amount to a hill of beans. But he wouldn't let go.

He went into one of his first meetings only to find a transformer had blown and the lights wouldn't work. But instead of canceling the meeting, he walked up to the podium and hollered, "Let there be light!"

Sure enough, the lights came on. He just wouldn't give in to fear. He stayed hooked up to faith.

I asked him once, "What would you have done if the lights hadn't come on?"

"I'd still be standing there hollering at them," he said.

That fellow is still hooked up to faith today. In fact, you've probably heard of him. His name is Jerry Savelle.

Just think what a loss it would have been to the Body of Christ if Jerry had unhooked from faith and let fear stop his ministry.

It would be just as great a loss to us all if you stop short of your calling as well. So stay hooked up to faith—and the anointing will stay hooked up with you!

## *Speak the Word*

*The Lord is on my side. I do not fear what man can do to me.*
*Psalm 118:6*

FOR FURTHER STUDY:

Joshua 10:1-14

DAILY SCRIPTURE READING:

Isaiah 15-16;
Psalm 34

# The Best Timesaver of All!

"I'm just too busy!"

That's the number one reason believers give for failing to spend time in the Word of God. Homemakers run from one chore or errand to the next taking care of their family's pressing needs. Business people rush out the door early every morning and fall into bed exhausted at night. It seems we spend hours thinking how to squeeze more time out of each day. Our schedules are so packed, the demands on our lives are so heavy, that it just doesn't seem we have time to give much attention to the Word.

But the truth is, we don't have time *not* to!

When you have the Word of God in abundance—you have more of *it* inside you than anything else! You're so full of the Word that when trouble comes, the Word is the first thing out of your mouth.

To lay hold of that kind of abundance, you need to do what Joshua 1:8 said. You need to "meditate the Word." To *meditate* means "to fix your mind." So fix your mind on the Word of God every day. Apply it to yourself, personally. Allow the Holy Spirit to make it a reality in your heart.

> "Wisdom is the principal thing; therefore get wisdom: and with all thy getting get understanding. Exalt her, and she shall promote thee: she shall bring thee to honour, when thou dost embrace her."
> PROVERBS 4:7-8

Carefully ponder how the Word you've read applies to your life. Ask yourself, "What does this Word from God say to me? What does it mean in my life? How can it change my situation?"

Then place yourself in agreement with what God says about you in that Word. Make up your mind that you are who God says you are. You can do what God says you can do. And you can have what He says you can have. Put yourself in agreement with Him, then receive it.

I know you're busy. There are tremendous demands made on you every day. But God promises that if you'll keep His Word in front of you, if you'll put it first place in your life, you'll know how to prosper and succeed in all you do. Now, that sounds like a real timesaver to me!

## Speak the Word

*I get and exalt wisdom. Wisdom promotes me and brings me honor.*
*Proverbs 4:7-8*

FOR FURTHER STUDY:

Proverbs 3:1-8

DAILY SCRIPTURE READING:

Isaiah 17-18;
Psalm 35

# Paint Those Pictures!

Hope is a living thing. Paul says hope "abides." To *abide* means "to live." Only living things abide, so hope is a living thing and you have to guard it and nourish it with the Word of God. You have to feed it with the Word so it can grow.

If you'll do that, hope will paint a picture of God's promise fulfilled in your life. It will give you an inner image of yourself healed and prosperous, with your loved ones saved, your marriage restored or whatever else you've been hoping for. Hope will paint that picture so clearly inside you and make it so real, you'll begin to be blind to what you see on the outside.

As you meditate on those inner pictures hope has painted with God's Word, you'll begin to believe you are what the Word of God says you are. You'll begin to realize you're not what the world says you are. You're not what your parents or your friends say you are. You're not even what you think you are. You are what GOD says you are! You're the righteousness of God in Christ Jesus (2 Corinthians 5:21)!

Let me give you an example: You've prayed for your son to be set free from a drug habit. You can get such a clear picture of what that child is going to be like after he has been delivered that he starts looking great to you now—even though he still may be giving you trouble!

You'll actually get to the point where you won't see what a challenge he is being right now, because you've seen him in Jesus with the eyes of your spirit.

If you'll continue to look at him that way and not let the devil shake you, if you'll refuse to jump up in that child's face and tell him how sorry he is, one of these days that child of yours will look on the outside just like you see him on the inside. He'll be delivered!

That's what hope does. It is strong spiritual stuff!

So how do you get some? You go to the same place you do to get faith—the Word of God. You bathe your brain and your spirit in that Word every day. You think about it all the time, wherever you are and whatever you are doing. You keep your faith tapes going. In short, you just keep feeding your spirit...and allow the Word to paint those pictures! That's hope at work in you.

## Speak the Word
*Hope surely and steadfastly anchors my soul.*
*Hebrews 6:19*

FOR FURTHER STUDY:

2 Corinthians 3:12-18

DAILY SCRIPTURE READING:

Isaiah 19-21; Psalms 36-37

*Gloria*

# He's Coming Back for You!

The *King James Version* of the Bible translates this verse as, *"Having therefore these promises, dearly beloved, let us cleanse ourselves from all filthiness of the flesh and spirit, perfecting holiness in the fear of God."* Perfecting holiness is simply the continual act of perfecting being separated unto God, in the fear of God.

Now, fear of God doesn't mean you are afraid of Him, but rather you reverence Him. The more fear of God you have, the more obedient you are—and the more you give of yourself to God. That reverential fear of God increases in you as you study the Word, as you spend time with God, as you grow in the Lord.

*The Amplified Bible* says we're to cleanse ourselves from everything that contaminates and defiles the body and spirit, everything that would prevent us from being separated unto God.

For example, if you and I believe adultery is wrong, and we have no intention of committing adultery or fornication, then we ought not watch adultery. We ought not feed ourselves with adultery that's on television, in a movie or in a book. I like to say it this way, "If you don't want to do it, don't watch it." And that applies to everything, not just adultery.

We simply don't have any business contaminating our spirit and mind with the trash the world sells. We're to cleanse ourselves from *everything* that contaminates and defiles the body and spirit. And everything is not as blatant as the sin of adultery. There are subtle ways we can contaminate our spirit.

> "Therefore, since these [great] promises are ours, beloved, let us cleanse ourselves from everything that contaminates and defiles body and spirit, and bring [our] consecration to completeness in the (reverential) fear of God."
> 2 CORINTHIANS 7:1, AMP

The greatest sin you and I can commit is not walking in love. Jesus said, *"A new commandment I give unto you, That ye love one another..."* (John 13:34). So when we walk in hate, when we walk in unforgiveness, our spirit is contaminated.

Ken had a vision one time of a pipe. And this pipe was so clogged up that any liquid in it just dripped out little by little. God showed him that our spirit is the same way. When we don't walk in love, our spirit gets so clogged up that the power of God can't come through. We're not living separated unto God.

We've got to unclog our pipes. We've got to perfect holiness to which we are called (1 Thessalonians 4:7). We've got to stop contaminating our spirits. Jesus is coming back soon! And He's coming for a Church that's holy! He's coming for a people who have separated themselves unto Him. He's coming back for you.

FOR FURTHER STUDY:

1 John 2:15-17

DAILY SCRIPTURE READING:

Isaiah 22-23; Psalm 38

## Speak the Word

*I cleanse myself from everything that contaminates and defiles my body and spirit. I consecrate myself to God.*
2 Corinthians 7:1, AMP

> "We have the
> mind of
> Christ."
> 1 CORINTHIANS
> 2:16

# You Can Change Your Mind

Some people are baffled by everything about God. You'll often hear them say something like this: *"Yes, amen, but you know that's the way the Bible says it will be. After all, God's ways are higher than our ways and His thoughts are higher than our thoughts."*

Yes, the Bible says that, but if that's all it says, we can never hope to be anything except stupid. But praise God, the Bible doesn't stop there. According to Isaiah 55:11, God says, *"So shall my word be that goeth forth out of my mouth: it shall not return unto me void, but it shall accomplish that which I please, and it shall prosper in the thing whereto I sent it."*

In other words, you don't have to stay below God's thoughts. Your thoughts can come up to His level. How? Through His Word. God's thoughts are His Word, so if you'll think His Word, you'll think His thoughts.

*"But wait a minute. To think God's supernatural thoughts, you'd have to have a 'supernatural mind,' wouldn't you?"*

Yes—and if you're a believer, you already have one. You have the mind of Christ (1 Corinthians 2:16). I read that for years, but I didn't really understand it until I translated the word *Christ.* It means "the Anointed One."

So to have the mind of Christ is to have a mind that is under the influence of the Anointing of God. A mind that's not under the influence of God is in opposition to Him. It always goes contrary to His ways. And since God's ways are right, then a mind without the anointing will think wrong.

But hang on...just because you've made Jesus Lord doesn't mean you'll automatically think God's thoughts. You only begin thinking God's thoughts when you begin to fill your mind and heart with the Word of God and make yourself subject to His Anointing.

Romans 12:2 calls that process *"the renewing of your mind."* It also says that process will transform you. Why does it have such a dramatic effect? Because when you change your mind, you change your choices—and that changes everything.

So learn to stir up the anointing on the inside of you. Subject your mind to it. Allow the anointing to transform the way you think. Allow it to change your mind!

### *Speak the Word*

*I have the mind of the Anointed One.*
*1 Corinthians 2:16*

FOR FURTHER
STUDY:

Isaiah 55:6-11

DAILY SCRIPTURE
READING:

Isaiah 24-25;
Psalm 39

*Gloria*

# Nothing Intimidates God

No matter what difficult situation you may be facing today, God can turn it around! The doctors may have told you there's no hope. Your bank account may be empty and the creditors knocking on the door. There may be trouble in your family or on your job. You may have a loved one headed for prison. Your problems may be stacked so high, you feel like you can never overcome them. But don't let the devil fool you. He has never devised a problem that faith in God can't fix! Nothing intimidates God.

It's just as easy for God to heal cancer as it is for Him to heal a headache. It's as easy for Him to buy you a new home as it is for Him to pay your rent.

Think about that! If you'll dare to believe God's Word, you can have light in the midst of a dark world. You can have protection in the midst of a dangerous world. You can live healed in the midst of a sick world. You can live prosperously in the midst of an impoverished world. You can live free in the midst of a captive world.

But you can't do it by dragging around in an attitude of defeat.

If you want to walk in constant victory, you must develop a spirit of faith and persevere when the devil is putting pressure on you.

Faith believes God's Word just because God said it—whether natural circumstances seem to agree or not. That means if you want to maintain a spirit of faith in the area of healing, you must start by getting your Bible and finding out what God has said about healing. Then you must choose to receive that Word as the truth. Then say it! Say, "The Word says healing belongs to me and I believe it!" Keep putting the Word in your heart day after day until faith rises up within you and your body begins to line up with that Word.

People with the spirit of faith always receive the blessings of God. They may go through tests and trials, but they come out victorious every time.

I like those odds, don't you? I like to beat the devil every time. And, glory to God, we can do it if we'll walk continually in the spirit of faith.

Keep faith stirred up. Get your expectancy up and out there ahead of where you are now. Dare to believe God. It won't shake Him up! NOTHING intimidates Him!

FOR FURTHER STUDY:

Exodus 10:16-23

DAILY SCRIPTURE READING:

Isaiah 26-27; Psalm 40

## *Speak the Word*

*I have the spirit of faith!*
*2 Corinthians 4:13*

> "And on my servants and on my handmaidens I will pour out in those days of my Spirit; and they shall prophesy: And I will show wonders in heaven above, and signs in the earth beneath."
>
> ACTS 2:18-19

# The Place of Prayer

Now, more than ever before, it is vital for every Christian to understand that we are in the last of the last days. We are on the edge of the greatest outpouring of God's Glory this earth has ever seen. Amazing, supernatural things are beginning to happen just as the Bible said they would.

Yet many believers are sitting back, watching these events like spiritual spectators. They seem to think God will sovereignly empty some great Glory bucket, spilling signs and wonders over the earth. But it won't happen that way.

It will happen the way Acts 2 reveals it. If you'll read that last phrase in today's scripture, taking out the punctuation that was put in by the translators, you'll see a divine connection. You'll see that God is saying when His servants and handmaidens prophesy, when they speak out His divine will and purpose in intercession and faith, then in response to their speaking, He will work signs and wonders.

That means, if this last outpouring of Glory is to come in its fullness, all of God's servants and handmaidens must be in their place. What place? The place of prayer!

Some years ago, I had been studying the authority of man, and I had seen over and over in the Word how the prayers of God's people precede His actions on the earth. Yet I hung on to the idea that God still did His most important works independently of man.

One day, as I was praying about it, I said, "Lord, You brought Jesus into the earth sovereignly, didn't You?"

*No, I didn't,* He answered.

"You mean, there were people who interceded for the birth of Jesus?"

*Yes,* He said. Then He told me about Simeon.

As the Lord revealed to me the account of Simeon in Luke 2, I saw how he was led by the Holy Spirit to the Temple the day Joseph and Mary dedicated Jesus. I read how he had fervently prayed, asking God to send the Redeemer.

It's amazing enough that when Simeon saw Jesus, he immediately recognized Who Jesus was. It's even more amazing that he knew Jesus was bringing salvation to the Gentiles (verse 32)—a fact the rest of the Church didn't find out until Peter went to Cornelius's house, 10 years after the Day of Pentecost!

We must get on our knees and start praying for the fullness of the final outpouring in these last days. We must start speaking out God's Word and His will for this last hour in prophecy and intercession so He can do signs and wonders. We must enter into that place of prayer.

## *Speak the Word*

*I am constant in prayer.*
*Romans 12:12,* AMP

FOR FURTHER STUDY:

Luke 2:25-35

DAILY SCRIPTURE READING:

Isaiah 28-29;
Psalm 41

*Gloria*

# Claim What's Yours

Jesus told us in Matthew 6:19-21 that we're to lay up treasure in heaven and not on earth, where moth and rust corrupt and where thieves can break in and steal. I call this our heavenly account!

We have been blessed by God to be able to deposit and withdraw from this account. How do we do that?

> "So shall your storage places be filled with plenty."
> PROVERBS 3:10, AMP

You make deposits by giving to God's work.

The foundation for that giving is the tithe. When you give the first tenth of your income to the Lord, you open the door for God to come into your finances and move supernaturally. Proverbs 3:9-10 says that when you honor the Lord with the first fruits of your increase, your storage places will be filled with plenty.

In addition to your tithe, you can also deposit to your heavenly account by giving offerings into the work of the gospel. When you give, be sure you are giving into good ground. You have to put your seed (money) into good ground if you want a return. (Study Mark 4.)

If you are like me, you're already eager to get to the bottom line here. You're saying, "OK, I know that I have an account. I know where it is, and I know how to make deposits. But when can I get the money? When can I make a withdrawal?"

The answer is in Mark 10:29-30. There Jesus was answering the disciples who had asked Him what they were going to get in return for the giving they had done for the gospel's sake.

He told them they would receive a hundredfold return from their heavenly account today, in this time! Although our deposits are going to be bringing us reward for eternity, we don't have to wait until we die and go to heaven to draw on those resources. We can make withdrawals on our heavenly account here and now!

And you make those withdrawals with your faith. You do that by releasing your faith in what God has already spoken about the financial blessings that belong to you in Christ Jesus. Then say it with your mouth and believe it in your heart until it comes to pass (Mark 11:22-24).

You reach out with the hand of faith and claim what's yours!

## Speak the Word

*I honor the Lord with my money and with the first fruits of all my income. My storage places are filled with plenty!*
*Proverbs 3:9-10, AMP*

FOR FURTHER STUDY:

Mark 4

DAILY SCRIPTURE READING:

Isaiah 30-31; Psalm 42

> "So, come out from among (unbelievers), and separate (sever) yourselves from them, says the Lord, and touch not [any] unclean thing; then I will receive you kindly and treat you with favor."
> 2 CORINTHIANS 6:17, AMP

# Walking in Favor

If God's favor is manifested in your life, it is the blessing of God. I've been in the Christian walk for a long time, and over the years I have grown to be more dedicated than ever before. Through this I've learned a valuable truth about God's favor: However much you give of yourself to God, that's how much favor you'll receive in return.

When you do what God says, favor is the result. When you do what He says, things work together for your good. The Scripture says for those who love God, all things work together for their good (Romans 8:28). Well, who loves God? Jesus Himself taught that those who love God keep His Word and obey it (John 14:23).

The Scripture teaches us to give God glory in our body and spirit. Our actions are to glorify God. Whatever we do, we're to do it to the glory of God (1 Corinthians 10:31).

Well, you're not going to be sinning to the glory of God. You're going to be walking in love to the glory of God. You're going to be giving to the glory of God. You're going to be kind and good to the glory of God. You're going to be ministering to others to the glory of God. Whatever you do, do it to the glory of God.

God is to be worshiped. He's God! He is to be served. He is to be obeyed. When we treat Him as God and obey Him and serve Him and do whatever He tells us, favor comes to us. SUPERnatural favor and blessings can't help but come to us.

So honor Him. Obey Him. Walk with Him. Expect favor from God and man, and you'll be walking in favor everywhere you go.

## *Speak the Word*

*I am received of the Lord. He shows me kindness and treats me with favor.*
*2 Corinthians 6:17, AMP*

FOR FURTHER STUDY:

Psalm 5:11-12

DAILY SCRIPTURE READING:

Genesis 29-30; Matthew 16

*Gloria*

# Shine On!

SEPTEMBER 24

⸎

> "All that will live godly in Christ Jesus shall suffer persecution."
> 2 TIMOTHY 3:12

If you do anything that makes a mark for God in this world, persecution is going to come. It goes with the territory. Second Timothy 3:12 leaves no room for doubt about that.

But why is it that simply living a godly life causes so much trouble in this world? First John 5:19 tells us it's because *the whole world lieth in wickedness."* We're living in a world that is ruled by the spirit of darkness. And the brighter our light becomes, the more offensive we are to that realm of darkness.

The reverse is also true. As long as we aren't doing much for God, we're not bothered with persecution. If we look like the world, talk like the world and act like the world—worldly people will think we're all right. A little crazy maybe, but no real threat.

So you might as well know right now, if you're very turned on to God, the world isn't going to like you much. Actually, that's an understatement. Jesus put it this way:

*"If the world hate you, ye know that it hated me before it hated you. If ye were of the world, the world would love his own: but because ye are not of the world, but I have chosen you out of the world, therefore the world hateth you"* (John 15:18-19).

You may be thinking, *Well, I'm sure that's true, but it's also not very pleasant. Why do we have to talk about it?*

We need to prepare ourselves so that when persecution comes, it doesn't slow us down, much less stop us. That's what persecution is designed to do, you know. It's designed to discourage us and keep us from completing God's plan for our lives.

But, praise God, if we learn how to handle it in advance, it won't even slow us down.

So don't be afraid of the darkness of this world. It may persecute you, but it can't overcome you. Your family may even persecute you, but they can't overcome you either. *"For whatsoever is born of God overcometh the world: and this is the victory that overcometh the world, even our faith"* (1 John 5:4). Just turn up your light a little brighter...and shine on!

## Speak the Word

*Though I suffer persecution, I continue to live godly.*
*2 Timothy 3:12*

FOR FURTHER STUDY:

Matthew 10:16-26

⸎

DAILY SCRIPTURE READING:

Isaiah 34-36;
Psalms 44-45

> "So mightily grew the word of God and prevailed."
> ACTS 19:20

# The Word Prevails

Even though you might be the one speaking God's Words, they have the same power as if Jesus Himself were speaking them.

"But how can that be, Brother Copeland? I'm not Jesus!"

No, you're not. But when you speak and act upon God's Words in faith, they always release His power, just like they did for Jesus.

Peter and John proved that the day they walked up to the lame man at the Beautiful gate in Acts 3. At the time, they only had a few words of the New Covenant. They just had the words Jesus spoke to them before He ascended (Mark 16:15-18).

But those were all the words they needed. When they believed and acted upon those words, the Holy Spirit went into action for them just as He had for Jesus—and a miracle happened. When they opened their mouths and said, *"In the name of Jesus Christ of Nazareth rise up and walk,"* that lame man *"leaping up stood, and walked, and entered with them into the temple, walking, and leaping, and praising God"* (Acts 3:6-8).

They didn't stop with that one miracle either. Peter and John and the rest of the early disciples took those first few words of the New Covenant and turned the whole known world upside down! (Acts 17:6).

"Well, Brother Copeland, you know those men were apostles. That's the reason they were anointed to do such miracles."

No, it's not! If that were the reason, then Acts 19:20 would say, *Mightily grew the apostles and they prevailed.* But it doesn't say that. It says *the Word of God grew mightily and prevailed.* Those early apostles were anointed to do such miracles because they spoke and acted on the Word of God. It was the Word and the anointing released by that Word that did the work.

Since the Word never changes, you can be confident that it will prevail for you just as surely as it prevailed for Peter and John. It will prevail for you as surely as it prevailed for Jesus. It will prevail for you as powerfully as when God Himself said, *"Let there be light!"* (Genesis 1:3).

What are you waiting for? You have the very power and Anointing of God Himself moving in your reborn spirit. You have the Word of God at your fingertips. And the more you fill your heart with that Word, the more you act on it, and speak it out in faith, the more freely that anointing can function through you. So stop stalling! Get moving! Grab your Bible, take your stand on it and let's go! God's Word prevails!

## *Speak the Word*

*God's Word grows mightily and prevails in me.*
*Acts 19:20*

FOR FURTHER STUDY:

Acts 17:1-10

DAILY SCRIPTURE READING:

Isaiah 37-38;
Psalm 46

*Gloria*

# A Divine Appointment

"He hath appointed a day, in the which he will judge the world in righteousness by that man whom he hath ordained; whereof he hath given assurance unto all men, in that he hath raised him from the dead."

ACTS 17:31

*"It shall come to pass."*

When this statement appears in the Bible, it means that event is eternally fixed.

While we can grasp that about events that have already occurred, we sometimes aren't too sure about the ones still in the future.

For example, God had an appointed time for the children of Israel to come out of Egypt. He set that date in Genesis 15:13 when He told Abraham, *"Know of a surety that thy seed shall be a stranger in a land that is not theirs, and shall serve them; and they shall afflict them four hundred years."*

Sure enough, after the Israelites went to Egypt, they were afflicted. And 400 years to the day after Egypt began to afflict Israel, God brought the Israelites out just as He promised (Exodus 12:40-41). He wasn't even one day late!

What's more, He saw to it that day that the Israelites were blessed, equipped and ready to go on.

"Well, that's easy to believe, Gloria. I believe God's Word."

Yes, it's easy to believe an event that's passed. But what about one that is still to come—like the second coming of Jesus?

Just as surely as God set an appointment with the children of Israel, He has set an appointment with us. As Acts 17:31 says, *"He hath appointed a day...."*

The end of things as we know them in the earth is drawing near. God has notified us both through His written Word and by His Spirit within us that Jesus is coming back for us. It's not some fairy tale someone made up. It really will happen.

We don't need to fear the coming of the Lord, or, choose to disbelieve it because we can't comprehend it. We're to be excited about it. God's plans are always good. They always turn out right. It will be a glorious time. He ordained it years ago. It's a perfect plan. It's a divine appointment.

## Speak the Word

*I believe God, that it shall be even as it was told me.*

*Acts 27:25*

FOR FURTHER STUDY:

Isaiah 46:9-11

DAILY SCRIPTURE READING:

Isaiah 39-40;
Psalm 47

*Kenneth*

❧

"We exhorted and comforted and charged every one of you, as a father doth his children, That ye would walk worthy of God, who hath called you unto his kingdom and glory."

1 THESSALONIANS
2:11-12

# Prepare for the Unusual

My friend, we are about to hit the spiritual gusher that all generations have longed to see! It's not far off either. In fact, prophecies the Spirit of God has given through me and other ministers are coming to pass. Some time ago, for example, a man in a denominational church whose voice had been damaged by a physical condition was teaching that healing had passed away. As he did, God healed him right in front of the people he was teaching!

I want you to know, it's exciting to go to church these days. The more God pours out His Glory, the more unusual things we'll see.

One of these days, you may just be talking to somebody, asking them how things went at church last Sunday, and they may say, "Oh, it was great! The Glory of God was so strong it healed 10 cripples, opened the ears of 30 deaf people, cured seven cases of cancer, and killed Brother Bigmouth and Sister Strife."

I can just hear you thinking, *Now hold on a minute, Brother Copeland. The Glory of God is a good thing. It doesn't kill people.*

It did in the New Testament Church. Acts 5 tells the story of Ananias and his wife, Sapphira. They lied to the Holy Ghost and withheld part of what they were to give. And they died!

Please understand, I'm not trying to dampen your enthusiasm about this wonderful move of God's Glory we're experiencing. I just want you to realize that in the midst of a move like this, willful sin and an unrepentant heart are dangerous.

A Christian might be able to get away with hanging on to sin when the rest of the congregation is as cold as he is. But when the fire of God begins to burn and the rivers of the Spirit start to flow, he'll have to do one of two things: He'll either have to yield to the Spirit and let go of that sin by repenting, or he'll have to resist the flood of God's Spirit and be swept away.

I realize that's a sobering truth, but we need to be sober in this hour. We need to be watchful and keep ourselves in submission to God. If we'll do that, we can have a wonderful time. That's what the Church in Acts 5 did.

They were having such a glorious time in God that even when Ananias dropped dead right there in front of the preacher, they just went right on praising and worshiping. We know they did because the Bible says three hours later when Sapphira came in, lied and died, they were still having church!

Those believers had seen so many outstanding things that death didn't even slow them down. So prepare yourself. Get ready for the Glory. Repent of any sin and get excited when the unusual happens all around you! The Glory is here!

## Speak the Word

*I walk worthy of God, Who has called me unto His kingdom and glory.*
1 Thessalonians 2:12

FOR FURTHER STUDY:

Acts 5:1-11

❧

DAILY SCRIPTURE READING:

Isaiah 41-42;
Psalm 48

*Gloria*

# God's Success Formula

May I ask you a very direct question? How much do you want to succeed in life?

I've been amazed over the years at the people who have come across the formula for success, only to leave it lying on the table while they stay broke, sick and defeated.

Such people initially think success is easy for those who are gifted with great abilities. When they run into the truth, however, it stops them cold. The reality of it is this: *Real supernatural success is no picnic for anyone. It takes courage. It takes faith. And it is not dependent on natural ability.*

If Joshua were around today, he could tell you just how true that is. When God called him to lead Israel after Moses' death, he faced an overwhelming task. As Moses' successor, Joshua had some big shoes to fill. Several million people were under his command, and he knew if they didn't stay in line with God, His blessing would not be on them. Without God's blessing, they would never be able to take the Promised Land.

Joshua had to succeed.

"But Gloria, you don't know *me!* I've tried and failed with every formula in the book. I just don't have what it takes to succeed."

If that's what you're thinking, you haven't tried the formula in God's Book. Read again what He said in Joshua 1:5. God said the same thing to Moses in Exodus 3:12, *"Certainly I will be with thee."* In other words, "It doesn't matter who you are, Moses. It matters Who I am. For I am with you!"

That's the great thing about God's success formula. It's not based on our abilities, it's based on His abilities. We may be inadequate in a dozen different ways, but the One Who is with us is more than enough.

> "There shall not any man be able to stand before thee all the days of thy life: as I was with Moses, so I will be with thee: I will not fail thee, nor forsake thee."
> JOSHUA 1:5

## *Speak the Word*

*God is with me. He will never fail me or forsake me.*
*Joshua 1:5*

FOR FURTHER STUDY:

Exodus 3:11-14

DAILY SCRIPTURE READING:

Isaiah 43-44;
Psalm 49

"I know that this shall turn to my salvation through your prayer, and the supply of the Spirit of Jesus Christ, According to my earnest expectation and my hope, that in nothing I shall be ashamed."
PHILIPPIANS
1:19-20

# Don't Give Up Hope!

When you have hope, you have a supernatural expectancy that what God has promised will come to pass in your life. In today's Scripture verses, the Apostle Paul talks about this kind of supernatural expectancy. Paul uses two different words from the Greek language, each of which can be translated "hope." One of them means "the happy anticipation of good." The other can be defined as "eager longing, strained expectancy, watching with an outstretched head, an abstraction from anything else that might engage the attention." So, for example, Hebrews 11:1 says, *"Now faith is the substance of things hoped [intensely expected] for."*

When you're so locked in on the Word of God, you can't be distracted from it. Divine hope will come alive in you. I know what that's like. There have been times in my life when I was so focused on something God had called me to do, and I was so tuned in to what the Word said about it, I couldn't think about anything else.

People would try to have a conversation with me and I'd always end up talking about my hope. It would come up so big inside me that, at those times, I was bigger on the inside than I was on the outside. On the inside of me it was as though everything I was believing for had already come to pass.

When your hope gets that strong, it doesn't matter what kind of unbelief, opposition or situation contrary to the Word the devil tries to throw your way. It just bounces off you. You're so one-track-minded, you can't be drawn off course. The divine inner image of your success that the Word of God's promise gave birth to is just too strong.

So whatever you're believing God for, get your supernatural expectancy up for it. Eagerly long for it. Stretch your neck out and refuse to be distracted by all the things that would get you off course and tell you it won't happen. Keep the promise of God's Word before your eyes and that will keep your hope up, and you will see your desire come to pass!

## *Speak the Word*

*According to my earnest expectation and my hope,*
*I am ashamed in nothing.*
*Philippians 1:20*

FOR FURTHER STUDY:

Psalm 16;
Proverbs 13:12

❧

DAILY SCRIPTURE READING:

Isaiah 45-46;
Psalm 50

*Gloria*

# "Can I Afford It?"

You and I have been called to live the high life in Christ Jesus, not to be tied down to this natural realm. But all too often, instead, we allow ourselves to become tangled in the temporary affairs of this world. We allow those entanglements to drag us into defeat.

Don't let that happen to you. Simplify your life. If you don't have time for God, make time. Don't let your career, your family or anything else keep you from going on with God.

One thing I can promise you is that every part of your life will be more blessed if you take time to listen to God. Nothing you can do is better than hearing from heaven.

> "No man that warreth entangleth himself with the affairs of this life; that he may please him who hath chosen him to be a soldier."
> 2 TIMOTHY 2:4

Before I consider taking on any new activity, I always ask myself, *Can I afford this?* Not can I afford it financially, but can I afford it spiritually? Can I give time to this activity and still keep my priority time with God? If not, I can't afford it.

There's only one thing you absolutely can't afford to do without—and that's your time spent in prayer and in the Word of God. It is your very life. It is where your victory lies. You may forget that, but Satan never does. He'll constantly be sending time-stealers your way. So be alert and don't become entangled in them. Remember to ask yourself, "Can I afford this?" Then simplify your life. Make the time you spend with God your first priority every day.

## Speak the Word

*I do not entangle myself with the affairs of this life so that I may please the Lord Jesus Christ.*
*2 Timothy 2:4*

FOR FURTHER STUDY:

2 Timothy 3:14-17

DAILY SCRIPTURE READING:

Isaiah 47-48; Psalm 51

> "Having your conversation honest among the Gentiles: that, whereas they speak against you as evildoers, they may by your good works, which they shall behold, glorify God in the day of visitation."
>
> 1 PETER 2:12

# Honor—He Guarantees It

One time when I was shopping in a convenience store, a preacher came in to purchase some shotgun shells. He began trying to talk the clerk into giving him a discount on his shells because he was a minister. It embarrassed me so. It made me so mad that he would do that to our God.

It almost made me ashamed for the clerk to know I was a preacher! The clerk didn't have any authority to give the minister a discount even if he had wanted! The young man got really irritated. I wonder if that preacher has any idea how much damage his preoccupation with a petty discount might have caused in that clerk's life.

I get so embarrassed at what people try to do as believers walking in dishonor. We are never to use our positions as preachers of the gospel or as children of God to defraud anyone.

It's situations like these, and others on a much larger scale, that often cause the world to look at the Body of Christ with a raised eyebrow. They've not seen enough honor. They've seen too much dishonor. But you can help change that. You can guard your manner of life, your conversation. You can be honorable.

My parents were honorable people. I grew up seeing example after example of what it was to live honorably. That taught me valuable lessons...like the fact that real honor isn't hard to recognize. It may be hard to find, but not to recognize. Honor stands out in a crowd because it appears foolish in the system of the world.

You see, to be honorable requires an act of the will, an act which triggers and releases all that God has provided for us. It requires a choice between God's Word and the subtleties and deceptions of the world. It requires a choice between the spirit and the flesh. It comes down to a choice between standing and falling.

If you are honorable, you will stand. If you are dishonorable, you are guaranteed to fall—and bring even more dishonor to the Body of Christ. If you don't know how to live honorably, start learning.

You can begin with God and His Word. As you get into His Word and allow it to get on the inside of you, honor will well up in you so full, you'll have no desire to walk in anything else. Your spirit will experience conviction about the smallest of commitments. You'll become so tuned to His Spirit that you will become honorable in everything. You'll be honest about the smallest details. You won't exaggerate or hedge on the truth. Your word and your commitments will become as good as His. Believe me, He's guaranteed it. He's given you His Word.

## *Speak the Word*

*I bring glory to God by conducting myself properly,*
*honorably and righteously among the Gentiles.*
*1 Peter 2:12, AMP*

FOR FURTHER STUDY:

1 Peter 2:1-12

DAILY SCRIPTURE READING:

Isaiah 49-51;
Psalms 52-53

*Gloria*

# Change What You're Hearing

OCTOBER 2

❧

"This book of
the law shall
not depart out
of thy mouth."
JOSHUA 1:8

Have you ever been frustrated with yourself...because of what you hear coming out of your mouth? Jesus said that out of the abundance of the heart, the mouth speaks (Luke 6:45). If you're focusing most of your attention on natural things—watching secular television, going to the movies, thinking about worldly matters, worrying about your job and family—then that's what you're going to talk about.

What you need to do is refocus your attention. Turn your attention toward God's Word and keep it there.

In everyday terms, Joshua 1:8 says, "Talk the Word."

When I say talk the Word, I don't mean just every now and then when you're feeling spiritual. I mean continually. In Deuteronomy 6:7 (NIV), God said you should talk His Word, *"when you sit at home and when you walk along the road, when you lie down and when you get up."*

That's pretty much all the time, isn't it? At home, at work, in the grocery store—wherever you are, keep the Word of God in your mouth.

Romans 10:17 tells us that *"faith cometh by hearing, and hearing by the word of God."* So when you're continually talking about what God says, what He'll do, and what His promises are, you're going to be growing in faith because you're hearing the Word from yourself all the time.

Isn't that exciting? You can change what you're hearing. So start today to fill your heart with an abundance of the Word. Then listen as your mouth gets in line with what God says about you and your circumstances.

## Speak the Word
*The Word of God does not depart out of my mouth.*
Joshua 1:8

FOR FURTHER
STUDY:

Deuteronomy
6:1-9

❧

DAILY SCRIPTURE
READING:

Isaiah 52-53;
Psalm 54

> "If ye continue in my word, then are ye my disciples indeed; And ye shall know the truth, and the truth shall make you free."
>
> JOHN 8:31-32

# The Sweetest Victory

One afternoon, as I was studying that scripture, the Lord spoke something to me that nearly knocked me out of my chair. He said, *Jesus was not free because He didn't sin. He didn't sin because He was free.*

I want you to let that statement sink in a moment. Can you see what it means? It means that many times as believers, we've been going at things backward. We've thought, *If I could just kick this smoking habit, if I could just get rid of this disease, if I could just get some money in the bank, then I'd be free.*

But we need to go after the freedom itself. Once we lay hold of real freedom, those cigarettes, that disease and that financial lack will fall powerless at our feet. They'll have no more ability to bind us than they had to bind Jesus.

You may say, "Yeah, but people have laid hands on me until they've nearly rubbed all the hair off my head trying to get me that freedom—and I still don't have it."

Listen, Jesus didn't say you'd have hands laid on you and the laying on of hands would make you free. He said you'd know *the truth, and the truth* would make you free! He said, "Continue in *My Word* and you'll be free like Me! Get in the Word and act on it. Then the laying on of hands will work."

I know it's thrilling to have hands laid on you for healing and feel the power of God go through your body. But let me tell you, there's an even stronger joy that comes when you get your healing or your deliverance by standing in faith in God's Word.

You know you're growing up in Jesus when trouble comes and instead of running to the pastor crying for help, you go into your place of prayer, take your Bible and find the answer. You begin to read and, as you do, you hear God talking to you. Every scripture you find that quickens your spirit, you write down.

Then, every night before you go to bed, you read those scriptures again—and you believe them. Your body may not feel any different. The devil may be standing by your bedside saying, *You won't get healed this time. I'll kill you in the morning.*

But instead of wilting in fear, you just say, "Shut up, devil, and take your hands off my body. I don't belong to you and I never will. The Word says I'm healed and as far as I'm concerned, that's the end of it."

The next morning, you get your Bible and read those scriptures again. Suddenly you catch yourself and think, *Praise God, I got so excited about these verses, I've forgotten to hurt for the last 30 minutes!*

That kind of victory is the sweetest kind there is.

## *Speak the Word*

*I continue in the Word of God, and I am a disciple of Jesus.*
*I know the truth and the truth makes me free.*
*John 8:31-32*

FOR FURTHER STUDY:

Luke 8:11-15

DAILY SCRIPTURE READING:

Isaiah 54-55;
Psalm 55

*Gloria*

# God Is a Good God

The simple message that God is good often worries traditional, religious people. It bothers them when faith preachers say that God wants His people healed, prosperous and blessed in every way.

I realize that sounds strange, but it has always been true. Years ago, when Oral Roberts first began preaching, a fellow minister complained, "I wish he wouldn't preach that God is a good God," he said. "People will get the wrong idea!"

That minister was afraid, like so many are today, that people will hear that message and start expecting too much. They think gullible people will get the idea that God wants us all to live like kings.

Personally, I'm not afraid of that, because that's what the Bible teaches. When I say the Bible teaches it, I'm not talking about a few isolated scriptures. God's will and plan to bless His people can be seen from Genesis to Revelation.

> "Every good gift and every perfect gift is from above, and cometh down from the Father of lights, with whom is no variableness, neither shadow of turning."
> JAMES 1:17

If you'll read the Book, you'll see that man has never had to shout up at heaven and say, "Hey God, I want to be blessed so let's make a deal. I'll do these certain things—and You give me good things in return. How about it?"

No, that's a scene you'll never see in the Bible because God always beats man to the punch. Blessing was originally His idea! That's because HE IS good! He is totally innocent and pure, untouched by evil. So everything He creates is the same way.

God created the earth and every good thing in it as a gift for man. And when it was finished, *"the Lord God planted a garden eastward in Eden; and there he put the man whom he had formed"* (Genesis 2:8).

I want you to know, man had it made in the Garden. He had close communion with God Himself. Man's every need and desire was abundantly supplied. He had perfect food, an ideal temperature, beautiful surroundings and even a perfect wife! And Eve had a perfect husband.

If you want to see how blessed God wants us to be, just look at the Garden. That was His perfect will for man. That's how He wanted us to live. All man had to do to remain in that blessed environment was believe and obey the Word of God.

God never changes. He has always operated just like He did in the Garden. He wants us to live in continual blessing. And all we have to do is believe Him and obey His Word. Don't listen to the devil like Adam and Eve did. Tell him to get out of your garden! Then live in the land of blessing, worshiping your God, Who is a good God!

FOR FURTHER STUDY:

Genesis 2:7-25

DAILY SCRIPTURE READING:

2 Kings 19-20; Colossians 4

## Speak the Word

*God is a good God. Every good and perfect gift comes from Him.*
*James 1:17*

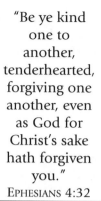

> "Be ye kind one to another, tenderhearted, forgiving one another, even as God for Christ's sake hath forgiven you."
>
> EPHESIANS 4:32

# Drive Out Unforgiveness

Forgiveness. Lots of people talk about it. But many fail to actually do it. Oh, they try...and try and try. But trying just doesn't get the job done. You can come around and talk to those "try-ers" years later, and they're still carrying around hurts and resentments. They're still saying, "Well, I'm trying to forgive that person, but what they did to me was so bad that I just haven't been able to do it."

That's why the Word of God doesn't say anything about "trying" to forgive. It simply commands us to forgive one another, *"even as God for Christ's sake hath forgiven you."* Since God has never commanded us to do anything without providing us with the ability to do it, we can be sure He has given every believer the power to forgive in any and every situation.

You may think it is hard to forgive. It's not. Nothing you do by the power of God is hard. You can make it hard by trying to do it in your own strength. But if you'll learn to rest in God through faith in His Word, the struggle will disappear.

You see, if you'll trust God's Word, that Word will fight for you in any area of life. You won't have to wrestle your problems to the ground and solve them with your own great will power. All you'll have to do is open your Bible and start speaking out God's Word about the situation. Release your faith in that Word and it will conquer any problem—including unforgiveness.

That's right! God's Word will fight unforgiveness for you. If you'll find out what God has to say on the subject—and believe it—it will drive unforgiveness completely out of your life.

## *Speak the Word*

*I am kind to others, and tenderhearted. I forgive others as God has forgiven me.*
*Ephesians 4:32*

FOR FURTHER STUDY:

Colossians 3:12-17

DAILY SCRIPTURE READING:

Isaiah 58-59; Psalm 57

*Gloria*

# The Ministry of Grace

Did you know it's possible to be a Christian and live without the ministry of grace that's offered by the Holy Spirit? Certainly it is. Read the book of Galatians and you'll see. When Paul said the Galatians had fallen from grace (Galatians 5:1-4), he didn't mean they had lost their right to go to heaven. He meant they had fallen from their dependence on the Holy Spirit. They were reverting to the traditions of the Law, and in doing so they had deprived themselves of the Holy Spirit's ministry of grace for daily living.

You see, the Spirit of God didn't quit ministering grace to us the day we were born again. He remains in us to minister grace—God's favor and bless-ing—to us every day. But when we don't trust and depend on His ministry, we hinder Him from performing it.

How can you demonstrate your trust in Him? By simply being obedient. You can start by obeying what you know God's Word says. The Spirit of God is the author of the Bible, so you can be sure when you're obeying that Word, you're in line with the Spirit.

And we need to learn to hear the Holy Spirit in our spirit. By fellowship-ing with the Lord in prayer and in the Word, we can develop our spiritual hearing and our sensitivity to the Spirit.

We need to develop our confidence to the point we know, *I won't be led astray. My heart is right before Him. I fellowship with Him. I study the Word. I walk in the fear of God and I expect to walk in the comfort of the Holy Ghost.*

Once you know those things—step out and obey the promptings you receive. Don't be afraid of making a mistake. You have the protection of knowing that the Holy Spirit will never lead you contrary to God's written Word.

By following the Holy Spirit day by day in the big things and the small, you won't compromise God's ministry of grace—His divine favor and blessing. You'll keep the door open to hearing and knowing His promptings, and what He wants you to do. All that's left is to follow through.

For Further Study:

1 Corinthians 2:10-16

Daily Scripture Reading:

Isaiah 60-61; Psalm 58

## Speak the Word

*I stand fast in the liberty wherewith Christ has made me free. I refuse to be entangled again with the yoke of bondage.*
*Galatians 5:1*

---

October 6

"Stand fast therefore in the liberty wherewith Christ hath made us free, and be not entangled again with the yoke of bondage. Behold, I Paul say unto you, that if ye be circumcised, Christ shall profit you nothing. For I testify again to every man that is circumcised, that he is a debtor to do the whole law. Christ is become of no effect unto you, whosoever of you are justified by the law; ye are fallen from grace."
Galatians 5:1-4

> "And he could there do no mighty work, save that he laid his hands upon a few sick folk, and healed them. And he marvelled because of their unbelief."
>
> MARK 6:5-6

# He Answers the Cry of Faith

Would it be possible for someone to starve right in the middle of a supermarket? Certainly it would. It would be absurd and unnecessary, but it could be done. A person could be wasting away of hunger, lying in the middle of the produce section with people offering him food left and right. But if he refused to receive it, eventually he would be as dead as can be.

I can just hear you, "That's the silliest thing I've ever heard. It would never happen!" Naturally speaking, you're probably right. But in the realm of the spirit, things like that happen every day.

Take healing for example. God has already provided it for every believer on the face of the earth. As far as He's concerned, it's an accomplished fact. Yet countless believers are sick and dying today. God's provision isn't helping them because they haven't received it.

"But Brother Copeland, this receiving business is easier said than done. It's tough to reach out and receive invisible blessings from a God I can't see. If Jesus were here on the earth, I'd have it made."

Would you? Jesus didn't walk around meeting the needs of everyone He met. In a crowd of people, you might see Him stop and respond to a single individual. What caused Him to single out one person when we know that God is no respecter of persons (Acts 10:34)? *Faith.*

Jesus did not operate apart from the faith of the people. His ministry was not directed by the multitudes, nor by His own personal preferences, nor by the severity of a need. It was directed by the cry of faith.

Why didn't Jesus say to Jairus and Bartimaeus, "According to *My* faith be it done unto you" instead of *"Thy faith hath made thee whole"*? (Luke 17:19; Mark 10:52). Didn't Jesus have any faith? Certainly He did! There's no question that Jesus had faith. His faith connection to God was never broken, so He was always full of the Holy Ghost and power. He was always anointed. But for that power and anointing to be delivered to someone, it had to be touched by the faith of a receiver.

Faith and receiving are intimately connected. If you are starving for something you need, remember: Everything you need has been given to you if you're born again. All you have to do is believe you receive it. He answers the cry of FAITH!

## *Speak the Word*

*I have faith in God. I have the God kind of faith.*
*Mark 11:22*

FOR FURTHER STUDY:

Mark 5:25-34

DAILY SCRIPTURE READING:

Isaiah 62-63;
Psalm 59

*Gloria*

# Fellowship With the Faithful

Living the Christian life was never meant to be done alone. Many people withdraw from taking the time to fellowship with other believers, because they become busy...they have hectic jobs, they move to a new town, life becomes stressful in many ways.

But being isolated will only lead you down the road to defeat.

If you want to live in victory, you need to fellowship with people who know God. Don't try to fellowship with the world and live like an overcomer. It won't work.

We get strength from one another. We also get weaknesses from one another. If you want to grow strong, find someone who is stronger in the Lord than you are and fellowship with them. They'll bring you up.

On the other hand, if you fellowship with people who don't live for God and trust His Word, they'll bring you down. Don't try to go to a church, for example, where people tell you healing has passed away and then try to live in divine health. It just doesn't work.

Listen to me. Your very life depends on whom you fellowship with and where you go to church. Fellowship with people who are strong and walk in power, who preach God's Word and get results when they pray.

You may have to take the initiative. You may be the one to introduce yourself. You may need to go shake hands with the pastor...not sit back and wait to see if he notices you. But go ahead. Invite people over for dinner. Go to the prayer meeting. Go to the Bible study. Go to church!

Fellowship with the faithful. If you do, it will help you be the one who ends up living in victory every day.

> "Shun youthful lusts and flee from them, and aim at and pursue righteousness... faith, love, [and] peace... in fellowship with all...who call upon the Lord out of a pure heart."
> 2 TIMOTHY 2:22, AMP

## *Speak the Word*

*I aim at and pursue righteousness, faith, love and peace.*
*I fellowship with all who call upon the Lord out of a pure heart.*
*2 Timothy 2:22, AMP*

FOR FURTHER STUDY:

Hebrews 10:22-25

DAILY SCRIPTURE READING:

Isaiah 64-66;
Psalms 60-61

> "But we all, with open face beholding as in a glass the glory of the Lord, are changed into the same image from glory to glory, even as by the Spirit of the Lord."
>
> 2 CORINTHIANS 3:18

# Like a Rocket Headed Home

We're headed for Glory like a rocket locked on a target. The Bible says as we behold as in a glass the Glory of the Lord, we are being *"changed into the same image from glory to glory, even as by the Spirit of the Lord."*

Notice the Word says we're changed as we behold the Glory. How do we do that? By attending to the "glorious gospel." The gospel that is in the book you carry to church every Sunday is the Word of the living God, and it is filled with His Glory! When you read it under the Anointing of God, you're changed more and more into the very image of that Glory. That's why the Apostle Paul said, *"Be not moved away from the hope of the gospel...Whereof I am made a minister...Even the mystery which hath been hid from ages and from generations, but now is made manifest to his saints: To whom God would make known what is the riches of the glory of this mystery among the Gentiles; which is Christ [the Anointed One and His Anointing] in you, the hope of glory"* (Colossians 1:23, 25-27).

You have an anointing in you that's the Anointing of Jesus, and it is crying out for the Glory. There's something inside you that cries for the Glory of God. You have the hope of Glory inside you. *Hope* translated there doesn't mean *wish*. It means "absolute expectancy."

It's time for us, as believers, to take a faith stand concerning the Glory! When you take a faith stand, go to the Word of God and find out what God has already said, and then take an uncompromising stand on that Word. You say, "That's mine! I settle it now in the Name of Jesus, according to the Word of the living God. I fully expect to see the Glory of God in my life!"

It is your destiny to know the Glory of God. Don't let the devil steal it from you through lack of knowledge. Get into the Word. Study it. Take that faith stand. You'll be like a rocket headed home!

## *Speak the Word*

*As I behold the glory of God through the Word,*
*I am constantly transfigured into His very own image.*
*2 Corinthians 3:18, AMP*

FOR FURTHER STUDY:

Isaiah 60:1-3

DAILY SCRIPTURE READING:

Jeremiah 1-2; Psalm 62

*Gloria*

# Living in Love

> "Love...takes no account of the evil done to it—pays no attention to a suffered wrong."
> 1 CORINTHIANS 13:5, AMP

Did you know that walking in love is good for your health? That's right! I saw a documentary that focused on stress. It explained that researchers had discovered there are two kinds of stress.

The first is the kind you experience when you're working hard to achieve something, pressing yourself to reach a goal. That kind of stress, they said, is natural and good. It doesn't hurt you. The second kind of stress, however, has such a negative effect that it's physically dangerous.

Do you know what they said causes that kind of stress? Hostility. Or, we could say, failing to walk in love.

Now when you think of hostility, you may think of the type of anger you feel when something serious happens, but according to this program, that kind of thing isn't what really causes the problem with most people. It's the little things. When the dry cleaners ruins your favorite outfit, for example. Or when the cafeteria lady puts gravy on your mashed potatoes, especially after you've asked her not to.

In short, what researchers have discovered is what God has been telling us all along. We need to *live* in love.

Isn't that something? God is so smart. And the longer I walk with Him, the more He proves that everything He instructs us to do is for our good.

Just think of all the stress we could avoid if we were quick to forgive. If we truly took no account of a suffered wrong. We'd be so healthy—both physically and spiritually! You see, our bodies weren't made to live with hostility flowing through them. They were designed to live according to love.

So why don't we all constantly walk in love? Very often, it's because we're still wrapped up in old, worldly habits of thinking and reacting. We continue to live from the outside instead of from the inside where God (Who is love) dwells.

So shake off that stress. Learn to walk in love. Renew your mind according to the Word and what it says about love. Choose to walk in forgiveness. Pretty soon you'll be feeling like the new person you really are...a new person living in love!

FOR FURTHER STUDY:

Luke 17:1-4

DAILY SCRIPTURE READING:

Jeremiah 3-4;
Psalm 63

## *Speak the Word*

*I take no account of evil done to me. I pay no attention to a suffered wrong.*
*1 Corinthians 13:5,* AMP

*Kenneth*

❧

"Which hope
we have as an
anchor of the
soul, both
sure and
stedfast."
HEBREWS 6:19

# The Creative Aspect of God

Plant your hope. If you focus it on a particular problem in your life, it will grow up and become greater. Greater than what? Greater than the problem!

Hope is a very powerful force. And it is inside you if you are born of God. Do you understand that? The moment you received Jesus Christ as your Lord, the Spirit of the living God came to live inside you. Your inner man was reborn in His image. God literally became the Father of your spirit. Just as your body took on the same genes and traits of your natural mother and father when you were born, your spirit took on the spiritual "genes," so to speak, of your Heavenly Father when you were reborn.

Your spirit took on His hope, His faith, His love—and all the other spiritual forces that are characteristic of Him. All of them together are called eternal life. The Greek word for it is *zoe*. It's a word that defies definition. So the best way I can explain *zoe* is by saying it's the part of God that makes Him God. And He invested *zoe* in your spirit when you made Jesus the Lord of your life.

This isn't a human kind of hope. It's God's kind. It's one of the supernatural forces He used to create the universe, and He put it inside you when you were born again. But before you can use it, *you* have to be absolutely certain that you have it.

"But, Brother Copeland, you don't understand. My circumstances have been bad for so long, I don't have any hope anymore!"

Yes, you do! Hebrews 6:19 says so. You may feel totally hopeless right now. This may be the most hopeless moment of your entire life. But, according to the Word of God, you have hope. God Himself is your hope. So the first thing you need to do is acknowledge that. Say, "Thank God, I have hope!" You have to get in agreement with God and His Word.

Hope. You have it living within you right now. Realize that. Use it. Feed it. Speak it. Guard it. Put it to work with the Word of God for a blueprint to victory.

## *Speak the Word*

*Hope is the anchor of my soul, both sure and steadfast.*
*Hebrews 6:19*

FOR FURTHER
STUDY:

1 Peter 3:15-22

DAILY SCRIPTURE
READING:

Jeremiah 5-6;
Psalm 64

*Gloria*

# Separate Yourself!

God is calling His Church to be separate. That means He wants you to be set apart, to be disunited from your old ways of living. When He saved you, you were set apart for His use. After all, you are no longer your own. You were bought with a price (1 Corinthians 6:19-20).

First Corinthians 1:2 says those who are set apart are called saints.

"No, not me, Gloria. I'm not a saint."

Yes, you are, if you're born again. The verse says, *"Unto the church of God which is at Corinth, to them that are sanctified in Christ Jesus, called to be saints...."*

In other words, "to them that are made holy, set apart or separated unto God in Christ Jesus, called saints." So you're a saint! A Bible saint is one who's born of God.

OCTOBER 12

"Wherefore come out from among them, and be ye separate, saith the Lord, and touch not the unclean thing: and I will receive you."
2 CORINTHIANS 6:17

What does it mean to be set apart for His use? It means that whatever He wants you to do, you should do. If He asks you to go to your neighbors and tell them the good news, or if He asks you to go to another land, or if He asks you to go into the ministry, or become a teacher or a nurse, then you do it!

Why is that? Because you've been redeemed.

When you put something in a pawnshop, you later go back and redeem it. You buy it back. In the same way, as a born-again believer, you've been bought back from darkness. You are no longer your own. You have been paid for by the precious blood of Jesus. You now belong to God. And if you intend to let God be God in your life, and you plan to walk in the reverence and fear of the Lord to honor Him, then you will do whatever He tells you to do.

If He calls you to a particular occupation, then that's what you should do. That's obedience. That's being separated unto God. And it's not just being separated in your job, but in your lifestyle, in your conduct.

He reveals His will to us "as we go." He may say one day, *This thing is holding you back. Make a change.* Maybe it's not a sin. Maybe it is. What matters is that you obey and get rid of it. That's separating yourself.

So, whatever it is that He's been speaking to you about, acknowledge it. Make that change. Go where He's saying to go. Do what He's been saying to do. Separate yourself!

FOR FURTHER STUDY:

Ephesians 5:1-17

DAILY SCRIPTURE READING:

Jeremiah 7-8; Psalm 65

## Speak the Word

*I come out and separate myself from among the world so that the Lord may receive me.*
*2 Corinthians 6:17*

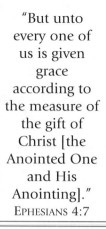

"But unto every one of us is given grace according to the measure of the gift of Christ [the Anointed One and His Anointing]."
EPHESIANS 4:7

*Kenneth*

# Live the Gospel!

According to this scripture, we're headed toward a time when we'll be walking in the anointing to its fullest expression! I want to see that, don't you? I want to see the entire Body of Christ flowing in the anointing so powerfully that the whole earth is filled with God's Glory.

I believe with all my heart, we're the generation who will see that.

But before we do, we must lay aside the things that block that anointing. We must rid ourselves of religious traditions that cause us to take offense at the idea that ordinary believers like us, or the pastor of our little church, can operate in the Anointing of Almighty God.

I asked the Lord once what was the greatest problem in the Body of Christ. Here's what He told me: *It's your dogged determination to correct one another.*

It's time for us to change that. We must stop strife, stop the criticism, and stop taking offense at one another—and we must do it now because the end of the age is at hand. The anointing needs to flow in measures we have never seen or even dreamed were possible.

We need that flow in our families, in our jobs, in our ministries and in our marriages. It's the anointing that will change things.

So let's rise up in unity and show the world that what was once true in Jesus' own life and ministry is now true in the lives of His servants throughout the earth. Let's dare to believe the Word of God and say, "Because I belong to Jesus, the Spirit of the Lord is upon me and He hath anointed me!"

Let's preach—and live—the gospel of *Christ*.

## *Speak the Word*

*God has given me grace according to the measure of the gift of Christ,*
*the Anointed One and His Anointing.*
*Ephesians 4:7*

FOR FURTHER STUDY:

Ephesians 4:7, 11-13

DAILY SCRIPTURE READING:

Jeremiah 9-10; Psalm 66

*Gloria*

# Continue in the Word

Reading, studying and listening to the Word of God is vital to walking in the spirit. Fellowship with God through His Word opens the door to your heart so the fruit of the spirit can flow out of it. They're listed in Galatians 5:22-23 and are a part of your new nature as a believer.

When you think about it, you can easily understand why. The Word is spiritual food. The more of it you put in your heart, the stronger your spirit becomes. If you'll continue to feed on the Word, eventually your spirit will be so dominant that it can overcome your flesh every time (Hebrews 5:14).

The opposite is also true. If you spend your time feeding on soap operas, romance novels and the 6 o'clock news, your flesh will grow stronger and your spirit will weaken. And though you'll still have the inner desire to be loving and kind, the flesh will bully you into acting like the devil!

"But strong meat belongeth to them that are of full age, even those who by reason of use have their senses exercised to discern both good and evil."
HEBREWS 5:14

If you're especially wanting to strengthen your spirit in the area of one particular fruit of the spirit, one of the wisest things you can do is feed on what the Word has to say about that particular fruit. If you've been running short of joy lately, for example, make it a point each day to read and meditate on what the Bible has to say about joy and rejoicing. Build up your spirit in that particular area. The moment light comes, faith is there.

Jesus said, *"If ye continue in my word, then are ye my disciples indeed; And ye shall know the truth, and the truth shall make you free"* (John 8:31-32). Continuing in the Word will help the fruit of the spirit to flow, to make you free from the bondages of the flesh. *"Walk in the spirit, and ye shall not fulfil the lust of the flesh"* (Galatians 5:16).

## Speak the Word

*I will continue in God's Word and walk in the spirit, and I will not fulfill the lust of the flesh.*
John 8:31; Galatians 5:16

FOR FURTHER STUDY:

Hebrews 6:9-14

DAILY SCRIPTURE READING:

Jeremiah 11-12;
Psalm 67

> "The law of the Spirit of life in Christ Jesus hath made me [us] free from the law of sin and death."
> ROMANS 8:2

# Living in the Life Cycle Every Day

This world is caught in a death cycle. You don't have to read the Bible to know that. All you have to do is look around. Inflation, recession, depression, sin, sickness, disease and death. They're all part of the cycle of death that has been keeping this world in check ever since Adam joined Satan in the Garden of Eden.

Sadly enough, they often have kept the children of God in check too. They shouldn't have. But they have.

Read today's scripture one more time. This verse means that you and I, as born-again believers, aren't locked into the death cycle of the world anymore. We can step out of it and into the life cycle of God. We've been set free!

"Brother Copeland, how can you say we're free? This last swing in the economy ruined my business!"

No, it didn't. It was your participation in it that ruined your business.

*"The law of the Spirit of life in Christ Jesus hath made [us] free from the law of sin and death."*

Hallelujah! We can live debt free, poverty free and recession free right in the middle of a world filled with financial ruin.

"Nobody can do that!"

Yes, Somebody can. In fact, Somebody did...Jesus.

He healed the sick, raised the dead, cast out demons, rebuked the storm. Nothing could control Him—not disease, not circumstances, not finances, not criticism, not conspiracy, not demonic forces, not even death itself! Now that's freedom!

You can live the same way by copying Him. Imitate Jesus. He lived His life by doing what He saw His Father do and by saying what He heard His Father say (John 8:28-29). He lived His life by copying His Father!

So how do you know what to copy? By reading the Word and by spending time in prayer and continual fellowship with your Father, beginning today. He'll tell you what to do. He'll show you how to do it. He'll teach you how to live in the life cycle—every day.

## *Speak the Word*

*The law of the Spirit of life in Christ Jesus has made me free from the law of sin and death.*

*Romans 8:2*

FOR FURTHER STUDY:

Romans 8:1-8

DAILY SCRIPTURE READING:

Jeremiah 13-15;
Psalms 68-69

*Gloria*

# No Time to Faint

"If thou faint
in the day
of adversity,
thy strength
is small."
PROVERBS 24:10

This *is* the day of adversity! Whatever you are facing today, you can't afford to be weak. You can't afford to faint spiritually in the trials of life. If you do, you'll be in trouble because, naturally speaking, things aren't going to get better in this world, they're going to get worse.

But don't let that scare you. For 1 John 5:4 tells us that *"whatsoever is born of God overcometh the world: and this is the victory that overcometh the world, even our faith."*

Did you know you can become just as strong as you want to from the Word? The only one who can put limits on you is you. If you'll give the Word more time, it will give you more strength.

That's what wise believers do. They keep themselves strong by spending time in the Word every day. They stay strong and ready because they know this is an evil day we live in.

Wake yourself up to the Word by getting out your Bible and meditating on it every day. Get tapes and books of anointed men and women preaching the Word. Listen to them and read them again and again.

Keep that Word in your heart. Keep it going in your eyes and in your ears until it takes over the very thoughts that you think. Keep yourself strong and ready...and free to operate in the Spirit of God.

If you do, when adversity strikes, you'll have supernatural strength to overcome and walk in the victory. Remember, this is no time to faint.

## *Speak the Word*

*I refuse to faint in the day of adversity for I am strong.*
*Proverbs 24:10*

FOR FURTHER
STUDY:

Isaiah 40:28-31

DAILY SCRIPTURE
READING:

Jeremiah 16-17;
Psalm 70

# Brother Big, Mother Smith and You

God cannot sit still when He hears the cries of His people! The problem is, most of us are too busy with other things to take the time to intercede and cry out to Him. We don't make prayer a priority. Many become so occupied "working" for God, we think we don't need to pray.

But in the end, we'll find out it was the intercessors who were behind every success in ministry. Someday in heaven when the rewards are being handed out, Brother Big will be sitting on the front row, expecting a gold trophy because he started the first Full Gospel church in his county. He'll lean over to the fellow next to him and say, "Yes, amen. I pastored that church for 47 years. I led 2,000 people to the Lord and had 1,000 baptized in the Holy Ghost in 1919. I'll tell you boys all about it as soon as I get my trophy."

But when the Lord starts to give the trophy, instead of calling Brother Big's name, He'll say, "Where's Mother Smith?" Then He'll send an angel down to row 7 million to fly Mother Smith up to the front.

When she gets there, He'll put that trophy in her hands and say, "Mother Smith, I want to give you this in honor of those 25 years you prayed and interceded and lay on your face before Me. Because of your prayers, I called Brother Big to come start the Full Gospel church in your county. Because of your prayers, thousands of people were saved and filled with the Holy Spirit in that church."

Then He'll turn to the front row and say, "Brother Big, I'm rewarding you by allowing you to carry Mother Smith's trophy for her."

I can tell you whose trophies I will get to carry when that day comes. One of them will belong to my mother and the other one will belong to a little woman who used to pray with her all the time.

I'm saved and preaching the gospel today because of those two women. I don't get any credit for it. I do have some credit coming for the times I interceded and cried out to God on behalf of someone else. But rewards aren't the reason you pray those kinds of prayers. You pray them because you're a bondservant of the One Who laid His blood on the line for you. You pray them because of love.

Pray those things stirring in your spirit. Answer that call to intercede. Speak forth those things God is wanting to do in the earth today.

## *Speak the Word*

*I make supplications, prayers, intercessions and giving of thanks for all men.*
*For this is good and acceptable in the sight of God.*
*1 Timothy 2:1-4*

FOR FURTHER STUDY:

Acts 12:1-17

DAILY SCRIPTURE READING:

Jeremiah 18-19;
Psalm 71

*Gloria*

# Faith in All the Right Places

> "A good man out of the good treasure of the heart bringeth forth good things: and an evil man out of the evil treasure bringeth forth evil things."
>
> MATTHEW 12:35

Have you ever heard someone say, "I'd have no problem at all believing God's Word would heal me if He'd speak to me out loud like He did in Genesis, but He hasn't!"?

The correct answer is, "No, and He probably won't either." You see, God no longer has to thunder His Word down at us from heaven. These days He lives in the hearts of believers, so He speaks to us from the inside instead of the outside. What's more, when it comes to covenant issues like healing, we don't even have to wait on Him to speak.

He has already spoken! He has already said, *"By whose [Jesus'] stripes ye were healed"* (1 Peter 2:24). He has already said, *"I am the Lord that healeth thee"* (Exodus 15:26). He has already said, *"The prayer of faith shall save the sick, and the Lord shall raise him up"* (James 5:15).

God has already done His part. So we must do ours. We must take the Word He has spoken, put it inside us and let it change us from the inside out. You see, everything—including healing—starts inside you. Your future is literally stored up in your heart. Matthew 12:35 confirms that.

In other words, if you want external conditions to be better tomorrow, you'd better start changing your internal condition today. You'd better start taking the Word of God and depositing it in your heart just like you deposit money in the bank. Then you can make withdrawals on it whenever you need it. When sickness attacks your body, you can tap into the healing Word you've put inside yourself and run that sickness off!

Exactly how do you do that? You open your mouth and speak—not words of sickness and disease, discouragement and despair, but words of healing and life, faith and hope. You follow the last step of God's divine prescription in Proverbs 4:20-24: *"Put away from thee a froward mouth, and perverse lips put far from thee."* In short, you speak the Words of God and call yourself healed in Jesus' Name. Initially that may not be easy for you to do. But you must do it anyway, because for faith to work, it must be in two places—in your heart and in your mouth. *"For with the heart man believeth unto righteousness; and with the mouth confession is made unto salvation"* (Romans 10:10).

So get into the Word. Fill your heart with the good treasure of God's Word for your healing...and speak forth from your heart that Word in faith. Then you'll have your faith in all the right places!

FOR FURTHER STUDY:

Proverbs 6:20-23

DAILY SCRIPTURE READING:

Jeremiah 20-21; Psalm 72

## *Speak the Word*

*By the stripes of Jesus I am healed. He is the Lord that heals me.*
*1 Peter 2:24; Exodus 15:26*

*Kenneth*

> "Walk by faith,
> not by sight."
> 2 CORINTHIANS
> 5:7

# Get That Bulldog, Never-Let-Go Kind of Faith

When I think of the spiritual tenacity we'll need in the days ahead, I think of a story I once read about a young man who was in pilot training during World War II. He was a bomber pilot training on the Martin Marauder.

One day this young pilot was sitting with his instructor in this airplane at the end of the runway, preparing to take off on a training flight. His roommate, who was training in the same kind of plane, was coming in for his final approach. About one-fourth of a mile from the end of the runway, right in front of this young pilot's eyes, his roommate flipped that airplane upside down, it hit the ground and exploded in a ball of flames.

Stunned, the young man simply sat and stared in silence. Then he heard the firm voice of his instructor, "Don't just sit there! Take the runway!"

The young pilot was astonished. "Surely we're not going to train today! My buddy just got killed!"

"Take the runway!" the instructor ordered. "We are in the middle of a war. We have no time to grieve. Take the runway!" He taxied through the smoke of his friend's burning airplane and put that bomber in the sky!

I know as well as anyone that living by faith isn't easy. There are times when the devil blindsides you and hurts you so badly that your flesh just wants to lie down and cry. There are times when you want Jesus to appear to you and give you some tangible manifestation to help you go on. But crying won't get the war won. And neither will fleshly manifestations. You have to keep going.

Walking by faith will win the war, because faith is our link to the Anointing of God. Faith releases within us and through us the yoke-destroying, burden-removing power of God. If you'll keep your faith strong and your spirit activated through the Word of God, when the devil takes a punch at you, you can rise up.

I can tell you from personal experience what will happen when you hammer away at the devil with faith and refuse to let up. The Anointing of God will come on you. Your spirit will be activated. You'll get bigger on the inside than you are on the outside. Instead of whimpering in the corner, you'll begin to roar like the Lion of the tribe of Judah!

So commit to live by faith. Make a quality decision to walk by faith and not by sight. Determine to keep feeding on the Word, to keep your spirit activated by believing, speaking and acting on it. Get tenacious. Get that bulldog, never-give-up faith. Satan will be the one who gives up. He will flee!

## *Speak the Word*

*I refuse to walk by sight. I walk by faith.*
*2 Corinthians 5:7*

FOR FURTHER
STUDY:

1 Kings 17:1-16

DAILY SCRIPTURE
READING:

Jeremiah 22-23;
Psalm 73

*Gloria*

# Live in the Highest Measure

The Church, as a whole, is discontent with carnal ways and immaturity. We want to put childish things behind us and grow up spiritually. We want to be more like Jesus.

The Apostle Paul had that same desire. He prayed fervently for the day when we would all arrive *"at really mature manhood—the completeness of personality which is nothing less than the standard height of Christ's own perfection—the measure of the stature of the fullness of the Christ, and the completeness found in Him"* (Ephesians 4:13, AMP).

Paul not only prayed about that kind of spiritual maturity, he exhorted us as believers to move actively toward it (Ephesians 4:15).

As I've studied the fruit of the spirit, I've come to realize more and more that love is the single most important key to growing up in God. I've seen that if we don't grow up in love...we won't grow up at all.

We won't enjoy the fullness of God we've been longing for until we start walking consistently in love. Our love life has everything to do with the manifestation of God's presence and His power in our lives.

That might come as a surprise to some people. They think that love is so basic, something only beginners need to study. They might consider the gifts of the Spirit—things like tongues and interpretation, gifts of healings and miracles—as more relevant to the mature believer. But according to 1 Corinthians, the gifts are not marks of spiritual maturity. Paul referred to the Corinthian church as mere infants in Christ, still unspiritual, ruled by the flesh (1 Corinthians 3:1, 3).

As wonderful as the gifts are, it's the fruit of the spirit that indicate a person is walking in the spirit and not in the flesh.

So, if you want to know whether you're a spiritual person or not, don't look to see what mighty gifts of the Spirit are flowing out of you, look at the fruit in your life. Specifically, look to see if you are walking in love. You simply can't walk in the spirit or be a spiritual person without being ruled by love. The quality of our life depends on it. Living a life ruled by the love of God is what opens us up to walk in the spirit and live in the highest measure of blessing and power of God!

## *Speak the Word*

*I grow up in every way and in all things into Him by walking in love.*
*Ephesians 4:15, AMP*

OCTOBER 20

"Let our lives lovingly express truth.... Enfolded in love, let us grow up in every way and in all things into Him, Who is the Head, [even] Christ, the Messiah, the Anointed One."
EPHESIANS 4:15, AMP

FOR FURTHER STUDY:

1 Corinthians 3:1-3

DAILY SCRIPTURE READING:

Jeremiah 24-25; Psalm 74

> "This book of the law shall not depart out of thy mouth; but thou shalt meditate therein day and night, that thou mayest observe to do according to all that is written therein: for then thou shalt make thy way prosperous, and then thou shalt have good success."
>
> JOSHUA 1:8

# Turn on the Light!

Just because you can't see something doesn't mean it isn't there. For example, you can look out your back window on a moonless night when it's dark as pitch, and you won't be able to see your patio. But that doesn't mean your patio is gone. It simply means you can't see it. You need to turn on the light.

Sometimes we become concerned that we can't "see" God's promises coming to pass in our lives. But that doesn't mean His Word is of no effect. We just can't see it because we haven't spent enough time in the Word of God for the light to dawn in our hearts. But if we'll start meditating on those promises, the Bible says, "you will observe." In other words, you'll start to see!

Let me show you what I mean. Perhaps God has instructed you to be completely debt free. But you don't have enough cash yet to buy everything you need. Instead of meditating on the problem and thinking, *I'm afraid not to borrow money, I'm afraid I'll never be able to afford to buy anything,* you make a change. You start meditating on what God said.

You think, Jesus said, *"Give and it shall be given to you again." I wonder what would happen if I applied that principle?*

If fear tries to rise up (and I assure you it will), just slap it down. You don't have to be afraid. When the "yeah-but-what-ifs" come up, just go back over what the Word says again.

Begin to see how your life would change if you became a giver. Let the Holy Spirit use the Word to paint a picture of that promise coming to pass in your life.

It will take awhile, but if you do this long enough, giving will start looking like the only intelligent thing for you to do. Courage will overwhelm your fear. You'll find yourself saying, "God said He'd never leave me or forsake me! He said He'd meet my needs! He said if I'd give, it would be given to me again. So praise God, I'll act on that. I'll cross over into the promised land and be debt free!"

So what happened? What changed? You did. You turned on the light!

## *Speak the Word*

*I meditate on the Word of God and contemplate all His ways.*
*Psalm 119:15*

FOR FURTHER STUDY:

Psalm 119:1-24

DAILY SCRIPTURE READING:

Jeremiah 26-27;
Psalm 75

*Gloria*

# A Gift of Honor

In God's economy, giving equals receiving. Seeds planted bring a harvest. All of us who've studied what the Bible has to say about prosperity know that. But we've also looked around enough to know that despite their giving, many of God's people are struggling financially. They plant seeds, but instead of reaping abundance, lack continues to dog their footsteps.

I believe the difference is giving a gift of honor.

For example, just because you've been in the habit of setting aside 10 percent for God doesn't mean you are a tither. True tithing must be done in a way that honors God. It must be done with heart worship for God, not just plunked in the plate and deducted in the checkbook register.

Just like tithing must be done in a way that honors God, so must all our giving. Here are six principles that will guarantee a return on your giving.

> "If the willingness is there, the gift is acceptable according to what one has, not according to what he does not have."
> 2 CORINTHIANS 8:12, NIV

*1) Start Where You Are*—Some people get discouraged before they even begin because they can only give small gifts. "All I can give is $2. That's not enough to matter." Don't be deceived. Every gift matters to God. The poor widow in Mark 12 gave only two mites, yet Jesus said she gave the biggest gift of all.

*2) Give in Faith*—When you give, believe God. You can't tithe in faith and in heart and not increase. Expect God to prosper you when you tithe and you will get exactly what you believe for.

*3) Tithe, No Matter What*—Commit to tithe consistently, not just when things are going well financially. You won't increase if you aren't consistent. You may even decrease!

*4) Sow What You Want to Reap*—Don't give God your leftovers. Give Him quality gifts (Malachi 3).

*5) Watch Your Words*—When people get under pressure financially (or in any other area of life), there's a temptation to start spouting their frustration and talking unbelief. A good place to check for this is to consider what you say in front of your spouse. You are probably OK in front of your faith and Word friends.

*6) When You Give, Rejoice!*—Worship before the Lord. Rejoice in all the good things He has given to you. Rejoice in the goodness He's brought into your life (Deuteronomy 26).

FOR FURTHER STUDY:

Proverbs 3:9-10; 2 Corinthians 9:7

This is the kind of giving that honors God. When you begin to give according to these principles, something exciting will happen. Your spirit will rise up inside you. You will take authority over doubt and fear and lack in the Name of Jesus. Instead of expecting the natural shortages that have dogged you, you'll start expecting supernatural abundance. And you know what? You're going to get it!

DAILY SCRIPTURE READING:

Jeremiah 28-30; Psalms 76-77

## Speak the Word

*I give and it is given to me, good measure, pressed down, shaken together and running over do men give to me.*

*Luke 6:38*

> "Therefore being justified by faith, we have peace with God through our Lord Jesus Christ [the Anointed One]: By whom also we have access by faith into this grace wherein we stand, and rejoice in hope of the glory of God."
> ROMANS 5:1-2

# God's Word + Hope + Faith = Manifestation

God's Word + Hope + Faith = Manifestation. This spiritual process always works the same way. Hope forms the image according to the Word, then faith rises up and gives substance to that image, making it a reality in the natural, physical realm.

Now, I have a question I'd like you to seriously consider: In the light of all God has promised us in His Word, what are you and I to expect? What should we be hoping for? What inner image should be so capturing our hearts and minds that it is all we can see?

Certainly, healing is great. Financial supply is wonderful. But could it be that God has something even more grand for us to fix our hope upon?

Yes, He does. And He tells us what it is in Romans 5:1-2.

This scripture, in the last phrase, says we're to rejoice in the hope of the Glory of God! We're to expect the Glory, not just the healing! or the finances!

As long as you're just expecting healing, you'll always be battling it out with your flesh. But if you're expecting the Glory, you'll be raising your spiritual sights to something bigger than healing. You'll be expecting the very presence of God to rise up in you so powerfully that instead of believing for healing every six weeks, you'll walk in divine health every day!

I've experienced touches of Glory, and believe me, I'm eager for more! So start expecting the Glory. Raise your expectations to a new level, a new level of understanding. The results will be glorious!

## Speak the Word

*I have access by faith into this grace wherein I stand, and I rejoice in hope of the Glory of God.*
*Romans 5:2*

FOR FURTHER STUDY:

Exodus 40:34-38;
1 Kings 8:10-11

DAILY SCRIPTURE READING:

Jeremiah 31-32;
Psalm 78

*Gloria*

# No Fear!

> "Nay, in all these things we are more than conquerors through him that loved us."
> ROMANS 8:37

Did you know we're not supposed to fear the devil? We're supposed to fear God. We're to have so much reverence and respect for Him that we immediately make any adjustment in our lives just to please Him.

When He tells us to do something that looks risky from a natural point of view, we ought to be more concerned about what we'll miss if we don't obey Him, than of what will happen if we do.

In other words, when He tells you that you *are more than a conqueror,* and instructs you to march in and take back some part of your life that the devil has stolen from you, you shouldn't sit around debating about whether or not you can do it. You should just start marching!

*Well, I just couldn't do that. After all, I've been defeated in that area of my life for so long that I have a poor self-image.*

If that's what you're thinking, let me tell you something. If you'll serve God, your poor self-image will begin to change, and you'll start to see yourself as He sees you. We look so much better in Him!

We've got to get away from being so self-conscious, so aware of what we think we can or can't do. That's what keeps us from entering into our promised land. Instead of simply obeying God, we start to wonder, *Now what will people think of me if I do that? What if I lay hands on someone and they don't get healed? What if I start believing for prosperity and go broke? What will people think of me? How will I look?*

It doesn't matter how you look! What counts is that you obey God. Once you do that, your reputation will only get better. It's a funny thing, but once you lose that desire to protect your image, your image gets better. Why? Because then the image of the Lord Jesus can come forth instead of that image you had of yourself.

*"Certainly I will be with thee."* God promised that to you just as surely as He did to Moses (Exodus 3:12). So whatever God is telling you to do today... or has been telling you to do for some time now, do it! Grab hold of His promise to be with you. That's what will cause you to live in the supernatural and do impossible things. Don't fear the devil and let that fear stop you. You are more than a conqueror! Rise up and obey God. You'll have victory for everyone to see!

FOR FURTHER STUDY:

Hebrews 3:12-19

DAILY SCRIPTURE READING:

Jeremiah 33-34; Psalm 79

## *Speak the Word*

*In all things I am more than a conqueror through Him that loves me.*
*Romans 8:37*

> "We have this treasure in earthen vessels, that the excellency of the power may be of God, and not of us."
>
> 2 CORINTHIANS 4:7

# You Have the Treasure

There's an old religious cliché that used to be especially popular among ministers: "We're just going to burn ourselves out for God," they'd say. That's not what God wants for any of us. That's what the devil wants! He would love to see you work yourself until you "burn out" and die. He'd kick up his heels at your funeral!

Don't give him that opportunity. Take time to feed your inner man so you won't burn out. Keep feeding your spirit until you increase in strength. Burn brighter and stronger every year.

Be transformed from Glory to Glory by *"beholding as in a glass the glory of the Lord"* (2 Corinthians 3:18). Increase the wattage of your spiritual generator by spending time focusing on the Lord. Begin to work *with* Him instead of just *for* Him. Take your focus off the things of the world and look at Him.

Where must you look to see Jesus? First, in the Word. Second, in your own spirit.

We can see Jesus great and magnificent in the Word. We can envision Him sitting grandly in heaven at the right hand of the Father. But we haven't developed our ability to see Him living inside us. And that is the key.

You must have that ability to survive the pressure in these last days. You'll need to be able to see Jesus within you just as clearly as you can see Him in the Word. You'll have to know—not just with your brain, but with every fiber of your being—that He Who is within you is greater than he that is in the world.

Never forget this: Once you truly see that the very Spirit and power of Jesus resides on the inside of you, nothing—no amount of debt, no disease, no problem of ANY kind—will be able to defeat you. When your inner image of the Jesus Who lives in you becomes bigger than your image of the problems around you, you'll conquer any challenge the devil brings your way.

The answer to everything is inside you right now. Everything you'll ever need is in your spirit. All the money...all the health...all the strength...all the wisdom...all of it is in you because that's where Jesus is!

Remember, we have this treasure in earthen vessels, that the excellency of the power may be of God, and not of us!

## *Speak the Word*

*I have this treasure...that the excellency of the power may be of God and not of me.*
*2 Corinthians 4:7*

FOR FURTHER STUDY:

John 17:20-26

DAILY SCRIPTURE READING:

Jeremiah 35-36; Psalm 80

*Gloria*

# Make Those Faith Deposits

Whatever you do in life, whether you're a surgeon, a garbage collector or a schoolteacher, spending time with God and keeping your heart full of His Word is your number-one priority.

That's right. The most important thing you'll do each day is to make those faith deposits. Don't just make them in times of crisis, either. Make them before you need them. Go to Psalm 91 and proclaim the things that belong to you by faith every day.

I remember a letter Ken and I received from a family whose child drowned in the swimming pool. When they came out and found the baby in the pool, he had already turned blue and quit breathing.

But because they had made deposits of the Word of God before that time, the moment it happened, they were ready. Nobody said, "Go get the Bible and look up a scripture." (Sometimes you don't have time to get your Bible. That's why you'd better get the Word in your heart. It will save your life.)

Immediately that family began to pray and rebuke death and command the spirit of that baby to come back. As a result, that child is alive and well today.

Do you have enough faith in your heart to handle a situation like this? If you don't, start making big deposits of God's Word in your heart now. Start speaking the Word day and night...not just when you're praying or being spiritual, but all the time—at the office, at the dinner table, over your coffee break, even in your bed at night. The words you speak either work for you or against you. They are either words of faith or words of doubt.

Frankly, I think it's time we quit being so focused on our financial accounts and turn our attention on the account that's ultimately responsible for all the rest. We need to become spiritual tycoons, with hearts so full of faith that we foil the devil's every scheme.

If we'll do that, we will be able to buy back every piece of ground he's ever stolen from us. We can enjoy the riches of our inheritance at last!

## Speak the Word

*I hide God's Word in my heart, so that I might not sin against Him.*
*Psalm 119:11*

FOR FURTHER
STUDY:

Psalm 18:20-30

DAILY SCRIPTURE
READING:

Jeremiah 37-38;
Psalm 81

**OCTOBER 27**

"In righteousness shalt thou be established."
ISAIAH 54:14

*Kenneth*

# You Are Established!

Do you know what it means to be established in righteousness? It means to be in a right place with God. To be able to stand in the presence of a holy, awesome, almighty, pure God without a sense of guilt or inferiority.

Think about that! What must it be like to be established in righteousness? What must it be like to know without a shadow of a doubt that there's absolutely nothing wrong between you and God? No sin. Nothing. Everything is so right that every time you walk in the door, the Father says, *Yes, yes, yes,* before you can even ask Him for anything.

It's easy for us to believe things are that way between God and Jesus. But realize this: You were made the righteousness of God with exactly the same miraculous occurrence that made Him sin with your sin.

Second Corinthians 5 says, *"Therefore if any man be in Christ, he is a new creature: old things are passed away; behold, all things are become new.... For he hath made him to be sin for us, who knew no sin; that we might be made the righteousness of God in him"* (verses 17, 21).

You have just exactly the same entrance to the Heavenly Father as Jesus does. He loves you just as much as He loves Jesus. (Read John 17:23.)

I know that's hard for you to grasp. It's hard for me too, but we have to keep working on it. We have to keep thinking about it all the time. We have to keep meditating on it and developing a righteousness-consciousness instead of a sin-consciousness. We have to keep becoming skillful in the Word of righteousness. (See Hebrews 5:13.)

Do you know what will happen as you do that? You won't be afraid to do exploits in Jesus' Name. You won't be afraid to act like Him. You won't be afraid to boldly claim what is yours in Christ Jesus. You won't be afraid to lay hands on the sick, believing they will recover. You won't be afraid to believe God for your own healing, or for the finances you need.

So become skillful in the Word of righteousness. Receive that you have been made the righteousness of God in Christ Jesus. Receive that you are established in righteousness...stand before Him without any sense of guilt or inferiority...and live in victory every day!

## *Speak the Word*
*I am established in righteousness.*
*Isaiah 54:14*

FOR FURTHER STUDY:

1 Corinthians 1:26-31

DAILY SCRIPTURE READING:

Jeremiah 39-40; Psalm 82

*Gloria*
# We're Not Civilians!

A soldier in boot camp will jump out of bed before dawn every morning to run and do push-ups. He may not like it, but he'll do it because his commanding officer has ordered him to do it. He endures the discomfort because he knows it's an inescapable part of military life.

A civilian, on the other hand, might start an exercise program, but when the going gets tough, his muscles feel sore and his schedule gets busy, he'll just quit exercising. If someone asks him about it, he might just shrug and say, "I tried exercise, but it didn't work for me."

Some Christians are like that. They hear the Word of faith and they think, *Well, I'll try that.* Then when the hard times come, they give up.

But that's not how it should be. After all, we're not civilians! We're soldiers! We don't *try* faith, we make it our lifestyle. We walk by faith, whether it's hard or easy. We don't do it so we'll be blessed. We do it because we're determined to be pleasing to Jesus. He is our commander in chief, and the Bible says without faith, it is impossible to please Him.

Of course, we will end up blessed if we'll walk by faith. We'll end up healed and delivered and prospering in every area of life because God promised we would. That, however, is not our motivation. We're motivated by our desire to serve the Lord. That's what makes us believe His Word, stand fast and endure when the hard times come.

## *Speak the Word*
*I walk and live by faith so that I can please God.*
*Hebrews 11:6*

FOR FURTHER STUDY:

1 Peter 1:1-7

❧

DAILY SCRIPTURE READING:

Jeremiah 41-42; Psalm 83

"The Lord is
on my side;
I will not
fear."
PSALM 118:6

*Kenneth*

# He Will See You Through

Notice in Psalm 118:6 that David didn't say, "I'll pray and ask God to take the fear away." He didn't say, "I try not to be afraid." He said, *"I WILL NOT FEAR."*

Refusing to fear is first of all a matter of the will. But, as that verse indicates, it is also a matter of choosing to believe that in every situation God is on your side and by His power, He will see you through.

Of course, to successfully walk by faith and not fear, we need to know exactly how to tap into that power. Second Peter 1:3-4 tells us: *"His [God's] divine power hath given unto us all things that pertain unto life and godliness, through the knowledge of him that hath called us to glory and virtue: Whereby are given unto us exceeding great and precious promises: that by these ye might be partakers of the divine nature, having escaped the corruption that is in the world through lust."*

God makes available everything we could possibly need, every conceivable blessing, through the promises in His Word. If we'll believe them and activate the Law of the Spirit of Life, those promises will manifest in our lives. They will open the way for us to escape the destruction brought into the earth by the Law of Sin and Death.

Satan, however, challenges those promises with fear. He brings us contrary circumstances to convince us those promises can never come to pass. He tells us lies. He contradicts the Word of God and says, *You'll never make it. You're too weak. Other people can walk by faith because they're stronger than you. You don't have the background they have. There's something wrong with you.* And so on.

But no matter what, the choice is still yours. You can listen to the Word of God or the lies of the devil. Which will it be?

"But, Brother Copeland, I'm not really listening to the devil. I believe the Word of God. But I can't just forget what happened to me in the past. I failed. I didn't receive my healing. I was mistreated...."

You'd better forget those things! You'd better put them under the blood of Jesus and wash them away forever. If you don't, you'll find yourself meditating on them. And just as faith comes by hearing and hearing by the Word of God, fear comes by hearing the word of the devil. Fear comes when you entertain his threats about the future and his boasts about the past.

So make the right choice...even if you have to make it every 60 seconds. Don't let the devil's lies swirl through your head for even a minute. Fill your thoughts with God's Word...remember He is on your side and will see you through.

## *Speak the Word*

*The Lord is on my side. I do not fear.*
*Psalm 118:6*

FOR FURTHER
STUDY:

Deuteronomy
31:1-6

DAILY SCRIPTURE
READING:

Jeremiah 43-45;
Psalms 84-85

*Gloria*

# In My Name, YOU Will...

> "In My name they [you] will cast out demons."
> MARK 16:17, NKJV

*Wait a minute,* you may be thinking, *I've been saved for 20 years and Jesus has been in me the whole time. But He has never preached any sermons or healed any sick people through me.*

That's because you haven't expected Him to do those things. You see, even though the Anointed One is in you, He is not going to be revealed through you unless you use your faith. That shouldn't surprise you. After all, everything we receive from God—even the new birth—must be activated in our lives by faith.

Thus, if you want the Anointed One Who lives in you to begin to be manifested through you, you'll have to believe God for it. You can't just sit back and wait to see what happens. You must lay hold of the promise of God and believe what the Word says, rather than what your circumstances or experiences say.

You may feel as though you have no power or anointing at all. But the Word of God says, *"After...ye believed, ye were sealed with that holy Spirit of promise"* (Ephesians 1:13). To be sealed means "to be stamped with an image." That means, when you were born again, you were stamped with the likeness of the Anointed One. You were made to look like the Lord Jesus Christ on the inside.

What you need to do now is believe that, and let what God put on the inside of you come out! Seek to yield to the Anointed One within you every day. Let Him have His way. Expect the divine Life already in you to begin to flow, so others can see the Lord Jesus Christ through you!

Put your faith into action by spending time with Him. Set your affections on those things that are above. Desire Him to reveal Himself through you so much that you're willing to set aside other things and seek Him first.

I firmly believe that the more important Jesus becomes to us, the more He will reveal Himself through us. So make up your mind to hunger for Him and to give Him His way in you every day. As you do, He'll begin to bless people through you.

## Speak the Word

*Jesus lives in me. He is my Hope of Glory.*
*Colossians 1:27*

FOR FURTHER STUDY:

Colossians 1:25-29

DAILY SCRIPTURE READING:

Jeremiah 46-47; Psalm 86

> "Submit yourselves therefore to God. Resist the devil, and he will flee from you."
>
> JAMES 4:7

# Resist Him in the Name of Jesus

How many times have you seen footage on the 6 o'clock news of someone resisting arrest? Have you ever noticed their behavior? They refuse to cooperate. They fight back. They kick, scream, hit and do anything and everything they can except what the arresting officer wants them to do. What are they doing? They are resisting. The law calls it "resisting arrest."

In the same way, when you act that way toward the devil, he'll flee from you. James 4:7 guarantees it. The word *flee* in that scripture doesn't just mean he leaves the scene. It literally means he runs as in terror.

The reason he runs is because you bear the Name of Jesus. That Name strikes terror into every fiber of the devil's twisted being.

If you could see things from his viewpoint, you'd see why. Philippians 2:9-10 describes the situation clearly: *"God also hath highly exalted him [Jesus] and given him a name which is above every name: That at the name of Jesus every knee should bow, of things in heaven, and things in earth, and things under the earth."* That includes the devil. He has to bow his knee at the Name of Jesus.

Now you can see why, when you resist the devil in Jesus' Name, he flees from you. He has no choice. Jesus is the One Who defeated him. In fact, after Jesus spoiled principalities and powers, Colossians 2:15 says He made an open show of them publicly, triumphing over them!

Satan was humiliated in front of all the angels of heaven and the demons of hell. He is a defeated foe and he knows it. Jesus is the One Who defeated him—and it's His Name you're wearing!

So the next time you're tempted, or the next time Satan tries to put something over on you, resist him in the Name of Jesus. Say, "Satan, I take authority over you. I resist you in the Name of Jesus and I'll not receive (whatever he's trying to tell you or give you). According to Colossians 2:15, you are defeated! And I am victorious! Amen."

## *Speak the Word*

*I submit myself to God, and I resist the devil. The devil flees from me.*
*James 4:7*

FOR FURTHER STUDY:

Colossians 2:9-15

DAILY SCRIPTURE READING:

Jeremiah 48-49;
Psalm 87

*Kenneth*

# Vote Holy Spirit

"If any of you lack wisdom, let him ask of God, that giveth to all men liberally, and upbraideth not; and it shall be given him."
JAMES 1:5

As a believer, you have probably stood for your nation for years. I know I have. I pray for the leaders of the United States government from the president down to our local level regularly. I specifically release my faith and believe God for the deliverance and preservation of our spiritual heritage. I thank God that we are a free nation, that we can worship our God openly.

On the local level, on a regular basis, we have the opportunity to vote for elected officials. And every four years, we vote for the next president. It's a tremendous privilege and a tremendous responsibility.

Many believers are tempted to be discouraged by the things they see wrong with the political system. But that is never a reason not to vote. No matter where you live, voting is putting feet to your faith. Voting brings to life your faith by taking the action real faith demands.

Yes, we should pray. And vote. We can never underestimate the importance of elections. They establish the spiritual climate of a nation's government. There are spiritual battles that rage over political positions. Satan is always trying to tell people that their vote won't matter, that their one vote won't make a difference. But that is a lie from the devil himself. Don't listen to his deceptions.

If you don't know whom to vote for, then go to the Lord and ask Him. He has specific ideas on how you should vote, and He will give you the wisdom you need (James 1:5). Take the time to get that wisdom from Him. Vote Holy Spirit!

Then, as Ephesians 6:13 says, *"Having done all...stand."*

Stand in line to register to vote.

Stand in line to vote.

Stand in faith, believing His will to come to pass.

And then, no matter who wins, stand in prayer for them. Your job isn't finished in the voting booth...it continues in your prayer closet. You can make a difference, before, during and after the elections. Your vote counts and your prayer counts!

## Speak the Word

*I ask God for wisdom, and He gives it to me liberally.*
*James 1:5*

FOR FURTHER STUDY:

1 Timothy 2:1-4

DAILY SCRIPTURE READING:

Jeremiah 50-51; Psalm 88

# Lions Go Hungry

It doesn't matter how dark the world around us may become in the coming days. It doesn't matter how hard the devil tries to bring us down, if we're steadfast, dependable and trustworthy—constantly serving the Lord and doing what is right—God will bring us through in victory.

If you have any question about that, just take a look at what He did in the life of Daniel. When Daniel was just a young man, he served as one of three presidents directly under the king. Daniel did his job so faithfully that he was preferred above the other presidents, and the king considered putting him over the whole realm.

When the other presidents found out about the king's promotion plan for Daniel, they were jealous. So they began looking for some wrongdoing to accuse him.

The Bible records that they could find no fault in him. And since they couldn't dig up any real dirt on him, they decided to scheme and trap him. That trap led to Daniel's being thrown into the lions' den to be eaten.

Daniel 6:16, 18-20 records the king's words to Daniel as he was being thrown to the lions, and then the morning after he was NOT eaten by the lions. In these verses, the king mentions twice that Daniel continually served God. What stood out to the king was Daniel's faithfulness. He was faithful—both in spiritual things and in natural things. Because of that faithfulness, God preserved Daniel.

What God did for Daniel, He'll do for you. If you'll be faithful with what God has given you right now, with what He's told you to do, He'll preserve you. He wants you to be faithful spiritually by fellowshiping with Him in the Word and praying every day. He wants you to put yourself in a position of increase in the natural realm by being faithful with the material things He's given you.

For example, if you live in a rented house, and you want a house of your own, treat that rented house as though it belongs to you. Don't tear it up and be careless with it. Jesus said, *"If ye have not been faithful in that which is another man's, who shall give you that which is your own?"* (Luke 16:12).

Until now, you may have acted like the most unfaithful person around. You may feel like you have made disastrous mistakes in your life by being undependable and untrustworthy. You may have always been a quitter. But you can start changing that today because as a child of God, you have inside you His very own force of faithfulness. So start yielding to it. Begin to strengthen that force by meditating on God's Word. Read and study what it says about faithfulness. You can be among those who *"are called, and chosen, and faithful!"* (Revelation 17:14).

Remind the devil of that the next time he pressures you to quit. Remind him of it when he tempts you to do less than your best. Determine to be the kind of person God can trust to follow through, no matter what the inconvenience or discomfort. Say, "Lord, I am a faithful person. I will get my job done and do it well. I will trust You to help me, energize me and create in me the power and desire. And I'll stay with it at any cost."

## *Speak the Word*

*I am faithful, and the Lord preserves me.*
*Psalm 31:23*

FOR FURTHER
STUDY:

Daniel 6:16-22

DAILY SCRIPTURE
READING:

Jeremiah 52;
Lamentations 1;
Psalm 89

*Kenneth*

# Pull a New Trigger

NOVEMBER 3

"Even so the tongue is a little member, and it can boast of great things. See how much wood or how great a forest a tiny spark can set ablaze!"
JAMES 3:5, AMP

Think right now about the sourest lemon you've ever tasted. Picture it in your mind. Pick it up, squeeze it just a little and watch the sour juice just trickle out. Now work up your nerve, put that lemon in your mouth and bite down.

What kind of physical response are you having right now? Your mouth is watering, right? Your lips are probably puckered up like a prune. Science calls that a conditioned response. It's a physical reaction triggered by a mental stimulus.

Our lives are filled with conditioned responses like that. Every one of us has scores of reactions that, through repeated experiences, have become totally automatic. There are certain triggers you can use that will affect your spirit as surely as the thought of that lemon affected your body. What are those triggers?

Words, words, words!

Words are seemingly little things that produce very big results. They put in motion the inner working of your spirit.

Words trigger faith or fear, joy or despair, courage or discouragement. That's a spiritual principle and it works all the time whether you know it or not.

What's all this got to do with conditioned responses? If you start listening to yourself, you'll find you have many, many phrases and expressions you use automatically, without even thinking. "It's blue Monday again.... If it weren't for bad luck, I wouldn't have any luck at all.... My memory gets worse and worse every year...." The list goes on and on.

What I want to challenge you to do today is to begin turning those expressions around. Pull a new trigger. Start conditioning yourself to respond to every situation with words of faith instead of words of unbelief. Learn to connect faith words with everything you do all day long. Teach yourself to talk in such a way that every situation becomes a trigger to your faith. You'll be blessed at the difference it makes!

## Speak the Word

*Death and life are in the power of my tongue.*
*I determine to speak words of life.*
*Proverbs 18:21*

FOR FURTHER
STUDY:

Hebrews 4:14-16

DAILY SCRIPTURE
READING:

Lamentations 2-3;
Psalm 90

*Gloria*

# Keep Your Eyes on the Word

> "We look [Faith looks] not at the things which are seen, but at the things which are not seen: for the things which are seen are temporal; but the things which are not seen are eternal."
> 2 CORINTHIANS 4:18

If you want to maintain the spirit of faith, you'll quit considering the natural impossibilities that might be piling up around you this very moment. God is not sweating them, so neither should you. Ken and I have found that out by experience!

More than 30 years ago, when Ken was praying down in the riverbed in Tulsa, Oklahoma, God began speaking to him about preaching to nations. God told him way back then that he would have a worldwide ministry.

It was clear God hadn't considered our bank account. We hardly had enough money to get across town—much less go to the nations! But God didn't expect us to fulfill that call. He intended to do it Himself through our faith in His Word. He intended to provide the power, the resources, the ability—everything! All He expected us to do was believe and obey.

That's all He expects you to do today.

Right now you may be thinking, *I really want to do that. I want to walk and talk by faith. The problem is, every time I look at the mess I'm in, I get discouraged!*

Then stop looking at that mess!

Instead, focus your attention on the promise of God. Keep His Word in front of your eyes and in your ears until you can see it coming to pass with the eyes of your spirit.

That's what the spirit of faith does. It looks not at the things which are seen, but at the things which are not seen.

Of course, I'm not saying you should ignore your problems or close your eyes to them as if they aren't real. They are real. But according to the Word they are *temporal.* That means "subject to change." And you can be assured that if you keep looking at what the Word says, they will change!

You can develop your faith. You can walk by faith. You can. You can. You can. Just keep your eyes on the Word.

## *Speak the Word*

*I do not look at the things which are seen, but at the things which are not seen. I look through the eyes of faith.*
*2 Corinthians 4:18*

FOR FURTHER STUDY:

Psalm 108:1-6

DAILY SCRIPTURE READING:

Lamentations 4-5; Psalm 91

*Kenneth*

# Let the Word Change Things

If you're in a fix of a situation today, I have good news. You don't have to do a thing about it—except abide in the Word. The Word can change everything.

You see, the Word of God is alive. It will go into the very marrow of your bones. It will go into your mind, your will and your emotions and change them. It will go into your spirit and get you born again.

When you spend time meditating on that Word—when you abide in it—it will begin to change your thinking. Then it will convert your way of living and turn you around. It will bring your body into health. It will make your mind sound. It will make you prosperous. It literally has the power of God within it!

Although we work and put forth effort to learn that Word, to spend time in it, speak it and obey it—it is actually the Word itself that brings about the changes in our lives. That's what the writer of Hebrews means when he said we "labour therefore to enter into that rest."

We rest on the Word, knowing it will accomplish what God has promised.

Some believers wear themselves out trying to make the Word of God come to pass. But that's not our job! Our job is not to make things happen. Our job is to let the Word abide in us. Our job is to abide in Jesus. Our job is to replace our thoughts with His thoughts—to speak and act in line with His Word.

But it is God Who performs it. He's the One Who will cause His promises to become a living, manifested reality in your life.

What's more, He can do it right in the midst of the worst trouble the world has ever seen. He can do it in the midst of the worst trouble you may find yourself. He can prosper you in the midst of famine. He can heal you in the midst of plagues. He can keep you safe when danger is on every hand. In fact, He can—and will—give you anything you ask, IF you're abiding in Him and His Word is abiding in you. In this position you are always asking according to His will. *"And this is the confidence that we have in him, that, if we ask any thing according to his will, he heareth us: And if we know that he hear us, whatsoever we ask, we know that we have the petitions that we desired of him"* (1 John 5:14-15).

So let not your heart be troubled! Just set your heart on Jesus. Just let the Word of God answer the situation...and you'll make it through in the glorious victory of God.

> "Let us labour therefore to enter into that rest, lest any man fall after the same example of unbelief. For the word of God is quick [alive!], and powerful, and sharper than any twoedged sword, piercing even to the dividing asunder of soul and spirit, and of the joints and marrow, and is a discerner of the thoughts and intents of the heart."
> HEBREWS 4:11-12

FOR FURTHER STUDY:

Psalm 33

DAILY SCRIPTURE READING:

Ezekiel 1-3;
Psalms 92-93

## *Speak the Word*

*The Word of God is alive and powerful, therefore I can enter into rest.*
*Hebrews 4:11-12*

> ❧
>
> "So is the kingdom of God, as if a man should cast seed into the ground...For the earth bringeth forth fruit of herself... But when the fruit is brought forth, immediately he putteth in the sickle, because the harvest is come."
> MARK 4:26-29

# A Harvest of Health

People want to be well. No one wants to be sick. But to be well, you have to make choices. How often have you seen someone with a hacking cough still smoking a cigarette? Or an overweight person eating ice cream?

Our fleshly nature likes to take the easy way. And it's much easier to give in to habits than to break them. It's easier to give in to your flesh and watch television every night like the rest of the world, than to spend your time putting God's healing Word into your heart.

I heard Charles Capps say that some people try to build the third story of a building on a vacant lot. That sounds funny, but spiritually speaking it's true. A lot of people want to enjoy the benefits of healing without building the foundation for it from the Word of God.

It can't be done. If you want a building, you have to start below ground level and lay a foundation. If you want a harvest, you will have to plant something first.

Everything in the natural world works that way. Ken calls it the law of genesis. This law of sowing and reaping works in the spirit realm too. It governs health, prosperity—in fact, everything in God's kingdom is governed by the law of sowing and reaping. Jesus taught about it in Mark 4:26-29.

According to the law of sowing and reaping, if you want health, you need to do more than just want it. You even need to do more than believe in healing. You need to plant seed—and the seed you plant is the Word of God concerning healing. So look up healing scriptures. Begin sowing them into your spirit man. Speak them out loud every day. Soon, they will grow up and yield a harvest of health.

## *Speak the Word*

*I serve the Lord my God. He blesses my bread and my water and takes sickness away from my midst.*
*Exodus 23:25*

FOR FURTHER STUDY:

James 1:22-25

❧

DAILY SCRIPTURE READING:

Ezekiel 4-5; Psalm 94

*Kenneth*

# The Fiery Glory

"Said I not
unto thee,
that, if thou
wouldest
believe, thou
shouldest see
the glory
of God?"

JOHN 11:40

These are the words Jesus spoke to Martha when Lazarus died. They are just as true today for you and me as they were for her. If we'll believe for the Glory, if we'll meditate on the Word of God until we develop our hope and begin to intently expect the Glory, then faith will become the substance of it—and we'll begin to see it.

Does that sound wild to you? Well, it's not!

If you'll go back and read the Bible, you'll see that's what Christianity is all about. God intended for the Body of Christ to walk through this earth with such manifestation of His presence in our lives, that it would draw people into the kingdom of God!

He intended us to live in such Glory that sickness and disease flee at our presence. He intended us to have a foretaste of the resurrected body right here on the earth. The Apostle Paul was reaching for that in his ministry: "*[For my determined purpose is] that I may know Him...And that I may in that same way come to know the power outflowing from His resurrection...That if possible I may attain to the... resurrection [that lifts me] out from among the dead [even while in the body]* (Philippians 3:10-11, AMP).

I've experienced little touches of that kind of Glory. And more is on the way! There are evidences of it all around the world. A good friend of mine pastors a church where the Glory of God manifested so powerfully that someone called the fire department. All they were doing was having a prayer meeting—but the Glory of God settled in the top of that church and made it look like the church was on fire!

When the firemen arrived, they crawled up in the attic and, sure enough, the fiery Glory of God was still blazing up there. Those firemen couldn't figure it out. They knew it wasn't fire, but they didn't know what it was.

They checked it out to see if it was the result of some peculiar ray of the sun shining in there. Finally they just left. It was beyond their realm of expertise!

More and more, that kind of Glory will manifest as we start building our hope, expecting to see the Glory, and then releasing it with our faith. Sickness and disease will flee. Lack will go. And the manifest presence of God will flow from us.

FOR FURTHER
STUDY:

John 11:18-44

DAILY SCRIPTURE
READING:

Ezekiel 6-7;
Psalm 95

## Speak the Word

*I believe, and I shall see the Glory of God.*
*John 11:40*

> "A faithful man shall abound with blessings."
> PROVERBS 28:20

*Gloria*

# Prosperity—From Genesis to Revelation

Prosperity. Everybody wants it. We've heard much teaching on it. We've been told to owe no man anything except to love him (Romans 13:8). We've been told that God wants us to prosper (3 John 2). We've been encouraged to live debt free. But what many believers haven't heard is how their everyday decisions to obey, or not to obey, seemingly unrelated Bible commands directly impact their financial prosperity.

You see, you can't separate God's financial principles from any of His other principles. All of them work together. So you have to live according to the entire Bible to have a good foundation for godly prosperity.

For example, the primary commandment Jesus gave us is to *"love one another"* (John 15:12). To the casual observer, that commandment may seem to have nothing to do with money, yet to have true prosperity, love must be the guiding force of your life.

Think of it this way. Every action you take, every godly decision you make, every time you go love's way, you're putting another block on your foundation of prosperity.

When you pray for your enemies instead of hating them, you become a candidate for increase. When you turn away from immorality, you're turning toward blessing. When you see things in your life that you know aren't right and you correct them according to the Word of God, you're preparing yourself to handle greater financial abundance.

In Proverbs, you'll find out, for example, that the quality of faithfulness and blessing of prosperity are tied together closely (28:20). Wherever you find one, you'll find the other.

According to *Webster's Dictionary*, a *faithful* man is one who "adheres to duty, of true fidelity, loyal, true to allegiance, and constant in the performance of duties or services."

Luke 16:10 (AMP) says, *"He who is faithful in a very little [thing], is faithful also in much; and he who is dishonest and unjust in a very little [thing], is dishonest and unjust also in much."* So if you want to be trusted with more and be promoted to a better job, you have to be faithful and honest in the job you have right now.

If you really want to prosper...apply all of the principles of God's Word—from Genesis to Revelation.

## Speak the Word

*I am faithful, and I shall abound with blessings.*
*Proverbs 28:20*

FOR FURTHER STUDY:

1 Peter 3:8-11

DAILY SCRIPTURE READING:

Ezekiel 8-9;
Psalm 96

*Kenneth*

# Dare to Believe It!

You are the victory of Almighty God! You are more than a conqueror in Christ Jesus! You are everything to the Father that Jesus is. John 17:23 says God loves you as much as He loves Jesus.

"But Brother Copeland," you may say, "how could He?"

I don't know! You'll have to ask Him. I just know that's what He said, and I believe it. By faith it's mine! His victory is my victory because He said it was. If I don't believe it, then He wasted His time. If I don't believe it, then Jesus went through hell to win a victory He already had. He didn't need that victory. I did. He won it to give it to me. The moment I believe it, that victory is mine. Until I do believe it, I don't have any victory at all.

Once you dare to accept that fact, your life will be forever changed. You'll no longer be satisfied to just sit around whining and wishing things were different. You'll want to step up to the position of authority that Jesus has given you, to take your rightful place beside Him, and learn to operate the way He does.

If we'll receive that message, if we'll dare to believe it, if we'll dare to put it into action, the world around us will never be the same again!

## *Speak the Word*

*Thanks be to God, Who gives me the victory through my Lord Jesus Christ.*
*1 Corinthians 15:57*

> "I in them, and thou in me, that they may be made perfect in one; and that the world may know that thou hast sent me, and hast loved them, as thou hast loved me."
> JOHN 17:23

FOR FURTHER STUDY:

Hebrews 2:5-18

DAILY SCRIPTURE READING:

Ezekiel 10-11; Psalm 97

> "The time of my departure is at hand. I have fought a good fight, I have finished my course, I have kept the faith: Henceforth there is laid up for me a crown of righteousness, which the Lord, the righteous judge, shall give me at that day: and not to me only, but unto all them also that love his appearing."
>
> 2 TIMOTHY 4:6-8

# Victorious Words From a Victorious Soldier

In every army there are good soldiers and sloppy soldiers. There are soldiers who win battles and conquer enemy territory, and there are soldiers who fail and lose ground. I want to be a good soldier for the Lord, don't you? I want to drive the devil back and advance the kingdom of God.

The Apostle Paul was that kind of soldier. He was a man of victory. He triumphed in every circumstance. The devil tried to stop him again and again with persecutions, beatings and trouble of every kind. But Paul kept right on marching in victory, preaching the gospel, healing the sick, working miracles and building the Church of the Lord Jesus Christ.

Eventually, Paul was put in prison and in chains. Imagine how terrible the conditions in prison must have been in those days! No doubt, the devil expected that to stop Paul—but it didn't. Instead of lying down and feeling sorry for himself, Paul used his time in prison to pray and write letters to minister to people. He didn't know he was writing letters that would become a major part of the New Testament. He was in prison, but he was also in the Spirit. Prison didn't even slow him down.

It was during this time that he wrote 2 Timothy 4:6-8, *"I have fought a good fight, I have finished my course...."*

Aren't those wonderful words? I want to be able to say words like that when I come to the end of my earthly life. I want to know that I have fought the good fight—and won!

Someone might say, "Well, Gloria, that was the Apostle Paul! He was special. We can't all be like him."

Why not? We have the same Savior Paul had. We're filled with the same Holy Spirit. We even have the words he wrote to Timothy, his precious son in the faith, just before he departed this life—instructions that Paul knew would enable Timothy to be a victorious soldier of the Cross just as he had been.

So, yes, you can be a victorious soldier. You can conquer enemy territory, push the devil back, and advance the kingdom of God.

## Speak the Word

*I fight a good fight. I finish my course.*
*Therefore, there is a crown of righteousness laid up for me.*
*2 Timothy 4:7-8*

FOR FURTHER STUDY:

2 Corinthians 11:22-33

DAILY SCRIPTURE READING:

Ezekiel 12-13; Psalm 98

*Kenneth*

# Be Courageous!

After reading the book of Joshua many times, I'm convinced that, as God began to give Joshua his instructions (Chapter 1), Joshua was deeply shaken by the magnitude of the task that lay before him.

Yet God didn't speak to Joshua about the impossibilities. He simply kept repeating to him, "Be strong and of good courage!"

God didn't tell Joshua to do a great many things. He didn't say, "Go figure out how to get across the river."

He didn't say, "Check your military might and see if you have firepower to conquer this land."

He said, *"Only...."* (Did you see that? *Only!)* *"Only be thou strong and very courageous!"* In other words, "Joshua, your part in this assignment is to be strong and of a good courage. I'll take care of everything else. I'll win the battles. I'll keep the people in line. I'll show you how to divide the land. You just be courageous!"

"Well, Brother Copeland, He's never said that to me!"

Yes, He has. In fact, He had it written for you in the New Testament.

*"He hath said, I will never leave thee, nor forsake thee. So that we may boldly say, The Lord is my helper, and I will not fear what man shall do unto me"* (Hebrews 13:5-6). Therefore, *"my brethren, be strong in the Lord, and in the power of his might"* (Ephesians 6:10).

For whatever impossible challenge that may be lying before you, God has already given you your instructions. "Be strong and very courageous." If you'll do that, He'll take care of the rest.

## *Speak the Word*

*I am strong and of good courage.*
*Joshua 1:6*

FOR FURTHER
STUDY:

Joshua 1

DAILY SCRIPTURE
READING:

Ezekiel 14-15;
Psalm 99

> "Fight the good fight of faith."
> 1 TIMOTHY 6:12

*Gloria*

# Fight On!

*"I'm tired of fighting! As soon a I whip one problem, there are a hundred more knocking on my door!"*

Some years ago a friend of mine said those very words to the Lord. At the time she was weary from the battles of life and ministry. She was fatigued from the constant pressure of pushing back the powers of darkness in her own life and in the lives of those around her. I'll never forget the Lord's response to her as she voiced her frustration.

*What is an army for, if not to fight?!* He said. *You'll either be fighting or retreating from now until Jesus returns!*

Those words come as a shock to many Christians. They don't want to be warriors. They want a comfortable, easy life. They want to lie back and go on a spiritual vacation. But that's not what we as believers are called to do.

We're called to *"fight the good fight of faith."* We are an army and we are at war, *"not against flesh and blood, but against principalities...powers...rulers of the darkness of this world...spiritual wickedness in high places"* (Ephesians 6:12).

God has given us spiritual weapons (2 Corinthians 10:4) and His own armor (Ephesians 6:10-18). He has equipped us to be spiritual soldiers!

Right now you may be thinking, *My, this soldier business sounds rough. I'm not sure if I can do it.*

Yes, you can! When you face the pressure of battle, when stress and trouble come, when you are about to faint, look up! Focus your attention on the truth that Jesus is risen from the dead and you are in Him! When He arose, you arose. When He defeated the devil, you defeated the devil. His victory is your victory!

Think about that when the devil is telling you that you're not going to make it. Then turn the tables on him and tell him a few things for a change! Say: *"Satan, I remind you that Jesus triumphed over you. I remind you that He spoiled you and made a show of you, that He took away all the authority you had. The Bible says you've been brought to naught! You're nothing, but I am Jesus' own representative here on the earth. I have His power and act in His Name. I'm seated with Him in heavenly places. All I have to do is stand in the victory Jesus has already won. The only way you can defeat me is by convincing me to quit, and that's the one thing I won't do! I won't accept defeat. I won't let you talk me out of my victory. I will stand and endure until I win—so you might as well surrender right now."*

Or if you are short on time, just say, "Get out in the Name of Jesus!"

That's the way a good soldier talks. And that's the way you'll talk too when you constantly keep in mind Christ Jesus has risen from the dead!

## *Speak the Word*

*I fight the good fight of faith.*
*1 Timothy 6:12*

FOR FURTHER STUDY:

2 Corinthians 10:1-6

DAILY SCRIPTURE READING:

Ezekiel 16-18; Psalms 100-101

*Kenneth*
# Paint Your Destiny!

How many times have you heard someone say, "I sure do wish God would do something for me"? The rest of the statement hangs unspoken in the air: "but He probably won't."

That's not faith. That's unbelief. But it works the same way faith works—only backward. Fear is actually faith going the wrong way. Fear is faith in the negative dimension. It's faith in failure, danger or harm. When someone is meditating on negative thoughts or "worrying," as we call it, he or she is developing inner pictures. Not pictures of hope, but pictures of despair.

Just as fear is the flip side of faith, despair is the flip side of hope. It's an inner image of failure, sickness, poverty or whatever else the devil wants to inject into you. Despair is actually hope in the negative, and fear, like faith, brings it to pass.

Do you see how powerful this process is that controls the course of your life? These inner images, whether they be of hope or despair, become the blueprint for your faith or fear, and ultimately control your destiny.

What you must do is dig into the Word and begin building your hope. Start developing God's pictures within you. As long as you have an image of your own defeat on the inside of you, you're destined to be defeated on the outside as well. But change that inner image with the Word of God and no demon in hell will be able to hold you down.

Jesus came to change the inner man. *"If ye continue in my word,"* He told us, *"then are ye my disciples indeed; And ye shall know the truth, and the truth shall make you free"* (John 8:31-32).

Get that truth working on the inside of you. Put it in there until hope begins to paint new pictures in your heart. Then hang on to those pictures relentlessly. Don't ever let them go. Eventually, inevitably, faith will make those pictures as real on the outside as they are on the inside.

"For as a man thinketh in his heart, so is he...." It's the pictures inside you that determine your destiny. Paint some new pictures. God's Word is full of them. The question is—are you?

## Speak the Word

*As I think in my heart, so am I.*
*Proverbs 23:7*

FOR FURTHER STUDY:

Titus 3:4-7

❧

DAILY SCRIPTURE READING:

Ezekiel 19-20;
Psalm 102

> *"Lay aside every weight, and the sin which doth so easily beset us."*
> HEBREWS 12:1

# Victory Is a Sure Thing

God has called us all to holiness. He has called us to a life that is consecrated to Him. He has called us to a life that is fully dedicated to walk in His ways.

I'll warn you though, some of the things the Lord may ask you to lay down on this road to holiness may not necessarily be sinful. They may simply be the weights referred to in Hebrews 12:1.

What are the weights? They are natural interests or pursuits that take up your time or energy and hold you down in this natural realm. They are earthly distractions that may not necessarily be bad in themselves, yet they keep you from going higher in spiritual pursuits.

Weights are also anything that takes God's place in your heart. God is supposed to have the first and supreme place in your affections. He is not meant to be one of many treasures in your life. He is meant to be THE treasure of your life, your first love.

Colossians 3:1-2 says, *"If ye then be risen with Christ, seek those things which are above, where Christ sitteth on the right hand of God. Set your affection on things above, not on things on the earth."*

Once again, notice that verse doesn't say the Lord will set your affection for you. It says you must set your affection. It's your responsibility.

If you don't devote much time to the Lord, you will find it very difficult to overcome your fleshly desires. You will find yourself laying them down one day...and picking them back up the next, because spiritually you're just not strong enough to do what you know you should do.

When you find yourself in that condition, immediately begin to spend more time reading and meditating on the Word of God. Start spending more time in prayer and fellowship with Him. Your union with the Lord is what makes your spirit strong, so focus on maintaining that union. You'll soon find you have more than enough strength to overcome that stubborn sin, or turn off that television program, or set aside that golf game to hear the Word, or cancel that trip to the mall when the Lord prompts you to spend time with Him.

Remember this: The Lord can change anything about you. He can take care of any situation in your life if you'll give Him enough of your time. As you spend time with Him in the Word and in prayer, you'll begin to get victory on the inside of you. And once you get victory on the inside, victory on the outside is a sure thing!

## *Speak the Word*

*I set my affection on the things of God.*
*Colossians 3:2*

FOR FURTHER STUDY:

1 John 3:1-3

DAILY SCRIPTURE READING:

Ezekiel 21-22;
Psalm 103

*Kenneth*

# The Greatest Satisfaction

Several years ago I was snow skiing down the back side of a mountain when suddenly, I hit a patch of ice and went down like a derailed freight train. My goggles flew one way, and my skis, poles and hat flew every other direction. By the time I landed, it looked like I was having a yard sale!

I landed on my right shoulder. Man, it hurt! After I finally stood up, gathered my stuff together and started to ski again, I hit another patch of ice. Wham! I fell, hitting that same shoulder.

By the time I got back home to Texas, I could hardly use my right arm properly. I couldn't even raise it high enough to comb my hair. But every time it would hurt, I'd say, "Praise God, forever, I am a well man. This injury is not the perfect will of God for me, so I don't have to have it. I am healed." Then I'd read the Word. I'd read it when I went to bed, and I'd read it when I got up.

During those first few days, I went to a service to preach and all the people had their hands raised, praising God. I tried to raise my hands too, but I just couldn't get that right arm to go up. I pushed it and shoved it, but it just wouldn't budge.

Later, I went to preach at a conference in New Orleans. That morning I read all my scriptures, praised God, confessed the Word and thanked God that I was healed. Then I tried to comb my hair...and I still couldn't raise my arm high enough to do it.

Of course, all kinds of thoughts ran through my mind. *You'll never get your healing! When is this ever going to happen? I wonder why this isn't working.* But I just took authority over those thoughts, thanked God for His faithfulness, and walked across the street to the conference where I was to preach.

When I walked in, the praise and worship had already started. So I stepped up on the platform, put my Bible down in the chair and just threw both arms up in the air and started praising God!

I never did feel a thing. No goose bumps. No tangible power. But I want you to know, manifested victory, when it comes by faith, brings a satisfaction nothing else can.

It's so satisfying because when you lay hold of victory by faith in God's Word, you're truly being like Jesus. You're not just getting His blessing, you're living the lifestyle He lived. You're living by faith, just like He did. You're being His disciple!

The next time you're faced with a challenge, be it physical or financial or relational, apply the Word, stand on the Word...and when the victory is manifested, you'll have a satisfaction you've never known! You'll have acted like Jesus!

FOR FURTHER STUDY:

Psalm 19:7-14

DAILY SCRIPTURE READING:

Ezekiel 23-24; Psalm 104

## *Speak the Word*

*The righteousness of God is revealed from faith to faith. I live by faith.*
*Romans 1:17*

*Gloria*

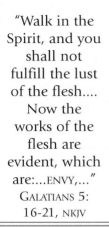

"Walk in the Spirit, and you shall not fulfill the lust of the flesh.... Now the works of the flesh are evident, which are:...ENVY,..."
GALATIANS 5: 16-21, NKJV

# Envy—The Devil's Poison

It's an experience we've all had at one time or another. It is so common, in fact, most people think it is no big deal. They see it as just a harmless, human emotion. But they are gravely mistaken.

As innocent as it may sometimes seem, envy is actually the devil's own poison, designed to turn love into hate and immobilize the force of faith in your life.

"Well, Gloria. That all sounds so awful. I don't really think I'm envious of anyone."

That may be true. But let me encourage you to search your heart carefully just to be sure, because many times, we aren't even conscious of envy. We may feel it stirring within us, but we fail to identify it because we assume such feelings are "natural."

Envy sneaks in without announcing itself. It slips in unnoticed.

Suppose you go to church, for instance, and you see Brother Smith with a new car. Suddenly a thought comes to your mind: *Why does he have a new car? He didn't even need it. I'm the one who needs a new car.* And you resent that he received a new car.

Or suppose you see Sister Jones in a beautiful, new dress. As you sit down next to her, you notice how dowdy your dress is compared to hers. Suddenly, you feel ugly and self-conscious, and resentment comes that you don't have as nice a dress as she does.

You may not think much more about it consciously. But later, you notice you're a little irritated or depressed. You can't quite put your finger on why you feel that way. After all, you were having a good day until a little while ago. What happened?

Envy crept in and poisoned you with a feeling of ill will and discontent because of another's success or advantages. Envy made a move on you.

But listen, if you're a born-again believer, envy is not part of your spiritual nature. It's something the devil tries to pressure you into receiving. He dangles it in front of you like bait on a hook, hoping you'll take a bite. But don't do it! Taking the bait will produce hate in your life. It will stop the force of faith in your life. It will stop the plans of God in your life. It stops your success cold. So get before God and rid yourself of all envy. Make a quality decision never to allow it in again. It's the devil's personal poison. Let him keep it to himself!

## *Speak the Word*

*I walk in the Spirit and do not fulfill the lust of the flesh.*
*I refuse to give place to envy in my life.*
*Galatians 5:16-21, NKJV*

FOR FURTHER STUDY:

James 3:13-18

DAILY SCRIPTURE READING:

Ezekiel 25-26;
Psalm 105

# Let Your Faith Temperature Rise!

There are so many things in our lives that can be solved by simply making a quality decision. They can't be solved by begging God, "Oh, God, take this habit away from me!"

If God was going to do it that way, He'd have done it already!

"But Brother Copeland, making a decision like that isn't easy!"

No, it isn't. But it is possible to do and I can tell you how to get started.

First, dig into the Word and into the promises of God. Spend some time finding out what belongs to you in Christ Jesus.

The phrases "in Christ," "in Him" or "in Whom" are used more than 100 times in scriptures of promise and statement throughout the New Testament. Search them out. Read every book from Acts through Revelation looking for them. As you find them, make a decision right then and say, "That's mine. I'm in Christ and He's in me and I lay claim to that now. That verse is talking about me."

Then begin to see yourself according to the Word of God in your imagination. See yourself operating in power, love, discipline and self-control. (See 2 Timothy 1:7, AMP). Begin to see yourself making these firm, concrete decisions. See yourself the way God sees you.

Instead of considering your body, begin to consider Jesus! Don't let your mind and your senses lock you into this natural realm. Consider Jesus! Fix your mind on Him. Start programming your spirit with the Word of God. Decide in advance that no matter what happens, you are going to choose Jesus and His Word instead of what your body and your circumstances say.

If you'll do that, when the unexpected hits, your spirit will take over and see you through. And the temperature of your faith will rise and rise!

>
> "I am crucified with Christ: nevertheless I live; yet not I, but Christ liveth in me: and the life which I now live in the flesh I live by the faith of the Son of God, who loved me, and gave himself for me."
> GALATIANS 2:20

## *Speak the Word*

*I am crucified with Christ, nevertheless I live; yet not I, but Christ lives in me. I live by the faith of the Son of God.*
*Galatians 2:20*

FOR FURTHER STUDY:

2 Corinthians 5:17-21

DAILY SCRIPTURE READING:

Ezekiel 27-28; Psalm 106

> "Say not ye,
> There are yet
> four months,
> and then
> cometh
> harvest?
> behold, I say
> unto you, Lift
> up your eyes,
> and look on
> the fields; for
> they are white
> already to
> harvest."
> JOHN 4:35

# They're Coming On In

I believe holiness is the final frontier before Jesus comes. I believe these are the last of the last days. And as we get lined up with His Word, as we separate ourselves unto God, I believe there is going to be such a harvest of souls, the likes of which the Church has never seen. And you and I are seeing the beginnings of it.

I'm telling you, it is going to shake the world. The demonstrations of the power of God that we will see will be awesome. The prophets have prophesied about it, they've seen visions of it, and I'm expecting it.

One person has prophesied that the power of God from the Old Covenant, plus the power of God from the New Covenant, plus the multiplying of the power of this age is what's coming to pass.

That's what we expect to see...the multiplying of the power of this age resulting in all people, both Christians and unbelievers, seeing the power of God manifested.

People are hungry for the manifestation of God. They prove it all the time. Every time there's some kind of phenomenon, some kind of sign in the world, like blood appearing or a statue that sheds tears, thousands of people will go to see it. People are hungry for spiritual power.

And before the end they are going to see plenty of it. Miracles this world has never seen will begin to happen. People from all over the world will flow into the kingdom of God. It's harvest time. There's a harvest to get in before Jesus comes. God is going to get the people in, and then the end will come.

So our part in the Church is to be prepared and ready. We're to put ourselves in such a place that we can be used of God to do whatever He wants in this hour. Doing that is what holiness is. It's separating yourself unto God for His use. So get ready. All those people you've been believing to be saved, your friends, your family, your spouse...they're coming on in!

## *Speak the Word*

*I lift up my eyes and look to the fields, for they are ripe unto harvest.*
John 4:35

FOR FURTHER
STUDY:

Romans 10:9-13;
2 Timothy 2:19-22

DAILY SCRIPTURE
READING:

Ezekiel 29-30;
Psalm 107

# What Kind of Faith Do You Have?

> "Blessed are they that have not seen, and yet have believed."
> JOHN 20:29

Signs and wonders. Miraculous manifestations of the Spirit of God. If you haven't witnessed them already in your own life and in the lives of believers around you, you soon will because they are happening everywhere...and they are on the increase.

I don't mind telling you, I love it! I love to watch God work. I love to see miracles and feel the move of the Holy Ghost. It's the most thrilling, wonderful kind of fun there is. It's so much fun, in fact, that if we're not alert—we can get so caught up in watching and feeling these great manifestations of God that we neglect the Word and allow our faith to slip.

"Whoa! Wait a minute now, Brother Copeland. How could my faith slip while I'm watching miracles and feeling spiritual goose bumps? Don't those things increase my faith?"

Not according to the Bible. Romans 10:17 says faith comes by hearing and hearing by the Word of God. It doesn't say anything about faith coming by what you see or feel.

Some people might argue with that. They might think that since they saw a miracle and believed it, faith had come to their heart. But what actually happens when you see something and then believe it is that faith comes to your head!

Head faith (or sense-knowledge faith) and heart faith (or the God kind of faith, Mark 11:22) operate in two entirely different realms. The God-kind of faith operates in the realm of the spirit. It takes hold of the Word of God in the unseen realm and brings that Word to pass in the natural world.

That is the kind of faith God used to bring this earth into existence. It's a powerful force. And when it flows from the hearts and mouths of believers, real spiritual faith changes natural things.

Sense-knowledge faith, on the other hand, has no real power. It doesn't change things. On the contrary, natural things change it! Everybody in the world has sense-knowledge faith. They believe certain things just because they can see them, or because they've experienced them. People believe, for example, that when they flip a light switch, the light will come on. They have faith in that process because they've seen it work time and again. But the light-switch kind of faith comes strictly from the mind. When you exercise it, your spirit is dormant. Believing only what you can see and feel does not activate your spirit.

FOR FURTHER STUDY:

John 4:43-54

So what kind of faith do you have? The God kind generates spiritual power and blessing. It's believing before you can see or feel a natural manifestation. It's the kind you want to have. It comes by hearing the Word of God and believing it. So get into the Word. And watch the right kind of faith come alive!

DAILY SCRIPTURE READING:

Ezekiel 31-33; Psalms 108-109

## *Speak the Word*

*I am blessed because I believe, whether I see or not.*
*John 20:29*

> "If ye be
> Christ's, then
> are ye
> Abraham's
> seed, and heirs
> according to
> the promise."
> GALATIANS 3:29

# Your Circumstances Can't Stop the Blessing

Once, when there was a famine in the land, Isaac considered moving to Egypt to escape it. But the Lord appeared to him and said, *"Do not go down to Egypt.... Dwell temporarily in this land, and I will be with you and will favor you with blessings...and I will perform the oath which I swore to Abraham your father"* (Genesis 26:2-3, AMP).

Keep in mind, famines back then were just as awful as they are today. I'm sure it was just like the pictures we see where the babies' bellies are swollen from starvation and their arms and legs are little more than skin and bone. Yet right in the midst of it all, *"Isaac sowed seed in that land, and received in the same year 100 times as much as he had planted, and the Lord favored him with blessings"* (verse 12).

I want you to know, that's what the blessing of Abraham will do. It will enable you to prosper, no matter what's happening around you. It will cause you to increase in the midst of recessions, depressions and every other kind of economic calamity the devil can dream up.

If you're the seed of Abraham—and you are if you are born again—you shouldn't even worry about such things. They don't have to affect you. You're not dependent on the economic cycles of this natural realm. You're not dependent on what the Federal Reserve does. You are dependent on your covenant with Almighty God—and that never changes! He never alters the Word that comes out of His mouth, and He has said you are BLESSED!

What's more, He's said you're a BLESSING! That means the company or corporation you work for will be blessed just because you're there.

"Well, I don't know about that," you may say. "I'm just a clerical worker, and the company I work for is full of heathens!"

So what! Genesis 41 tells us that Abraham's great-grandson, Joseph, started out as a slave in the ungodly nation of Egypt. But because he was the seed of Abraham—just like you are—he ended up saving that nation from being destroyed by famine. Not only that, he became the most powerful man in the nation next to the Pharaoh himself. The entire country was blessed because of Joseph and his covenant with God.

You were re-created to live above the circumstances of this world—not in subjection to them. Stand up. Release your faith. Put the Word first place in your life. Put your name in the promises of the Bible and speak them to your circumstances. The truth is, they can't stop the blessings of Almighty God!

FOR FURTHER
STUDY:

Genesis 41

DAILY SCRIPTURE
READING:

Ezekiel 34-35;
Psalm 110

## *Speak the Word*

*I am Christ's, therefore I am Abraham's seed and*
*an heir according to the promise.*
*Galatians 3:29*

*Kenneth*

# Get Your Glory Bag Packed!

You need to understand that when those verses talk about *"blood, and fire, and pillars of smoke,"* they are not talking about destruction. No, those come before the day of destruction. Those are the signs and wonders in the heavens above and in the earth beneath during this outpouring of the Spirit. Notice the next line: *"Whosoever shall call on the name of the Lord shall be delivered [saved]."* That's not destruction. That's revival!

I asked the Lord one time, "Lord, how will You do that? How will You make the sun not shine?"

He told me He will block out its light with the cloud of His Glory. That *shekinah* cloud of God has been manifested both in the Old and New Covenant. In the Old, Israel saw it as a pillar of smoke in the daytime and a pillar of fire at night. In the New Covenant, that same fire was manifested on the Day of Pentecost.

God said to me, *I'll make that cloud get so thick on whole cities, that people can't see the sunshine.* Then He added, *That's the reason you need to be ready.*

What He said to me, I'm saying to you. If you want to be in on this, you need to get ready. You need to quit criticizing your fellow believers and get the sin out of your life. You need to fast, pray and learn how to win souls. Go practice! Learn how because when God's power falls and His Glory cloud hits a whole city at one time, men and women will fall under the power of it, crying out to God.

Then when it hits, they'll be looking for it and the only place they'll see it is on God's people and His churches. Thousands of people will come running to those churches. God will give us whole cities at once. Not only that, this move of the Spirit will grow until we get whole nations flowing into the mountain of God.

Then the voice of the Lord will come more plainly and clearly to you than you've ever heard in your life. He'll begin to tell you what to do, what to say, what song to sing, how to pray, and we'll see multitudes healed and born again. We'll see homes put back together, and the Glory of the Lord will be throughout the land.

When that happens, you'd better have your Glory bag packed because we'll be raptured out of this place!

NOVEMBER 21

"Fear not, O land; be glad and rejoice: for the Lord will do great things.... I will show wonders in the heavens and in the earth, blood, and fire, and pillars of smoke. The sun shall be turned into darkness, and the moon into blood, before the great and the terrible day of the Lord come. And it shall come to pass, that whosoever shall call on the name of the Lord shall be delivered."
JOEL 2:21, 30-32

FOR FURTHER STUDY:

Acts 2:14-21

DAILY SCRIPTURE READING:

Ezekiel 36-37;
Psalm 111

## *Speak the Word*

*I call upon the Name of the Lord, and I am saved.*
*Joel 2:32*

> "But you shall (earnestly) remember the Lord your God; for it is He Who gives you power to get wealth."
> DEUTERONOMY 8:18, AMP

# Pass the Prosperity Test

The very idea of wealth scares some Christians. They think having a lot of money is ungodly—but that's not what the Bible says.

God doesn't object to our having money. On the contrary, He *"takes pleasure in the prosperity of His servant"* (Psalm 35:27, AMP). What God doesn't want us to do is covet money. He doesn't want money to have us! He doesn't want us to love money and make it our god.

So He gave us a safeguard. He gave us in His Word a foundational instruction about prosperity that enables us to be wealthy and godly at the same time... *"Seek for (aim at and strive after) first of all His [God's] kingdom, and His righteousness [His way of doing and being right], and then all these things taken together will be given you besides"* (Matthew 6:33, AMP).

That is the foundation of biblical prosperity. It's based on God's way of doing and being right. It comes to those who operate in this earth according to His system of life, instead of the world's system.

The world's system has money for its god. It loves and seeks after money. But the kingdom of heaven has the Father for its God. And in His economy, you can't prosper supernaturally unless you give Him and His ways first place in your life.

Granted, there are times when godly people begin to prosper and then get off track. Those people pass the poverty test, but fail the prosperity test. They start out seeking first God's kingdom. But when they begin to experience the financial blessings of that kingdom, they become overly preoccupied with the things that have been added to them. Their hearts begin to grow cold toward God because they don't continue to give Him first place in their lives.

God doesn't want that to happen to His people. That's why He told the Israelites not to forget Him when they entered the Promised Land and started living in goodly houses and enjoying material abundance... *"But you shall (earnestly) remember the Lord your God; for it is He Who gives you power to get wealth."*

So don't just release your faith to pass the poverty test. Pass the prosperity test as well!

## *Speak the Word*

*I earnestly remember the Lord my God, for it is He Who gives me power to get wealth.*
*Deuteronomy 8:18, AMP*

FOR FURTHER STUDY:

Deuteronomy 8:11-18

DAILY SCRIPTURE READING:

Ezekiel 38-39; Psalm 112

*Kenneth*

# Make That Decision

If God has called you to do something, something that you think in the natural is impossible, chances are the devil has been bombarding you with thoughts of doubt, fear and discouragement.

But don't let him lead you down that road. Don't let him keep you from meditating on God's ability and faithfulness to get the job done. Resist the temptation to meditate on your problems and inabilities...which is worrying.

Stop struggling. And start resting. Relax. God knows that what He has called you to do is impossible. He knows you are having a problem with that fact. And He doesn't mind waiting while you draw on His Word and develop the courage you need for the task.

You see, you don't have to panic. Just keep reminding yourself that as long as you have your Bible and your faith, you can do anything God tells you to do.

Put thoughts about your own weaknesses behind you and focus instead on the awesome ability of God. Start saying to yourself, *Hallelujah. God is with me! He will not, He will not, HE WILL NOT in any degree leave me helpless, nor forsake me, nor let me down!*

Then open your Bible and choose to believe what it says about you. Treat it as God's blood-sworn oath to you. Keep it in front of your eyes. Keep it in your ears. Keep it on your lips. Make a quality decision to stick with it until the might of God Himself rises up within you and overwhelms the fear.

Once you make that decision, there's no turning back. It's on into the promised land!

> "[I will] not in any degree leave you helpless, nor forsake nor let [you] down...!"
> HEBREWS 13:5, AMP

## *Speak the Word*

*The Lord does not in any degree leave me helpless, nor forsake me, nor let me down!*
*Hebrews 13:5, AMP*

FOR FURTHER STUDY:

Philippians 4:4-9

DAILY SCRIPTURE READING:

Ezekiel 40-41;
Psalm 113

> "Be ye holy;
> for I am holy."
> 1 PETER 1:16

# I'm Doing the Best I Can

When Max, our grandson, started kindergarten, he had quite an awakening. Max is the youngest in his family and is used to being pampered by his three big sisters. So he was very surprised to find out that in kindergarten, he wasn't the center of attention. He was especially distressed to discover he was actually expected to sit still!

For the first few weeks, Max just didn't seem to be able to do it. He got in trouble again and again. One day, his mother was talking to him about it, and he threw his hands up in desperation, "I'm doing the best I can."

"Well, Max, that's not good enough," his mother replied. "You are going to have to do better."

In all exasperation with his mother, Max said, "I told you, I'm doing the best I can!"

Within a few weeks, Max grew tired of having to stay on the sidewalk during recess (that's the consequence for misbehaving in his class), and he discovered he could indeed do better.

I think about Max many times when God is dealing with me about some area of dedication and consecration. Max has ruined the old excuse, "Lord, I'm doing the best I can!" Now I say to myself, *Gloria, you're just doing the best you want to do!*

That's the way it's been with the Church in general. When it comes to being holy, and laying aside sin, we haven't done all we know to do. We've just done what we wanted to do. We may have put away what we considered to be major sins and even many minor sins, but there are worldly hindrances we've held on to because our flesh enjoys them.

When God tells us to make a change, we must obey. We have entered the last of the last days...and we have to become obedient. We have to become holy.

We can't feed on the garbage of the world and at the same time be separated to God, fit for any good work (2 Timothy 2:21).

I realize this makes your flesh uncomfortable...but we're told to crucify our flesh (Romans 8:13). We're to cleanse ourselves and consecrate ourselves to God (2 Corinthians 6:14-7:1). God has cleansed us on the inside, now it's our responsibility to let our born-again spirit have dominion.

When you do that, then you can say truthfully, "I'm doing the best I can!" And God will be pleased.

### Speak the Word

*I am holy for God is holy.*
*1 Peter 1:16*

FOR FURTHER
STUDY:

1 Corinthians
6:9-20

DAILY SCRIPTURE
READING:

Ezekiel 42-43;
Psalm 114

*Kenneth*

# Get Beyond the Requirements!

More than any other man, Paul knew what it was to be free. He was born a free Roman citizen. Then he was born again and received the revelation from God that he had been made free from the authority of darkness, and translated into the kingdom of God's dear Son. Yet he bowed his knee to Jesus and said, "I give away my freedom. I give away my will. I give it all away to serve You. I'll live for You and I'll die for You."

Jesus Himself set the pattern for such servanthood during His earthly ministry, and Philippians 2:5-7 exhorts us to follow His example.

As a servant, or handmaiden, your attitude will be like Jesus' attitude: *"Not my will, but thine, be done"* (Luke 22:42). You'll say, "I don't care what it takes, I will obey God. If He wants me to lock myself up in my closet and pray for eight hours every day, that's what I'll do, because I'm His bondslave!"

Some people like to argue that God would never require such sacrifices from us.

That's just proof that those people aren't servants or handmaidens, because servants and handmaidens aren't interested in doing only what God requires. True servants and handmaidens want to be totally committed to God and His Word. They want everything they do to be governed by Him. As a result, God rewards them. He entrusts to them the gifts of the Spirit. He anoints them, and He uses them to do great exploits in His Name.

If you want God to entrust His gifts to you, if you want to do great exploits in His Name, then you'll first need to become a servant, a bondslave...one who goes beyond the requirements.

> "Let this mind be in you, which was also in Christ Jesus: Who, being in the form of God, thought it not robbery to be equal with God: But made himself of no reputation, and took upon him the form of a servant."
> PHILIPPIANS 2:5-7

## Speak the Word

*I choose to be a servant, a bondslave of God.*
*I will do whatever it takes to please God in every area of my life.*
*Philippians 2:5-7*

FOR FURTHER STUDY:

Philippians 2:5-11

DAILY SCRIPTURE READING:

Ezekiel 44-45;
Psalm 115

> "For every creature of God is good, and nothing to be refused, if it be received with thanksgiving: For it is sanctified by the word of God and prayer."
>
> 1 TIMOTHY 4:4-5

# Stop! Before You Take Another Bite

Have you ever wondered why on earth we pray over our food? I pray over mine because I have to eat it!

I don't pray over my meals because my denomination or religion says that's what I should do. I don't have a denomination. If you do it just because religion or tradition says to, you'll wind up saying grace and praying for Jesus' sake.

Jesus said whatever you ask the Father in My Name, He will give it to you. He didn't say anything about praying for His sake. I don't pray for Jesus' sake. I pray for my belly's sake!

The Word of God says our food is sanctified by the Word, by thanksgiving and by prayer.

I pray over my food because I have to eat it. It's right to do, and I've eaten all over the world in all kinds of places. I've eaten stuff that I didn't have any idea what it was. And I didn't want any more of it, either!

I was in one place one time when they came out and honored me at 4:30 in the morning. So they came and took me to the breakfast they had prepared. I sat down in front of something green on my plate. I had no earthly idea what it was. I looked at it and thought, *I'm not going to eat this. I'm going to fast right now.*

The Spirit of God said, *What does My Word say?*

"I knew You would ask me that. The Word of God says when you're out in the field, eat whatever is set before you. It also says no deadly thing will hurt you. And it says the food is sanctified. OK, I know, I know. I got the message. I got the message."

Then He added, *That means do it with a smile on your faithful face.*

So I did, and then I went on a fast the next day.

When you pray over your food, do it in faith and simply follow what the Apostle Paul said in 1 Timothy and receive it with thanksgiving. Jesus broke Satan's power to contaminate your food. Praying in faith over your food allows it to minister nourishment and strength to your body, rather than pain and sickness. When we receive it with thanksgiving in Jesus' Name, it is sanctified, set apart for our use (John 16:23).

So stop right now before you take another bite of anything. Learn to pray according to the Word: *"Father, thank You for this food. I receive it blessed and set apart for my use according to Your Word. In Jesus' Name. Amen."*

## *Speak the Word*

*I receive my food with thanksgiving. It is sanctified by the Word of God and prayer.*
*1 Timothy 4:4-5*

FOR FURTHER STUDY:

Exodus 23:25

DAILY SCRIPTURE READING:

Ezekiel 46-48;
Psalms 116-117

*Kenneth*

# Go to War With Praise

Thanksgiving and praise are integral parts of prayer. When you believe you receive, then you begin to praise God for the answer. You thank God that it is done for you.

Thanksgiving and praise involve more than just speaking lovely words to God. There is power in the praise of God. Praise was ordained by God for a definite reason. It serves a purpose.

Psalms 8 and 9 point out some things about praise that every believer should know. Psalm 8:1-2 says, *"O Lord our Lord, how excellent is thy name in all the earth! who hast set thy glory above the heavens. Out of the mouth of babes and sucklings hast thou ordained strength because of thine enemies, that thou mightest still the enemy and the avenger."*

Jesus quoted this Psalm in Matthew 21:16, *"Out of the mouth of babes and sucklings thou hast perfected praise."* He equates praise with strength.

From these scriptures, we see that God brought praise into existence. He ordained it. Why? *"Because of thine enemies, that thou mightest still the enemy and the avenger."* Praise stops Satan right in his tracks. It is a weapon we are to use in calling a halt to Satan's maneuvers.

Psalm 9 says, *"I will praise thee, O Lord, with my whole heart; I will show forth all thy marvellous works. I will be glad and rejoice in thee: I will sing praise to thy name, O thou most High. When mine enemies are turned back, they shall fall and perish at thy presence. For thou hast maintained my right and my cause; thou satest in the throne judging right"* (verses 1-4).

*When* your enemies are turned back—not if! There is no question about it. Remember: We wrestle not against flesh and blood, but against Satan's forces (Ephesians 6).

Whatever adversity is challenging you today, begin to praise God. Exercise this vital weapon in your warfare against Satan and his forces. Your enemies will have to turn back. They will fall and perish at your presence. And the peace and victory that Jesus bought for you will be yours.

> "I will praise thee, O Lord, with my whole heart; I will show forth all thy marvellous works. I will be glad and rejoice in thee: I will sing praise to thy name, O thou most High. When mine enemies are turned back, they shall fall and perish at thy presence. For thou hast maintained my right and my cause; thou satest in the throne judging right."
>
> PSALM 9:1-4

FOR FURTHER STUDY:

2 Chronicles 20:20-30

DAILY SCRIPTURE READING:

Daniel 1-2; Psalm 118

## Speak the Word

*I praise the Lord with my whole heart.*
*I show forth all His marvelous works.*
*Psalm 9:1*

> "Let patience
> have her
> perfect work."
> JAMES 1:4

# The Pressure Is On

You have prayed the prayer of faith. You believe you have received the answer. You are confessing the Word. You are standing on God's promise. You are expecting a miracle.

But instead of getting better, you grow worse.

Soon all you can think about is how tired you are, how fed up you are with waiting for your answer to come. You've had it with this situation and you're about to say those two words that cost more believers their victory than anything else in the world: *I quit!*

Sound familiar? Sure it does. Everyone who has ever walked by faith has gone through times like that. Tough times. Maybe those times have tripped you up in the past. Maybe the devil has used them to pressure you into letting go of your faith. But I want you to know something. It doesn't have to be that way.

There is a force so powerful, it can carry you through those hard times in triumph. It is a force so dynamic, the devil cannot stop it. It is a force that comes from the heart and character of God Himself, and it will take you from here to victory...every time. It's the force of patience.

Patience is the force that keeps you from fainting under pressure. It is the quality that does not surrender to circumstances or succumb under trial.

"That sounds great, Gloria, but I don't have that kind of patience!"

If you've made Jesus the Lord of your life, you do! It's a fruit of the spirit and God equipped you with it the moment you were born again. He placed it into your re-created human spirit right along with the other fruit of the spirit (read Galatians 5:22-23).

God didn't give you just any old type of patience, either. He imparted to you His very own patience, and *The Amplified Bible* says He is *extraordinarily* patient (2 Peter 3:9). God has what it takes to get through hard times. He has the power to persevere until circumstances line up with His Word. Because you are born of His Spirit, you have that power too!

But just as water won't flow from a faucet unless you open the valve and let it through, the reservoir of patience God has put within you won't flow unless you release it by an act of your will.

I know that the pressure is on, and it can be intense. But patience will see you through. Open that valve, and let patience go to work!

## *Speak the Word*

*I develop the fruit of patience. I let her have her perfect work.*
*James 1:4*

FOR FURTHER
STUDY:

Luke 8:5-15

DAILY SCRIPTURE
READING:

Daniel 3-4;
Psalm 119:1-24

*Kenneth*

# From Galatians to the Garage

There was a time in my life when I had none of the blessings listed in Deuteronomy 28. Religion might have tried to explain the absence of those blessings in my life by telling me God made those promises to the Israelite nation, and not to me. But I had already found Galatians 3 that said everything God promised Abraham belongs to the Gentiles now through Christ Jesus. For *"if ye be Christ's, then are ye Abraham's seed, and heirs according to the promise"* (verse 29).

No, there was no doubt in my mind that these blessings were legally mine. The only question I had was, "How can I get my hands on them?"

As I dug into the Word, I found the answer. To enjoy the blessings of Abraham, I was going to have to walk in the same kind of faith he did. Now as in Abraham's day, faith opens the door to God's promises. To me, that was good news.

Not everyone sees it that way, however. Some people want the blessings without having to walk by faith. But like it or not, that's just not the way things work.

"Well," you say, "I wish they did!"

No, you really don't. God didn't set up the system of faith and prayer in order to make things difficult for you. He did it because Satan and his crew are always trying to steal our blessings. God's system is designed to keep them from pilfering our inheritance.

> "And the Lord shall make thee plenteous in goods, in the fruit of thy body, and in the fruit of thy cattle, and in the fruit of thy ground, in the land which the Lord sware unto thy fathers to give thee.... Thou shalt lend unto many nations, and thou shalt not borrow."
> DEUTERONOMY 28:11-12

God's promises belong to you. They're locked up in the spiritual treasure house of Almighty God. To access them, you'll have to take the time to learn the procedures. You'll have to study God's Word and discover His ways.

My willingness and even eagerness to do that was about all I had going for me back there in those early days, but it was enough. I was so desperate to learn faith that I locked myself in my garage with tapes of Kenneth Hagin's messages about our inheritance in Christ Jesus. I stayed out there with those tapes hour after hour. I couldn't get enough of the Word of God.

I'm the same way today. I can't get enough of it. I don't care what else is going on in the world, I'm going to stick with the Word. It brought me out of debt. It healed my children. It has taken me through everything that has ever come my way...and it will do the same for you.

FOR FURTHER STUDY:

Isaiah 48:15-19

DAILY SCRIPTURE READING:

Daniel 5-6;
Psalm 119:25-49

## *Speak the Word*

*The Lord makes me plenteous in goods, in the fruit of my body, and in the fruit of my cattle, and in the fruit of my ground. I lend unto many nations, but I do not borrow.*
*Deuteronomy 28:11-12*

> "I will rebuke the devourer for your sakes."
> MALACHI 3:11

# Don't Forget Faith

Do you realize what a wonderful privilege it is to have a financial covenant with Almighty God by tithing? Do you understand what it means to be connected to His heavenly economy?

It means we don't have to worry about depression or recession—there is no recession or depression in heaven. It means we can sleep peacefully at night when the rest of the world is tormented by fear of financial failure. It means when the devil comes to steal our increase, we can stand firmly on that covenant and say, "Get out of here, Satan! You're rebuked! We're tithers and the Word of God says you cannot devour our money. You can't devour our health. We've given God the first fruits of all our increase so we are blessed. And what God has blessed, you can't curse!"

Oddly enough, there are some Christians who shrink back at such bold words. "Well, I just don't know if I could say that," they protest. "I'm a tither, but I'm still not as prosperous as the sinner down the street. So I'm not sure tithing does that much good."

The people in Malachi's day said exactly the same thing. They said, *"It is useless to serve God; and what profit is it if we keep His ordinances?... And now we consider the proud and arrogant happy and favored; evildoers are exalted and prosper..."* (Malachi 3:14-15, AMP).

God didn't like those words. He said they were hard and stout against Him. Why? Because they were words of unbelief instead of words of faith.

You see, God not only wants us to tithe in honor and love, He also wants us to tithe in faith! It takes faith to please Him (Hebrews 11:6).

If you don't have faith that God will prosper you, then get your Bible and study the promises He has made to you as a tither. Meditate on the Word, so you can tithe believing that God will keep His end of the covenant and bless you abundantly.

God loves it when you tithe with that kind of confidence. He enjoys it when you give with an attitude of reverence and gratitude, trusting Him to take care of you. In fact, Malachi 3:16-17 says He considers you a special treasure! *"They shall be Mine, says the Lord of hosts, in that day when I publicly recognize and openly declare them to be My jewels—My special possession, My peculiar treasure. And I will spare them, as a man spares his own son who serves him"* (verse 17, AMP).

Don't you want to be counted as one of God's special treasures? I certainly do! First of all, because I love God and I want to be pleasing to Him. Second, because I know how I treat special treasures. I take good care of them, and if I'm God's special treasure, that's exactly how He'll treat me!

So, the next time you drop your tithe in the bucket, release your faith. Stand on God's promises for the tither...and receive the blessings that belong to God's special treasures—His tithers.

## *Speak the Word*

*I am a tither. Therefore the Lord rebukes the devourer for my sake.*
*Malachi 3:10-11*

FOR FURTHER STUDY:

Hebrews 7:1-9

DAILY SCRIPTURE READING:

Daniel 7-8;
Psalm 119:50-72

*Gloria*

# Don't Buy the Lie!

DECEMBER 1

❧

"Behold, I give
unto you
power to tread
on serpents
and scorpions,
and over all the
power of the
enemy: and
nothing shall
by any means
hurt you."
LUKE 10:19

Satan can't force you to do anything. He doesn't have the power. All he can do is make a presentation and try to sell you the lies he's peddling. He can't make you buy them. He can only present them. You have a choice whether to take him up on his sorry deal or rebuke him and command him to leave you.

So when he makes you a presentation, learn not to toy with it. Don't take the bait. Instead, learn to immediately turn away from his doubts and start thinking and speaking the Word of God instead. Ask yourself, *What does the Word say that guarantees me the very thing the devil just tried to make me doubt?*

Get in the Word of God and find out the real truth. That's where your authority is—in the truth. Satan will lie to you, cheat you, trick you, deceive you and bait you into bondage, if you'll let him. But God will always tell you the truth. And that truth will make you free.

So don't buy Satan's lies. Once you know the truth of your authority in Christ Jesus, you won't spend your days crying about how bad things are. You'll spend your days telling those mountains to be cast into the sea.

Instead of acting like a whiner, you'll be more than a conqueror in Christ. You'll kick the devil out of your affairs with the words of your mouth. And as you stand in triumph with your needs met, your body healed and your heart rejoicing, you can laugh right in the face of that snake as he slinks away complaining about his defeat.

## Speak the Word

*Jesus has given me power to tread on serpents and scorpions,
and over all the power of the enemy. And nothing by any means hurts me.*
Luke 10:19

FOR FURTHER
STUDY:

Luke 4:1-13

❧

DAILY SCRIPTURE
READING:

Daniel 9-10;
Psalm 119:73-96

"The night is far gone [and] the day is almost here. Let us then drop (fling away) the works and deeds of darkness and put on the [full] armor of light. Let us live and conduct ourselves honorably and becomingly as in the [open light of] day; not in reveling (carousing) and drunkenness, not in immorality and debauchery... not in quarreling and jealousy. But clothe yourself with the Lord Jesus Christ, the Messiah, and make no provision for [indulging] the flesh."

ROMANS 13:
12-14, AMP

# Live in the Light

In this day and hour we need God's blessing more than ever. As believers, we need to be walking in our full inheritance, because this age is about to be brought to a close. It's time for us to wake up. It's time we quit allowing the devil to darken our homes, our businesses, our churches and our individual lives with strife and envy. It's time we started living in the light!

You may be thinking, *That's easier said than done!*

I know. But you can do it.

Learn to watch over yourself. Pay attention to your state of mind. When you find yourself depressed or downcast, don't just ignore those feelings. Think back. Ask yourself, *What started this downturn?*

You may realize that a particular situation sparked feelings of aggravation, jealousy or strife within you. If so, look at that situation through the eyes of God and then talk to it (see Mark 11:23).

Say, "That situation has no power over me. I refuse to allow it to bring envy and strife into my life. I yield to the forces of love and joy within me."

Then just start praising God. Sing a song. Put on a tape that will lift you up, and force yourself to sing along. Before long, the love of God will be bubbling up out of your heart again and you'll be singing from a pure heart.

The coming of Jesus is near at hand. We want Him to find us standing tall in the spirit—full of love, faith and power—walking in the victory Jesus bought for us.

We want Him to find us living in the light!

## *Speak the Word*

*I put on the full armor of light.*
*I live and conduct myself honorably and*
*becomingly as in the open light of day.*
*Romans 13:12-13, AMP*

FOR FURTHER
STUDY:

Proverbs 10:12,
14:30, 20:3

DAILY SCRIPTURE
READING:

Daniel 11-12;
Psalm 119:97-120

*Kenneth*

# You Can Flood the Earth

Think about that for a minute. What do you have if something stretches from the west to the rising of the sun? You have something that has no boundary. You have something that has moved out of bounds.

What happens when water gets out of bounds? It becomes a flood! You no longer just have a lazy, old river. You have an unstoppable force that is roaring throughout the countryside with such power that nothing can stand in its way!

Now, with that in mind, I want you to move the comma in the next portion of that 19th verse. It was put in at the privilege of the translators to make that verse read, *"When the enemy shall come in like a flood, the spirit of the Lord will lift up a standard against him."*

But that could not possibly be correct. How could the devil be a flood? He is containable. Not only is he containable—he has been contained!

Satan wasn't a flood when he came against Jesus. He wasn't even a drop in the bucket. Jesus is the One Who came in like a flood. Jesus was the One Who was uncontainable. No matter what Satan tried to do, he couldn't contain Him. Everything Jesus did and everything He said shoved Satan out of the way and left him completely helpless.

So put that comma where it should be and read what that verse really says: *"So shall they fear the name of the Lord from the west, and His glory from the rising of the sun. When the enemy shall come in, like a flood the spirit of the Lord shall lift up a standard against him."*

Now, that's something to shout about! Jesus flooded the devil! And what's even better news is that the same Holy Ghost flood that flowed through Jesus is now flowing through you and me! You can flood the devil. The rivers of living water are inside of you! You can lay hands on the sick, cast out demons, intercede on people's behalf and watch them be set free. You can flood the earth with God's Glory as you purify your life and yield to the Spirit of God. You can do it!

So get started. Flood the earth today with His Glory, His mercy, His love for everyone around you.

> "So [as the result of the Messiah's intervention] they shall [reverently] fear the name of the Lord from the west, and His glory from the rising of the sun. When the enemy shall come in like a flood, the Spirit of the Lord will lift up a standard against him and put him to flight—for He will come like a rushing stream which the breath of the Lord drives."
>
> ISAIAH 59:19, AMP

FOR FURTHER STUDY:

Isaiah 59:16-21

DAILY SCRIPTURE READING:

Hosea 1-3;
Psalm 119:
121-144

## *Speak the Word*

*When the enemy comes in, like a flood the Spirit of the Lord will lift up a standard against him!*
*Isaiah 59:19*

DECEMBER 4

> "I come to do
> thy will, O
> God."
> HEBREWS 10:9

# For the Sake of the Glory

God wants to pour out His Glory in us and upon us. He wants us to lay hands on the sick and see them recover. He wants us to cast out demons and raise the dead. He wants us to have so much of His power flowing through our mortal flesh, that He can do signs and wonders through us. That is our destiny as sons and daughters of God.

But He cannot fully do what He desires until we are living sanctified, holy lives before Him, until He has our whole heart. He cannot do it until we surrender everything in our lives to Him and yield ourselves in total obedience to the promptings of His Spirit. He cannot pour upon us the full measure of His Glory until we so submit ourselves to Him that we can say as Jesus did, *"I come to do thy will, O God."*

I'm telling you, God is going to have a people who say that to Him before Jesus returns. He is going to have people who so hunger after Him and His Glory, that they are willing to set aside anything in their lives that might hinder it. He is going to have people who have heard and heeded the words Jesus spoke to His first disciples: *"Whosoever will come after me, let him deny himself, and take up his cross, and follow me. For whosoever will save his life shall lose it; but whosoever shall lose his life for my sake and the gospel's, the same shall save it"* (Mark 8:34-35).

I have determined in my heart once and for all that I am going to be one of those people. I have determined that I will walk this road of holiness day by day so that the Glory can rest increasingly upon me. I have made up my mind that when I stand before the Lord Jesus, I will hear Him say, *"Well done, thou good and faithful servant."*

It seems I see that day continually with the eyes of my heart. I know it's coming, and because of that, I cannot give up. I cannot quit. I must keep on becoming progressively more and more separated unto the Lord.

I urge you to make that same commitment today. Don't put it off another moment, for the time is very short. Jesus is surely coming soon. So bow your heart before the Lord and say:

*"Lord Jesus, I yield everything I have and everything I am to You today. I determine in my heart to set my affection on things above, and by the energizing power of Your Spirit to keep my flesh crucified, laying aside every sin and weight that would hinder me. I set myself to do Your will, O God. I'm asking You, Lord, to enlighten my heart, to speak to me and tell me what changes I need to make in my life. I set myself now to hear and obey Your voice. In Jesus' Name, Amen."*

## Speak the Word

*I deny myself and take up my cross and follow Jesus. I lose my life for Jesus' sake and for the sake of the gospel, and it shall be saved.*
*Mark 8:34-35*

FOR FURTHER STUDY:

Matthew 25:14-30

DAILY SCRIPTURE READING:

Hosea 4-5;
Psalm 119:
145-176

*Kenneth*

# Hook Up to the Power

DECEMBER 5

❧

"Be it unto me according to thy word."
LUKE 1:38

If you spend much time with the Lord, what I'm about to say is no surprise to you. You've already sensed it in your spirit. We are at the end time.

There is a greater urgency in the spirit now than ever before. It's much like a woman who is about to give birth.

That's what's happening in the realm of the spirit right now. A new millennium is about to be born. Everyone is having to move fast. All of us have a role to play—and this is no false alarm.

Every one of us needs to get in position and do what God has called us to do. Yet everyone seems to have some kind of excuse that would keep them from doing what God called them to, but it's not time for excuses! It's time for us to say what Mary said when the angel came in and told her she would have a baby supernaturally by the power of God. She said, *"Be it unto me according to thy word."*

Glory to God, what faith! Mary didn't know how the process would work. It was beyond anything she had ever heard. But she just said, "Yes, Lord. Let's get on with the program!"

Do you know what happened when Mary released that faith in response to the Word of God? It hooked her up with the realm of the supernatural. It connected her to the Anointing of Almighty God where *"nothing shall be impossible"* (Luke 1:37).

That is an unchangeable truth. A person without faith in action is bound to the realm of the natural, material and intellectual world of what's possible. But a person whose faith is in action hooks into Holy Ghost power—or what I like to call "the muscle" of God—and impossible things happen in his life.

That's how Jesus did all those impossible things when He was on earth. He fulfilled His calling the same way you and I have to do it—by using His faith to hook into supernatural power.

Remember this: It doesn't matter how impossible something may be, when you're hooked by faith to the supernatural, you're hooked up to God and all things are possible to Him!

*"Jesus said..., If thou canst believe, all things are possible to him that believeth"* (Mark 9:23).

## Speak the Word
*I am a believer and all things are possible to me!*
*Mark 9:23*

FOR FURTHER STUDY:

Luke 1:26-38

❧

DAILY SCRIPTURE READING:

Hosea 6-7;
Psalm 120

> "If ye abide in me, and my words abide in you, ye shall ask what ye will, and it shall be done unto you."
>
> JOHN 15:7

# Rise Up to His Way of Thinking

God's Words are living forces. Powerful forces that, if you allow them to take up residence in you, will produce holiness in your life.

To be holy is to be separated to God's use. Therefore, if you allow your choices to be bathed in the Anointing of God's Word, those choices will separate you from the destructive bent of this natural world and take you into the blessings of the SUPERnatural realm.

Just think how far-reaching the consequences of such a change would be. Your choices can affect an entire generation. You can make certain choices that can either damage or enrich lives all around you. What may not seem like a very important decision to you, may ultimately make vital differences in your own future and that of your family.

But God sees the whole picture. He knows what's around the corner that you can't see. So when you are walking in His choices, your life starts to fit. Things start working. All the pieces of the puzzle start coming together.

You can save yourself so much heartache and headache it isn't even funny, just by spending some quality time in God's presence and in His Word. If you'll let Him, He will help you with every choice you make.

To have abundant life on this death-bound planet, you'll have to live a SUPERnatural lifestyle by making SUPERnatural choices every day of your life!

So start now getting that Word into your heart. Start now letting the force of it and the anointing upon it direct your choices—big and small. Let God begin to lift you up to His way of thinking.

## Speak the Word

*I abide in Jesus, and His words abide in me. I ask what I will, and it is done for me.*
*John 15:7*

FOR FURTHER STUDY:

Deuteronomy 30:11-20

DAILY SCRIPTURE READING:

Hosea 8-9; Psalm 121

*Kenneth*

# A Winning Spirit

The spirit of faith speaks! It calls things that be not as though they were. It makes faith confessions—not because it's "supposed to" or out of desperation, but because it's so full of eager anticipation and confident expectation, it can't keep its mouth shut!

The spirit of faith says, "I don't care what God has to do, He'll turn the world upside down if He has to, but He will change this situation for me."

Every time I talk about the spirit of faith, I think about my high school football team. For years the school had losing teams. But something happened to the bunch on my team. A spirit of winning got into them.

When we were sophomores, we were on the B-squad. We were the nothings. But we somehow got the idea that we could win. Every year the B-squad would have to scrimmage the varsity team, and usually the varsity just beat the daylights out of the sophomores.

But the year our B-squad played them, that changed. We didn't just beat them, we had them down by several touchdowns, just daring them to get the ball, when the coach called off the game. He was so mad at the varsity team, he didn't even let us finish.

What happened to that little B-squad? We reached the point where we expected to win. We had an inner image of ourselves as winners, and it eventually took the best team in the state to beat us.

If a varsity giant is staring you in the face today, get that winning spirit in you. Get an inner image of yourself as the real winner. Stir up the spirit of faith. Confess over that situation, "I don't care what God has to do, He'll turn the world upside down if He has to, but He will change this situation for me. I am more than a conqueror in Christ Jesus (the Anointed One and His Anointing). I am an overcomer by the blood of the Lamb and the word of my testimony." And then celebrate the victory because you're a winner!

> "We having the same spirit of faith, according as it is written, I believed, and therefore have I spoken; we also believe, and therefore speak."
> 2 CORINTHIANS 4:13

## Speak the Word

*I have the spirit of faith. I believe, therefore I speak.*
*2 Corinthians 4:13*

FOR FURTHER STUDY:

Romans 4:16-21

DAILY SCRIPTURE READING:

Hosea 10-11; Psalm 122

> "[God] is able to do exceeding abundantly above all that we ask or think, according to the power that worketh in us."
>
> EPHESIANS 3:20

*Gloria*

# What Time Is It?

If you're a born-again child of God and you've been struggling financially, scraping along with just barely enough—it's time for that to change. It's time for you to wake up to the riches that belong to you in Jesus, kick the limits off your faith and receive your financial inheritance.

Even if you haven't been struggling, even if your bills are paid and your major needs are met, you need to step up to greater abundance. We all need to do that, because God has more in store for every one of us than we possess right now. He is able to do exceeding, abundantly above all that we ask or think, according to the power that worketh in us.

What's more, we are now closer than ever to the end of the age. Jesus is coming soon. God is desiring to pour out His Glory in greater measure than ever before, not just in our hearts, lives and church services, but in our finances as well.

Some time ago, the Lord began to speak to me about that. I began to hear, *Do you know what time it is? It's exceedingly-abundantly-above-all-that-you-can-ask-or-think time!*

I don't mind telling you, I was thrilled when I heard those words! And I've become even more excited about them as time has passed. I believe it. I believe it with all my heart!

We are in the days of the end-time transfer of wealth about which the Bible speaks. In these days, God is teaching us how to draw great riches from our heavenly account so we can glorify Him and get the gospel preached to the world. He is revealing to us how we can have more than enough to give to every good work and have plenty left over to enjoy! He *"giveth us richly all things to enjoy!"* (1 Timothy 6:17).

So stand up and stretch your faith. Believe God for more than enough! Not just what you need today, but what the Church needs to minister life to the world. Remember what time it is. If you can think it, then it's not "above all you can ask or think!" Think about that!

## *Speak the Word*

*God is able to do exceeding abundantly above all that I ask or think,*
*according to the power that works in me.*
*Ephesians 3:20*

FOR FURTHER STUDY:

1 Kings 10:1-24

DAILY SCRIPTURE READING:

Hosea 12-13;
Psalm 123

*Kenneth*

# Faith...or Desperation?

DECEMBER 9

Did you know you can make your faith lose its aim? You can have all the faith you need, yet let it scatter in every direction—without results!

"How?" By losing your hope. Most believers don't pay much attention to hope. They don't think of it as very important. They certainly don't consider it to be as important as faith. But the fact is, faith won't function without hope.

Hope is the blueprint of faith. When hope is lost, faith loses its aim. It no longer has a mission to accomplish. It just scatters.

I remember some years ago when that happened to me. I had given my airplane to another preacher, at God's instruction, and then ordered another to replace it. During the weeks while the new plane was being manufactured, I began to believe God for the full amount I needed to pay for it.

I hooked up my faith to the promises of God, and I was going along fine. But just a few days before the plane was scheduled to be delivered to me, I was $20,000 short.

I became more and more alarmed. I started confessing as fast as I could: "Thank God I have that $20,000. In Jesus' Name, I have it. I have it. I have it."

That sounded like faith, but it wasn't. I wasn't confessing in faith, I was confessing out of desperation.

I knew something had to change, so I gathered my Bible and my tapes, got in my boat, and went out to the middle of the lake so I could be totally alone with the Lord. When I got out there, I was still saying, "Thank God, I have that $20,000. In Jesus' Name, I have it. I have it. I have it. I have it."

Suddenly the Lord spoke up on the inside of me: *KENNETH, BE QUIET!* He said, *I'm tired of hearing that. Just hush and let Me show you what I can do.*

When He said that, hope came alive inside me again. Suddenly I was expectant instead of desperate. I started eagerly anticipating what God was about to do, instead of fearing what would happen if He didn't come through.

Sure enough, the $20,000 I needed for that airplane came in. It was a few days late, but it came (late because I let my hope get weak). The pilot who delivered the airplane to me got saved and filled with the Holy Spirit. But none of that would have happened if I hadn't pulled aside, locked myself away with the Word for several hours, and let the Spirit of God rebuild and rekindle the hope inside me. Hope is what took me from desperation to faith.

> "Faith is the substance of things hoped for."
> HEBREWS 11:1

FOR FURTHER STUDY:

Romans 8:18-25

DAILY SCRIPTURE READING:

Hosea 14;
Joel 1;
Psalm 124

Hope is a divine inner image that is born inside your spirit from God's precious promises. Faith is the heavenly substance that will bring that Word-born picture to pass. Without hope, faith has nowhere to go.

If you're facing serious circumstances, and your faith and confessions are splattering in every direction, stop. Get your Bible, get alone with God, and let that hope come alive inside you. Let the Spirit of God rise up on the inside of you and relight that fire. It will stop the desperation...and get your faith on target again.

## Speak the Word

*Faith is the substance of things that I hope for and expect.*
*Hebrews 11:1*

> "I will praise thee, O Lord, with my whole heart; I will show forth all thy marvellous works. I will be glad and rejoice in thee: I will sing praise to thy name, O thou most High. When mine enemies are turned back, they shall fall and perish at thy presence."
> PSALM 9:1-3

# Now, That's Power!

Joy and praise together release strength on the inside of you and power on the outside. Psalm 22:3 says God inhabits our praises. When God's presence begins to come into our midst, our enemies fall back. They can't stand the presence of God.

Psalm 68:1-3 says, *"Let God arise, let his enemies be scattered: let them also that hate him flee before him. As smoke is driven away, so drive them away: as wax melteth before the fire, so let the wicked perish at the presence of God. But let the righteous be glad; let them rejoice before God: yea, let them exceedingly rejoice."*

Now, that's power! When God's people rise up in praise and worship and celebrate the victories of God, His enemies are scattered.

No wonder Satan has tried so hard to get God's people to sit still. No wonder he has bound us up with traditions that taught us to sit back in "dignified" silence. For most of us, our traditions have taught us not to do the very things the Bible says we are to do when we worship and praise.

But tradition's day is over. I'm telling you, when the Spirit begins to move, inhibition has to flee. The Bible says, *"And they...shall be like a mighty man, and their heart shall rejoice as through wine..."* (Zechariah 10:7).

You know what happens when people drink wine—they lose their inhibitions! That's what happened to the disciples on the Day of Pentecost. They had been hiding out only a few days before, but when the Holy Ghost came upon them, suddenly they were on the streets acting so wild, everyone thought they had been drinking.

What God considers "dignified" and what you consider dignified are two different things. God wants you free. He doesn't want you bound up with traditions or fear of what other people might think.

He wants you to be free to laugh. He wants you to be free to leap and praise and sing. He wants you to be free to rejoice. He wants you so free that other people won't understand it—they'll just want it!

## *Speak the Word*

*I sing praises to the Name of the Lord. When my enemies are turned back, they fall and perish at the Lord's presence.*
*Psalm 9:2-3*

FOR FURTHER STUDY:

Psalm 98

DAILY SCRIPTURE READING:

Joel 2-3;
Amos 1;
Psalms 125-126

# More Than a Holy Ghost Giggle

DECEMBER 11

❧

"The joy of the Lord is your strength."
NEHEMIAH 8:10

If you've been in many services where the Holy Spirit is moving in recent years, you've probably heard the laughter—lots of laughter. You've seen and, perhaps, experienced spontaneous outbreaks of joy that range from a few, quiet chuckles to uproarious laughter that literally leaves believers rolling in the aisles.

It's wonderful. There's no denying that. But what is it all about? The answer to that question is even more thrilling than the laughter itself.

Jesus is building up His Church. He is strengthening us out of the rich treasury of His Glory. He is arming us with the spiritual might we will need to march out of every bondage and crush the devil under our feet—once and for all.

For example: The word *glory* in the Old Testament literally means "to be heavy-laden with everything that is good," and it relates directly to the presence of God's Spirit. On the other hand, the word for *grief* is the exact opposite. It means "to be heavy-laden with everything that is bad."

Grief is the satanic reciprocal of glory. So when the Glory of God comes on you, grief doesn't stand a chance. It has to flee! When it does, the joy of the Lord that's in you just starts bubbling out. There's nothing to hold it back.

Of course, that's a lot of fun. We all enjoy it. But actually, the Lord is not just out to give us a good time and a Holy Ghost giggle. He has a greater purpose. He wants us to be full of joy because it's the force that will make us strong enough to carry out His plan in this final hour. It will give us the spiritual, mental and physical fortitude to rise up in the fullness of God's Glory—fully healed, fully delivered, fully prosperous—so we can reap the final harvest and be gathered to Him in great triumph.

The Church will not slip out of this earth in defeat and disgrace. We will not leave here like some whipped pup. No, God will make us victorious. God will make YOU victorious. I don't care what low-level devil is harassing you with an aggravating problem...that low-level devil doesn't have the final say.

Laugh at the devil in the Name of Jesus. Laugh at the very idea that he thinks he could have victory over Jesus and His Body—over you as a member of His Body. Rise up and take your authority! The victory is yours but the battle is the Lord's. He always wins!

FOR FURTHER STUDY:

Psalm 105:37-43

❧

DAILY SCRIPTURE READING:

Amos 2-3;
PSALM 127

## *Speak the Word*

*The joy of the Lord is my strength.*
*Nehemiah 8:10*

'But as to the
suitable times
and the
precise
seasons and
dates,
brethren, you
have no
necessity for
anything
being written
to you. For
you yourselves
know perfectly
well that the
day of the
Lord['s return]
will come [as
unexpectedly
and suddenly]
as a thief in
the night."
1 THESSALONIANS
5:1-2, AMP

# God Wants Us Handy

At this moment in history, there is a shout going up in the spirit. A shout that rings out from the Word of God and from the voices of His prophets. A shout that is shaping the life of every wise believer on the face of the earth.

"BEHOLD, THE BRIDEGROOM COMETH!"

The signs of Jesus' return are all around us. Never before has there been such a time. Never before has it been so crucial that you and I be ready.

Some would say, "Oh, Gloria, you can't be sure of that. After all, the Bible says nobody knows when Jesus is coming. His return will overtake us like a thief in the night."

If that's what you've been thinking, you'd better go back to the Word and read that scripture again. First Thessalonians 5 goes on to say that we who are not in darkness won't be caught by surprise. It says we are to keep wide awake, alert, watchful, cautious and on our guard.

If you're a believer who is ready, Jesus' return will not take you by surprise. You're a child of the light and you'll know. You may not know the day or the hour, but you will know the season.

In fact, I just suspect that those who are ready will be walking so fully in the spirit on the day the Lord comes back, that in their prayer time, they'll sense something great is about to happen. A spiritual excitement will sound in their hearts. Suddenly they'll get goose bumps. Their hair might just stand straight up. Their spirit man will be so hooked up to God, that they'll just know something is happening.

There is no question about it. You and I have to be ready. Just like the military forces of our nation stay in combat readiness, we also must be in combat readiness all the time. We must be ready all the time, not only because Jesus is coming back, but also because there's an enemy out there. His name is Satan and his mission is to kill us, steal from us and destroy us. If we let him catch us off guard, he can make a serious mark on our life. But if we're ready and we resist him, he will flee from us.

If we're ready, we'll be prepared and equipped to act immediately. *Webster's Dictionary* says *ready* means "waiting to be used, unhesitant, willing, convenient, handy to use."

I like that last phrase. We ought to be handy for God to use at any time. He wants us willing! He wants us ready!

## *Speak the Word*

*The day of the Lord's return will come unexpectedly and suddenly
as a thief in the night. I am determined to be ready for Him.*
*1 Thessalonians 5:2*

FOR FURTHER
STUDY:

1 Thessalonians
5:1-6

DAILY SCRIPTURE
READING:

Amos 4-5;
Psalm 128

*Kenneth*

# Operate in Full Power

"Oh, God, I need more power! Please...please...please give me more power, Lord!"

Have you ever prayed like that? I have. In fact, years ago I was praying along those lines, earnestly beseeching God to give me greater power to minister. It was a fine, very spiritual-sounding prayer. But the Lord interrupted me right in the middle of it.

*Kenneth,* He said. *Where would I go to get you more power?*

The question stopped me cold.

*No one has more power than I do,* He continued. *And I've already filled you with My Spirit. I've put within you the same miraculous force that created heaven and earth, the same supernatural strength that raised Jesus from the dead. Where am I going to go to find something greater that that?*

The point was clear. As born-again, Holy Spirit-filled believers, you and I don't need more power. We simply need to more fully release what we've already been given. We need to allow the Spirit of God within us to flow through us in greater measure.

If we're not seeing miracles in our lives and ministries, it isn't God's fault. He isn't the one limiting us. We are!

That may not sound like good news to you, but it is. If you're the one who is keeping the lid on the power of God in your life, then you're the one who can take that lid off! You don't have to sit around waiting for some super-anointed prophet to come lay hands on you. All you have to do is make a quality decision to increase the flow of God's power in your life—starting today!

"Now, Brother Copeland, I don't believe we can just turn God's power on at will!"

I don't either. But thank God, we don't have to! His power is always on! He turned it on and made it available to every one of us almost 2,000 years ago on the Day of Pentecost, and He hasn't turned it off since. He is just waiting for us to get with the program and start using it and doing the works that Jesus did, and even greater works (John 14:12).

How? By operating in the same unlimited power that Jesus did. The same boundless power He enjoyed because He spoke the words of God.

Jesus didn't just speak the words of God when He was ministering. He didn't just speak the words of God when He was feeling spiritual. He *always* spoke God's Word (John 8:28). That was what brought the manifestation of the Spirit of His Father without reserve.

So quit asking God to give you more power. He couldn't, even if He wanted to. He doesn't have any more to give. You already have it all...just turn it on! Speak the Word of God every day, all day long, and operate in full power.

> "For since He Whom God has sent speaks the words of God...God does not give Him His Spirit sparingly or by measure, but boundless is the gift God makes of His Spirit!"
> JOHN 3:34, AMP

FOR FURTHER STUDY:

John 14:8-14

DAILY SCRIPTURE READING:

Amos 6-7;
Psalm 129

## Speak the Word

*I have the Holy Spirit, therefore I am full of power!*
*Acts 1:8*

❧

"And from the days of John the Baptist until now the kingdom of heaven suffereth violence, and the violent take it by force."

MATTHEW 11:12

# Worth It All

What does it take to be a winner? Everyone everywhere wants to know the answer to that question. Everyone wants to win. But when it comes right down to it, not everyone is willing to pay the price to do it.

During the Olympic Games, I listened to the athletes being interviewed. They talked about how hard they worked to compete in the games.

None of them just woke up one morning and said, "Hey! I think I'll be in the Olympics this year." They trained for years to get there. Some of them had trained most of their lives.

I heard one champion tell how she got out of bed every morning to run. She ran in the cold. She ran in the rain. She ran no matter what. Sometimes she would push herself so hard, she would become physically sick. But even then, she refused not to run. She was determined to win and she gave her very best.

That kind of commitment is what it takes to be a winner, not just physically, but spiritually. Jesus said so in Matthew 11:12. When He said those words, He wasn't talking about going to heaven. I believe He was talking about laying hold of the kingdom of God in this earth—taking hold of the promised blessings like healing and prosperity and peace.

You can have those kingdom blessings here and now. But it's not easy. You have to take them by force.

You have to become spiritually aggressive if you want to walk in the supernatural. You have to do it by faith with the Word of God or you won't do it at all.

Most people don't see faith as a violent force. But spiritually speaking, it is! Paul said, *"Fight the good fight of faith!"* (1 Timothy 6:12). Faith isn't passive, it's aggressive! It uses the Word of God as its weapon and brings down every stronghold of unbelief and every demonic obstacle in its path!

So start training for your race now. Don't waste another minute. Get into the Word. Build up your faith. Get aggressive with it. Do whatever it takes...just like the Olympic runner, it will be worth it all!

## *Speak the Word*

*I fight the good fight of faith! I take the kingdom of heaven by force!*
*1 Timothy 6:12; Matthew 11:12*

FOR FURTHER STUDY:

1 Timothy 6:11-12

❧

DAILY SCRIPTURE READING:

Amos 8-9;
Psalm 130

*Kenneth*

# Back the Truck Up, and Get Another Load!

DECEMBER 15

❧

"Rejoice in the Lord alway: and again I say, Rejoice."
PHILIPPIANS 4:4

Joy...it's a traditional part of the Christmas season. In December, people who hardly crack a smile all year send out cards with messages about joy. Carolers chirp out, "Joy to the World!" as grumpy shoppers push their way through crowded malls. Glittering banners, decked with sprigs of holly and silver bells, wave the word "JOY" over city streets jammed with irritated drivers who just want to get home.

Tradition aside, the fact is, with the busy schedules, high expectations and financial pressures people face this time of year, it's easy to let joy slip through your fingers. But don't do it. Instead, get a revelation of joy that will inspire you to hang on to it not only at Christmastime, but all year 'round.

You see, God is full of joy. Jesus is a man of joy. So if we're going to follow after Him, we'll have to be full of joy too.

Joy used to be my weakest area, spiritually. I spent so much time majoring on faith that I didn't pay much attention to it. But the Lord eventually taught me that you can't live by faith without joy.

That's because it takes strength to live by faith. We're surrounded by a world that is flowing toward death. The natural pull of it is always negative. When you leave things alone and don't work against that negative flow, they always get worse—not better. If you leave a garden unattended, it dies for lack of water or gets taken over by weeds. If you leave a house unattended, the paint peels off and the boards begin to rot.

To move toward life, you must constantly swim upstream. If you ever get too weak spiritually to do that, you'll find yourself being swept back toward sickness, lack or some other form of defeat. So you can never afford to run out of strength.

No wonder the Apostle Paul wrote to rejoice in the Lord always! To rejoice means to re-joy, to back the truck up and get another load!

Paul understood the link between joy and strength. That's why he prayed for the Colossians to be *"Strengthened with all might, according to his [God's] glorious power, unto all patience and longsuffering with joyfulness,"* (Colossians 1:11). The heart of that sentence says we are strengthened with all might and joyfulness!

Paul reaffirmed that what was true in Nehemiah's day under the Old Covenant is true today under the New Covenant...the joy of the Lord is our strength! So back your truck up...and get another load!

FOR FURTHER STUDY:

Acts 20:16-24

❧

DAILY SCRIPTURE READING:

Obadiah;
Jonah 1;
Psalm 131

## Speak the Word

*I rejoice in the Lord always!*
*Philippians 4:4*

> "The backsliding of the simple shall slay them, and the careless ease of [self-confident] fools shall destroy them. But whoso hearkens to me [Wisdom], shall dwell securely and in confident trust, and shall be quiet without fear or dread of evil."
>
> PROVERBS 1: 32-33, AMP

# Hearing From Heaven

There is nothing—absolutely nothing!—on this earth that's as valuable to you as the wisdom of God. It is the key that opens every good door. Prosperity and success. Health and long life. Peace and security. All of these are available to those who learn from and live by the wisdom of God.

But, oddly enough, many believers don't seek God's wisdom until their backs are against the wall. They wait until calamity strikes and then, in desperation, they listen hard for God's voice. But all too often they are unable to hear it.

Why? Because, as the voice of Wisdom says in Proverbs 1:24-28 (AMP): "*I have called and you refused [to answer],...you have treated as nothing all my counsel, and would accept none of my reproof, I also will laugh at your calamity; I will mock when the thing comes that shall cause you terror and panic, When your panic comes as a storm and desolation, and your calamity comes on as a whirlwind, when distress and anguish come upon you. Then they will call upon me [Wisdom], but I will not answer; they will seek me early and diligently, but they will not find me.*"

Don't ever let yourself get caught in a situation like that. Don't ever let yourself get to the point where you're unable to hear from heaven.

Hearing from heaven is the most important thing in your whole life! That's because you can never come up with a problem too big for God to solve. The important thing to remember, however, is that you can't turn the wisdom of God on and off like a water faucet. You've got to make a lifestyle of it.

If you want to be sure that the wisdom of God will be there for you when the crisis hits, you need to start listening for His guidance now. Learn to seek His wisdom, to listen for His instructions on the little, everyday matters of life. That way, when the big problems come, you'll be ready. You'll be in the habit of hearing from heaven.

## *Speak the Word*

*I hearken to wisdom, and I dwell securely and in confident trust.*
*I am quiet without fear or dread of evil.*
*Proverbs 1:33, AMP*

FOR FURTHER STUDY:

Proverbs 4:7-9

DAILY SCRIPTURE READING:

Jonah 2-3;
Psalm 132

*Kenneth*

# Think on These Things

When you begin to dwell on the Word of God, the first thing you discover is that the Word goes absolutely contrary to the way you're accustomed to thinking. But the only way for the Word to abide in you is to choose it over your old, worldly thoughts.

Second Corinthians 10:4-6 calls those old thought patterns "strongholds" and lets us know we have to overthrow them with the Word of God.

How do you take your old thoughts captive and bring them into obedience to Jesus? By replacing them with His thoughts and His Words.

Once you understand that, you can see how we can have untroubled hearts...and think on the things of Philippians 4:8.

Think about this: God isn't worried, is He? He isn't afraid He'll run out of money. He's not filled with anxiety about your problems. No! He has the supply. He has more than enough power to get you through every circumstance in victory. So when you think His thoughts, you won't be afraid either. You'll be full of the peace of God Himself.

If you're going to abide in the peace of God, if His Word is going to abide in you, you have to close the door to all other kinds of thought. You have to cast down every thought that disagrees with the Word and choose to think God's thoughts instead. You literally have to select what your mind thinks.

You have to be like my daughter Kellie was years ago when she was a little girl. One day I took her by the hand, led her into her room, opened the door of her closet (which was piled full of junk) and said, "Kellie Dee Copeland, this closet of yours is a mess! Now you're going to get in there and clean it up."

She just looked up at me and said, "That's not my thought."

She resisted that thought. She wouldn't accept it. I couldn't figure out how to get that thought into her either. Even when she went ahead and cleaned up the closet, it wasn't her thought. The only reason she did it is because her mother and dad made her.

> "Whatsoever things are true, whatsoever things are honest, whatsoever things are just, whatsoever things are pure, whatsoever things are lovely, whatsoever things are of good report; if there be any virtue, and if there be any praise, think on these things."
> PHILIPPIANS 4:8

That's the way we need to treat the devil. When he comes around with a thought of anxiety or disaster, we just need to tell him, "That's not my thought. I'm not touching that with my thought life." Then we need to immediately replace that thought with a thought from the Word of God. We need to think on things that are just, pure, lovely, of good report, of virtue and praise.

FOR FURTHER STUDY:

Psalm 119:40-64

DAILY SCRIPTURE READING:

Jonah 4;
Micah 1-2;
Psalms 133-134

## Speak the Word

*I think only on things that are true, honest, just, pure, lovely and of good report. I think on virtuous and praiseworthy things.*
*Philippians 4:8*

*Kenneth*

# Copy Him!

Just about everything I know, I learned from copying someone else. Take skiing, for example. Gloria and I love to ski. We had a good ski instructor. He did everything right. He always looked so great coming down the mountain.

I learned to ski by imitating him. I kept listening to everything he told me to do and then I went out there and did it. It worked! I didn't look as smooth as he looked, of course, but I skied.

I didn't *try* to ski. I skied. At first I only went about six feet down the slope, but I skied.

Every year I ski a little better. Every year I'm able to apply a little more of what that instructor taught me. Could someone accuse me of copying that ski instructor? Of course, they could! That's exactly what I'm doing. I'm trying to imitate him. I'm doing everything I possibly can to look just like him. Why? Because he's a better skier than I am!

There was a fellow once who was criticizing me. "That Copeland just runs around acting like a little Jesus," he said. He didn't realize it, but as far as I'm concerned, that's the highest compliment any man could pay me. That's exactly what I'm trying to do!

Jesus told me to do it. He said, *"As my Father hath taught me, I speak...."* In other words, "I'm standing here copying the Father. Now you copy Me."

Religion will try to convince you to say, "Oh, I could never be like Jesus! I'm too unworthy to ever act like Him."

Who will you act like then?

Know this: You *will* act like somebody. You'll copy what you see on television or what you read in magazines or what you hear from the world—or you'll copy Jesus.

The question is, which will you choose? If you choose to be like Jesus, you'll discipline your words by saying what He says. You'll discipline your actions by doing what He does. The more skilled you become with that discipline, the more you'll live in the dimension Jesus enjoyed.

So don't let religion or other wrong ideas hold you back. He's the best teacher and example you'll ever know. Copy Him!

## Speak the Word

*I imitate God. I copy Him and follow His example.*
*Ephesians 5:1, AMP*

FOR FURTHER STUDY:

John 8:25-29

DAILY SCRIPTURE READING:

Micah 3-4;
Psalm 135

# Get a Reputation

When Jesus trained the first 12 disciples, He taught them the same strategy He had been using on the earth: *"Go, preach, saying, The kingdom of heaven is at hand. Heal the sick, cleanse the lepers, raise the dead, cast out devils: freely ye have received, freely give"* (Matthew 10:7-8).

He also told the 70 disciples in Luke 10 the same thing in verses 8-9.

"Well, yes, that's how Jesus said to do it back then, but He has a different plan for us."

> "The person who is united to the Lord becomes one spirit with Him."
> 1 CORINTHIANS 6:17, AMP

No, He doesn't! His last words before He ascended to heaven were the same instructions: *"Go ye into all the world, and preach the gospel to every creature.... And these signs shall follow them that believe; In my name shall they cast out devils...they shall lay hands on the sick, and they shall recover"* (Mark 16:15, 17-18).

Praise God! We have the same new birth, the same Holy Spirit and the same commission those first disciples had. And you remember what happened to them after Jesus left, don't you?

They kept right on doing what Jesus had done—and the crowds treated them just like they had treated the Master. They brought the sick so they could be healed. In Jerusalem, they actually laid the sick in the street, so Peter's shadow might fall on them as he walked by.

Why did they do that? They had heard if you could get to where the Christians were, you could get healed. They had a reputation. It was the same reputation Jesus had. As a result, the early Church grew at a rate of thousands a day!

That's the way it should be for us today.

"But I can't heal the sick!," you say. "I can't cast out devils!"

Maybe not...but God can and He is in you. In fact, the Scripture says the person united to Him becomes one spirit with Him.

Jesus said it this way, *"At that day ye shall know that I am in my Father, and ye in me, and I in you"* (John 14:20).

You and Jesus are one. He is the Head and you are the Body. You are His instrument in the earth. Dare to believe that. Be bold enough to speak the words the Bible speaks and do whatever Jesus tells you to do. Believe me, people will come to you for help. The Spirit of God will anoint you—and great things will happen!

FOR FURTHER STUDY:

Ephesians 2:18-22

DAILY SCRIPTURE READING:

Micah 5-6; Psalm 136

## *Speak the Word*

*I am united with the Lord. I am one spirit with Him.*
*1 Corinthians 6:17, AMP*

> "For the kingdom of God is not meat and drink; but righteousness, and peace, and joy in the Holy Ghost."
>
> ROMANS 14:17

# Hook Up With the Holy Ghost

While there are several ways to stir up joy within yourself—such as meditating on God's Word, replacing your thoughts with His thoughts, and so on. Another way is to fellowship with the Holy Spirit.

According to Romans 14:17, there is joy in the Holy Ghost! So hook up with Him! Pray and sing in other tongues. Jump into the river of the Spirit with praise and thanksgiving. You may start out thinking you don't have anything to thank God for—but you'll quickly find out that you do.

You can begin by thanking Him for the blood of Jesus that has washed away your sin. You can thank Him that you're on your way to heaven. If you can't think of any other reason to praise Him, just center on those two things. Keep shouting, "Thank God, my sins are washed away!" until joy rises up within you.

"I can't do that. I just don't feel like it."

That doesn't matter! You don't have to feel any certain way to rejoice. Joy is bigger than your emotions. In the 27th Psalm, King David wrote, *"And now shall mine head be lifted up above mine enemies round about me: therefore will I offer in his [God's] tabernacle sacrifices of joy; I will sing, yea, I will sing praises unto the Lord"* (verse 6).

Rejoicing is an act of the will. When you don't feel like rejoicing, set your will and rejoice anyway.

If you're having financial problems, don't stay up all night worrying about how you will pay your bills. If you're going to stay up, stay up and praise God. Sing. Dance. Give thanks. Shout the Word of God and laugh at the devil until joy comes. Then keep on rejoicing until you're so filled with the strength and might of God that nothing can stop you.

Keep on rejoicing until your body is well. Keep on rejoicing until every chain the devil has used to keep you in bondage snaps like a thread. Keep on rejoicing until people start coming to you—and they will—saying, "Hey, I want some of that joy! Can you tell me how to get it?"

Think about it. Wouldn't it be wonderful if we started rejoicing this Christmas and just kept on rejoicing every day from now on until this whole earth was absolutely filled with the Glory of God? I believe with all my heart that's what God is calling us to do.

Let's get on with it so we can rejoice our way right into the rapture.

Let's rejoice in the Lord, always. Let's hook up with the Holy Ghost and get that joy!

FOR FURTHER STUDY:

Numbers 14:21;
Psalm 72:18-19;
Habakkuk 2:14

DAILY SCRIPTURE READING:

Micah 7;
Nahum 1-3;
Psalm 137

## *Speak the Word*

*I am in the kingdom of God, and therefore I have righteousness, and peace, and joy in the Holy Ghost.*
*Romans 14:17*

*Gloria*

# Center Your Life Around God

God doesn't just love the lovely. He loves the unlovely too. No matter how bad, mean or ornery someone might be, if they'll turn to Him, He'll cleanse them and forgive them. He'll let them partake of the sacrifice of His Son, Jesus, so they can have a new life in Him.

That's the way God loves us, and that's the way He expects us to love each other. In 1 Corinthians 13, He gives us a detailed description of that kind of love. That description is especially good in the *Amplified Bible.*

According to the Bible, that kind of love is the distinguishing mark of a Christian. It's God's love that sets you apart. You and I have a high calling. We're called to live a life of love just like Jesus did.

> "Love [God's love in us] does not insist on its own rights or its own way, for it is not self-seeking."
>
> 1 CORINTHIANS 13:5, AMP

Does that mean we'll have to die like He did? Literally speaking, probably not. But we will have to die to our own selfish tendencies and desires. We'll have to stop centering our lives on what *we* want and what *we* feel. We'll have to stop looking out for ourselves all the time. Walking in love means we lay down our own rights and look out for the other person's rights instead.

I realize that may sound tough, but it's actually the surest way to be wonderfully blessed, because when you walk in love, God takes care of you! You could never take care of yourself as well as He does. The Bible says, *"The eyes of the Lord run to and fro throughout the whole earth, to show Himself strong in behalf of those whose heart is blameless toward Him"* (2 Chronicles 16:9, AMP). So when you walk in love, you can rest assured He will see to it that you prosper in every way.

Not only that, when you stop being selfish, you'll be a happier person. When you're self-centered, you're always thinking about yourself. You're always thinking about someone who did you wrong...or how much you have to do.

It's impossible for a selfish person to stay happy for very long because everything centers around him. We're not made to live that way. We're not big enough or powerful enough for everything to center around us. The more we keep our minds on ourselves, the easier it is for the devil to upset us.

FOR FURTHER STUDY:

Ephesians 4:1-3

DAILY SCRIPTURE READING:

Habakkuk 1-3; Psalm 138

But praise God, you've been born again, you've been delivered from self-ishness. It's lost its dominion over you. You don't have to center your life around yourself. You have the power to center your life around God instead. You can keep your mind on obeying His Word and living a life of love! He will take care of everything else (Matthew 6:33).

## *Speak the Word*

*I walk in love. I do not insist on my own rights or my own way, for I am not self-seeking.*
*1 Corinthians 13:5, AMP*

> "In righteousness shalt thou be established."
> ISAIAH 54:14

# You Are a Tree

Jesus is the very picture of established righteousness. When He walked into the funeral of Lazarus, He was the only One not dressed in black. That's because He hadn't come to a funeral, He had come to a raising! He was so established in righteousness that He boldly said, "Roll the stone away from the door of the tomb" (John 11).

It was Righteousness Who commanded, *"Lazarus, come forth."* And when He did, God backed Him up. When the devil heard that, he just got out of the way. There's nothing he can do when Righteousness speaks but bow and leave.

"Sure, Jesus could speak like that," you say, "but I'm not Jesus!"

No, you're not. But your righteousness is of Him. When you understand that, you'll see why that angel shouted at Jesus' birth, *"Behold, I bring you good tidings of great joy, which shall be to all people"* (Luke 2:10).

What was so joyful about those tidings? Those angels were talking to Hebrew people who had been living under the strictness of the Law. They'd struggled all their lives to be righteous. They lived in bondage to the Law, trying to please and satisfy God. But they couldn't do it. So this angel was saying to them, "The One Who makes peace is in the earth! The Anointed One is here."

Talk about great joy! That was the best news those people could ever hear.

But the devil has come back into the Church and sowed that bondage all over again. He's told us that we're unrighteous. He's told us God is mad at us so we would be subject to oppression and fear and doubt.

He's told us there's something blasphemous about our standing up and saying, "I know my God and I have faith in Him. I stand on His Word and I reach out in the Name of Jesus to do exploits."

But friend, that's not blasphemy. That's the gospel!

Our covenant of peace says we're to be called *"trees of righteousness, the planting of the Lord, that he might be glorified"* (Isaiah 61:3).

So be a tree of righteousness planted by God. Not a bush—a *tree* planted! Stand tall because God put you there, and when the devil comes along, tell him just what Jesus told him, *"It is written."*

I'll warn you now, there are some Christians who will oppose you when you do that. They'll come along and try to climb all over you. Others will have sense enough to come hide under your foliage until they get established in righteousness.

Either way, it's all right. You're a tree. Just keep standing there digging your roots deeper and deeper into your covenant of peace. Keep healing the sick and raising the dead. Keep acting the same way that Jesus did. You'll be living proof to a frightened world that there truly is peace on earth, good will toward men!

## Speak the Word

*I am established in righteousness.*
*Isaiah 54:14*

FOR FURTHER STUDY:

Luke 2:1-20

DAILY SCRIPTURE READING:

Zephaniah 1-3;
Psalm 139

*Kenneth*

# It's Time to Rest

Ephesians 2:6 says God has *"raised us up together, and made us sit together in heavenly places in Christ Jesus."* And in Hebrews 3 and 4, we are commanded to enter God's rest. The literal translation says we ought to be afraid of getting *out* of God's rest.

Afraid of it? We haven't even heard of it!

Religious doctrine has told us to get agitated, sorry, bawl, squall or beat the altar with our fist. Yet all the while, God's Word is *commanding* us to enter into His rest...and then stay there.

Now I'll be the first to admit that entering God's rest has been the hardest thing for me to get hold of since I've been in the ministry, though I have done it more on a personal level. I have taken the Word, stood on it, believed God and entered into His rest when I've been faced with an attack of the devil, or the like.

> "Let us therefore fear, lest, a promise being left us of entering into his rest, any of you should seem to come short of it."
> HEBREWS 4:1

But I'm seeing that God intends for us to rest over the whole thing, over every situation—particularly with all that we have facing us in this end time, this sliver of time.

When those hungry people came up to Jesus in Matthew 14:19-21, He didn't fall on His face and start sobbing and kicking the dirt, saying, "Oh, God! Oh, God! I just don't know what I'm going to do. There are 5,000 of them—and that's just the men. We don't have enough money. Besides, we're out here in the middle of nowhere. And that thief I've got for a treasurer..."

No, Jesus just rested in God. He trusted and rested in His Father.

Today, as men and women of faith, our goal is to walk in the promises of God with such faith that, no matter what challenge or need comes our way, we do just like Jesus did when that multitude came to Him: We just smile and say, "Bring the loaves and fish here to me."

Then we take our seed, look to God, give thanks for it, bless it, break it and expect the abundance. Then we just rest. We are living in the last little sliver of time, a time of great harvest, a time when we can laugh, and a time when we can rest.

FOR FURTHER STUDY:

Psalm 37:7;
Hebrews 3-4

DAILY SCRIPTURE READING:

Haggai 1-2;
Psalm 140

## Speak the Word

*I believe, therefore I have entered into rest.*
*Hebrews 4:3*

# The Bridge Between Two Worlds

Everyone knows what a great place heaven is. It has everything—wealth so immense that the streets are made of gold, health so abundant that sickness can't exist there, joy so plentiful it forever extinguishes all sorrow.

Christians everywhere dream of going there when they die. But just imagine for a moment how wonderful it would be if you could have access to heaven right now. Think what it would be like if God would build a bridge between the realm of heaven and earth so that those boundless heavenly supplies could flow down to meet the needs in your life today.

It's a wonderful thought, isn't it? But do you know what's even more wonderful? The bridge has been built!

Most people can't even believe such a thing is possible! That's because, in their minds, the world of the spirit where heaven exists isn't quite real. So they can't understand how the "reality" of this physical world of matter and the "unreality" of the spiritual world could ever be connected.

I used to think that way too. But some years ago, when God began to teach me about these things, He set me straight and renewed my mind. He told me that the spectrum of reality includes both the spiritual world and the material world. He also informed me that, contrary to popular belief, the spiritual world is not only *just as real* as this physical world, but it is *more real!*

You see, 2,000 years ago, in the city of Bethlehem, an angel exploded with joy announcing the good news: "Peace on earth. Good will toward men!" (Luke 2:14). Jesus was born! The Word that brought life to Adam had come again as a way for you to have eternal life. Heaven and earth connected again...the bridge for your salvation was built...the separation that had existed since Adam chose to disobey God was over.

Because of that, today, you can have all your needs met in abundance. Every need...in your spirit, in your soul and in your body. That means your spiritual needs, your social needs, your mental needs, your physical needs, your health needs.

Jesus is born. You have been given the Savior! You have been given the Anointed One and His Anointing. Invite Him into your heart today...and walk across the bridge between two worlds.

## *Speak the Word*

*I believe in my heart that Jesus Christ is the Son of God,
and God has raised Him from the dead. I am saved!*
*Romans 10:9*

*Kenneth*

# Merry Christmas!

St. Nicholas should be an inspiration to us all. He was a godly man whose reputation for giving to people caused him to be a revered example of what compassion and giving are all about. He was not a jolly, fat man who climbed down chimneys and he didn't have flying reindeer!

Stories of his life—a life full of Christian beliefs and values—are the real background for today's mythical Santa Claus. So much of what Nicholas was— and what Santa Claus has become—has been distorted by Satan. What has been done to weaken and distort the testimony of this godly man is wrong.

Born in Turkey in the third century, Nicholas was raised by Christian parents. From the time he was born in A.D. 280, they considered him a gift from God. They diligently taught him devotion to God and to be very generous to the poor.

> "Behold, I bring you good tidings of great joy, which shall be to all people. For unto you is born this day in the city of David a Saviour, which is Christ the Lord."
> LUKE 2:10-11

At 19, Nicholas was ordained a priest. His uncle, a bishop, prophesied that Nicholas would offer guidance and consolation to many people, and that he would eventually become a bishop, and live a life of enlightenment. All of this was fulfilled in Nicholas' lifetime.

Many accounts have been written of his dedicated life. It has been said that he would spend all night studying God's Word to bring it to the people. He was known for helping the poor, for praying, fasting and standing steadfast in faith and goodness.

The true story of St. Nicholas is a beautiful picture of the giving that Christmas is all about. The greatest gift of all is the gift of Jesus Christ to us from God the Father. Jesus is our hope, redemption and victory. He is our advocate with the Father, our blood-covenant friend Who will never leave us nor forsake us. In Him we have the joy of living a heavenly life on earth.

He is the meaning of Christmas. *Christ mass* means "anointing celebration." It's the celebration of *"How God anointed Jesus of Nazareth with the Holy Ghost and with power."* It's the celebration of how the anointed Jesus *"went about doing good, and healing all that were oppressed of the devil"* (Acts 10:38). It's the story of our triumphant Savior, Jesus the Christ, the Lord of lords and King of kings! Now, that's a Merry Christmas!

FOR FURTHER
STUDY:

Matthew 1-2

DAILY SCRIPTURE
READING:

Zechariah 4-5;
Psalm 143

## Speak the Word

*God so loved me that He gave His only Son for me!*
*I believe in Him, and I have everlasting life.*
*John 3:16*

❧

# Ask for a Revelation

Some people think the fire and smoke in that verse refers to destruction. But it doesn't. Fire and smoke are manifestations of God's Glory. That scripture is talking about the greatest outpouring of the power and Anointing of God ever seen on this earth.

We are already in the beginning stages of that outpouring. Where is it coming from? It's coming from within believers like you and me. And it will keep increasing as the river of the anointing overflows the banks of our hearts and floods into our homes, our workplaces, our neighborhoods and our world.

But let me warn you, the increase is not going to come while we sit around watching TV and filling our time with the ordinary details of life. It's going to come as we dig into the Word of God and build our faith in the anointing. The more we learn to expect the anointing and align ourselves with it, the more manifestations of it we will see.

So get out your Bible and start studying. Every time you see the word *Christ*, translate it and meditate on the fact that it means "the Anointed One and His Anointing." Learn how to protect the anointing and how to live your life in such a way that the Holy Ghost can work freely through you.

In other words, ask God for a revelation of what it really means to be anointed with the Anointing of Jesus, to be baptized in the Holy Ghost with God's own burden-removing, yoke-destroying, world-changing, devil-chasing, healing, delivering, explosive, supernatural, universe-creating power. Ask for a revelation of what it really means to be a Christian.

Once you walk in that revelation, the world around you will never be the same again.

## *Speak the Word*

*I can do all things through the Anointed One
and His Anointing which strengthens me.*
*Philippians 4:13*

FOR FURTHER
STUDY:

John 7:37-39

❧

DAILY SCRIPTURE
READING:

Zechariah 6-7;
Psalm 144

*Kenneth*

# God Is Not a Liar

Everything that has to do with men, everything in this natural world, is subject to change, but the Word of God is not. The Word of God is true even when everything else around you is telling you otherwise. But notice that Romans 3:3-4 says you must let God be true in your life.

To do so, you must forever settle in your heart and mind that, there is no fault in God. There is no shadow of turning in Him. There's no weakness or shortcoming in His Word.

You will never catch God in a lie. You will never get in a situation where you exercise faith in God's Word and God fails to keep that Word. Never! The Bible says that God is active and alert, watching over His Word to perform it (Jeremiah 1:12, AMP).

Understand, however, that it's not enough just to know what the Word says. It must be reality to you—more real than the problem you face.

For example, maybe you or your children have experienced recurring symptoms of an illness for a long time. If so, you need to sit down and ask yourself, *Do I really believe that according to 1 Peter 2:24, by His stripes we were healed?*

However you honestly answered that question in your heart makes the difference in your situation. You have to choose to believe that God cannot lie and that His Word is true...regardless of what the circumstances are telling you. You cannot attempt to exercise your faith in His Word based on head knowledge. That's not enough!

That's why we must constantly center ourselves on God's Word, because it's that Word that produces faith in our hearts. In fact, you cannot deepen your faith in God without deepening your trust in His Word. Let God be found true...if you believe in His Word, it will come to pass.

> "What if some did not believe and were without faith? Does their lack of faith and their faithlessness nullify and make ineffective and void the faithfulness of God and His fidelity [to His Word]? By no means! Let God be found true though every human being be false and a liar."
> ROMANS 3:3-4, AMP

## Speak the Word

*God is true. I choose to believe God's Word and not my circumstances.*
*Romans 3:4*

FOR FURTHER STUDY:

Psalm 119:89;
John 17:17

DAILY SCRIPTURE READING:

Zechariah 8-9;
Psalm 145

# Get Caught Up!

> "I am convinced and sure of this very thing, that He Who began a good work in you will continue until the day of Jesus Christ—right up to the time of His return—developing [that good work] and perfecting and bringing it to full completion in you."
> PHILIPPIANS 1:6, AMP

From the moment you were born again, God began to peel things away from you that were holding you back, things that were stopping Him from operating in your life with power.

And He's still doing that. You're still growing. You keep growing and allowing God to talk to you and deal with you. He keeps speaking to you about things you need to change, things you need to drop out of your life.

But it's not just about dropping things, it's about taking on new things. Taking more of the things of God unto ourselves. We grow further by learning the Word and the truth of the Word. The old habits and old lifestyle lose their hold on us and fall away.

The more you get to know God, the less you want the old things. The more you know God, the more of the old is peeled away.

You could just say, "OK, I'm not going to smoke cigarettes anymore. I'm not going to do it anymore. I just won't."

That's better than saying you will do it. But there is a MUCH better way.

The best way is to get so caught up in the things of God that God's Spirit and His power begin to throw those things off you. You have to put your will in gear, and *will* to do what's right, but when you do, my, oh my, His power will change you.

So get in the Word. Meditate on it. Listen to tapes of the Word preached. Don't ever stop. Remember, you should always be growing.

Just get caught up in Him.

## *Speak the Word*

*God has begun a good work in me. He develops, perfects*
*and brings it to full completion in me.*
*Philippians 1:6, AMP*

FOR FURTHER STUDY:

2 Corinthians 5:17;
Ephesians 4

DAILY SCRIPTURE READING:

Zechariah 10-11;
Psalm 146

# Don't Let the Bullies Get You Down

Remember the class bully when you were in grade school? He intimidated everyone. He was nothing but a 5-foot, 140-pound heap of trouble who scared everyone silly. Well, you're over that situation by now, but trouble is still around.

In this life there is trouble...trouble with every opportunity the devil gets. The Apostle Paul said he was troubled by circumstances on every side...but on the inside he was not distressed.

Paul fixed his attention, not on external circumstances, but on the light of the gospel in his inner man, because that's where the excellency of God's power is. Knowing the truth will always make you free. "We're perplexed," he said. The Greek word for *perplexed* means "to be cornered by the circumstances."

"But we're not in despair." In other words, even when it looks like there's no way out, I can find a way out if I look to the Word that's living in me.

"Persecuted, but not forsaken." If I'm persecuted on the outside, how do I know God hasn't forsaken me? Because when I look on the inside, I can hear Jesus saying, "I'll never leave you nor forsake you, even to the ends of the earth."

> "We are troubled on every side, yet not distressed; we are perplexed, but not in despair; Persecuted, but not forsaken; cast down, but not destroyed."
> 2 CORINTHIANS 4:8-9

Perplexed...persecuted...cast down. There's no doubt about it, Paul was under more pressure than most of us today will ever experience. But he handled it...and so can you if you'll do the following three things:

ONE: Remember where the pressure is coming from—the outside! And remember where your life force comes from—the inside!

TWO: Stop running on a spiritual deficit. Take time to feed your inner man with the Word of God. Fast your body if necessary and feast your spirit on the Word so your inner man can get stronger more quickly.

THREE: Focus on Jesus inside you until your inner picture of Him is bigger than the outside situations you're facing.

If you'll build up your spirit man in those three ways, when pressure comes, it won't affect you like it may be doing today. Soon, the problems that are knocking you flat won't even bother you anymore.

FOR FURTHER STUDY:

2 Corinthians 4:8-12

DAILY SCRIPTURE READING:

Zechariah 12-13; Psalm 147

Remember the bully? He couldn't even make you blink today, now that you're 6 feet tall. What happened? What changed? You grew. You're stronger now. He's no longer a threat. That's what happened to Paul. He grew! He kept feeding on the Word until the image of Jesus within him grew bigger than the pressures around him. So just keep feeding your spirit man on the Word. Get strong on the inside. And don't let the bullies get you down!

## *Speak the Word*

*I am troubled on every side, yet not distressed; perplexed, but not in despair; persecuted, but not forsaken; cast down, but not destroyed. The life of Jesus is made manifest in me.*
*2 Corinthians 4:8-10*

December 30

"I believed...
therefore have
I spoken."
2 Corinthians
4:13

*Gloria*

# Why Didn't You Say Something?

Consider the following scenario:

"Where do you want to go eat, honey?" the husband asks.

"Oh, I don't care. Anywhere you want to go is fine with me," she'll answer.

Taking his wife at her word, the husband will go to his favorite restaurant. The problem is, the wife doesn't really like that one. Once they get there and start to order, she'll be acting a little aggravated.

"What's wrong?"

"Oh nothing," snaps the wife.

"Something is bothering you. What is it?"

"I didn't want to eat here. I want to eat somewhere else."

"Well, why didn't you say something?" he'll ask in exasperation.

Now, that's just a small example, but it illustrates a very solemn truth. Someday, when our earthly lives are finished, when we stand before Jesus, someone might say, "Lord, I really needed clothes for my children when I was on earth...I really needed healing for my body...I really needed deliverance from my circumstances."

And I can just hear Jesus saying to us just what the husband said to his wife, "Well, why didn't you *say* something?!"

Those words may shock you. You may be sitting around in the midst of a crisis waiting for God to act—when all the time, He's waiting for you. Jesus is waiting for each one of us to take the power and dominion He gave us and use it to put those devil-generated crises where they belong—under our feet!

Jesus said, *"All authority in heaven and on earth has been given to me. Therefore [you] go!..."* (Matthew 28:18-19, NIV). You lay hands on the sick and they'll recover. You cast out the devil. In other words, Jesus was saying, *I'm giving you My authority, so use it!*

Whatever crises you're facing right now, stand up, take authority over the devil and say something! Say, "Satan, in the Name of Jesus, I take authority over you and your assignment against me and my family. I take authority over you in this situation, and I declare deliverance and victory in the Name of Jesus! You take your hands off me. I am a child of the living God. I am covered by the blood of Jesus. And I am delivered! Amen."

Now the trick is to leave that place where you made your stand of faith and KEEP SAYING what you BELIEVED—what you want to come to pass (Mark 11:23).

If you want a change, why don't you SAY what you want? Jesus said you can have what you say!

**For Further Study:**

Matthew 28:16-20

**Daily Scripture Reading:**

Zechariah 14;
Malachi 1;
Psalm 148

## *Speak the Word*

*I believe, therefore I speak.*
*2 Corinthians 4:13*

*Gloria*

# Practice Righteousness

> "But strong meat belongeth to them that are of full age, even those who by reason of use have their senses exercised to discern both good and evil."
>
> HEBREWS 5:14

Whatever your body is exposed to, that's what it will practice. It can practice righteousness just as easily as it can practice unrighteousness. Read on and I'll prove it.

If you've ever smoked a cigarette, the first time you smoked, you probably got sick. You probably coughed and spit and carried on, because it's unnatural to put smoke inside your lungs. You had to learn how to do that. You had to practice until you could handle smoke in your lungs.

Does that make any sense? No. But, it seemed absolutely sensible to you when you were in darkness.

"I've got to learn how to get this smoke in my lungs so it will cut my life short and I can't breathe well."

Now, that's nonsense. But it made sense when you walked over there in darkness, before you were born again.

When you took your first slug of whiskey—I imagine it just about got you good. It was hard to swallow, particularly if you drank it straight. You had to learn how by repeating the procedure.

Well, that's exactly what happens to you in walking right before God. You learn by practice.

When you first start out, you might say to yourself, *I'm not going to smoke anymore.* And you'll start on your road and maybe you'll fail. Maybe you'll smoke. Ken quit smoking a lot of times. And so did I. But, one day, we quit for good.

If you mess up, what do you do? You repent and say, "Lord, I'm hanging on to You. I'm putting this behind me. Help me to do this! I believe I'm delivered from it." And you'll come out of it.

God's power will help you. It's not just willpower. Your willpower is there to make the choice. But the power of God is what empowers you to stand for what you know God wants you to do.

Now, a person who isn't born again doesn't have the power of God because their spirit is dead and there is no life of God in them. Willpower is all they have, and most of the time not much of that.

FOR FURTHER STUDY:

Colossians 3:1-17; 1 John 3:2-9

DAILY SCRIPTURE READING:

Malachi 2-4; Psalms 149-150

But you have an anointing to crucify the flesh. Call upon it. Say, "Flesh, you are not going to rule here. You're not going to have your way here. I'm serving God. I'm not going to do and practice the things that are displeasing to God. I'm going to practice righteousness!" Hallelujah!

## Speak the Word

*I follow after righteousness and godliness, faith and love, and patience and meekness.*

*1 Timothy 6:11*

# Topical Index to Devotions

⬧

"Attend to my words; incline thine ear unto my sayings.
Let them not depart from thine eyes; keep them
in the midst of thine heart. For they are
life unto those that find them."
PROVERBS 4:20-22

# Prayer for Salvation and Baptism in the Holy Spirit

Heavenly Father, I come to You in the Name of Jesus. Your Word says, *"Whosoever shall call on the name of the Lord shall be saved"* (Acts 2:21). I am calling on You. I pray and ask Jesus to come into my heart and be Lord over my life according to Romans 10:9-10. *"If thou shalt confess with thy mouth the Lord Jesus, and shalt believe in thine heart that God hath raised him from the dead, thou shalt be saved."* I do that now. I confess that Jesus is Lord, and I believe in my heart that God raised Him from the dead.

I am now reborn! I am a Christian—a child of Almighty God! I am saved! You also said in Your Word, *"If ye then, being evil, know how to give good gifts unto your children: HOW MUCH MORE shall your heavenly Father give the Holy Spirit to them that ask him?"* (Luke 11:13). I'm also asking You to fill me with the Holy Spirit. Holy Spirit, rise up within me as I praise God. I fully expect to speak with other tongues as You give me the utterance (Acts 2:4).

Begin to praise God for filling you with the Holy Spirit. Speak those words and syllables you receive—not in your own language, but the language given to you by the Holy Spirit. You have to use your own voice. God will not force you to speak. Worship and praise Him in your heavenly language—in other tongues.

Continue with the blessing God has given you and pray in tongues each day.

You are a born-again, Spirit-filled believer. You'll never be the same!

Find a good Word of God preaching church, and become a part of a church family who will love and care for you as you love and care for them.

We need to be hooked up to each other. It increases our strength in God. It's God's plan for us.

# About the Authors

**Kenneth and Gloria Copeland** are the best-selling authors of more than 60 books such as the popular *Walk With God, Managing God's Mutual Funds—Yours and His* and *God's Will for You.* Together they have co-authored numerous other books including *Family Promises.* As founders of Kenneth Copeland Ministries in Fort Worth, Texas, Kenneth and Gloria are in their 31st year of circling the globe with the uncompromised Word of God, preaching and teaching a lifestyle of victory for every Christian.

Their daily and weekly *Believer's Voice of Victory* television broadcasts now air on more than 500 stations around the world, and their *Believer's Voice of Victory* and *Shout!* magazines are distributed to more than 1 million adults and children worldwide. Their international prison ministry reaches an average of 60,000 new inmates every year and receives more than 17,000 pieces of correspondence each month. Their teaching materials can also be found on the World Wide Web. With offices and staff in the United States, Canada, England, Australia, South Africa and Ukraine, Kenneth and Gloria's teaching materials—books, magazines, tapes and videos—have been translated into at least 22 languages to reach the world with the love of God.

Learn more about Kenneth Copeland Ministries
by visiting our website at **www.kcm.org**.

**The Harrison House Vision**

Proclaiming the truth and the power
Of the Gospel of Jesus Christ
With excellence;

Challenging Christians to
Live victoriously,
Grow spiritually,
Know God intimately.

# Other Books Available

**Books Co-Authored by Kenneth and Gloria Copeland**

Family Promises

Healing Promises

Prosperity Promises

From Faith to Faith—A Daily Guide to Victory

**by Kenneth Copeland**

\* A Ceremony of Marriage

A Matter of Choice

Covenant of Blood

Faith and Patience—The Power Twins

\* Freedom From Fear

Giving and Receiving

Honor—Walking in Honesty, Truth and Integrity

How to Conquer Strife

How to Discipline Your Flesh

How to Receive Communion

Love Never Fails

Managing God's Mutual Funds

\* Now Are We in Christ Jesus

\* Our Covenant With God

\* Prayer—Your Foundation for Success

Prosperity: The Choice Is Yours

Rumors of War

\* Sensitivity of Heart

Six Steps to Excellence in Ministry

Sorrow Not! Winning Over Grief and Sorrow

\* The Decision Is Yours

\* The Force of Faith

\* The Force of Righteousness

The Image of God in You

The Laws of Prosperity

\* The Mercy of God

The Miraculous Realm of God's Love

The Outpouring of the Spirit—The Result of Prayer

\* The Power of the Tongue

The Power to Be Forever Free

The Troublemaker

\* The Winning Attitude

Turn Your Hearts Into Harvests

\* Welcome to the Family

\* You Are Healed!

Your Right-Standing With God

**by Gloria Copeland**

\* And Jesus Healed Them All

Are You Ready?

Build Your Financial Foundation

Build Yourself an Ark

Fight On!

God's Prescription for Divine Health

God's Success Formula

God's Will for You

God's Will for Your Healing

God's Will Is Prosperity

\* God's Will Is the Holy Spirit

\* Harvest of Health

Living Contact

\* Love—The Secret to Your Success

No Deposit—No Return

Pleasing the Father

Pressing In—It's Worth It All

The Power to Live a New Life

The Unbeatable Spirit of Faith

\* Walk in the Spirit

Walk With God

Well Worth the Wait

**Other Books Published by KCP**

\* Available in Spanish

**Available from your local bookstore.**

HARRISON HOUSE

Tulsa, OK 74153

# World Offices of Kenneth Copeland Ministries

For more information about KCM and a free
catalog, please write the office nearest you:

Kenneth Copeland Ministries
Fort Worth, Texas  76192-0001

Kenneth Copeland
Locked Bag 2600
Mansfield Delivery Centre
QUEENSLAND 4122
AUSTRALIA

Kenneth Copeland
Post Office Box 15
BATH
BA1 1GD
ENGLAND

Kenneth Copeland
Private Bag X 909
FONTAINEBLEAU
2032
REPUBLIC OF SOUTH AFRICA

Kenneth Copeland
Post Office Box 378
Surrey
BRITISH COLUMBIA
V3T 5B6
CANADA

UKRAINE
L'VIV 290000
Post Office Box 84
Kenneth Copeland Ministries
L'VIV 290000
UKRAINE

# We're Here for You!

### Believer's Voice of Victory Television Broadcast

Join Kenneth and Gloria Copeland, and the *Believer's Voice of Victory* broadcasts, Monday through Friday and on Sunday each week, and learn how faith in God's Word can take your life from ordinary to extraordinary. This is some of the best teaching you'll ever hear, designed to get you where you want to be—*on top!*

You can catch the *Believer's Voice of Victory* broadcast on your local, cable or satellite channels.

\* Check your local listings for times and stations in your area.

### Believer's Voice of Victory Magazine

Enjoy inspired teaching and encouragement from Kenneth and Gloria Copeland each month in the *Believer's Voice of Victory* magazine. Also included are real-life testimonies of God's miraculous power and divine intervention into the lives of people just like you!

**It's more than just a magazine—it's a ministry.**

### Shout! ...The dynamic magazine just for kids!

*Shout! The Voice of Victory for Kids* is a Bible-charged, action-packed, bimonthly magazine available FREE to kids everywhere! Featuring *Wichita Slim* and *Commander Kellie and the Superkids*sm, *Shout!* is filled with colorful adventure comics, challenging games and puzzles, exciting short stories, solve-it-yourself mysteries and much more!!

**Stand up, sign up and get ready to *Shout!***

To receive a FREE subscription to *Believer's Voice of Victory*, or to give a child you know a FREE subscription to *Shout!* write or call:

Kenneth Copeland Ministries

Fort Worth, Texas  76192-0001

Or call:

1-800-359-0075

(9 a.m. - 5 p.m. CT)